Another Stereotype Bites the Dust

Also by Darrin Bell

Candorville: Thank God for Culture Clash

Also by Darrin Bell and Theron Heir

Rudy Park: The People Must Be Wired
Peace, Love, and Lattes: A Rudy Park Collection

Another Stereotype Bites the Dust

a **CANDORVILLE**® collection

by Darrin Bell

Andrews McMeel
Publishing

Kansas City · Sydney · London

Candorville is distributed internationally by the Washington Post Writers Group.

Andrews McMeel Publishing, LLC
an Andrews McMeel Universal company
1130 Walnut Street, Kansas City, Missouri 64106

www.andrewsmcmeel.com

ISBN: 978-0-7407-6041-9

Library of Congress Control Number: 2006925703

Candorville can be viewed on the Internet at
www.candorville.com.

———— **ATTENTION: SCHOOLS AND BUSINESSES** ————

Andrews McMeel books are available at quantity discounts with bulk purchase for educational, business, or sales promotional use. For information, please e-mail the Andrews McMeel Publishing Special Sales Department: specialsales@amuniversal.com.

To my wife, Laura, who made me dance

candorville.com

http://www.candorville.com/

Daily Visits iCalX Mail Finances News (1348) Mac Comics Shopping Entertainment Resources

THE CANDORVILLE COURIER

a blog by Lemont Brown

Monday, 9:11 p.m.—"A Pretty Tolerant Guy"

I'm a pretty tolerant guy, but I'm not blind to the world. There are certain things I can't help but notice. For instance, the only thing worse than an Asian driver is a Black woman driver. That's what I decided about a half hour ago, as I was driving Susan's car home from Trader Joe's. I pulled out of the parking lot and was nearly sideswiped by a purple pickup truck. The first thing I noticed, after the ugly paint job and the Homer Simpson bobble-head on the dashboard, was the driver's race. Asian, of course.

I shook my head, and made a right onto 73rd Street—and right away, I was nearly rear-ended by an old yellow Nissan. My hospital bill flashed before my eyes. I had time for one thought: With 43 million medically uninsured people in this country, this clown—who shouldn't even have a driver's license—had to pick me to rear-end. I looked in my rearview mirror. I was disappointed, but not surprised, to see that the driver was a Black woman. Sort of looked beautiful like Mama, but deep down inside, she must've been ugly because she had the temerity to honk at me and flash her lights. I was the one who should be angry, not her. When she sped around me, I gave her a dirty look just so she'd know she didn't get the best of me.

I was almost hit three more times on the way home. I wasn't surprised by who was driving the cars. An elderly man who should've stopped driving years ago almost hit me head-on on a narrow side street. ("There should be an age limit for driving," I thought.) A Latino in a flatbed truck nearly sideswiped me at a four-way intersection. ("He probably isn't even legal," I thought.) A middle-aged White guy in a Hummer nearly ended my life when I tried to merge into his lane on the freeway. ("Obnoxious skinhead.") He yelled something at me as he sped past, but at this point I couldn't take it anymore, so I broke down and showed the jerk my favorite finger.

I finally pulled up to my apartment, heart pounding, and got out to open the garage. I couldn't see the keyhole. That's when I realized my headlights weren't on. They'd been off the whole time.

Those unforgivable idiots who made my ride home unbearable weren't idiots at all. They just couldn't see me because I had neglected to turn on my @#$% lights! That's when I realized I'm a bigot. Not the kind of bigot who wears a sheet and hood and carries a cross, but the kind who wears a T-shirt and jeans and carries around preconceived notions about other people. They're there, bubbling under the surface and waiting to explode under the slightest pressure, and I was completely in the dark about it. After all, I thought I was a pretty tolerant guy.

We don't need to be "tolerant." Tolerant means you're able to barely stand other people and you grudgingly accept that they have a right to exist, even though they disgust you. As long as they only remind you of what we all have in common, and they never bring up the differences we all have, you're willing to tolerate them. Big @#$% deal. There's far too much "tolerating" going on in our society. What we need is a little more "acceptance." Accept people who aren't like us.

Celebrate the differences we all have. Go through life with our headlights turned on.

Hang on just a sec. Phone's ringing . . .

Mama called; I told her how I almost died in five car accidents. Confessed I'm a bigot. She asked if I'm wearing clean underwear.

Monday, 8:01 p.m.—"Jonesin' for Mandarin"

Can't believe I ran out of Mandarin Orange Chicken. Better jet to Trader Joe's for more (if Susan loans me her Mini Coop). Looks like a nice night for a drive.

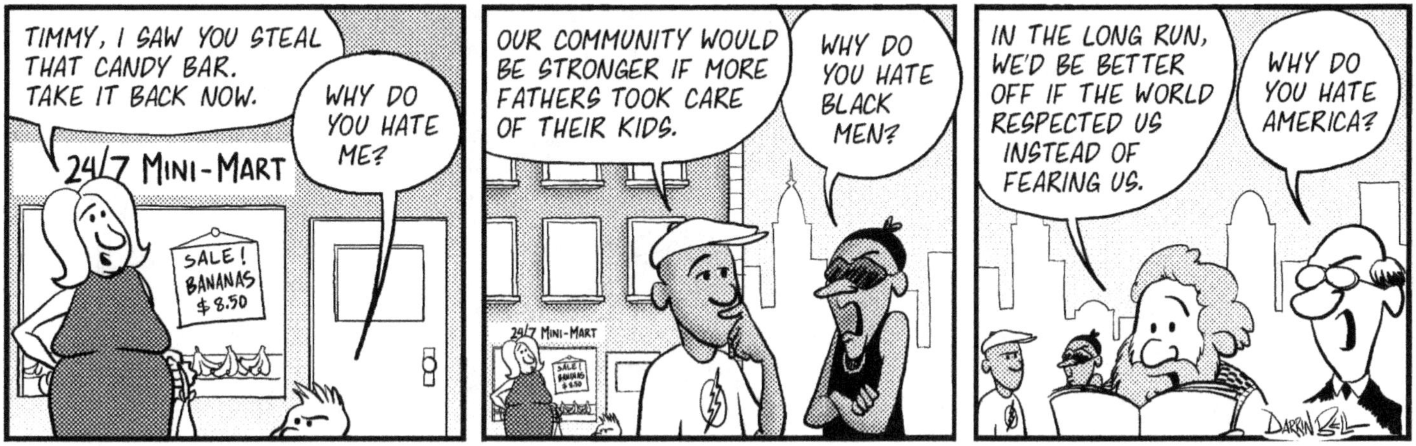
TIMMY, I SAW YOU STEAL THAT CANDY BAR. TAKE IT BACK NOW.
WHY DO YOU HATE ME?
24/7 MINI-MART
SALE! BANANAS $8.50
OUR COMMUNITY WOULD BE STRONGER IF MORE FATHERS TOOK CARE OF THEIR KIDS.
WHY DO YOU HATE BLACK MEN?
24/7 MINI-MART
IN THE LONG RUN, WE'D BE BETTER OFF IF THE WORLD RESPECTED US INSTEAD OF FEARING US.
WHY DO YOU HATE AMERICA?
DARRIN BELL

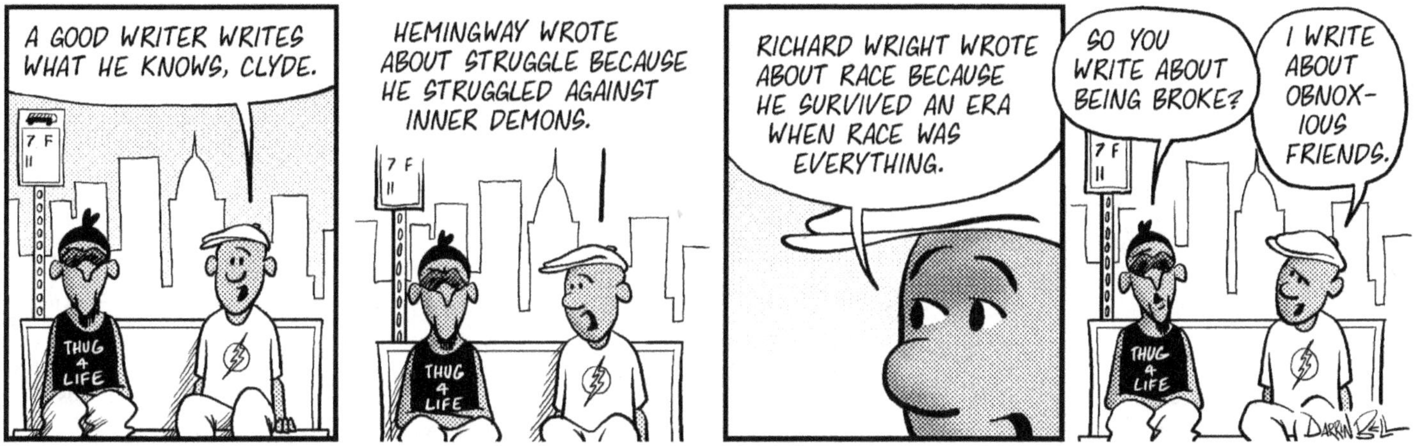
A GOOD WRITER WRITES WHAT HE KNOWS, CLYDE.
THUG 4 LIFE
HEMINGWAY WROTE ABOUT STRUGGLE BECAUSE HE STRUGGLED AGAINST INNER DEMONS.
THUG 4 LIFE
RICHARD WRIGHT WROTE ABOUT RACE BECAUSE HE SURVIVED AN ERA WHEN RACE WAS EVERYTHING.
SO YOU WRITE ABOUT BEING BROKE?
I WRITE ABOUT OBNOX-IOUS FRIENDS.
THUG 4 LIFE
DARRIN BELL

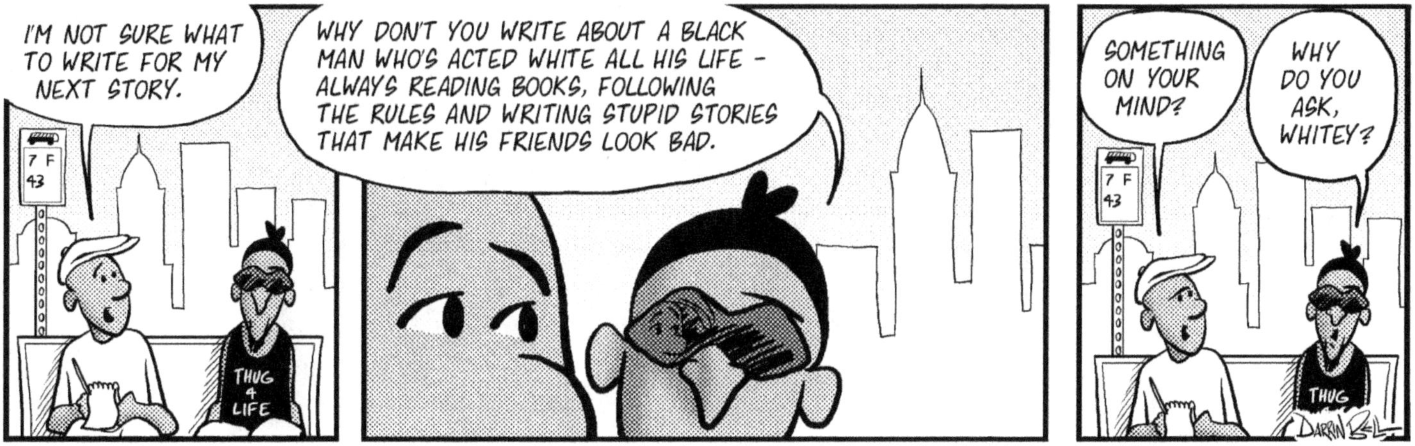
I'M NOT SURE WHAT TO WRITE FOR MY NEXT STORY.
THUG 4 LIFE
WHY DON'T YOU WRITE ABOUT A BLACK MAN WHO'S ACTED WHITE ALL HIS LIFE - ALWAYS READING BOOKS, FOLLOWING THE RULES AND WRITING STUPID STORIES THAT MAKE HIS FRIENDS LOOK BAD.
SOMETHING ON YOUR MIND?
WHY DO YOU ASK, WHITEY?
THUG
DARRIN BELL

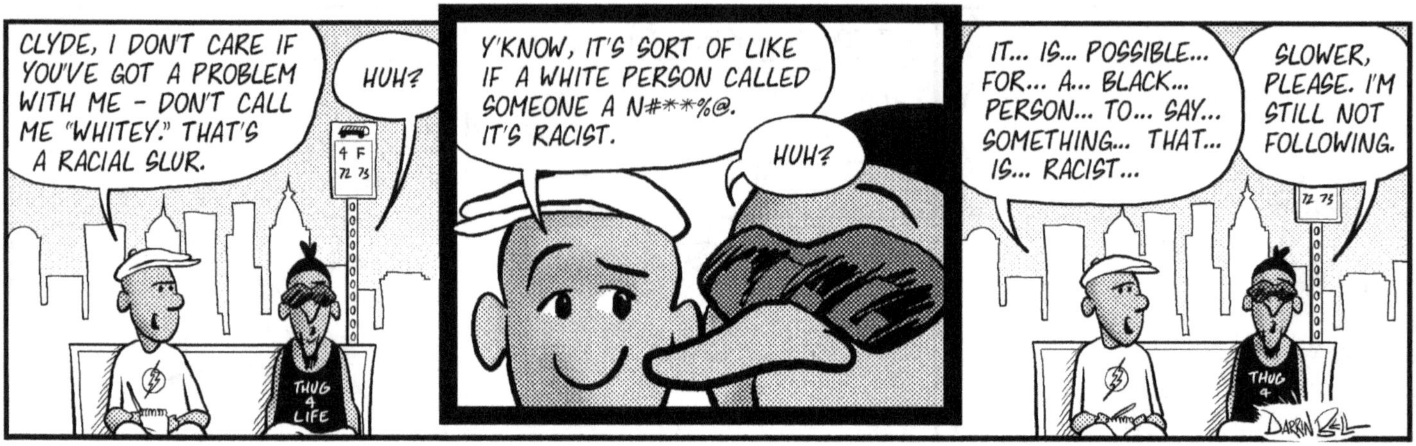
CLYDE, I DON'T CARE IF YOU'VE GOT A PROBLEM WITH ME - DON'T CALL ME "WHITEY." THAT'S A RACIAL SLUR.
HUH?
THUG 4 LIFE
Y'KNOW, IT'S SORT OF LIKE IF A WHITE PERSON CALLED SOMEONE A N#**%@. IT'S RACIST.
HUH?
IT... IS... POSSIBLE... FOR... A... BLACK... PERSON... TO... SAY... SOMETHING... THAT... IS... RACIST...
SLOWER, PLEASE. I'M STILL NOT FOLLOWING.
DARRIN BELL

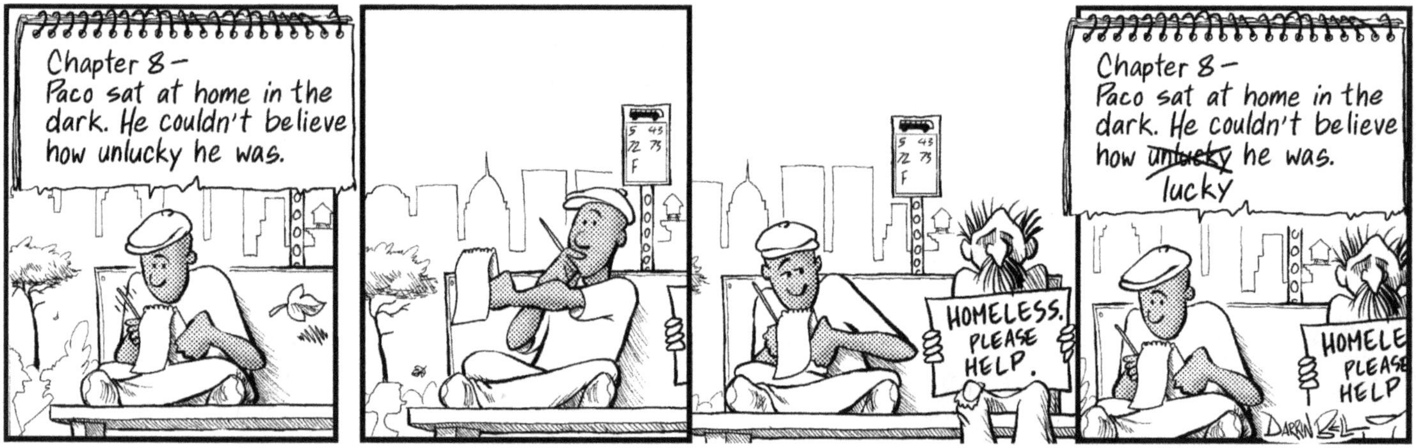
Chapter 8 — Paco sat at home in the dark. He couldn't believe how unlucky he was.
HOMELESS. PLEASE HELP.
Chapter 8 — Paco sat at home in the dark. He couldn't believe how ~~unlucky~~ lucky he was.
HOMELE PLEASE HELP
DARRIN BELL

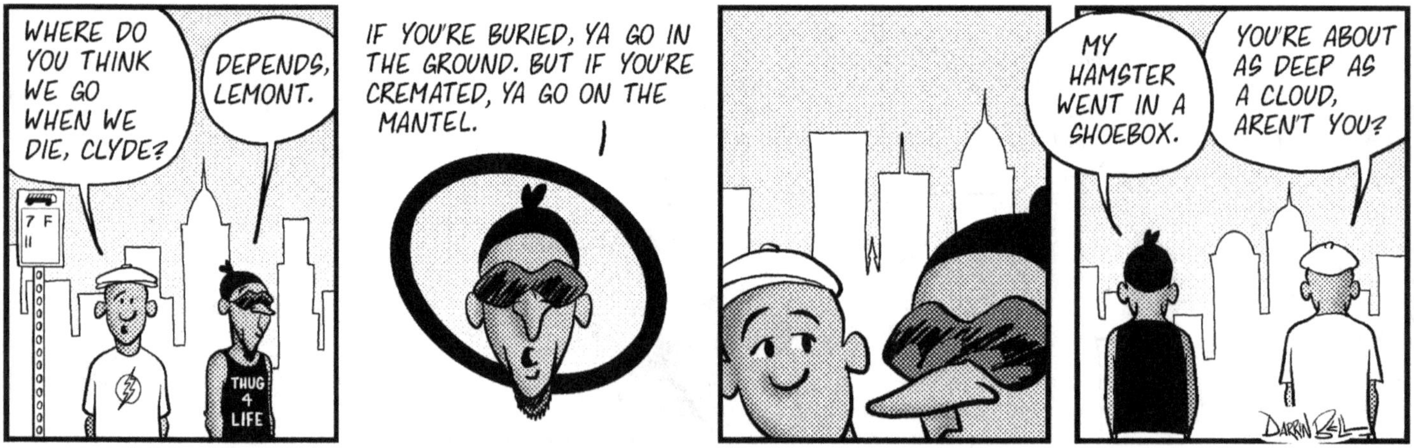
WHERE DO YOU THINK WE GO WHEN WE DIE, CLYDE?
DEPENDS, LEMONT.
THUG 4 LIFE
IF YOU'RE BURIED, YA GO IN THE GROUND. BUT IF YOU'RE CREMATED, YA GO ON THE MANTEL.
MY HAMSTER WENT IN A SHOEBOX.
YOU'RE ABOUT AS DEEP AS A CLOUD, AREN'T YOU?
DARRIN BELL

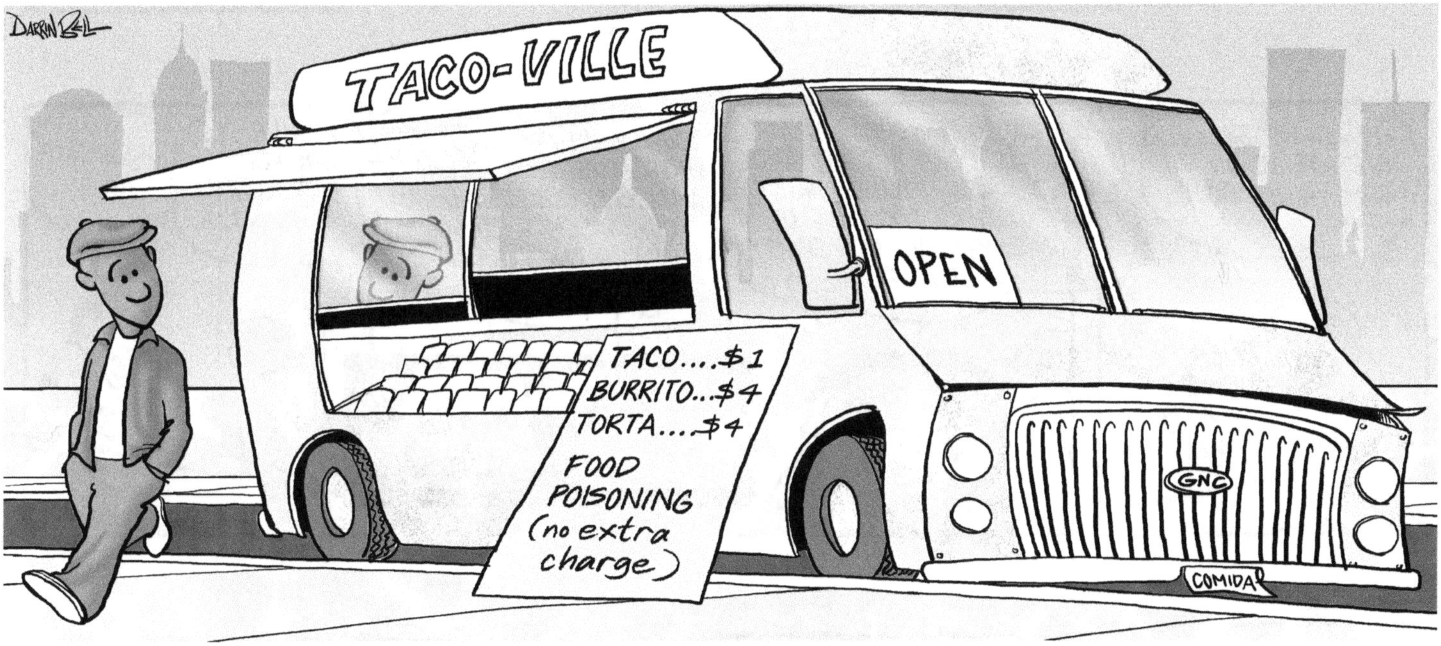
DARRIN BELL
TACO-VILLE
OPEN
TACO....$1
BURRITO...$4
TORTA....$4
FOOD POISONING (no extra charge)
GNC
COMIDA

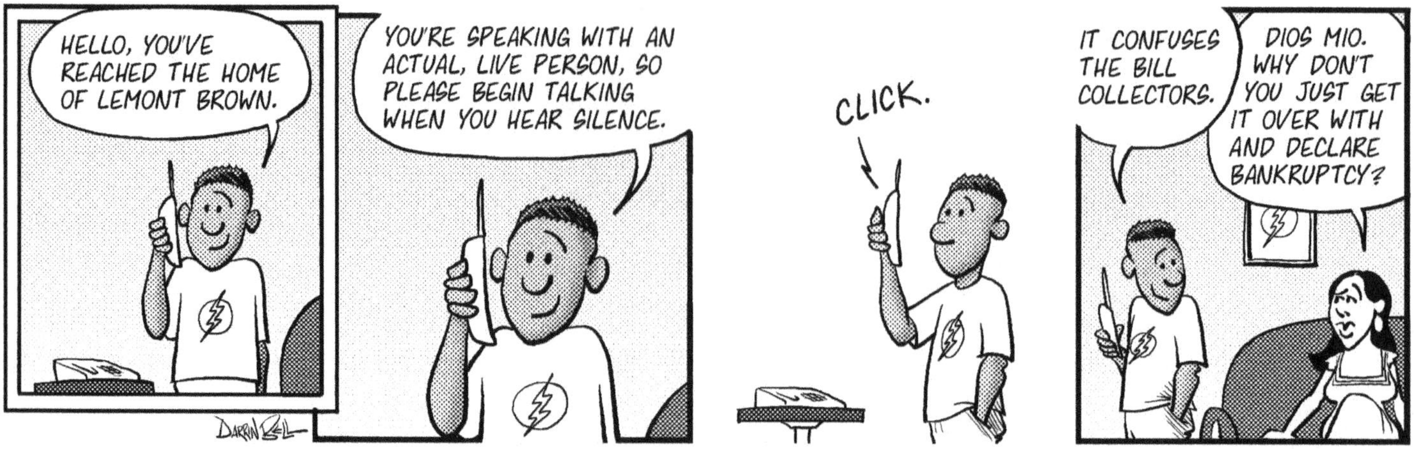
HELLO, YOU'VE REACHED THE HOME OF LEMONT BROWN.
YOU'RE SPEAKING WITH AN ACTUAL, LIVE PERSON, SO PLEASE BEGIN TALKING WHEN YOU HEAR SILENCE.
CLICK.
IT CONFUSES THE BILL COLLECTORS.
DIOS MIO. WHY DON'T YOU JUST GET IT OVER WITH AND DECLARE BANKRUPTCY?
DARRIN BELL

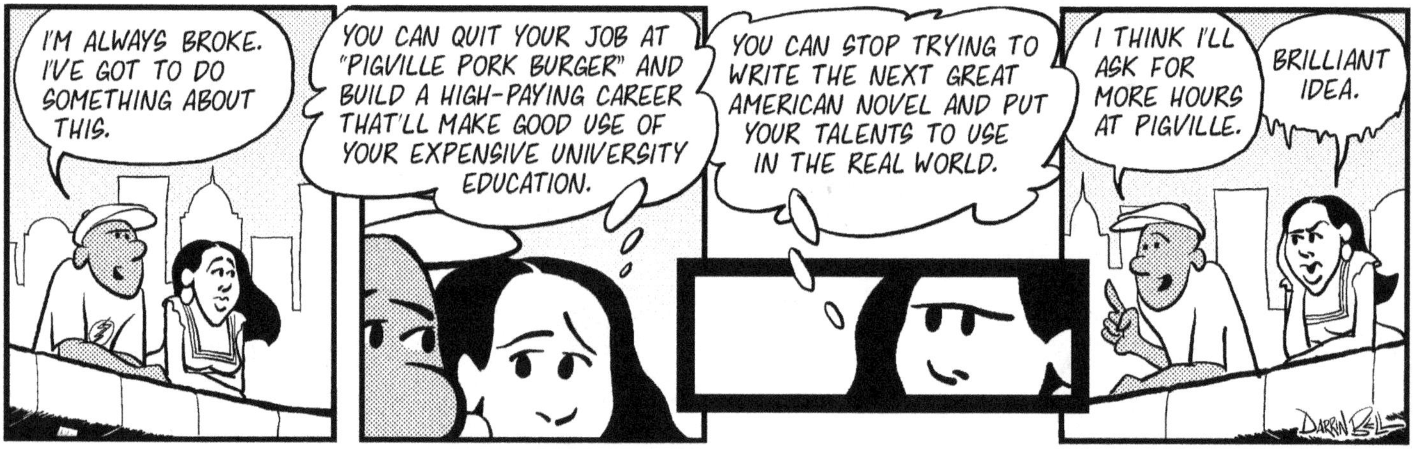
I'M ALWAYS BROKE. I'VE GOT TO DO SOMETHING ABOUT THIS.
YOU CAN QUIT YOUR JOB AT "PIGVILLE PORK BURGER" AND BUILD A HIGH-PAYING CAREER THAT'LL MAKE GOOD USE OF YOUR EXPENSIVE UNIVERSITY EDUCATION.
YOU CAN STOP TRYING TO WRITE THE NEXT GREAT AMERICAN NOVEL AND PUT YOUR TALENTS TO USE IN THE REAL WORLD.
I THINK I'LL ASK FOR MORE HOURS AT PIGVILLE.
BRILLIANT IDEA.
DARRIN BELL

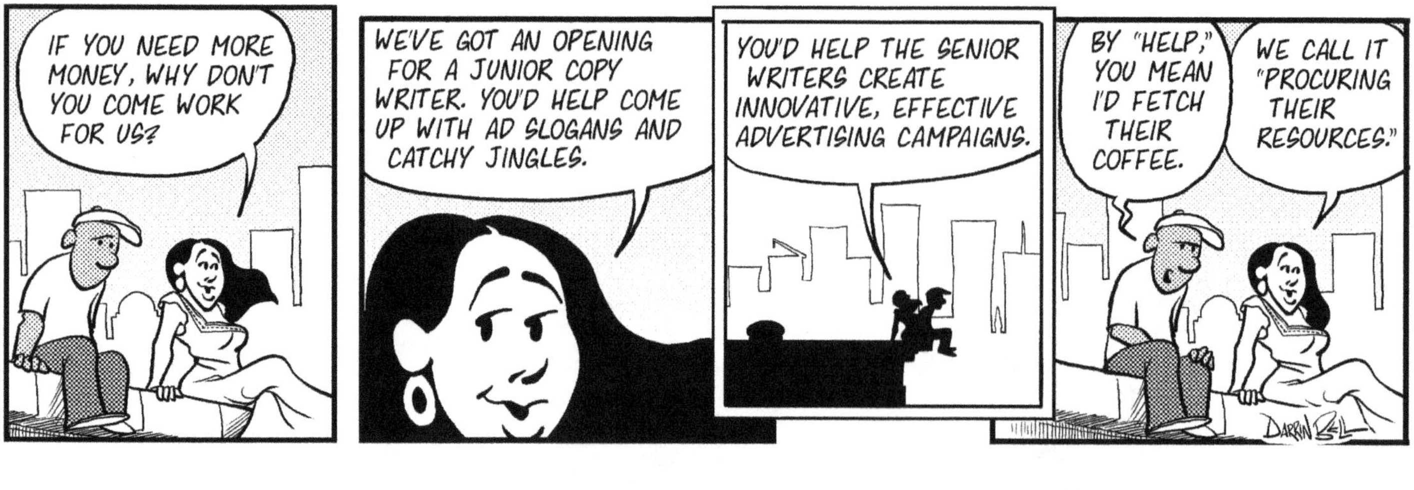
IF YOU NEED MORE MONEY, WHY DON'T YOU COME WORK FOR US?
WE'VE GOT AN OPENING FOR A JUNIOR COPY WRITER. YOU'D HELP COME UP WITH AD SLOGANS AND CATCHY JINGLES.
YOU'D HELP THE SENIOR WRITERS CREATE INNOVATIVE, EFFECTIVE ADVERTISING CAMPAIGNS.
BY "HELP," YOU MEAN I'D FETCH THEIR COFFEE.
WE CALL IT "PROCURING THEIR RESOURCES."
DARRIN BELL

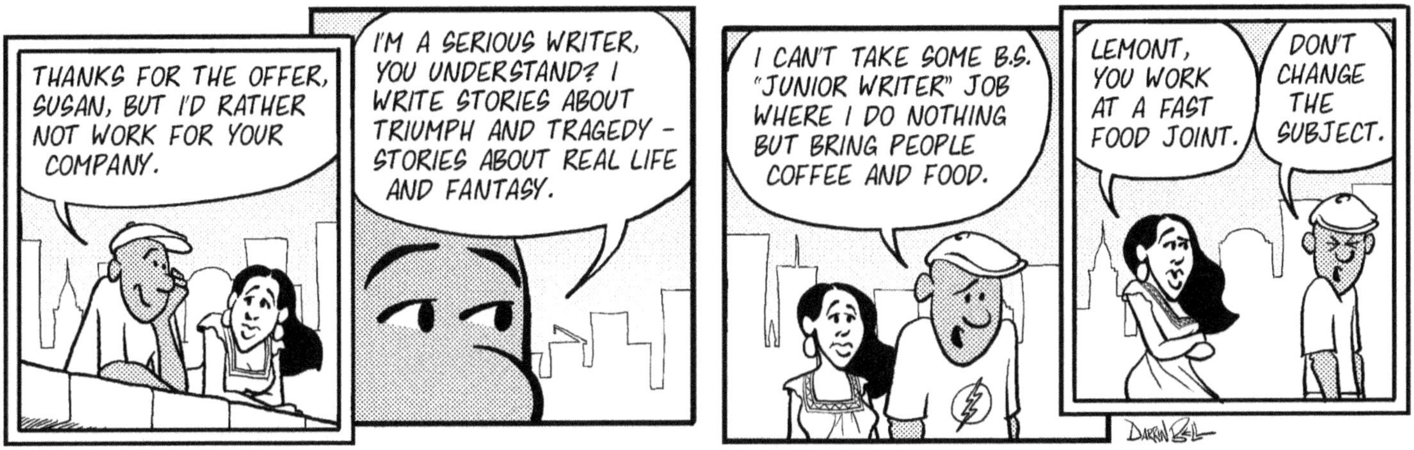
THANKS FOR THE OFFER, SUSAN, BUT I'D RATHER NOT WORK FOR YOUR COMPANY.
I'M A SERIOUS WRITER, YOU UNDERSTAND? I WRITE STORIES ABOUT TRIUMPH AND TRAGEDY - STORIES ABOUT REAL LIFE AND FANTASY.
I CAN'T TAKE SOME B.S. "JUNIOR WRITER" JOB WHERE I DO NOTHING BUT BRING PEOPLE COFFEE AND FOOD.
LEMONT, YOU WORK AT A FAST FOOD JOINT.
DON'T CHANGE THE SUBJECT.

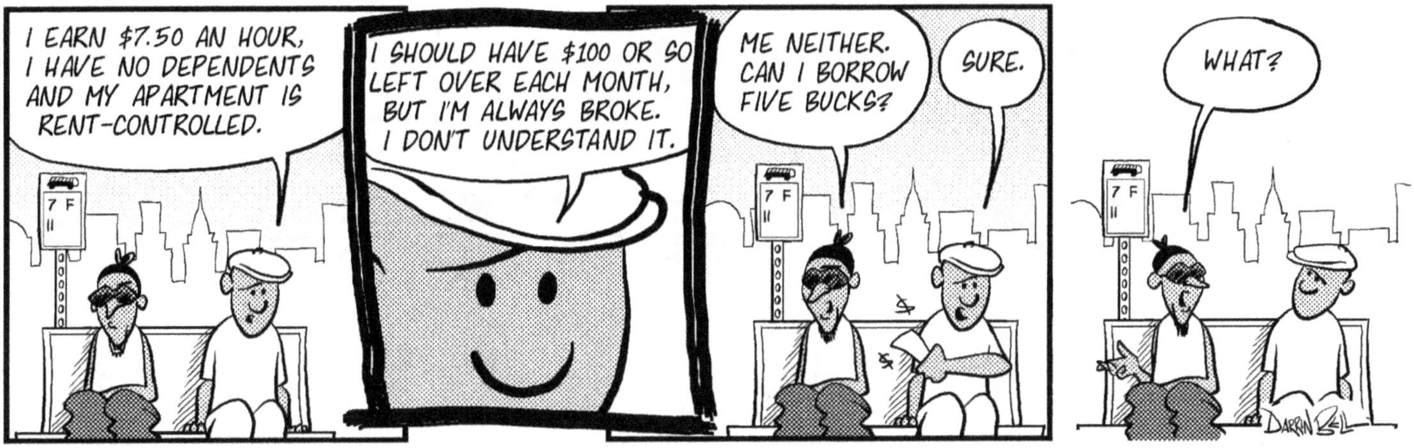
I EARN $7.50 AN HOUR, I HAVE NO DEPENDENTS AND MY APARTMENT IS RENT-CONTROLLED.
I SHOULD HAVE $100 OR SO LEFT OVER EACH MONTH, BUT I'M ALWAYS BROKE. I DON'T UNDERSTAND IT.
ME NEITHER. CAN I BORROW FIVE BUCKS?
SURE.
WHAT?

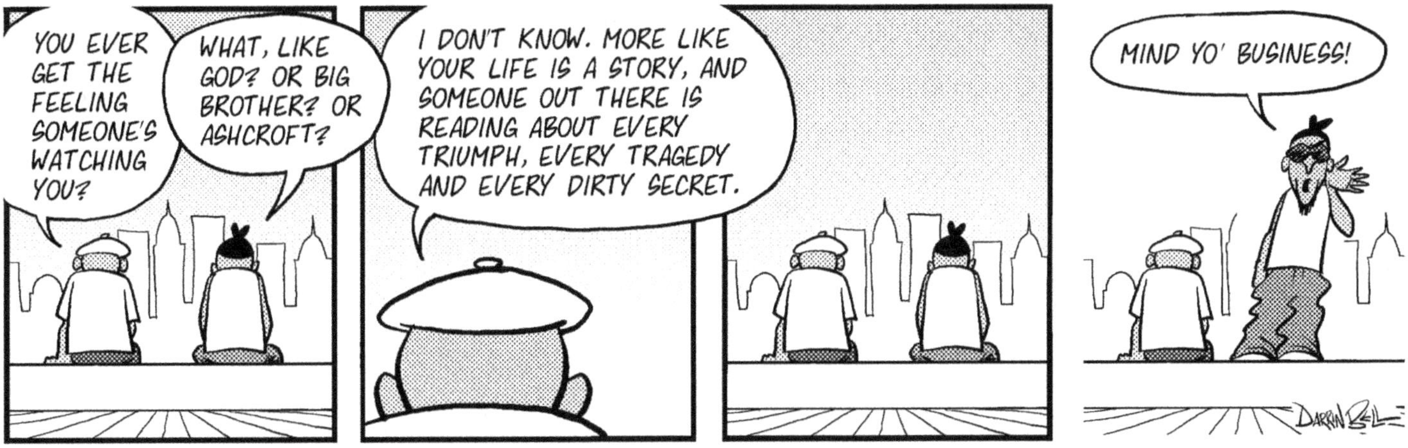
YOU EVER GET THE FEELING SOMEONE'S WATCHING YOU?
WHAT, LIKE GOD? OR BIG BROTHER? OR ASHCROFT?
I DON'T KNOW. MORE LIKE YOUR LIFE IS A STORY, AND SOMEONE OUT THERE IS READING ABOUT EVERY TRIUMPH, EVERY TRAGEDY AND EVERY DIRTY SECRET.
MIND YO' BUSINESS!

HELLO, WELLS FRAGGO BANK? I WAS JUST LOOKING AT MY BANK ACCOUNT ONLINE...

I'M WONDERING, WHY WAS I CHARGED A $220 "OVERDRAFT CHARGE" TODAY?

WELL, SIR, YOU HAD NINE DEBIT CARD PURCHASES PENDING, WHICH WOULD HAVE BEEN FINE. YOU HAD ENOUGH FUNDS TO COVER THOSE.

BUT THEN A MERCHANT CALLED "ROSCOE'S RIB SHACK" DEPOSITED A CHECK FOR $12, PUTTING YOU OVERDRAWN BY $1.

SO, RATHER THAN BOUNCE THAT ONE CHECK, WE GENEROUSLY PAID THEM ALL FOR YOU.

OF COURSE, WE HAD TO CHARGE A $22 OVERDRAFT FEE FOR EACH PURCHASE.

555-5555

I SEE. I JUST HAVE ONE MORE QUESTION.

YES, SIR?

WHY DIDN'T YOU JUST BOUNCE THE @$% $12 CHECK?!

DARRIN BELL

I'D THINK YOU WOULD BE GRATEFUL, SIR. THE MERCHANT MIGHT HAVE CHARGED YOU A $15 RETURNED-CHECK FEE.

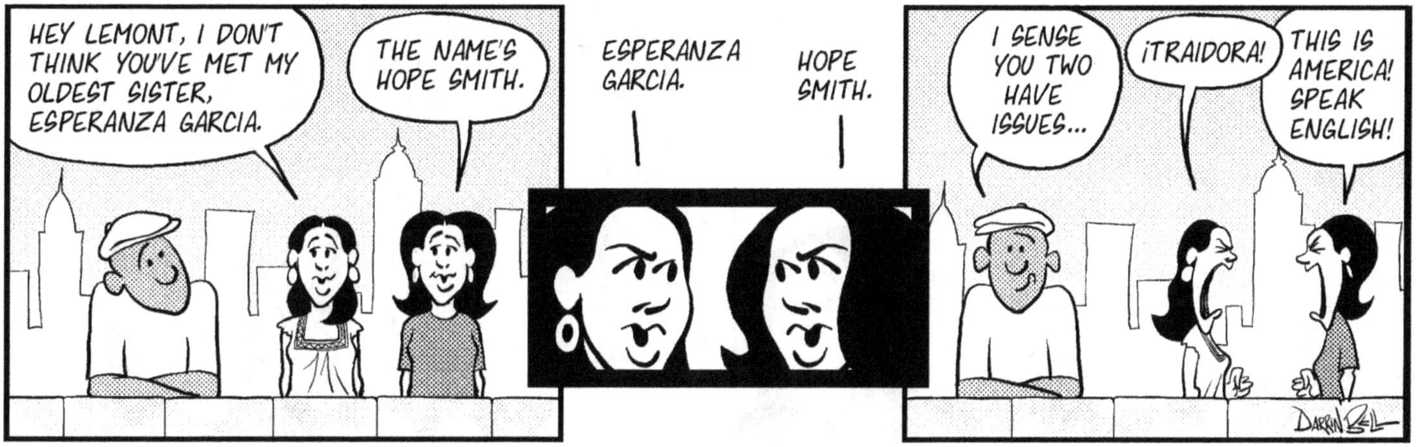
HEY LEMONT, I DON'T THINK YOU'VE MET MY OLDEST SISTER, ESPERANZA GARCIA.
THE NAME'S HOPE SMITH.
ESPERANZA GARCIA.
HOPE SMITH.
I SENSE YOU TWO HAVE ISSUES...
¡TRAIDORA!
THIS IS AMERICA! SPEAK ENGLISH!
DARRIN BELL

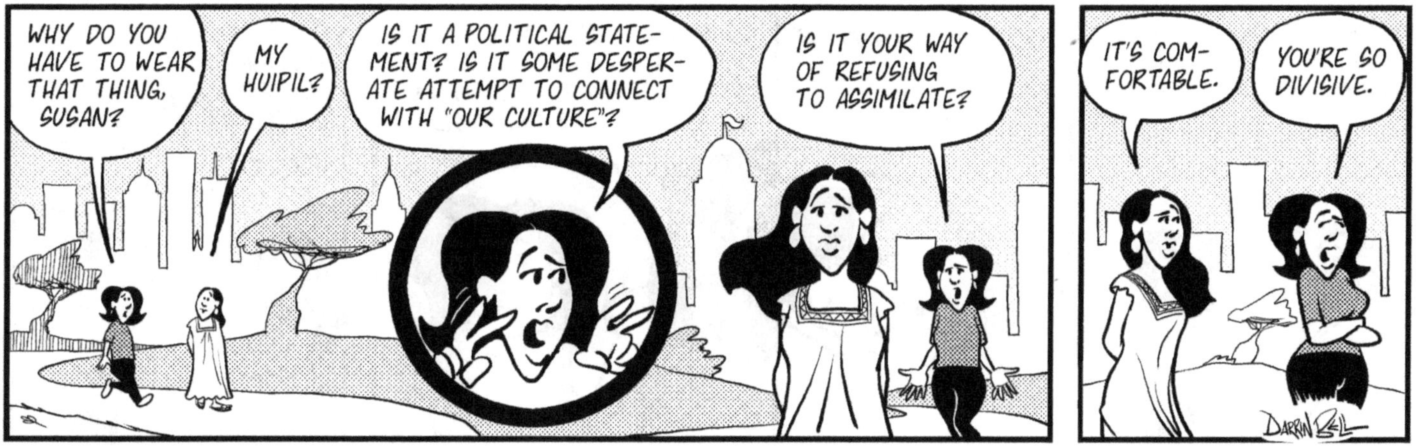
WHY DO YOU HAVE TO WEAR THAT THING, SUSAN?
MY HUIPIL?
IS IT A POLITICAL STATEMENT? IS IT SOME DESPERATE ATTEMPT TO CONNECT WITH "OUR CULTURE"?
IS IT YOUR WAY OF REFUSING TO ASSIMILATE?
IT'S COMFORTABLE.
YOU'RE SO DIVISIVE.
DARRIN BELL

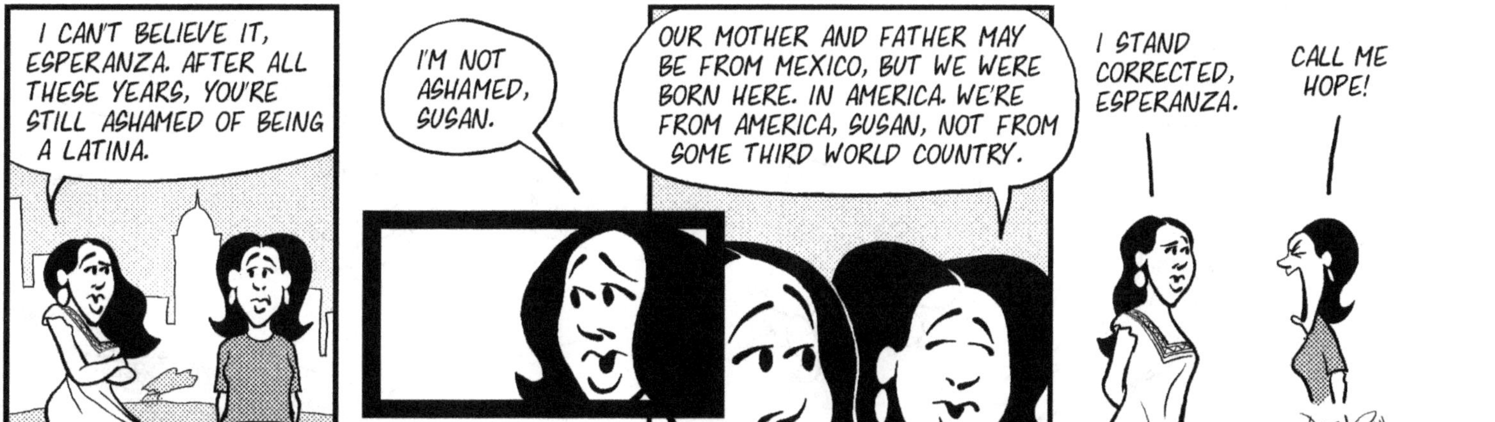
I CAN'T BELIEVE IT, ESPERANZA. AFTER ALL THESE YEARS, YOU'RE STILL ASHAMED OF BEING A LATINA.
I'M NOT ASHAMED, SUSAN.
OUR MOTHER AND FATHER MAY BE FROM MEXICO, BUT WE WERE BORN HERE. IN AMERICA. WE'RE FROM AMERICA, SUSAN, NOT FROM SOME THIRD WORLD COUNTRY.
I STAND CORRECTED, ESPERANZA.
CALL ME HOPE!
DARRIN BELL

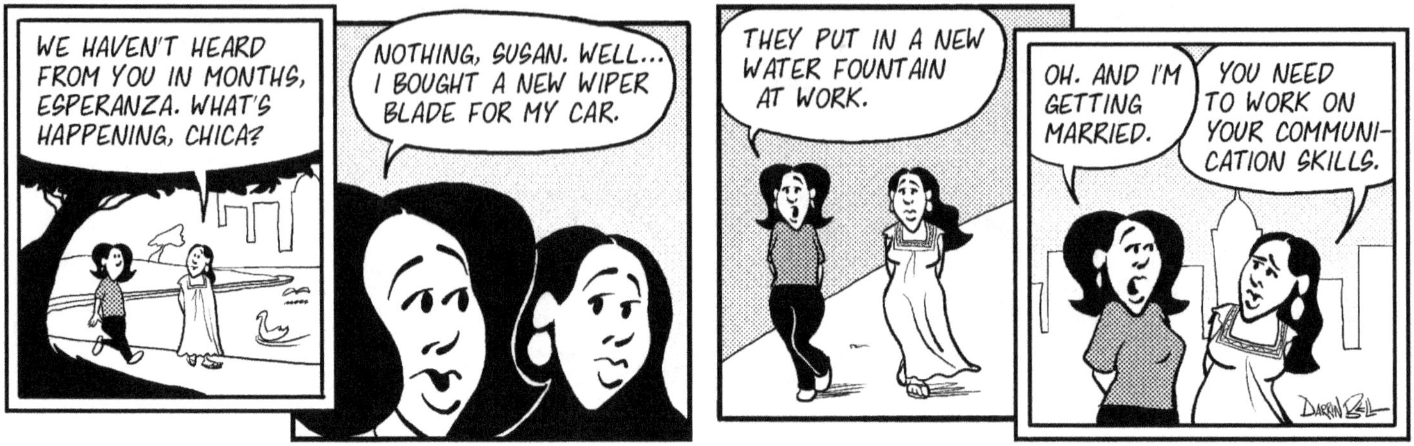
WE HAVEN'T HEARD FROM YOU IN MONTHS, ESPERANZA. WHAT'S HAPPENING, CHICA?
NOTHING, SUSAN. WELL... I BOUGHT A NEW WIPER BLADE FOR MY CAR.
THEY PUT IN A NEW WATER FOUNTAIN AT WORK.
OH. AND I'M GETTING MARRIED.
YOU NEED TO WORK ON YOUR COMMUNICATION SKILLS.
DARRIN BELL

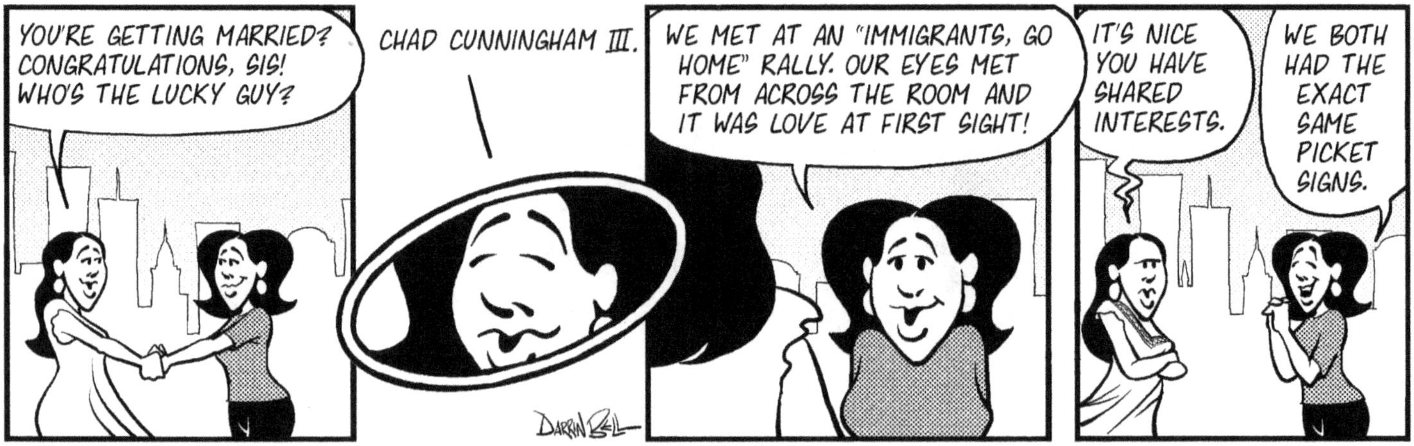
YOU'RE GETTING MARRIED? CONGRATULATIONS, SIS! WHO'S THE LUCKY GUY?
CHAD CUNNINGHAM III.
WE MET AT AN "IMMIGRANTS, GO HOME" RALLY. OUR EYES MET FROM ACROSS THE ROOM AND IT WAS LOVE AT FIRST SIGHT!
IT'S NICE YOU HAVE SHARED INTERESTS.
WE BOTH HAD THE EXACT SAME PICKET SIGNS.
DARRIN BELL

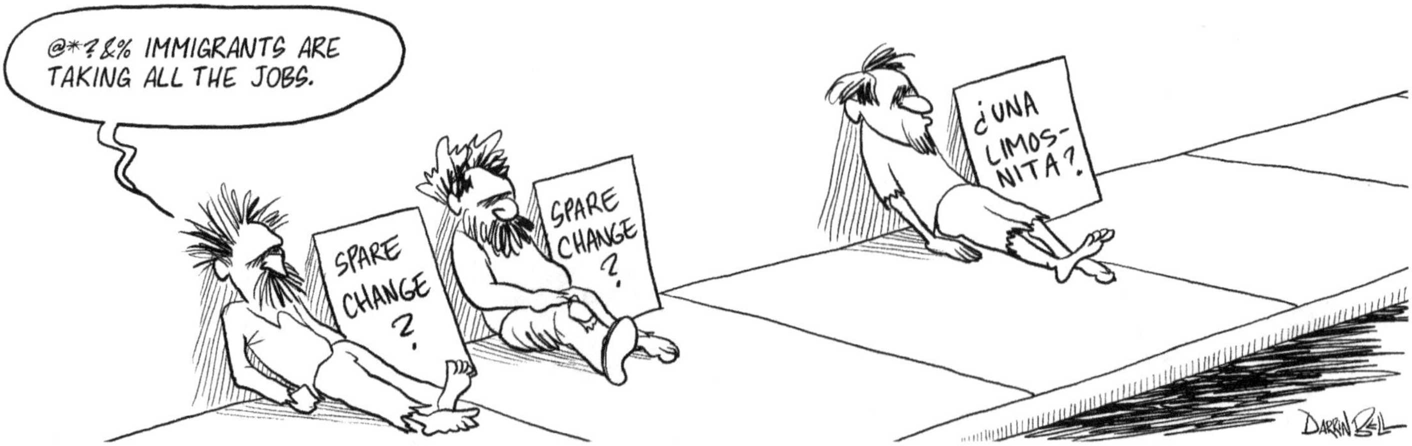
@*?&% IMMIGRANTS ARE TAKING ALL THE JOBS.
SPARE CHANGE ?
SPARE CHANGE ?
¿UNA LIMOSNITA?
DARRIN BELL

WELLS FRAGGO BANK. HOW MAY I HELP YOU?
I'M LEMONT BROWN. I CALLED LAST WEEK TO COMPLAIN ABOUT $220 IN FEES YOU CHARGED ME FOR BEING OVERDRAWN.
I TRANSFERRED ALL $300 FROM MY SAVINGS TO COVER THAT.
BUT NOW IT'S SAYING I'M OVERDRAWN AGAIN BY $155. WHAT'S GOING ON?
WELL, SIR, THERE WAS A $50 TRANSFER FEE, AND A $31 FEE BECAUSE YOU CALLED US ON THE PHONE MORE THAN THREE TIMES THIS MONTH.
WHAT THE-- THIS IS ABSURD.
THAT MADE YOU OVERDRAWN BY $1. YOU'VE BEEN OVER-DRAWN BY $1 FOR SEVEN DAYS, NOW, WHICH COMES TO $154 IN OVERDRAFT FEES.
WHAT? YOU PEOPLE ARE CRIMINAL. CRIMINAL! I'M TAKING MY BUSINESS ELSEWHERE, DO YOU HEAR ME?!
CLICK.
RRIIIING!
YOU'VE REACHED LEMONT BROWN. PLEASE LEAVE A MESSAGE.
A HANG-UP FEE OF $25 WILL APPLY.

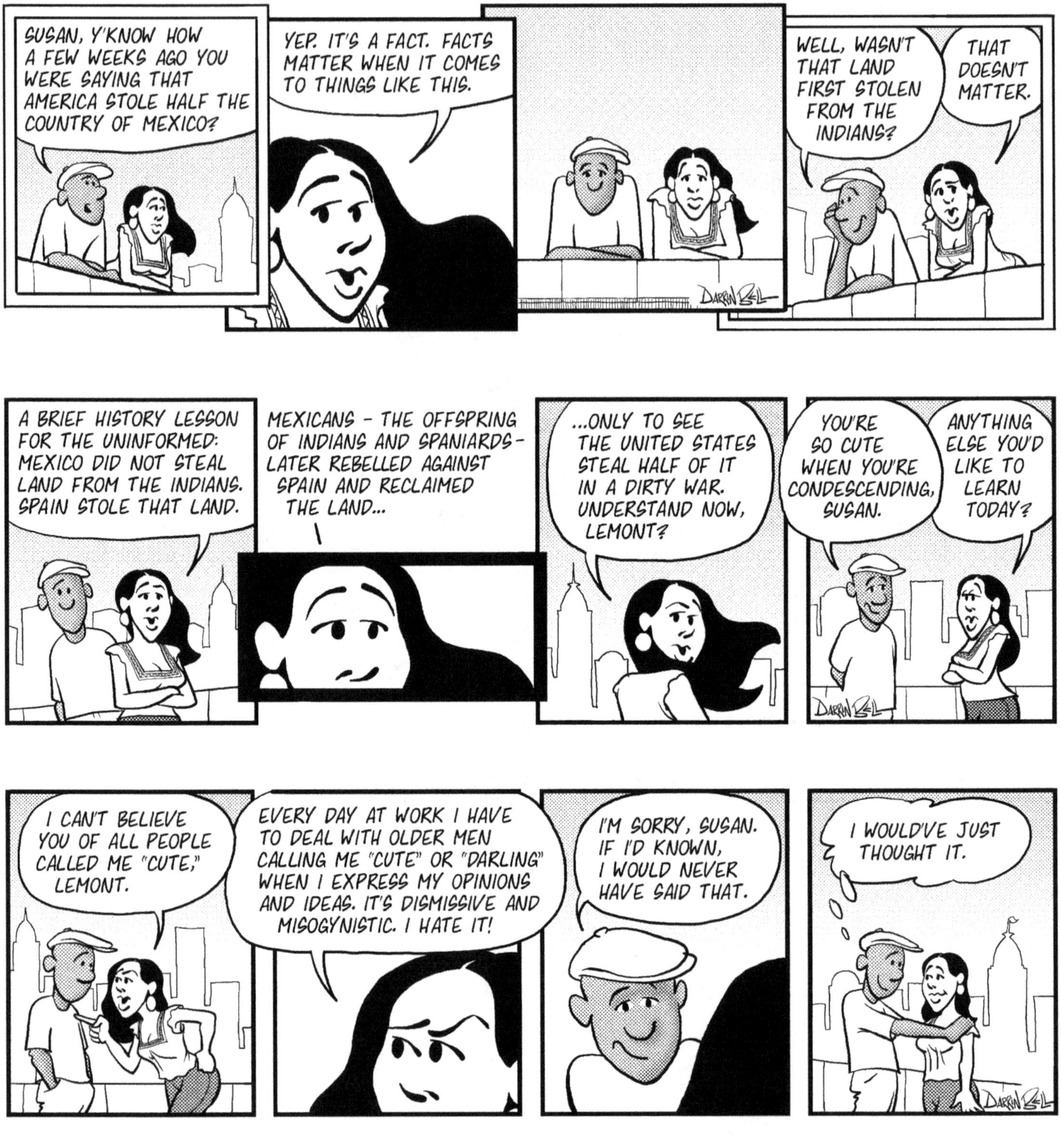
SUSAN, Y'KNOW HOW A FEW WEEKS AGO YOU WERE SAYING THAT AMERICA STOLE HALF THE COUNTRY OF MEXICO?
YEP. IT'S A FACT. FACTS MATTER WHEN IT COMES TO THINGS LIKE THIS.
WELL, WASN'T THAT LAND FIRST STOLEN FROM THE INDIANS?
THAT DOESN'T MATTER.
DARRIN BELL
A BRIEF HISTORY LESSON FOR THE UNINFORMED: MEXICO DID NOT STEAL LAND FROM THE INDIANS. SPAIN STOLE THAT LAND.
MEXICANS - THE OFFSPRING OF INDIANS AND SPANIARDS - LATER REBELLED AGAINST SPAIN AND RECLAIMED THE LAND...
...ONLY TO SEE THE UNITED STATES STEAL HALF OF IT IN A DIRTY WAR. UNDERSTAND NOW, LEMONT?
YOU'RE SO CUTE WHEN YOU'RE CONDESCENDING, SUSAN.
ANYTHING ELSE YOU'D LIKE TO LEARN TODAY?
DARRIN BELL
I CAN'T BELIEVE YOU OF ALL PEOPLE CALLED ME "CUTE," LEMONT.
EVERY DAY AT WORK I HAVE TO DEAL WITH OLDER MEN CALLING ME "CUTE" OR "DARLING" WHEN I EXPRESS MY OPINIONS AND IDEAS. IT'S DISMISSIVE AND MISOGYNISTIC. I HATE IT!
I'M SORRY, SUSAN. IF I'D KNOWN, I WOULD NEVER HAVE SAID THAT.
I WOULD'VE JUST THOUGHT IT.
DARRIN BELL

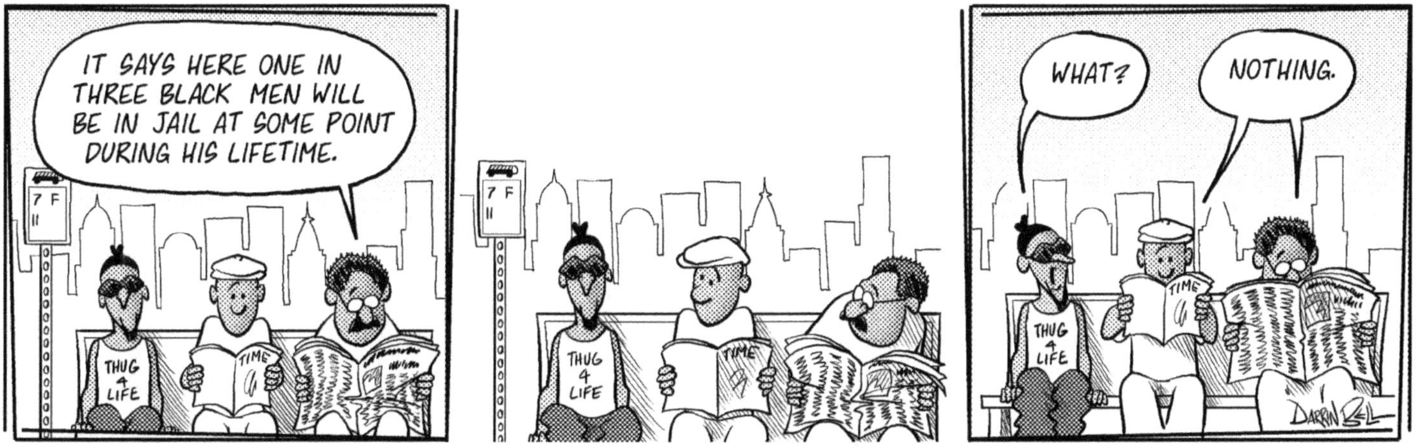
IT SAYS HERE ONE IN THREE BLACK MEN WILL BE IN JAIL AT SOME POINT DURING HIS LIFETIME.
THUG 4 LIFE
TIME
WHAT?
NOTHING.

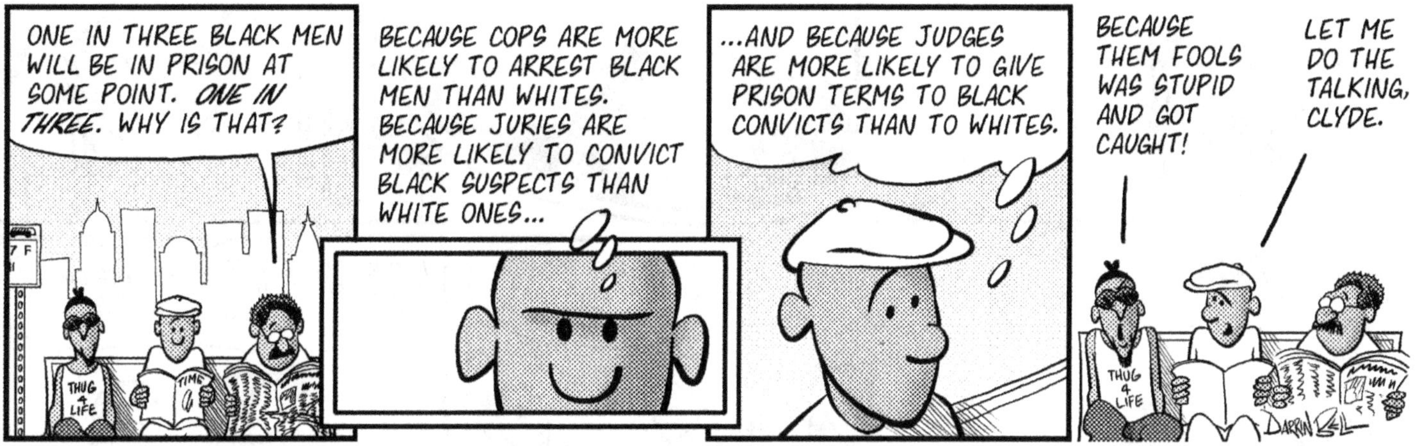
ONE IN THREE BLACK MEN WILL BE IN PRISON AT SOME POINT. *ONE IN THREE*. WHY IS THAT?
THUG 4 LIFE
TIME
BECAUSE COPS ARE MORE LIKELY TO ARREST BLACK MEN THAN WHITES. BECAUSE JURIES ARE MORE LIKELY TO CONVICT BLACK SUSPECTS THAN WHITE ONES...
...AND BECAUSE JUDGES ARE MORE LIKELY TO GIVE PRISON TERMS TO BLACK CONVICTS THAN TO WHITES.
BECAUSE THEM FOOLS WAS STUPID AND GOT CAUGHT!
LET ME DO THE TALKING, CLYDE.

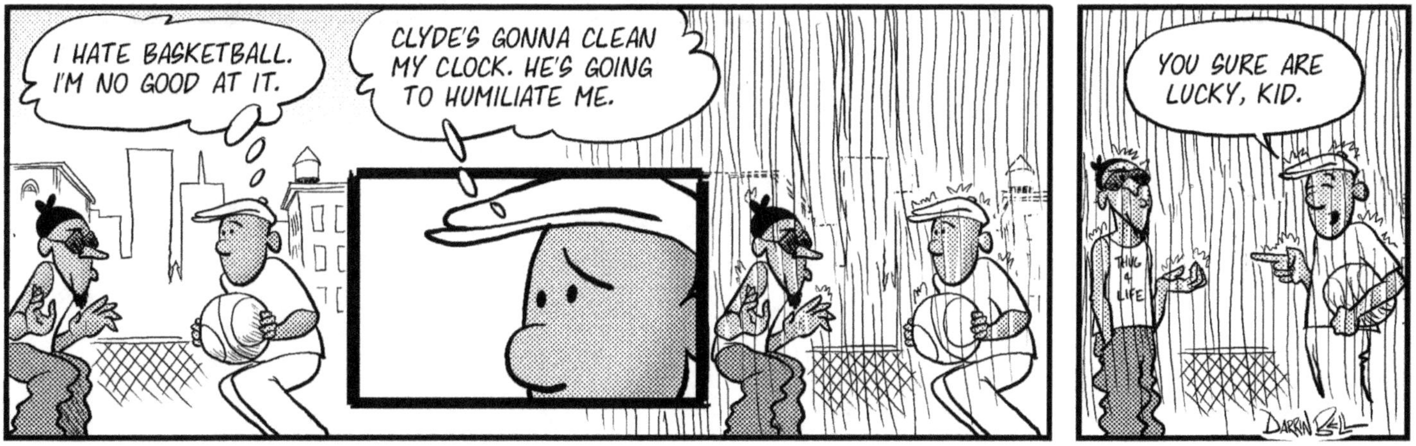
I HATE BASKETBALL. I'M NO GOOD AT IT.
CLYDE'S GONNA CLEAN MY CLOCK. HE'S GOING TO HUMILIATE ME.
YOU SURE ARE LUCKY, KID.
THUG 4 LIFE

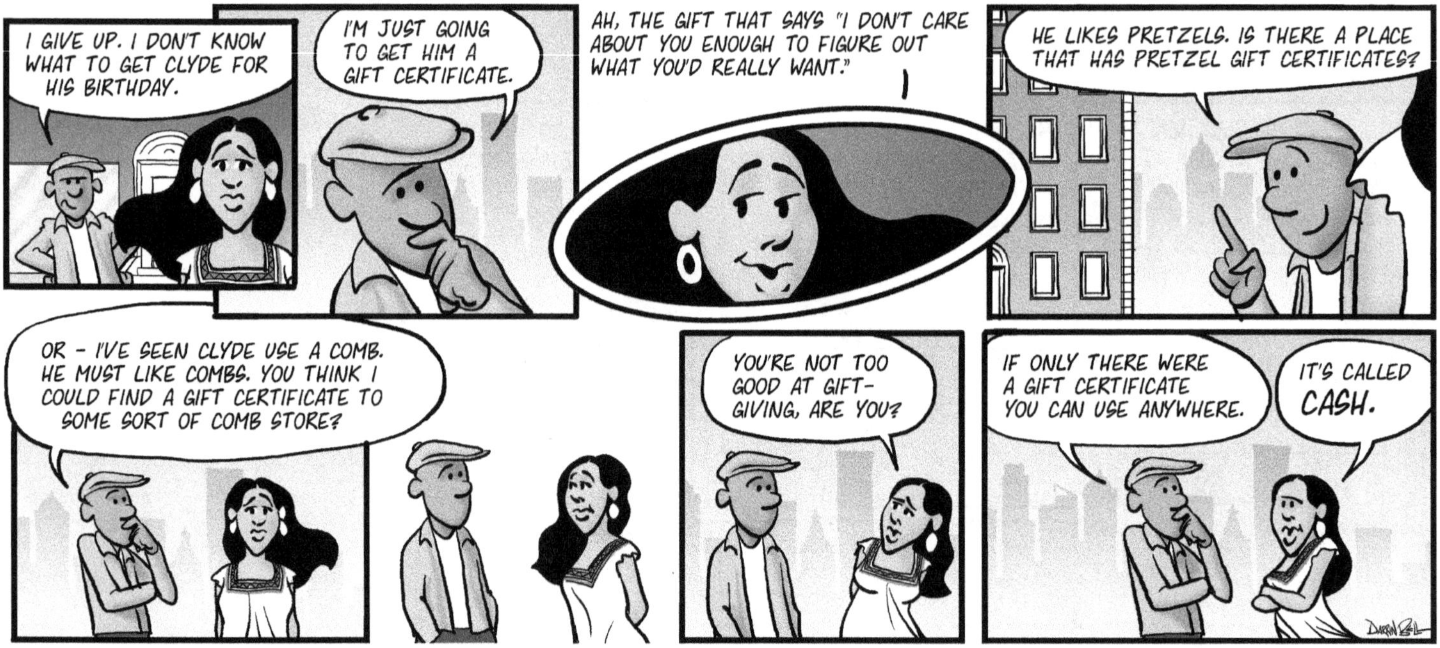
I GIVE UP. I DON'T KNOW WHAT TO GET CLYDE FOR HIS BIRTHDAY.
I'M JUST GOING TO GET HIM A GIFT CERTIFICATE.
AH, THE GIFT THAT SAYS "I DON'T CARE ABOUT YOU ENOUGH TO FIGURE OUT WHAT YOU'D REALLY WANT."
HE LIKES PRETZELS. IS THERE A PLACE THAT HAS PRETZEL GIFT CERTIFICATES?
OR – I'VE SEEN CLYDE USE A COMB. HE MUST LIKE COMBS. YOU THINK I COULD FIND A GIFT CERTIFICATE TO SOME SORT OF COMB STORE?
YOU'RE NOT TOO GOOD AT GIFT-GIVING, ARE YOU?
IF ONLY THERE WERE A GIFT CERTIFICATE YOU CAN USE ANYWHERE.
IT'S CALLED CASH.

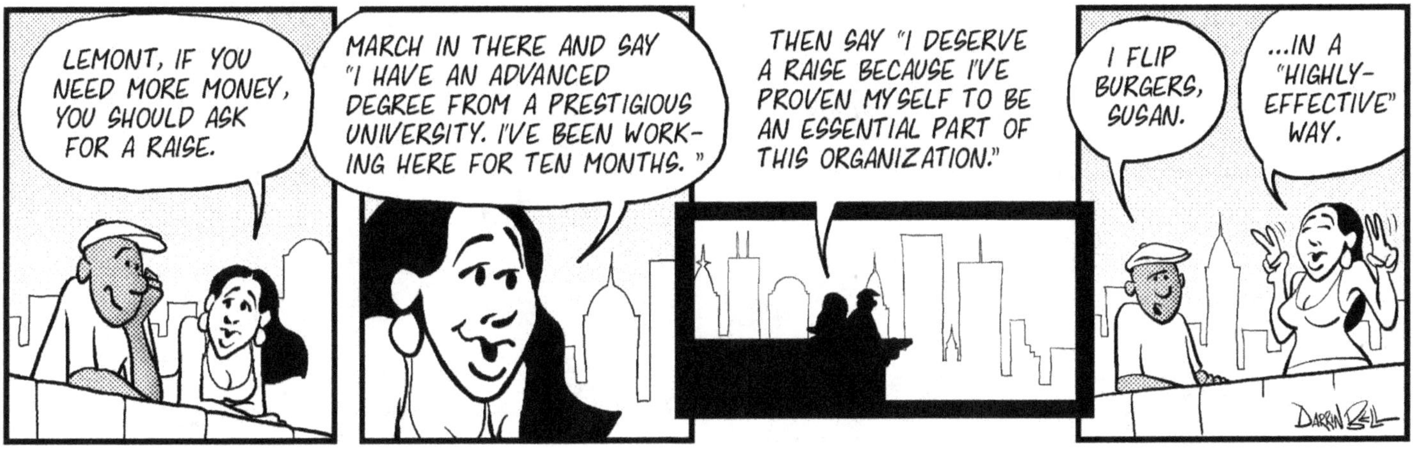
LEMONT, IF YOU NEED MORE MONEY, YOU SHOULD ASK FOR A RAISE.
MARCH IN THERE AND SAY "I HAVE AN ADVANCED DEGREE FROM A PRESTIGIOUS UNIVERSITY. I'VE BEEN WORKING HERE FOR TEN MONTHS."
THEN SAY "I DESERVE A RAISE BECAUSE I'VE PROVEN MYSELF TO BE AN ESSENTIAL PART OF THIS ORGANIZATION."
I FLIP BURGERS, SUSAN.
...IN A "HIGHLY-EFFECTIVE" WAY.

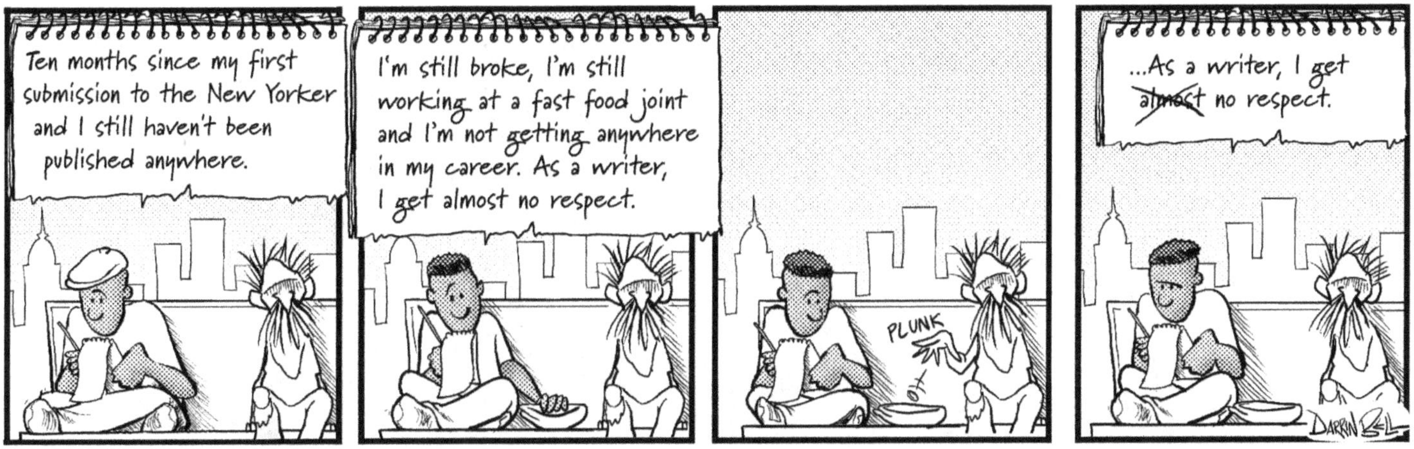
Ten months since my first submission to the New Yorker and I still haven't been published anywhere.
I'm still broke, I'm still working at a fast food joint and I'm not getting anywhere in my career. As a writer, I get almost no respect.
PLUNK
...As a writer, I get ~~almost~~ no respect.

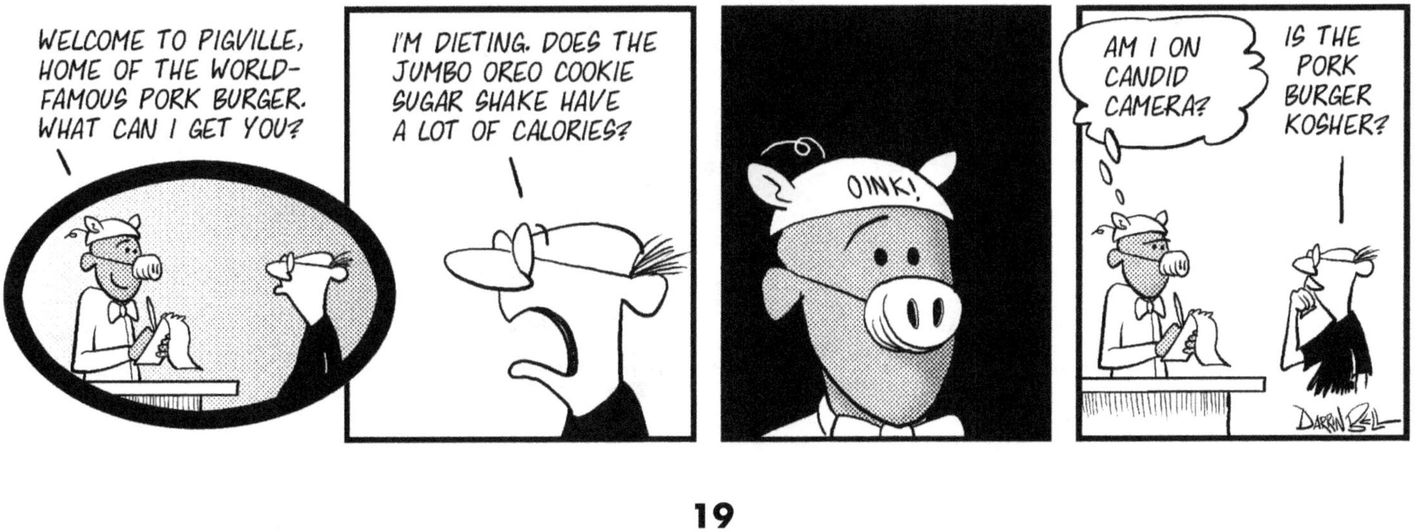
WELCOME TO PIGVILLE, HOME OF THE WORLD-FAMOUS PORK BURGER. WHAT CAN I GET YOU?
I'M DIETING. DOES THE JUMBO OREO COOKIE SUGAR SHAKE HAVE A LOT OF CALORIES?
OINK!
AM I ON CANDID CAMERA?
IS THE PORK BURGER KOSHER?

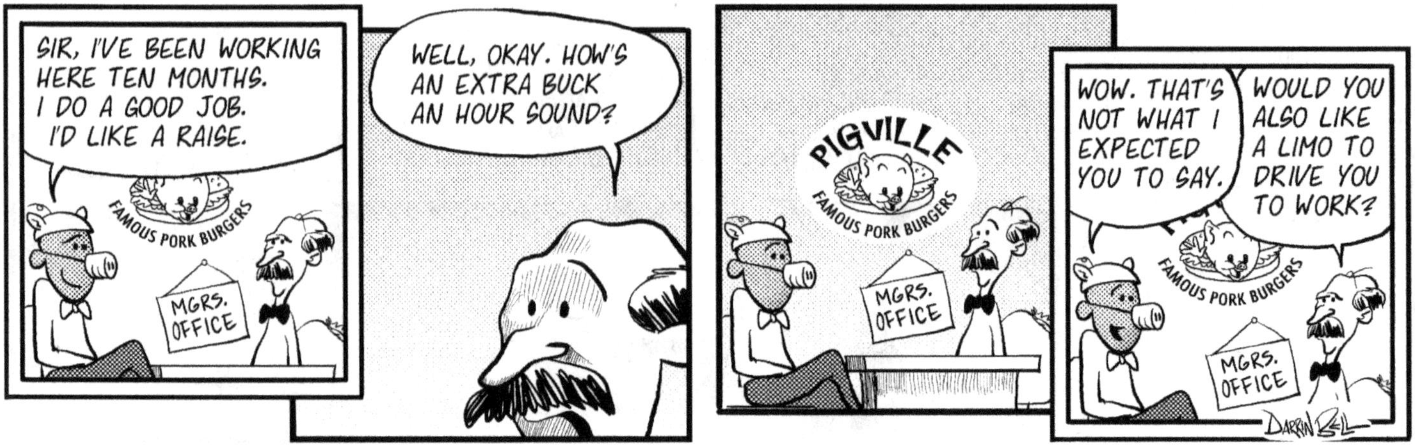
SIR, I'VE BEEN WORKING HERE TEN MONTHS. I DO A GOOD JOB. I'D LIKE A RAISE.
FAMOUS PORK BURGERS
MGRS. OFFICE
WELL, OKAY. HOW'S AN EXTRA BUCK AN HOUR SOUND?
PIGVILLE
FAMOUS PORK BURGERS
MGRS. OFFICE
WOW. THAT'S NOT WHAT I EXPECTED YOU TO SAY.
WOULD YOU ALSO LIKE A LIMO TO DRIVE YOU TO WORK?
FAMOUS PORK BURGERS
MGRS. OFFICE
DARRIN BELL

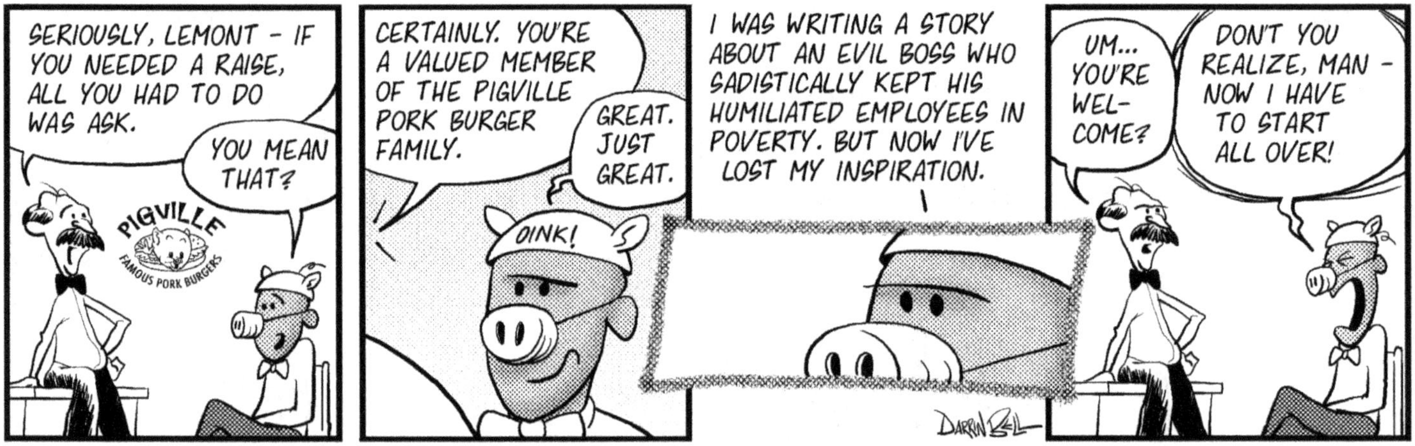
SERIOUSLY, LEMONT - IF YOU NEEDED A RAISE, ALL YOU HAD TO DO WAS ASK.
YOU MEAN THAT?
PIGVILLE
FAMOUS PORK BURGERS
CERTAINLY. YOU'RE A VALUED MEMBER OF THE PIGVILLE PORK BURGER FAMILY.
GREAT. JUST GREAT.
OINK!
I WAS WRITING A STORY ABOUT AN EVIL BOSS WHO SADISTICALLY KEPT HIS HUMILIATED EMPLOYEES IN POVERTY. BUT NOW I'VE LOST MY INSPIRATION.
UM... YOU'RE WEL-COME?
DON'T YOU REALIZE, MAN - NOW I HAVE TO START ALL OVER!
DARRIN BELL

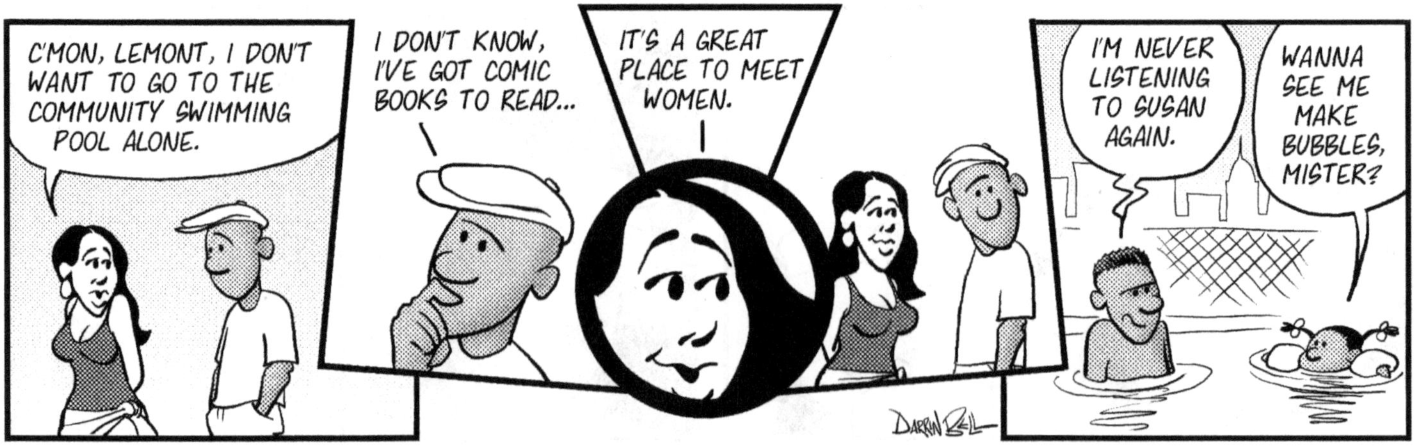
C'MON, LEMONT, I DON'T WANT TO GO TO THE COMMUNITY SWIMMING POOL ALONE.
I DON'T KNOW, I'VE GOT COMIC BOOKS TO READ...
IT'S A GREAT PLACE TO MEET WOMEN.
I'M NEVER LISTENING TO SUSAN AGAIN.
WANNA SEE ME MAKE BUBBLES, MISTER?
DARRIN BELL

STRAWBERRY TRUCK'S ALWAYS ON TIME.
GET A @#$% JOB!!!
DARRIN BELL

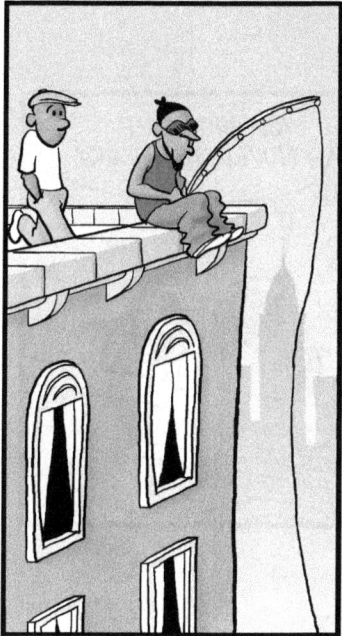

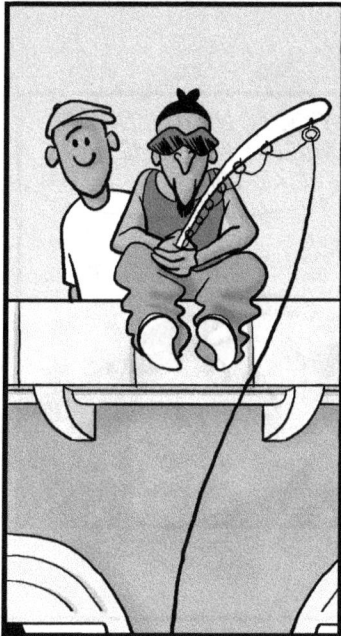

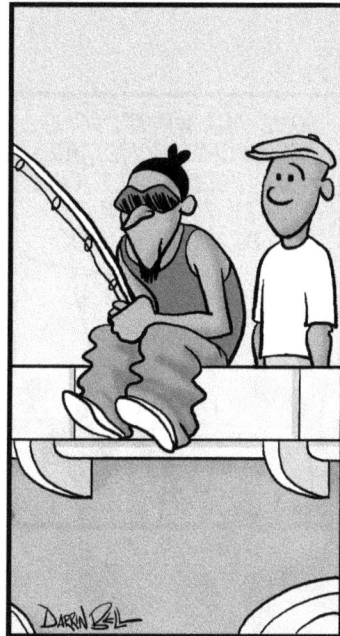

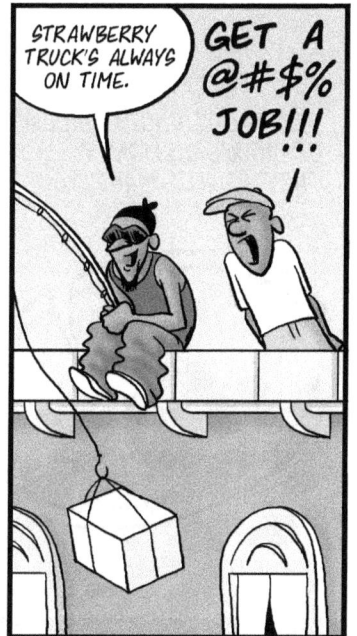

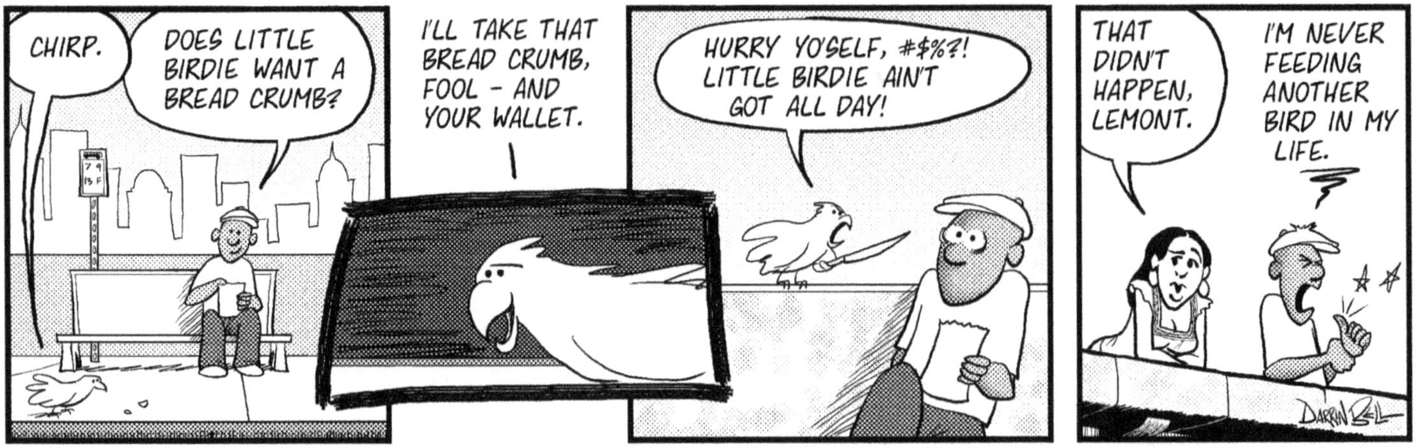
CHIRP.
DOES LITTLE BIRDIE WANT A BREAD CRUMB?
I'LL TAKE THAT BREAD CRUMB, FOOL - AND YOUR WALLET.
HURRY YO'SELF, #$%?! LITTLE BIRDIE AIN'T GOT ALL DAY!
THAT DIDN'T HAPPEN, LEMONT.
I'M NEVER FEEDING ANOTHER BIRD IN MY LIFE.
DARRIN BELL

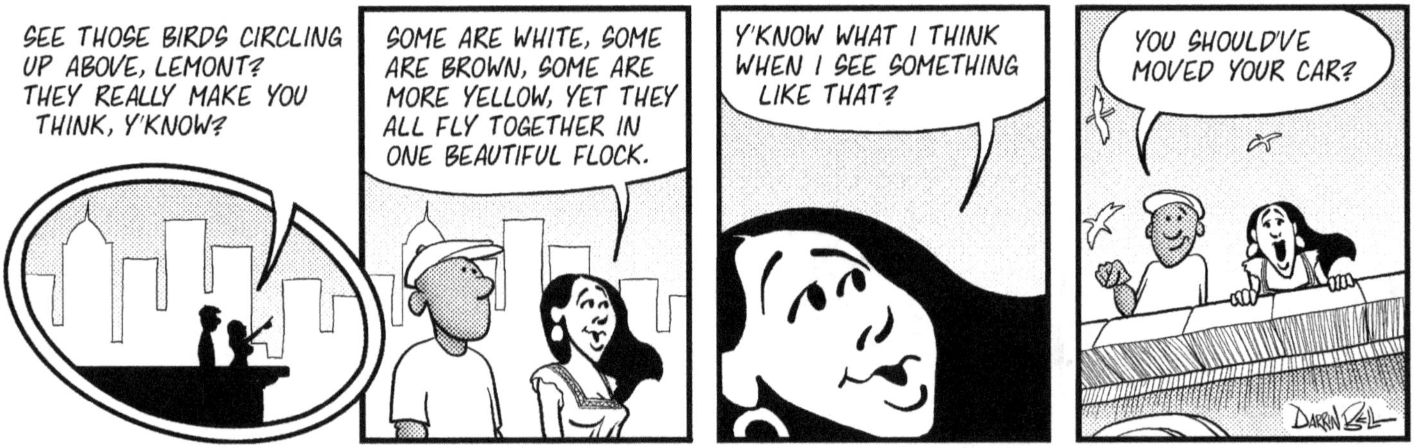
SEE THOSE BIRDS CIRCLING UP ABOVE, LEMONT? THEY REALLY MAKE YOU THINK, Y'KNOW?
SOME ARE WHITE, SOME ARE BROWN, SOME ARE MORE YELLOW, YET THEY ALL FLY TOGETHER IN ONE BEAUTIFUL FLOCK.
Y'KNOW WHAT I THINK WHEN I SEE SOMETHING LIKE THAT?
YOU SHOULD'VE MOVED YOUR CAR?
DARRIN BELL

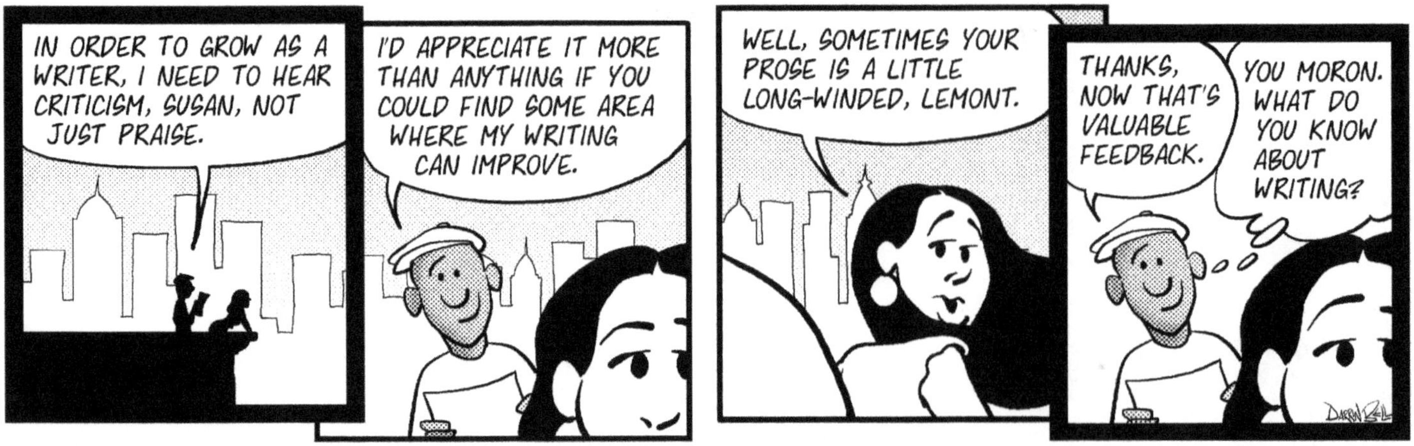
IN ORDER TO GROW AS A WRITER, I NEED TO HEAR CRITICISM, SUSAN, NOT JUST PRAISE.
I'D APPRECIATE IT MORE THAN ANYTHING IF YOU COULD FIND SOME AREA WHERE MY WRITING CAN IMPROVE.
WELL, SOMETIMES YOUR PROSE IS A LITTLE LONG-WINDED, LEMONT.
THANKS, NOW THAT'S VALUABLE FEEDBACK.
YOU MORON. WHAT DO YOU KNOW ABOUT WRITING?
DARRIN BELL

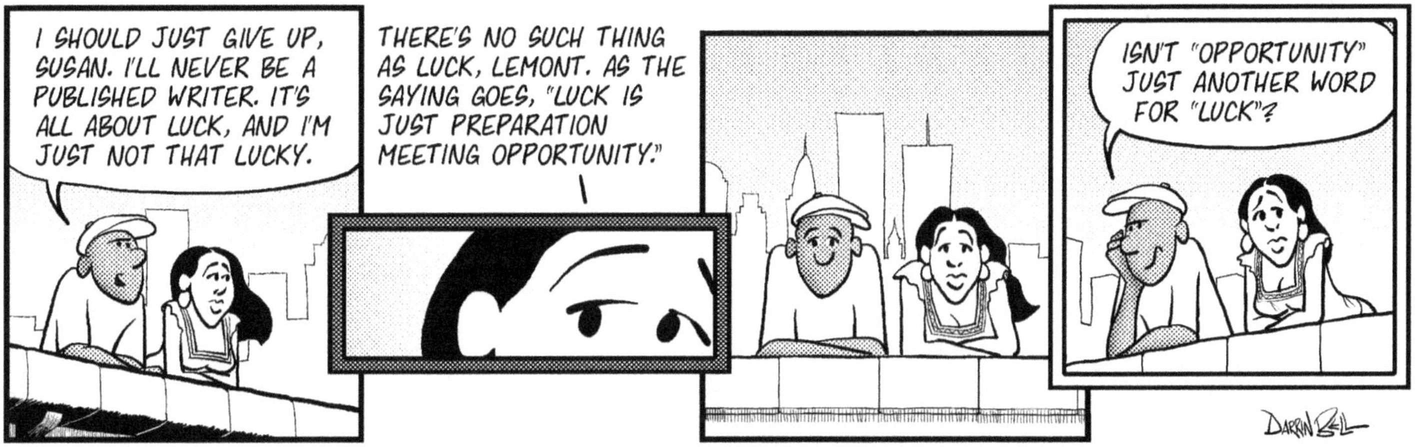
I SHOULD JUST GIVE UP, SUSAN. I'LL NEVER BE A PUBLISHED WRITER. IT'S ALL ABOUT LUCK, AND I'M JUST NOT THAT LUCKY.
THERE'S NO SUCH THING AS LUCK, LEMONT. AS THE SAYING GOES, "LUCK IS JUST PREPARATION MEETING OPPORTUNITY."
ISN'T "OPPORTUNITY" JUST ANOTHER WORD FOR "LUCK"?

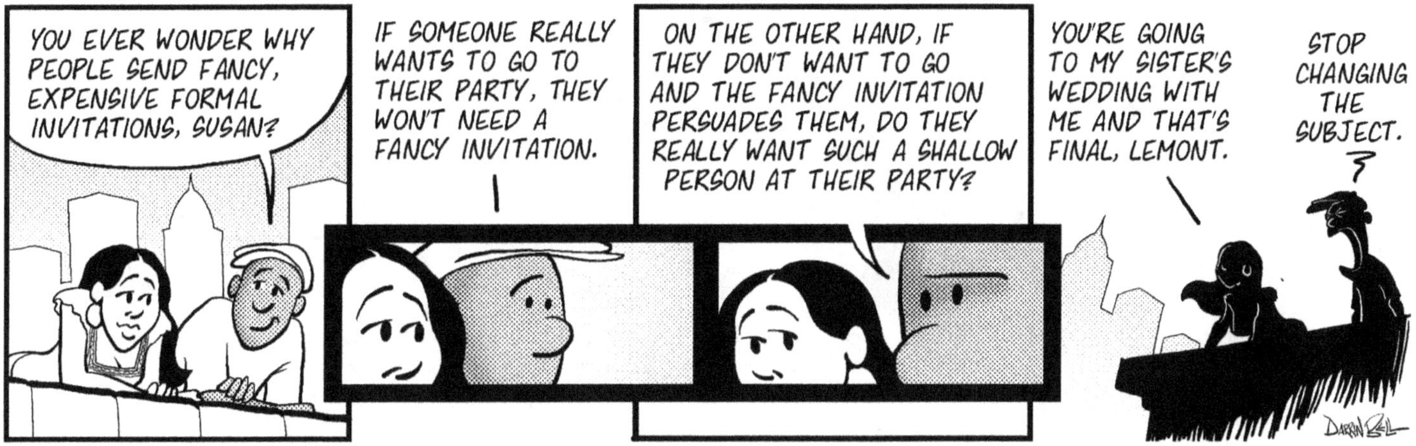
YOU EVER WONDER WHY PEOPLE SEND FANCY, EXPENSIVE FORMAL INVITATIONS, SUSAN?
IF SOMEONE REALLY WANTS TO GO TO THEIR PARTY, THEY WON'T NEED A FANCY INVITATION.
ON THE OTHER HAND, IF THEY DON'T WANT TO GO AND THE FANCY INVITATION PERSUADES THEM, DO THEY REALLY WANT SUCH A SHALLOW PERSON AT THEIR PARTY?
YOU'RE GOING TO MY SISTER'S WEDDING WITH ME AND THAT'S FINAL, LEMONT.
STOP CHANGING THE SUBJECT.

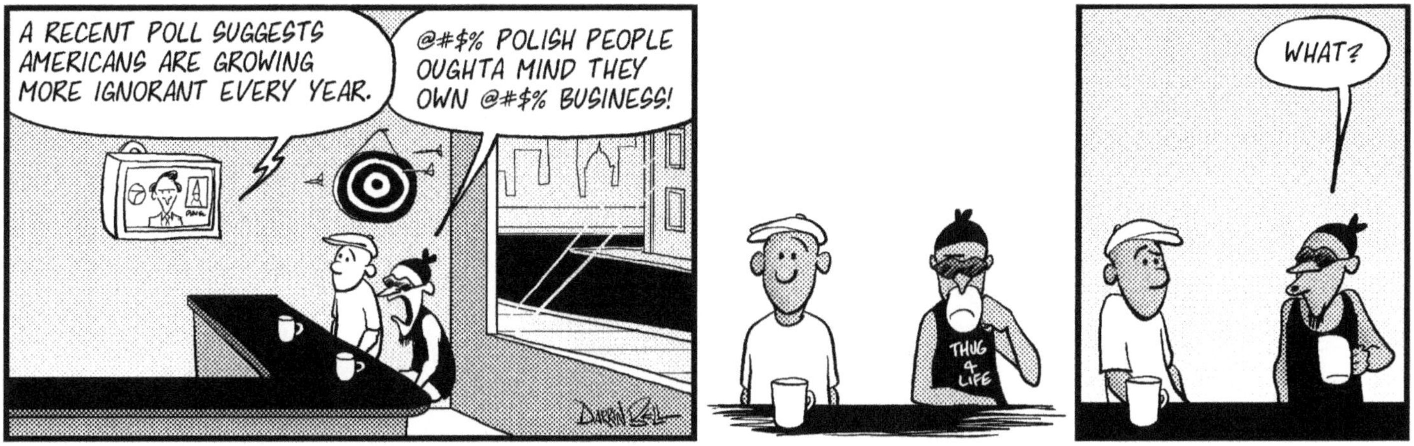
A RECENT POLL SUGGESTS AMERICANS ARE GROWING MORE IGNORANT EVERY YEAR.
@#$% POLISH PEOPLE OUGHTA MIND THEY OWN @#$% BUSINESS!
THUG 4 LIFE
WHAT?

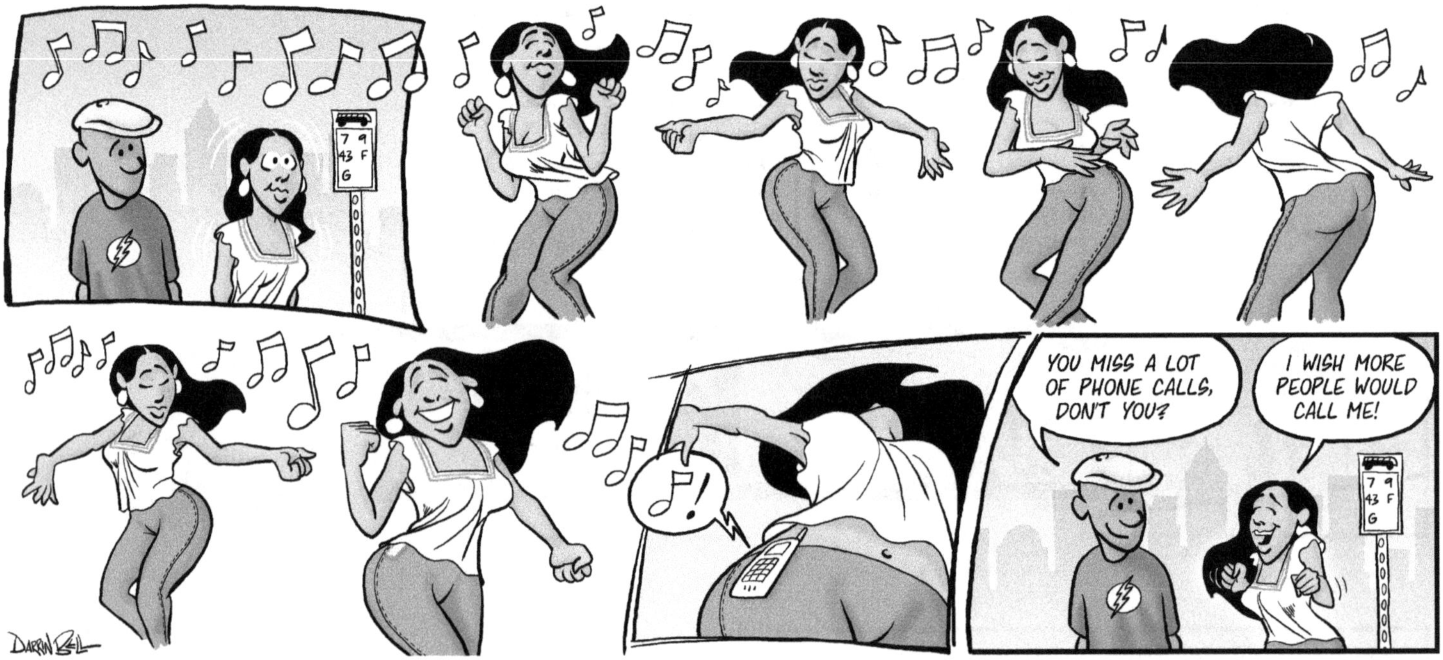

7 9
43 F
G
YOU MISS A LOT OF PHONE CALLS, DON'T YOU?
I WISH MORE PEOPLE WOULD CALL ME!

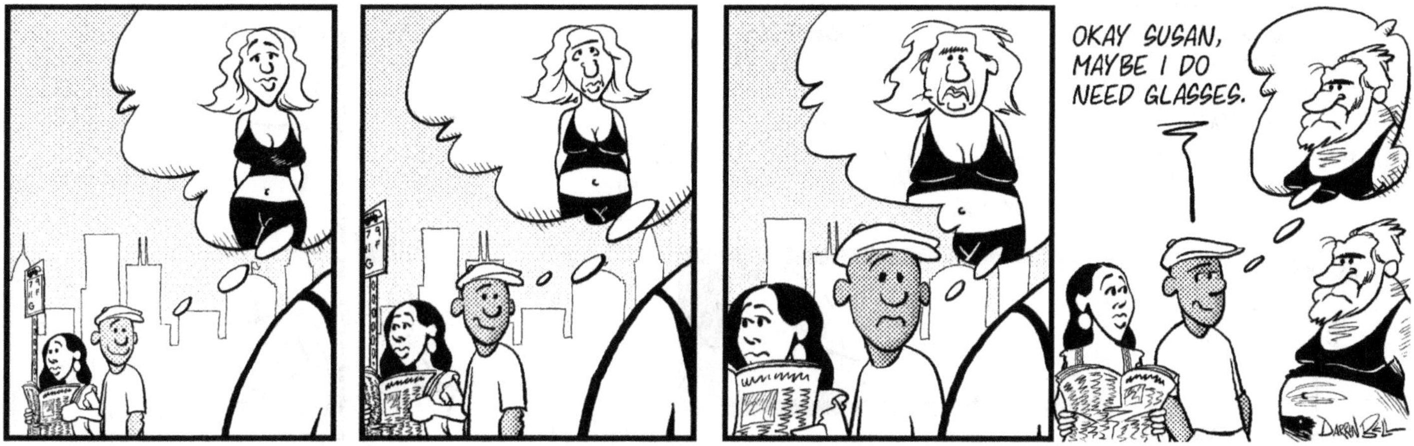
OKAY SUSAN, MAYBE I DO NEED GLASSES.

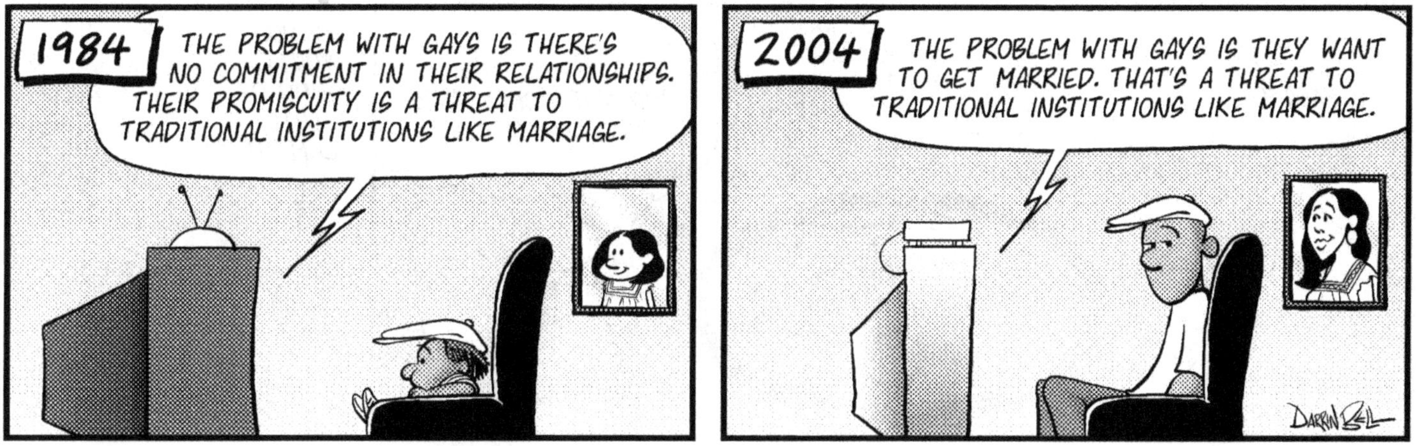
1984
THE PROBLEM WITH GAYS IS THERE'S NO COMMITMENT IN THEIR RELATIONSHIPS. THEIR PROMISCUITY IS A THREAT TO TRADITIONAL INSTITUTIONS LIKE MARRIAGE.
2004
THE PROBLEM WITH GAYS IS THEY WANT TO GET MARRIED. THAT'S A THREAT TO TRADITIONAL INSTITUTIONS LIKE MARRIAGE.

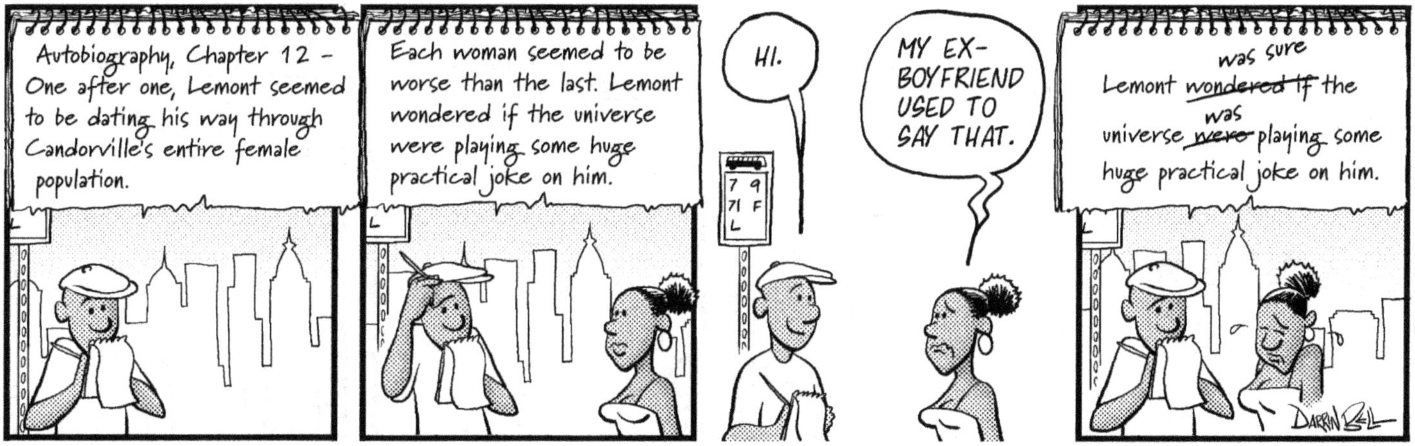
Autobiography, Chapter 12 - One after one, Lemont seemed to be dating his way through Candorville's entire female population.
Each woman seemed to be worse than the last. Lemont wondered if the universe were playing some huge practical joke on him.
HI.
MY EX-BOYFRIEND USED TO SAY THAT.
Lemont ~~wondered if~~ was sure the universe ~~were~~ was playing some huge practical joke on him.

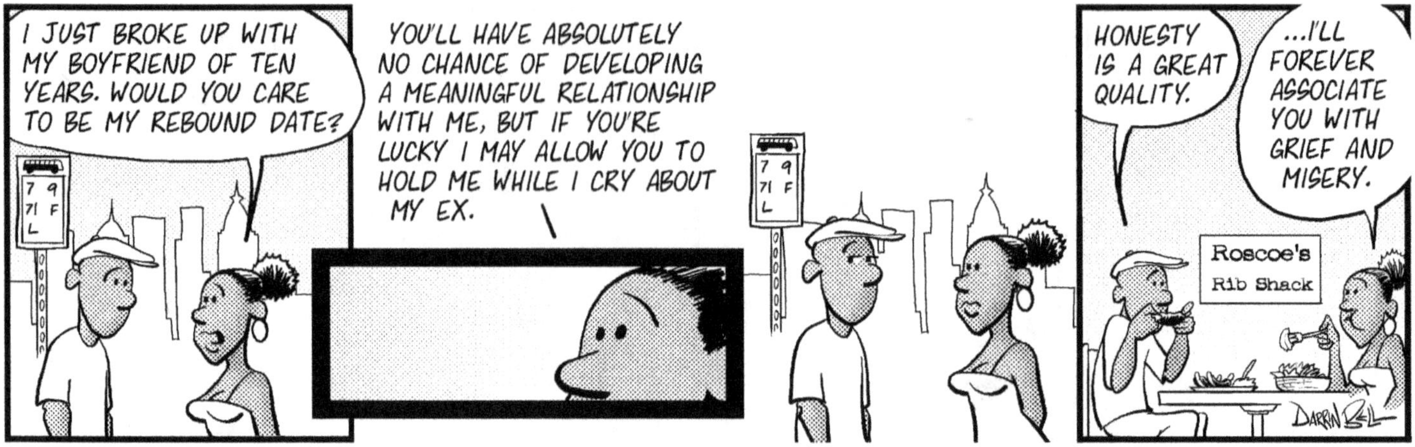
I JUST BROKE UP WITH MY BOYFRIEND OF TEN YEARS. WOULD YOU CARE TO BE MY REBOUND DATE?
YOU'LL HAVE ABSOLUTELY NO CHANCE OF DEVELOPING A MEANINGFUL RELATIONSHIP WITH ME, BUT IF YOU'RE LUCKY I MAY ALLOW YOU TO HOLD ME WHILE I CRY ABOUT MY EX.
HONESTY IS A GREAT QUALITY.
...I'LL FOREVER ASSOCIATE YOU WITH GRIEF AND MISERY.
Roscoe's Rib Shack
DARRIN BELL

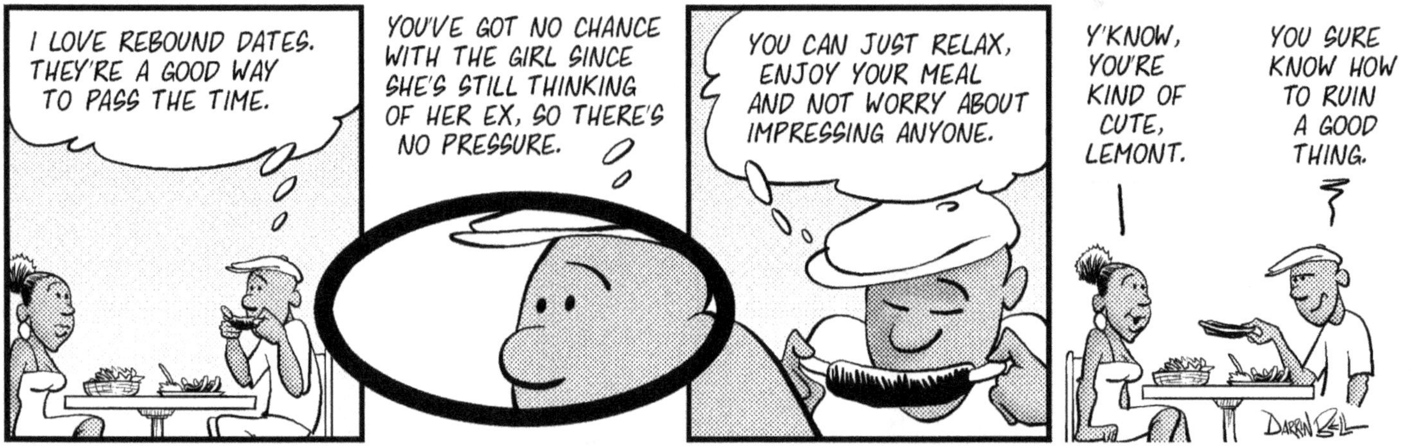
I LOVE REBOUND DATES. THEY'RE A GOOD WAY TO PASS THE TIME.
YOU'VE GOT NO CHANCE WITH THE GIRL SINCE SHE'S STILL THINKING OF HER EX, SO THERE'S NO PRESSURE.
YOU CAN JUST RELAX, ENJOY YOUR MEAL AND NOT WORRY ABOUT IMPRESSING ANYONE.
Y'KNOW, YOU'RE KIND OF CUTE, LEMONT.
YOU SURE KNOW HOW TO RUIN A GOOD THING.
DARRIN BELL

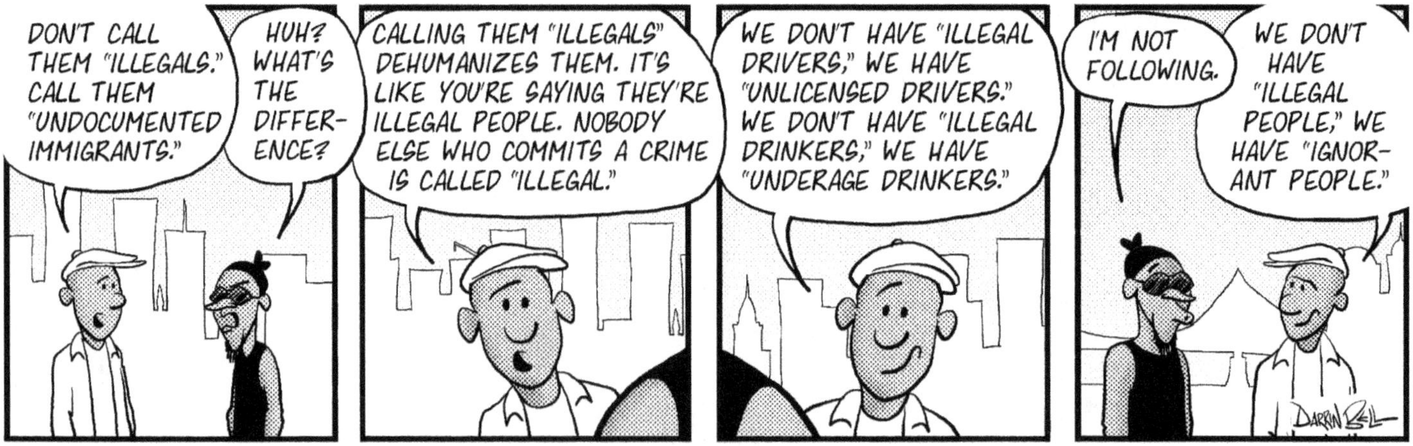
DON'T CALL THEM "ILLEGALS." CALL THEM "UNDOCUMENTED IMMIGRANTS."
HUH? WHAT'S THE DIFFER-ENCE?
CALLING THEM "ILLEGALS" DEHUMANIZES THEM. IT'S LIKE YOU'RE SAYING THEY'RE ILLEGAL PEOPLE. NOBODY ELSE WHO COMMITS A CRIME IS CALLED "ILLEGAL."
WE DON'T HAVE "ILLEGAL DRIVERS," WE HAVE "UNLICENSED DRIVERS." WE DON'T HAVE "ILLEGAL DRINKERS," WE HAVE "UNDERAGE DRINKERS."
I'M NOT FOLLOWING.
WE DON'T HAVE "ILLEGAL PEOPLE," WE HAVE "IGNOR-ANT PEOPLE."
DARRIN BELL

LOOK, LEMONT!
WHAT, SUSAN?
LOOK! LOOK! LOOK!
WHAT? WHERE? HUH?
RIGHT THERE! LOOK, QUICK, YOU'RE MISSING IT!
IT'S RIGHT OVER THERE!
AW, MAN... WHY DO YOU ALWAYS MISS EVERYTHING?
DARRIN BELL

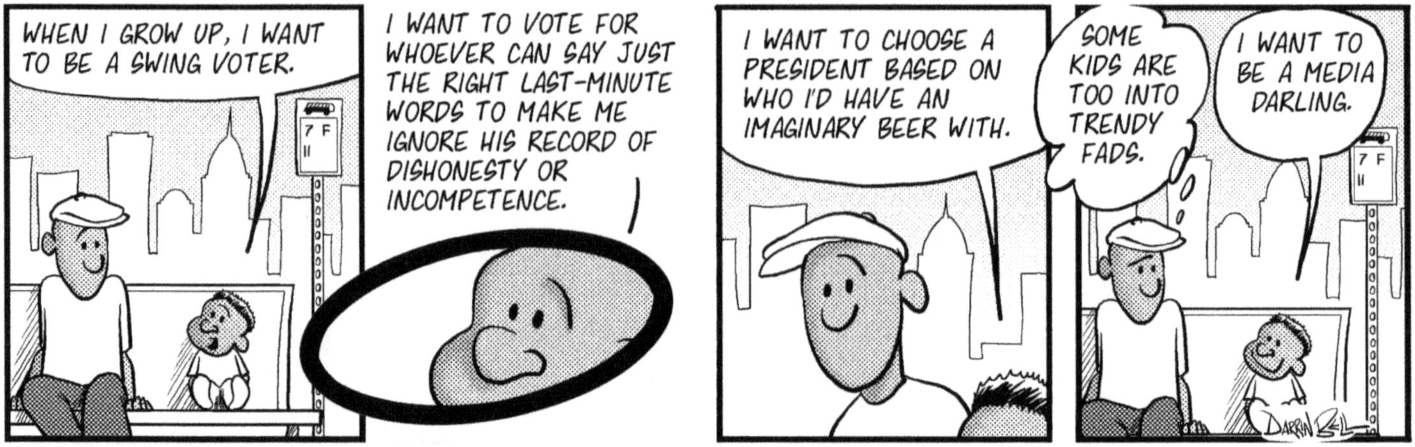
WHEN I GROW UP, I WANT TO BE A SWING VOTER.
I WANT TO VOTE FOR WHOEVER CAN SAY JUST THE RIGHT LAST-MINUTE WORDS TO MAKE ME IGNORE HIS RECORD OF DISHONESTY OR INCOMPETENCE.
I WANT TO CHOOSE A PRESIDENT BASED ON WHO I'D HAVE AN IMAGINARY BEER WITH.
SOME KIDS ARE TOO INTO TRENDY FADS.
I WANT TO BE A MEDIA DARLING.
DARRIN BELL

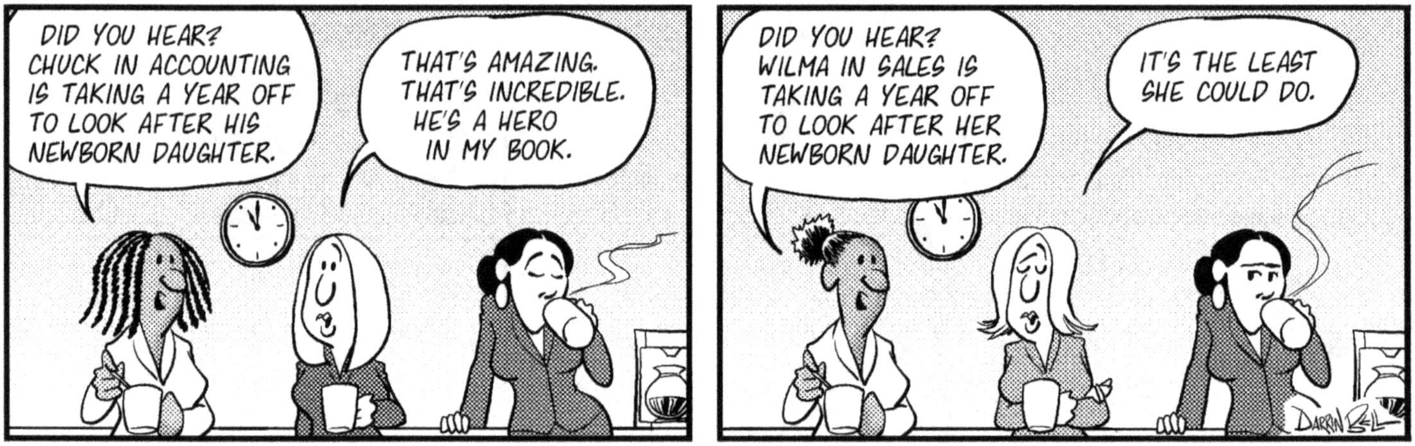
DID YOU HEAR? CHUCK IN ACCOUNTING IS TAKING A YEAR OFF TO LOOK AFTER HIS NEWBORN DAUGHTER.
THAT'S AMAZING. THAT'S INCREDIBLE. HE'S A HERO IN MY BOOK.
DID YOU HEAR? WILMA IN SALES IS TAKING A YEAR OFF TO LOOK AFTER HER NEWBORN DAUGHTER.
IT'S THE LEAST SHE COULD DO.
DARRIN BELL

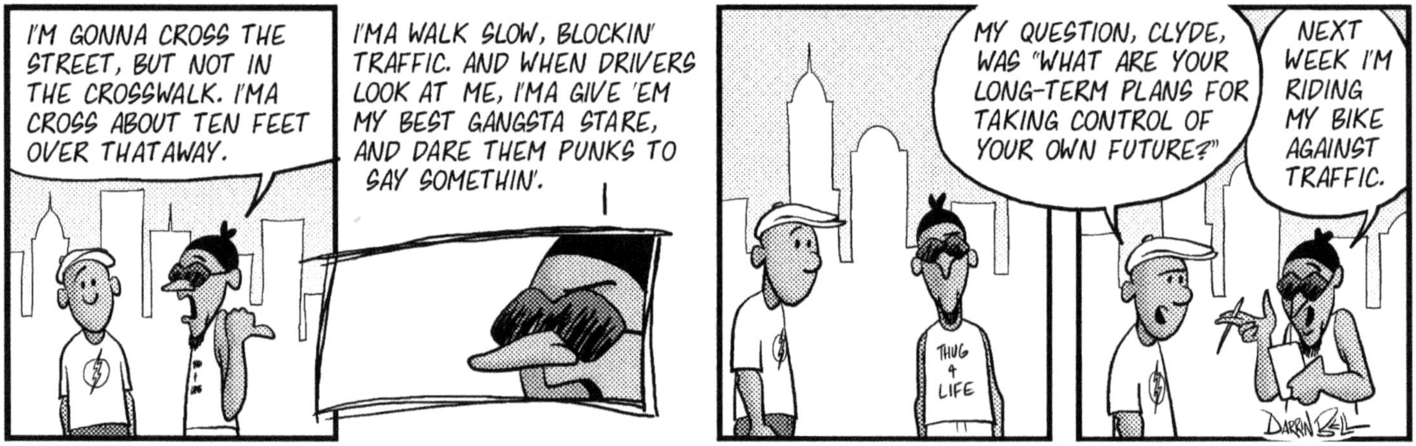
I'M GONNA CROSS THE STREET, BUT NOT IN THE CROSSWALK. I'MA CROSS ABOUT TEN FEET OVER THATAWAY.
I'MA WALK SLOW, BLOCKIN' TRAFFIC. AND WHEN DRIVERS LOOK AT ME, I'MA GIVE 'EM MY BEST GANGSTA STARE, AND DARE THEM PUNKS TO SAY SOMETHIN'.
MY QUESTION, CLYDE, WAS "WHAT ARE YOUR LONG-TERM PLANS FOR TAKING CONTROL OF YOUR OWN FUTURE?"
NEXT WEEK I'M RIDING MY BIKE AGAINST TRAFFIC.
THUG 4 LIFE
DARRIN BELL

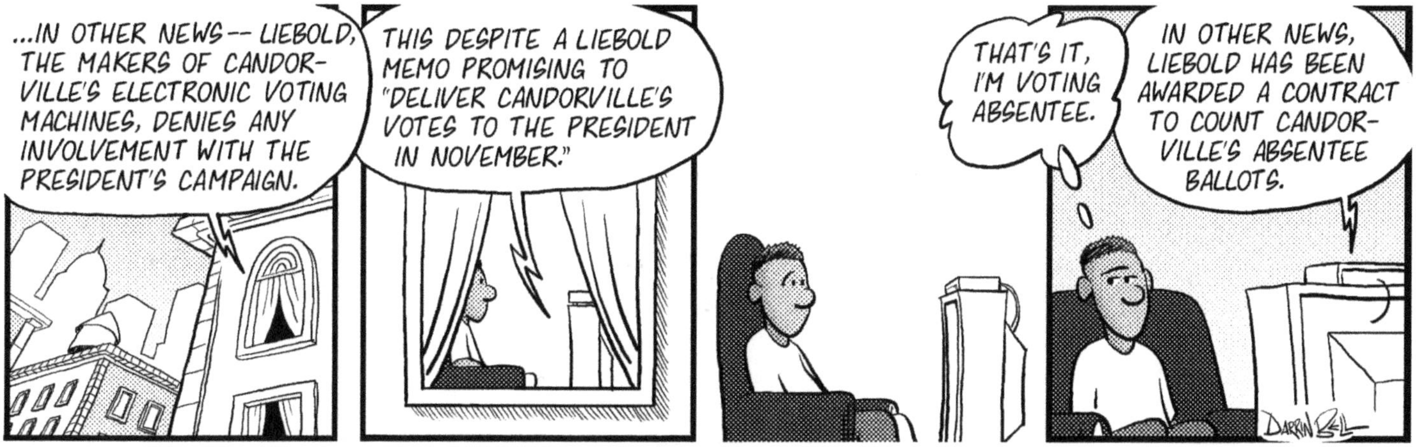
...IN OTHER NEWS-- LIEBOLD, THE MAKERS OF CANDORVILLE'S ELECTRONIC VOTING MACHINES, DENIES ANY INVOLVEMENT WITH THE PRESIDENT'S CAMPAIGN.
THIS DESPITE A LIEBOLD MEMO PROMISING TO "DELIVER CANDORVILLE'S VOTES TO THE PRESIDENT IN NOVEMBER."
THAT'S IT, I'M VOTING ABSENTEE.
IN OTHER NEWS, LIEBOLD HAS BEEN AWARDED A CONTRACT TO COUNT CANDORVILLE'S ABSENTEE BALLOTS.
DARRIN BELL

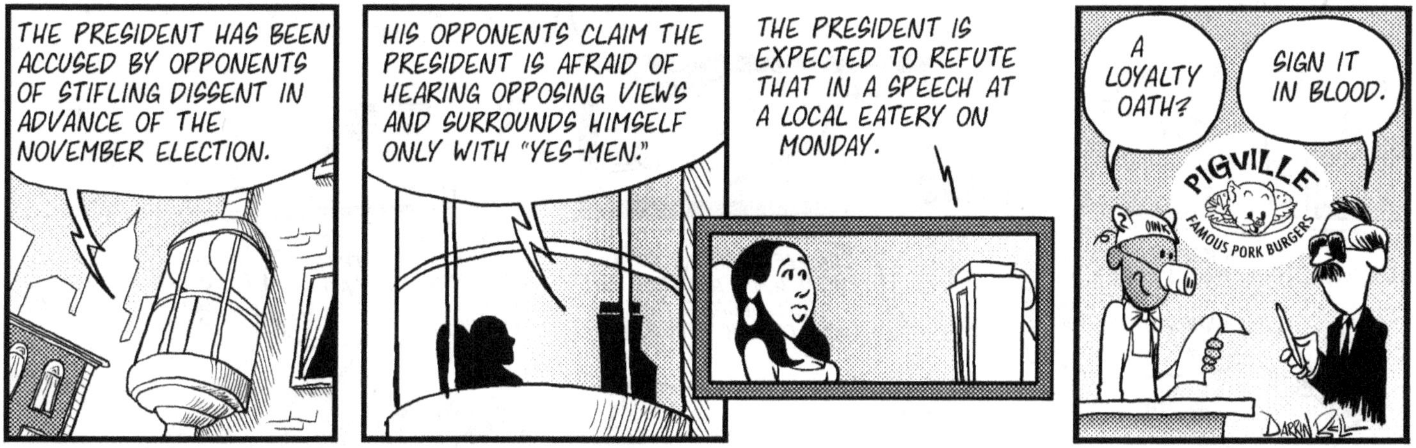
THE PRESIDENT HAS BEEN ACCUSED BY OPPONENTS OF STIFLING DISSENT IN ADVANCE OF THE NOVEMBER ELECTION.
HIS OPPONENTS CLAIM THE PRESIDENT IS AFRAID OF HEARING OPPOSING VIEWS AND SURROUNDS HIMSELF ONLY WITH "YES-MEN."
THE PRESIDENT IS EXPECTED TO REFUTE THAT IN A SPEECH AT A LOCAL EATERY ON MONDAY.
A LOYALTY OATH?
SIGN IT IN BLOOD.
PIGVILLE
FAMOUS PORK BURGERS
OINK
DARRIN BELL

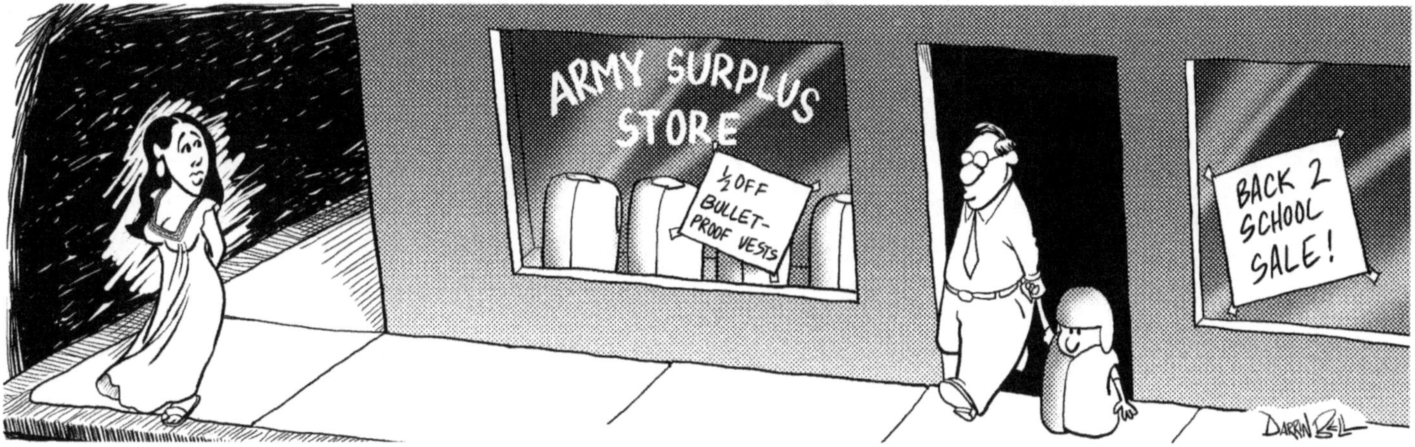
ARMY SURPLUS STORE
½ OFF BULLET-PROOF VESTS
BACK 2 SCHOOL SALE!
DARRIN BELL

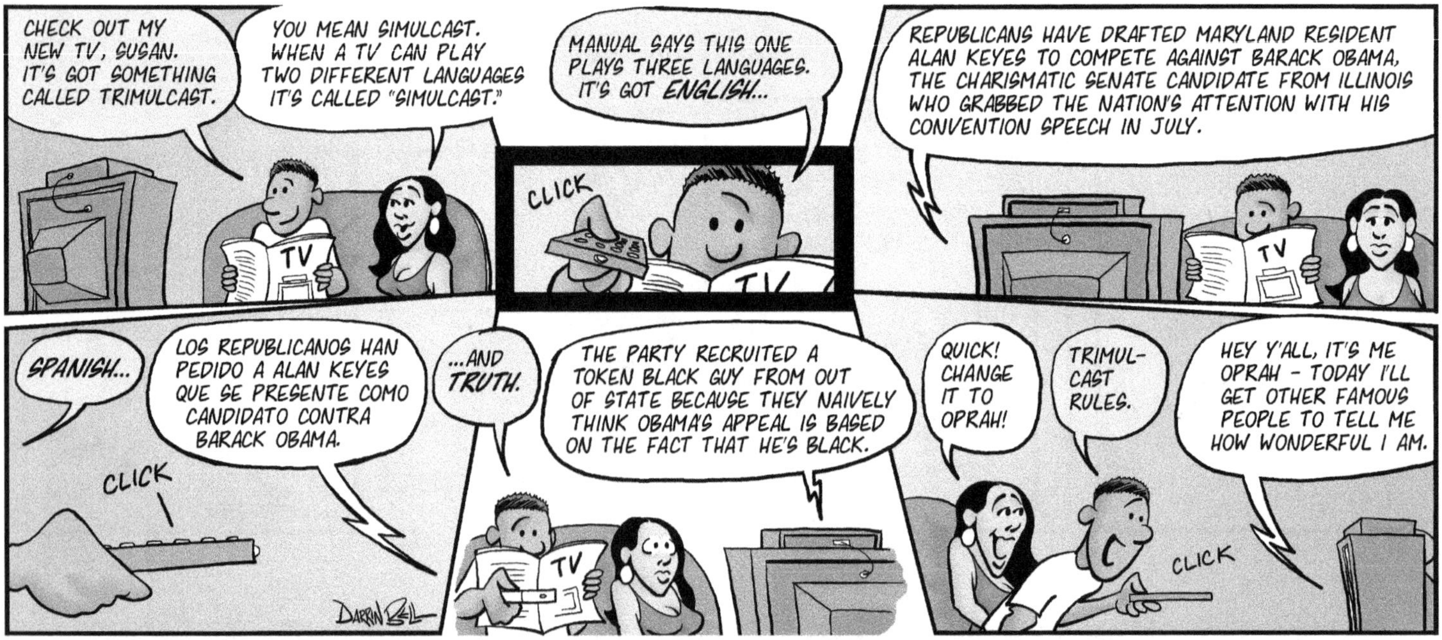
CHECK OUT MY NEW TV, SUSAN. IT'S GOT SOMETHING CALLED TRIMULCAST.
YOU MEAN SIMULCAST. WHEN A TV CAN PLAY TWO DIFFERENT LANGUAGES IT'S CALLED "SIMULCAST."
MANUAL SAYS THIS ONE PLAYS THREE LANGUAGES. IT'S GOT ENGLISH...
CLICK
TV
REPUBLICANS HAVE DRAFTED MARYLAND RESIDENT ALAN KEYES TO COMPETE AGAINST BARACK OBAMA, THE CHARISMATIC SENATE CANDIDATE FROM ILLINOIS WHO GRABBED THE NATION'S ATTENTION WITH HIS CONVENTION SPEECH IN JULY.
SPANISH...
LOS REPUBLICANOS HAN PEDIDO A ALAN KEYES QUE SE PRESENTE COMO CANDIDATO CONTRA BARACK OBAMA.
CLICK
DARRIN BELL
...AND TRUTH.
THE PARTY RECRUITED A TOKEN BLACK GUY FROM OUT OF STATE BECAUSE THEY NAIVELY THINK OBAMA'S APPEAL IS BASED ON THE FACT THAT HE'S BLACK.
QUICK! CHANGE IT TO OPRAH!
TRIMUL-CAST RULES.
HEY Y'ALL, IT'S ME OPRAH – TODAY I'LL GET OTHER FAMOUS PEOPLE TO TELL ME HOW WONDERFUL I AM.
CLICK

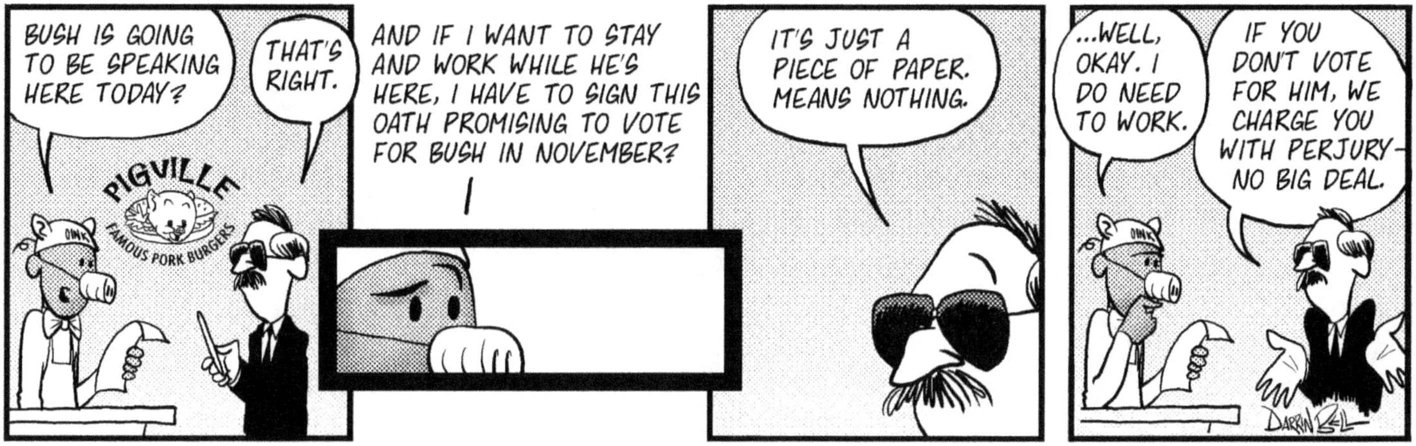
BUSH IS GOING TO BE SPEAKING HERE TODAY?
THAT'S RIGHT.
PIGVILLE
FAMOUS PORK BURGERS
OINK
AND IF I WANT TO STAY AND WORK WHILE HE'S HERE, I HAVE TO SIGN THIS OATH PROMISING TO VOTE FOR BUSH IN NOVEMBER?
IT'S JUST A PIECE OF PAPER. MEANS NOTHING.
...WELL, OKAY. I DO NEED TO WORK.
IF YOU DON'T VOTE FOR HIM, WE CHARGE YOU WITH PERJURY– NO BIG DEAL.
DARRIN BELL

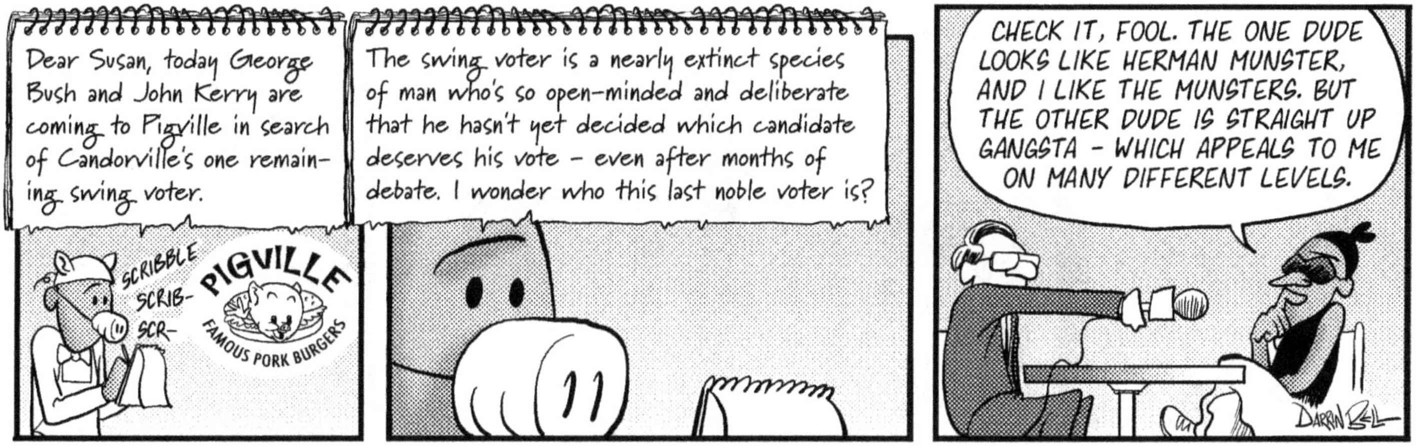
Dear Susan, today George Bush and John Kerry are coming to Pigville in search of Candorville's one remaining swing voter.
SCRIBBLE
SCRIB-
SCR-
PIGVILLE
FAMOUS PORK BURGERS
The swing voter is a nearly extinct species of man who's so open-minded and deliberate that he hasn't yet decided which candidate deserves his vote – even after months of debate. I wonder who this last noble voter is?
CHECK IT, FOOL. THE ONE DUDE LOOKS LIKE HERMAN MUNSTER, AND I LIKE THE MUNSTERS. BUT THE OTHER DUDE IS STRAIGHT UP GANGSTA – WHICH APPEALS TO ME ON MANY DIFFERENT LEVELS.
DARRIN BELL

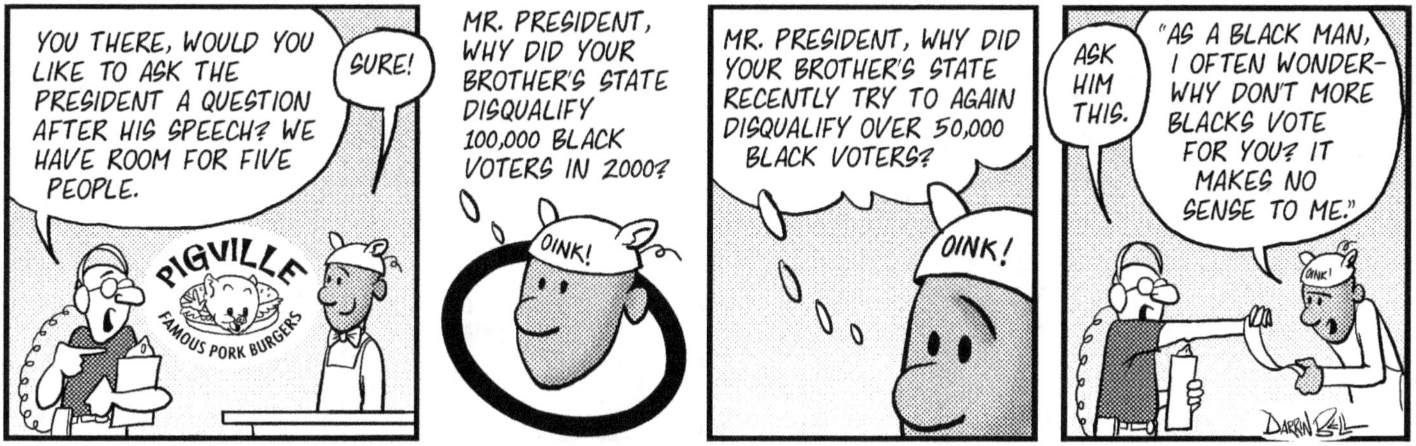
YOU THERE, WOULD YOU LIKE TO ASK THE PRESIDENT A QUESTION AFTER HIS SPEECH? WE HAVE ROOM FOR FIVE PEOPLE.
SURE!
PIGVILLE
FAMOUS PORK BURGERS
MR. PRESIDENT, WHY DID YOUR BROTHER'S STATE DISQUALIFY 100,000 BLACK VOTERS IN 2000?
OINK!
MR. PRESIDENT, WHY DID YOUR BROTHER'S STATE RECENTLY TRY TO AGAIN DISQUALIFY OVER 50,000 BLACK VOTERS?
OINK!
ASK HIM THIS.
"AS A BLACK MAN, I OFTEN WONDER– WHY DON'T MORE BLACKS VOTE FOR YOU? IT MAKES NO SENSE TO ME."
OINK!
DARRIN BELL

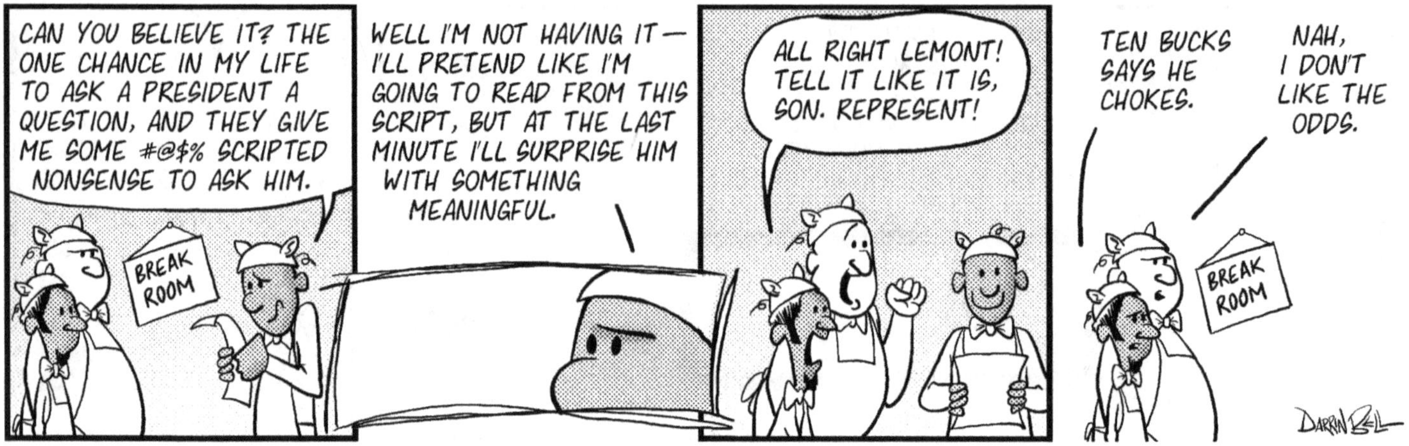
CAN YOU BELIEVE IT? THE ONE CHANCE IN MY LIFE TO ASK A PRESIDENT A QUESTION, AND THEY GIVE ME SOME #@$% SCRIPTED NONSENSE TO ASK HIM.
BREAK ROOM
WELL I'M NOT HAVING IT— I'LL PRETEND LIKE I'M GOING TO READ FROM THIS SCRIPT, BUT AT THE LAST MINUTE I'LL SURPRISE HIM WITH SOMETHING MEANINGFUL.
ALL RIGHT LEMONT! TELL IT LIKE IT IS, SON. REPRESENT!
TEN BUCKS SAYS HE CHOKES.
NAH, I DON'T LIKE THE ODDS.
BREAK ROOM
DARRIN BELL

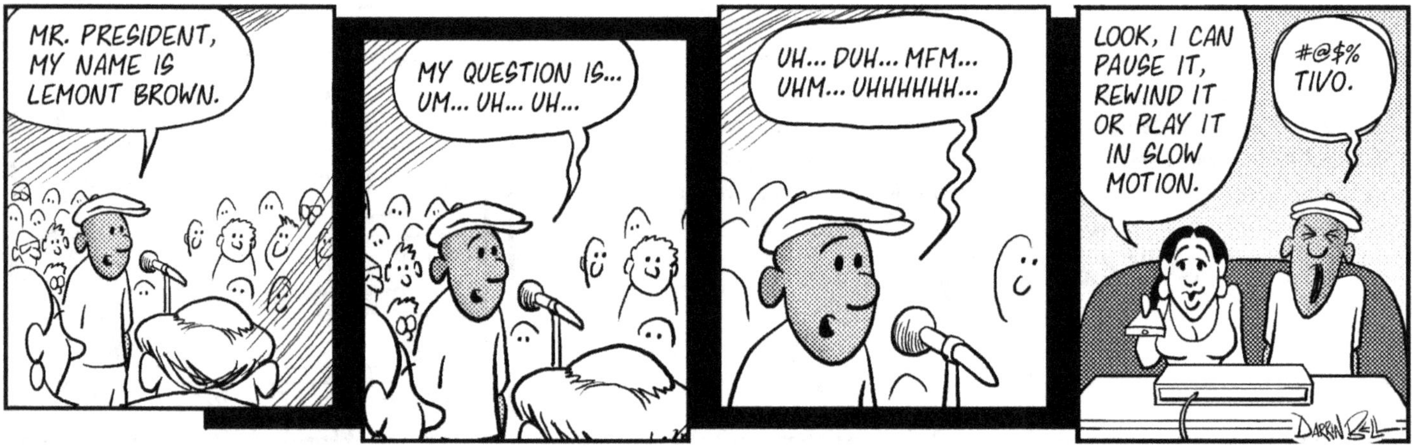
MR. PRESIDENT, MY NAME IS LEMONT BROWN.
MY QUESTION IS... UM... UH... UH...
UH... DUH... MFM... UHM... UHHHHHH...
LOOK, I CAN PAUSE IT, REWIND IT OR PLAY IT IN SLOW MOTION.
#@$% TIVO.
DARRIN BELL

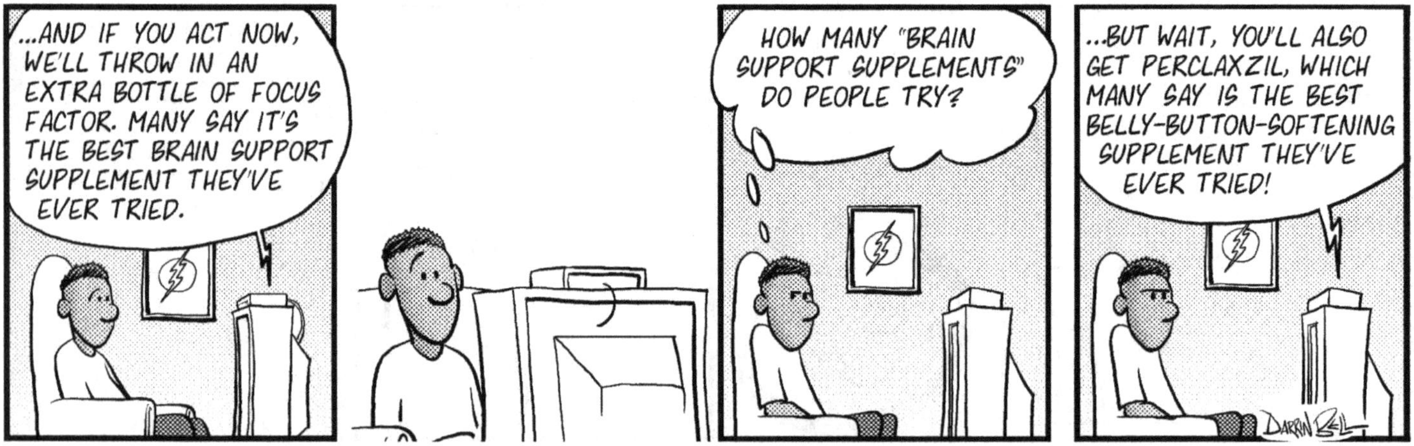
...AND IF YOU ACT NOW, WE'LL THROW IN AN EXTRA BOTTLE OF FOCUS FACTOR. MANY SAY IT'S THE BEST BRAIN SUPPORT SUPPLEMENT THEY'VE EVER TRIED.
HOW MANY "BRAIN SUPPORT SUPPLEMENTS" DO PEOPLE TRY?
...BUT WAIT, YOU'LL ALSO GET PERCLAXZIL, WHICH MANY SAY IS THE BEST BELLY-BUTTON-SOFTENING SUPPLEMENT THEY'VE EVER TRIED!
DARRIN BELL

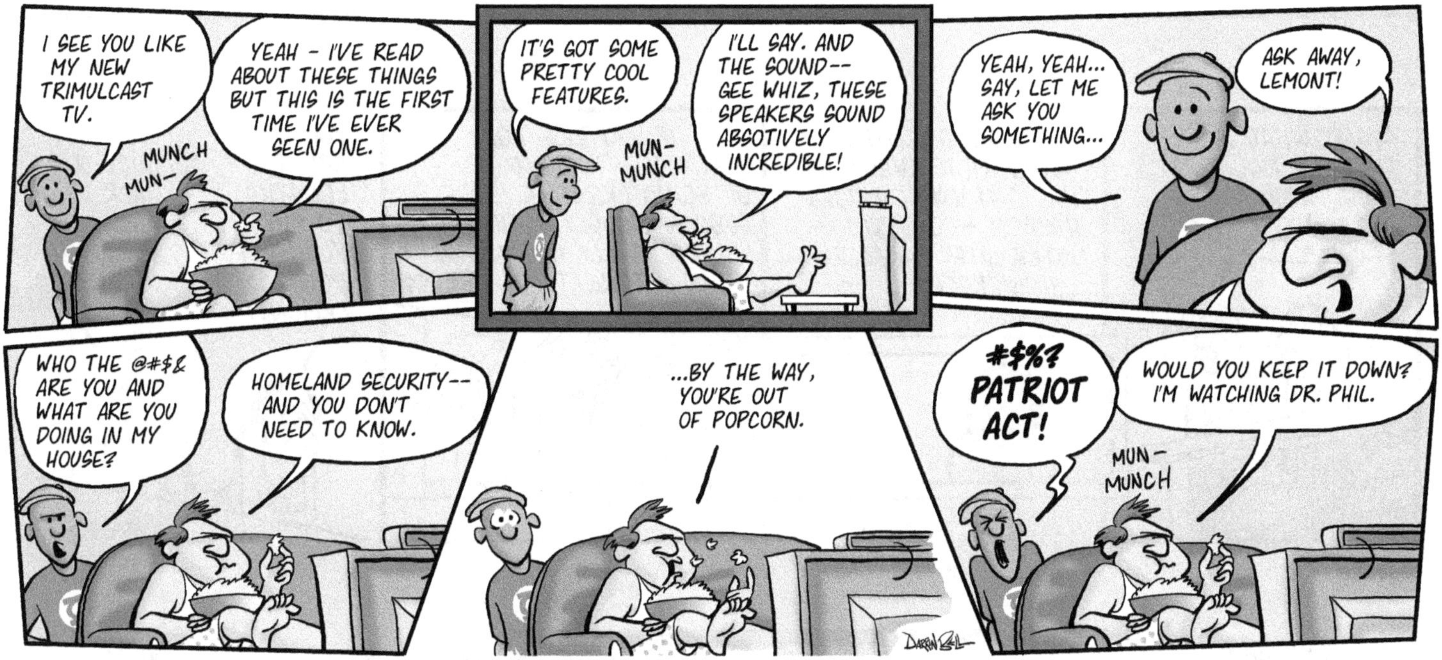
I SEE YOU LIKE MY NEW TRIMULCAST TV.
YEAH - I'VE READ ABOUT THESE THINGS BUT THIS IS THE FIRST TIME I'VE EVER SEEN ONE.
MUN- MUNCH
IT'S GOT SOME PRETTY COOL FEATURES.
I'LL SAY. AND THE SOUND-- GEE WHIZ, THESE SPEAKERS SOUND ABSOTIVELY INCREDIBLE!
MUN- MUNCH
YEAH, YEAH... SAY, LET ME ASK YOU SOMETHING...
ASK AWAY, LEMONT!
WHO THE @#$& ARE YOU AND WHAT ARE YOU DOING IN MY HOUSE?
HOMELAND SECURITY-- AND YOU DON'T NEED TO KNOW.
...BY THE WAY, YOU'RE OUT OF POPCORN.
#$%? PATRIOT ACT!
WOULD YOU KEEP IT DOWN? I'M WATCHING DR. PHIL.
MUN- MUNCH

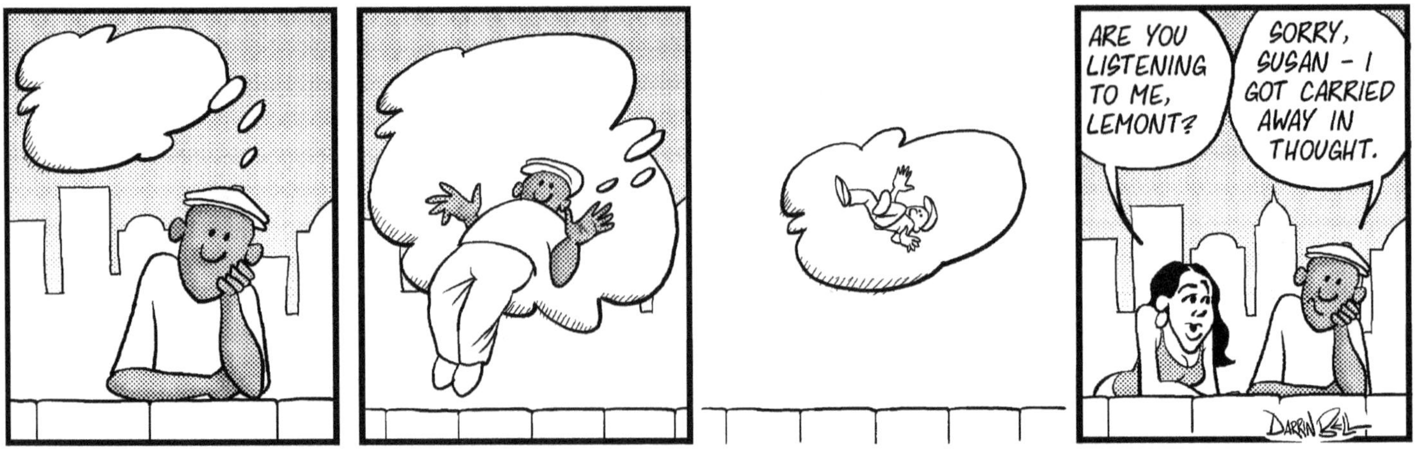
ARE YOU LISTENING TO ME, LEMONT?
SORRY, SUSAN - I GOT CARRIED AWAY IN THOUGHT.
DARRIN BELL

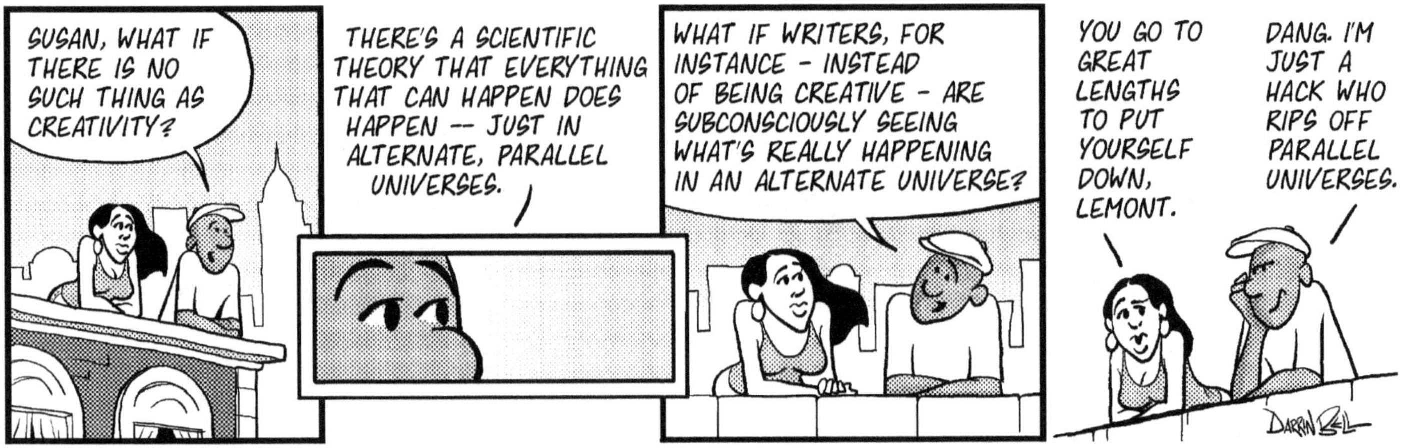
SUSAN, WHAT IF THERE IS NO SUCH THING AS CREATIVITY?
THERE'S A SCIENTIFIC THEORY THAT EVERYTHING THAT CAN HAPPEN DOES HAPPEN -- JUST IN ALTERNATE, PARALLEL UNIVERSES.
WHAT IF WRITERS, FOR INSTANCE - INSTEAD OF BEING CREATIVE - ARE SUBCONSCIOUSLY SEEING WHAT'S REALLY HAPPENING IN AN ALTERNATE UNIVERSE?
YOU GO TO GREAT LENGTHS TO PUT YOURSELF DOWN, LEMONT.
DANG. I'M JUST A HACK WHO RIPS OFF PARALLEL UNIVERSES.
DARRIN BELL

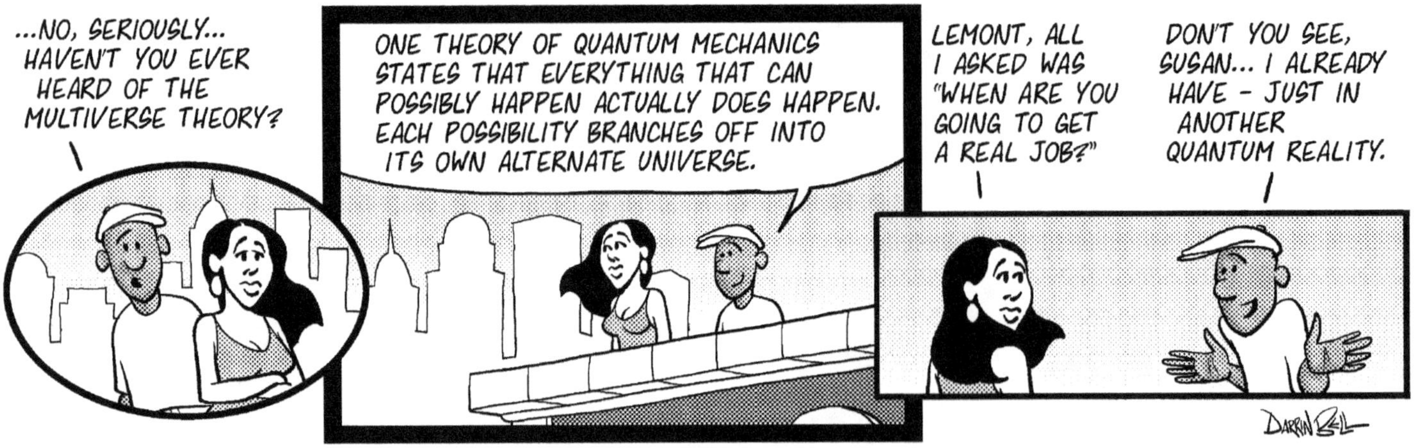
...NO, SERIOUSLY... HAVEN'T YOU EVER HEARD OF THE MULTIVERSE THEORY?
ONE THEORY OF QUANTUM MECHANICS STATES THAT EVERYTHING THAT CAN POSSIBLY HAPPEN ACTUALLY DOES HAPPEN. EACH POSSIBILITY BRANCHES OFF INTO ITS OWN ALTERNATE UNIVERSE.
LEMONT, ALL I ASKED WAS "WHEN ARE YOU GOING TO GET A REAL JOB?"
DON'T YOU SEE, SUSAN... I ALREADY HAVE - JUST IN ANOTHER QUANTUM REALITY.
DARRIN BELL

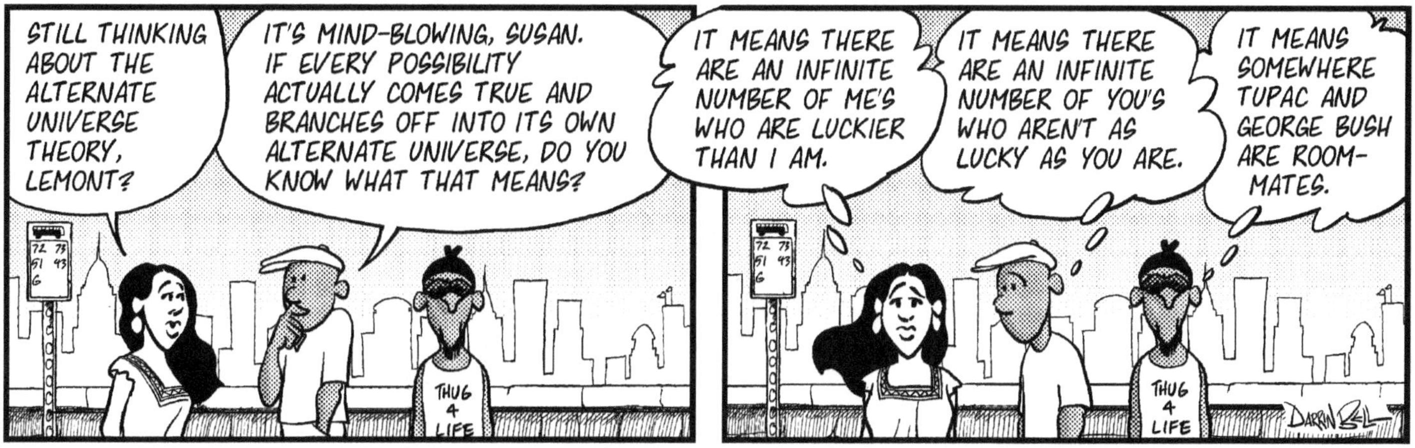
STILL THINKING ABOUT THE ALTERNATE UNIVERSE THEORY, LEMONT?
IT'S MIND-BLOWING, SUSAN. IF EVERY POSSIBILITY ACTUALLY COMES TRUE AND BRANCHES OFF INTO ITS OWN ALTERNATE UNIVERSE, DO YOU KNOW WHAT THAT MEANS?
IT MEANS THERE ARE AN INFINITE NUMBER OF ME'S WHO ARE LUCKIER THAN I AM.
IT MEANS THERE ARE AN INFINITE NUMBER OF YOU'S WHO AREN'T AS LUCKY AS YOU ARE.
IT MEANS SOMEWHERE TUPAC AND GEORGE BUSH ARE ROOM-MATES.
THUG 4 LIFE
DARRIN BELL

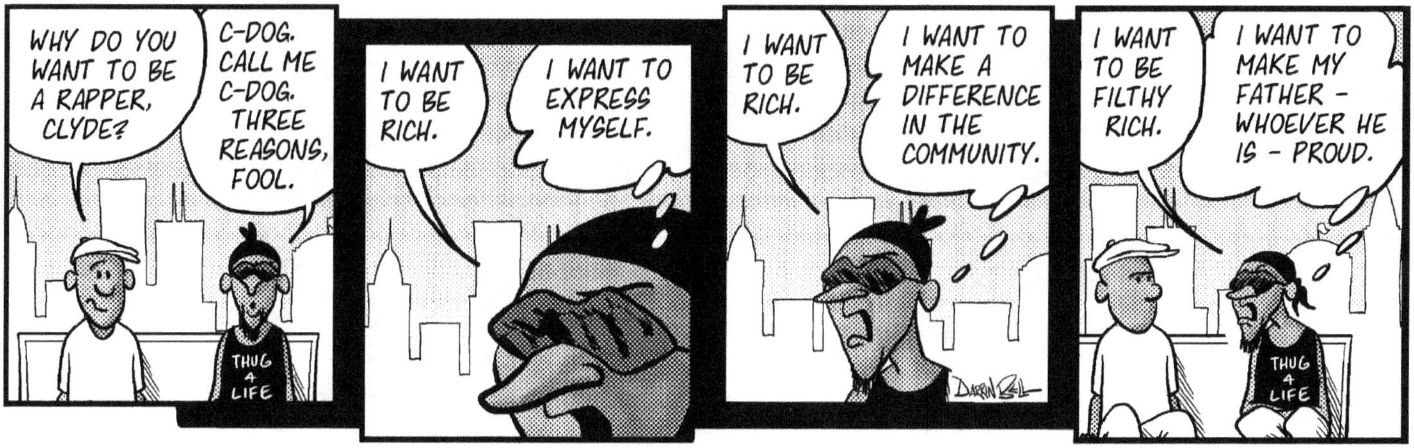
WHY DO YOU WANT TO BE A RAPPER, CLYDE?
C-DOG. CALL ME C-DOG. THREE REASONS, FOOL.
I WANT TO BE RICH.
I WANT TO EXPRESS MYSELF.
I WANT TO BE RICH.
I WANT TO MAKE A DIFFERENCE IN THE COMMUNITY.
I WANT TO BE FILTHY RICH.
I WANT TO MAKE MY FATHER – WHOEVER HE IS – PROUD.
THUG 4 LIFE
DARRIN BELL

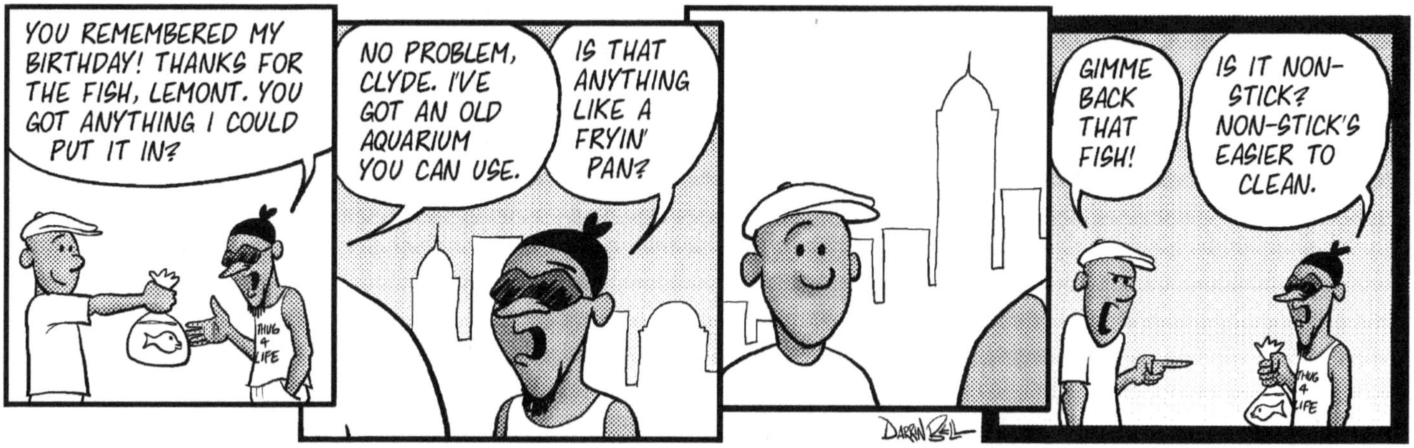
YOU REMEMBERED MY BIRTHDAY! THANKS FOR THE FISH, LEMONT. YOU GOT ANYTHING I COULD PUT IT IN?
NO PROBLEM, CLYDE. I'VE GOT AN OLD AQUARIUM YOU CAN USE.
IS THAT ANYTHING LIKE A FRYIN' PAN?
GIMME BACK THAT FISH!
IS IT NON-STICK? NON-STICK'S EASIER TO CLEAN.
THUG 4 LIFE
DARRIN BELL

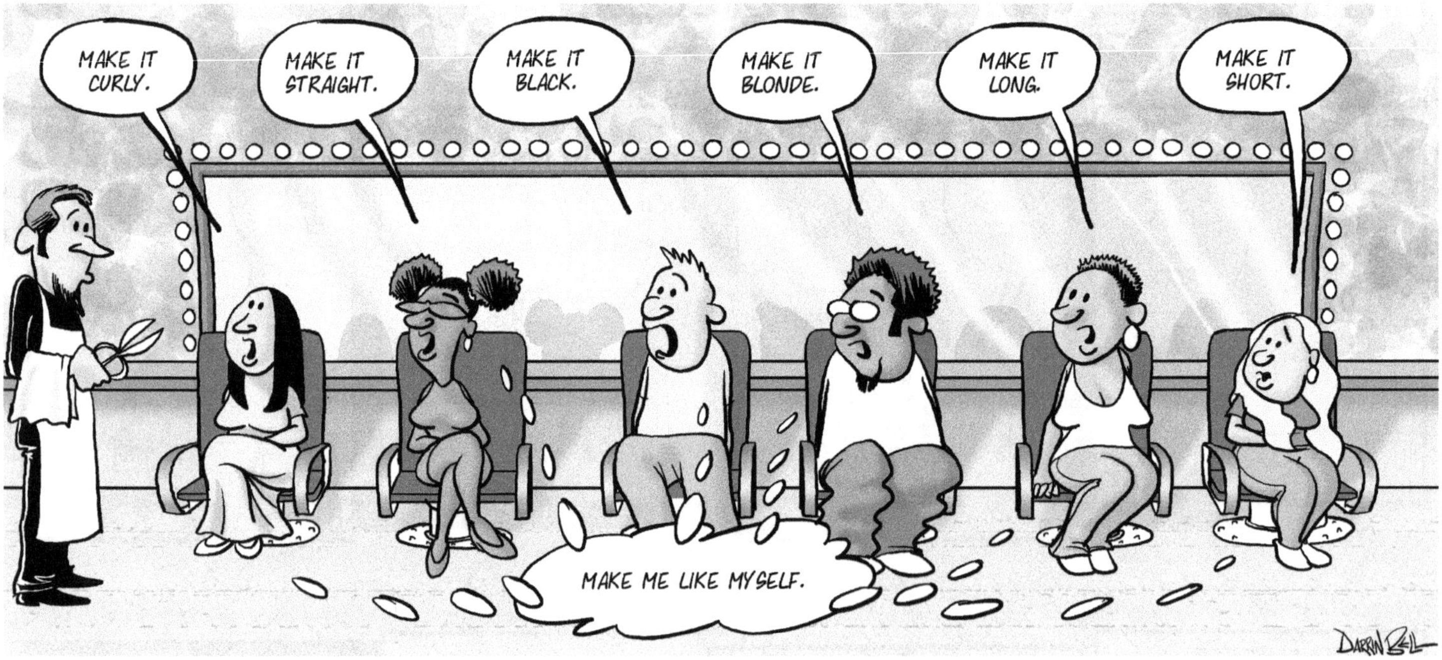
MAKE IT CURLY.
MAKE IT STRAIGHT.
MAKE IT BLACK.
MAKE IT BLONDE.
MAKE IT LONG.
MAKE IT SHORT.
MAKE ME LIKE MYSELF.
DARRIN BELL

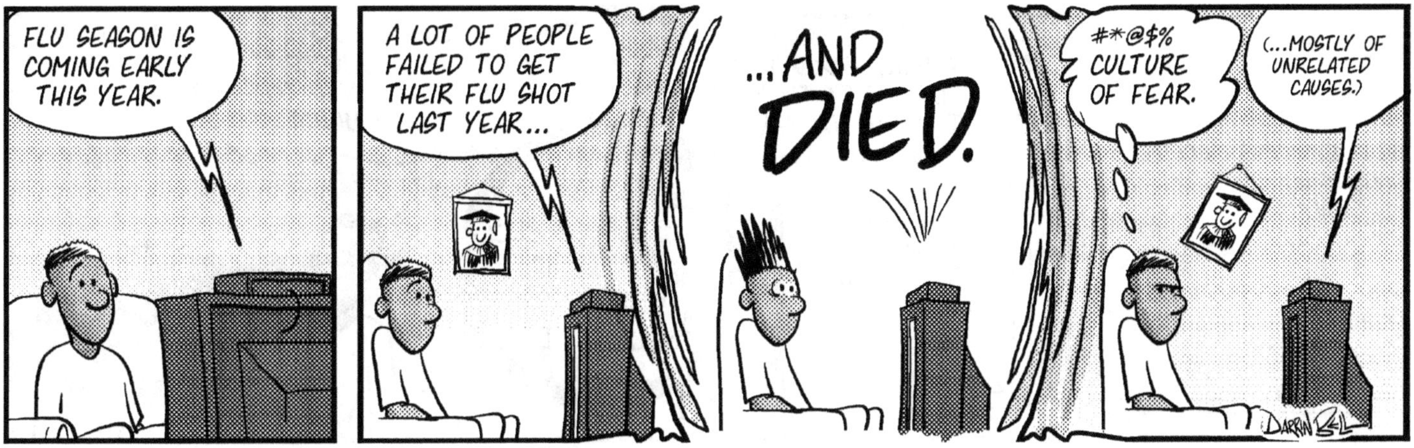
FLU SEASON IS COMING EARLY THIS YEAR.
A LOT OF PEOPLE FAILED TO GET THEIR FLU SHOT LAST YEAR...
...AND DIED.
#*@$% CULTURE OF FEAR.
(...MOSTLY OF UNRELATED CAUSES.)
DARRIN BELL

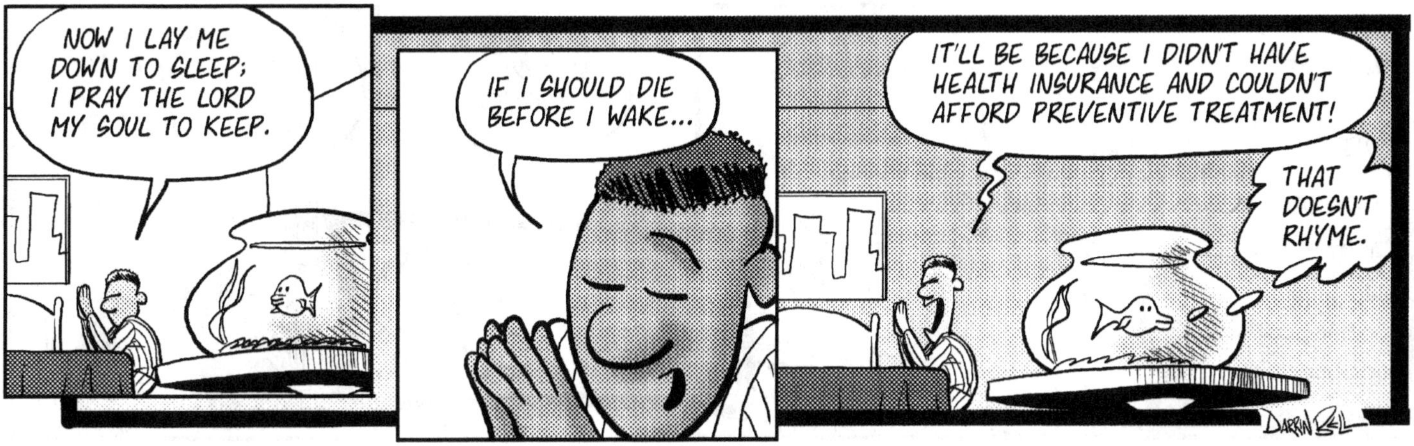
NOW I LAY ME DOWN TO SLEEP; I PRAY THE LORD MY SOUL TO KEEP.
IF I SHOULD DIE BEFORE I WAKE...
IT'LL BE BECAUSE I DIDN'T HAVE HEALTH INSURANCE AND COULDN'T AFFORD PREVENTIVE TREATMENT!
THAT DOESN'T RHYME.
DARRIN BELL

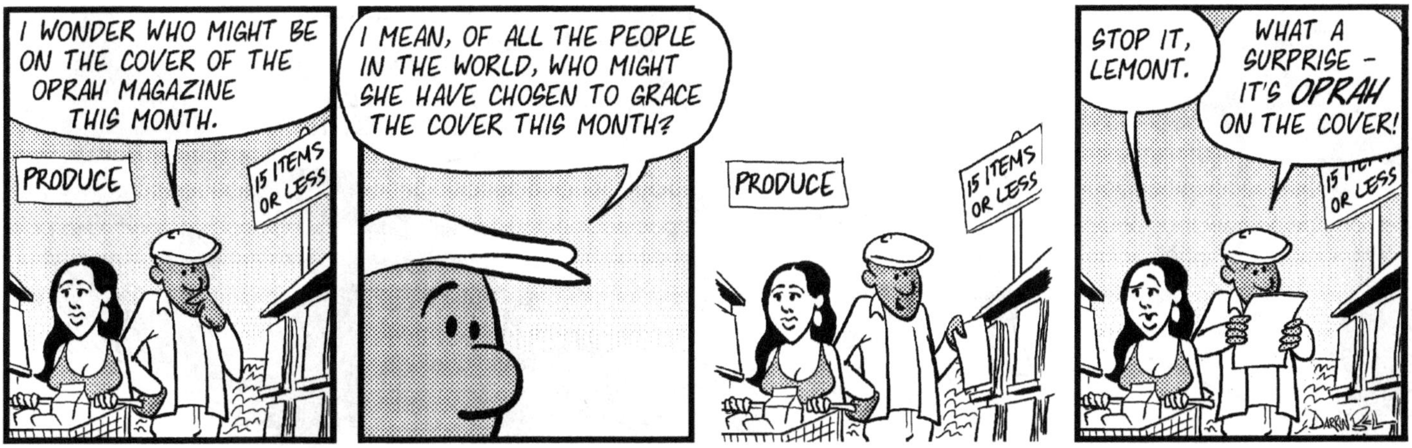
I WONDER WHO MIGHT BE ON THE COVER OF THE OPRAH MAGAZINE THIS MONTH.
PRODUCE
15 ITEMS OR LESS
I MEAN, OF ALL THE PEOPLE IN THE WORLD, WHO MIGHT SHE HAVE CHOSEN TO GRACE THE COVER THIS MONTH?
PRODUCE
15 ITEMS OR LESS
STOP IT, LEMONT.
WHAT A SURPRISE - IT'S *OPRAH* ON THE COVER!
DARRIN BELL

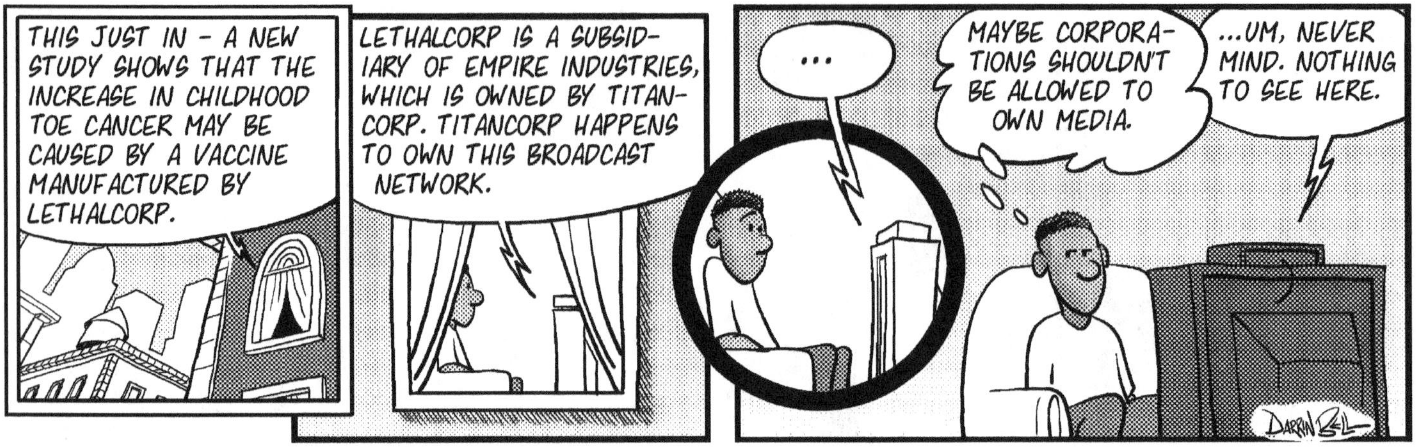
THIS JUST IN - A NEW STUDY SHOWS THAT THE INCREASE IN CHILDHOOD TOE CANCER MAY BE CAUSED BY A VACCINE MANUFACTURED BY LETHALCORP.
LETHALCORP IS A SUBSIDIARY OF EMPIRE INDUSTRIES, WHICH IS OWNED BY TITANCORP. TITANCORP HAPPENS TO OWN THIS BROADCAST NETWORK.
...
MAYBE CORPORATIONS SHOULDN'T BE ALLOWED TO OWN MEDIA.
...UM, NEVER MIND. NOTHING TO SEE HERE.
DARRIN BELL

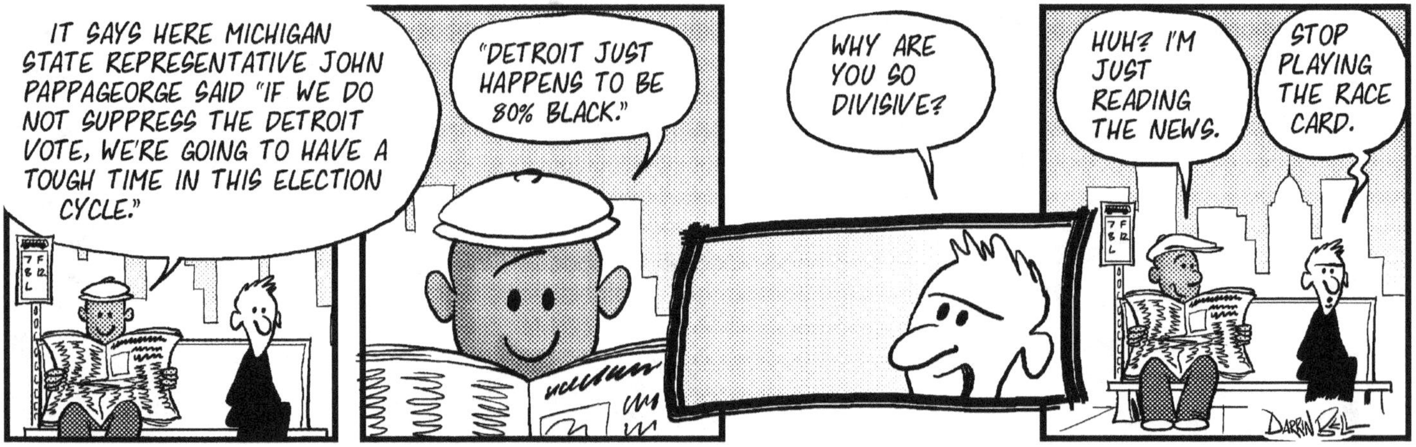
IT SAYS HERE MICHIGAN STATE REPRESENTATIVE JOHN PAPPAGEORGE SAID "IF WE DO NOT SUPPRESS THE DETROIT VOTE, WE'RE GOING TO HAVE A TOUGH TIME IN THIS ELECTION CYCLE."
"DETROIT JUST HAPPENS TO BE 80% BLACK."
WHY ARE YOU SO DIVISIVE?
HUH? I'M JUST READING THE NEWS.
STOP PLAYING THE RACE CARD.
DARRIN BELL

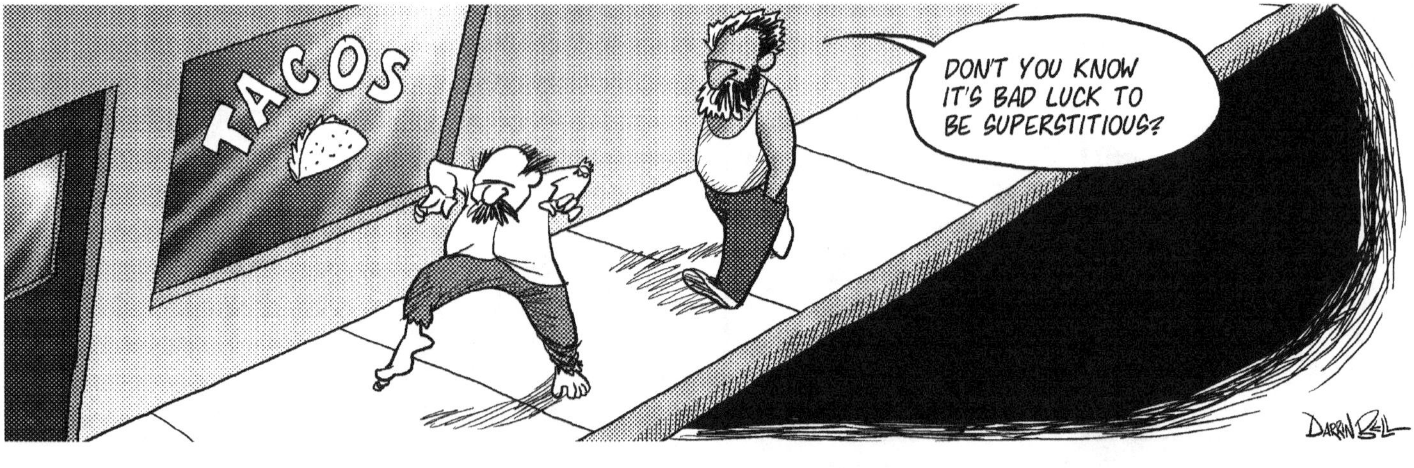
TACOS
DON'T YOU KNOW IT'S BAD LUCK TO BE SUPERSTITIOUS?
DARRIN BELL

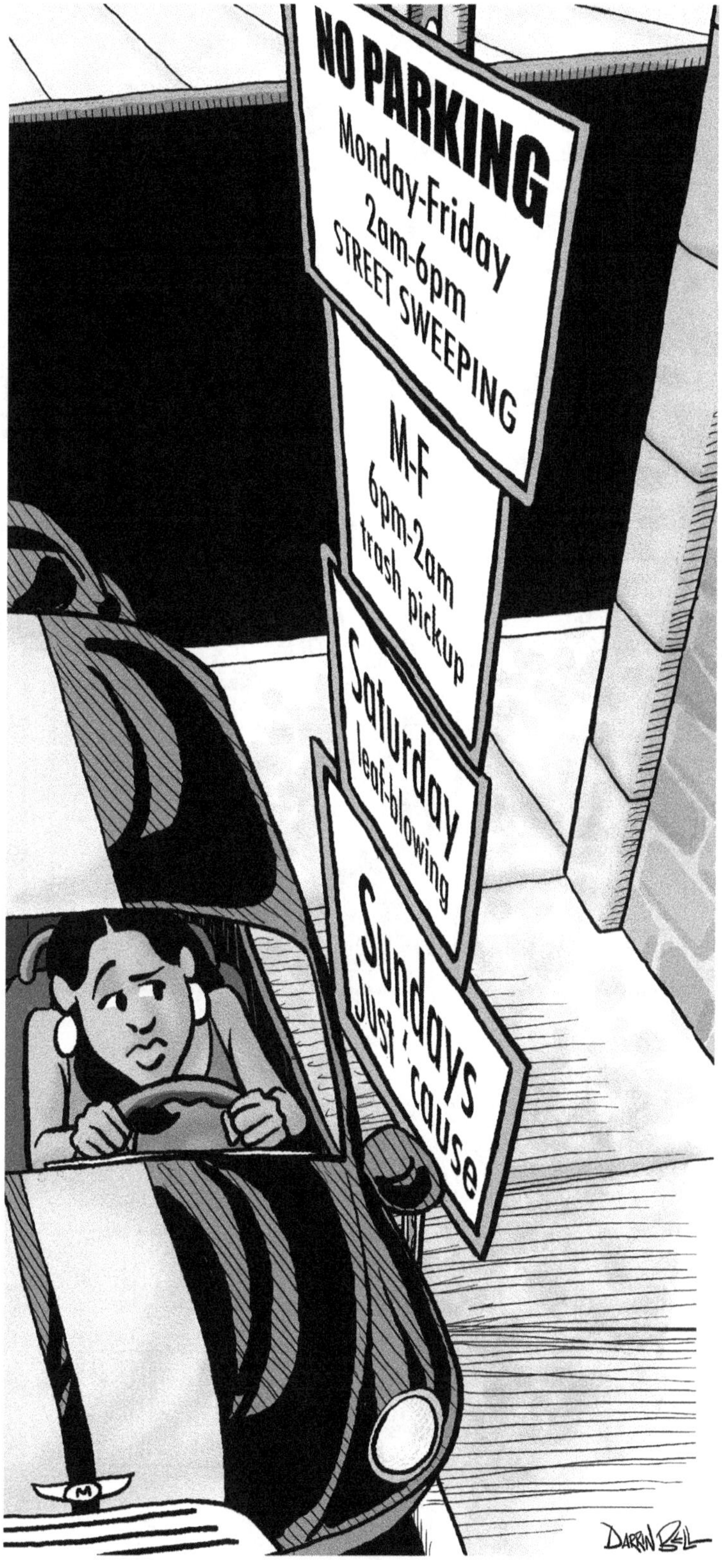
NO PARKING
Monday-Friday
2am-6pm
STREET SWEEPING
M-F
6pm-2am
trash pickup
Saturday
leaf-blowing
Sundays
just 'cause
DARRIN BELL

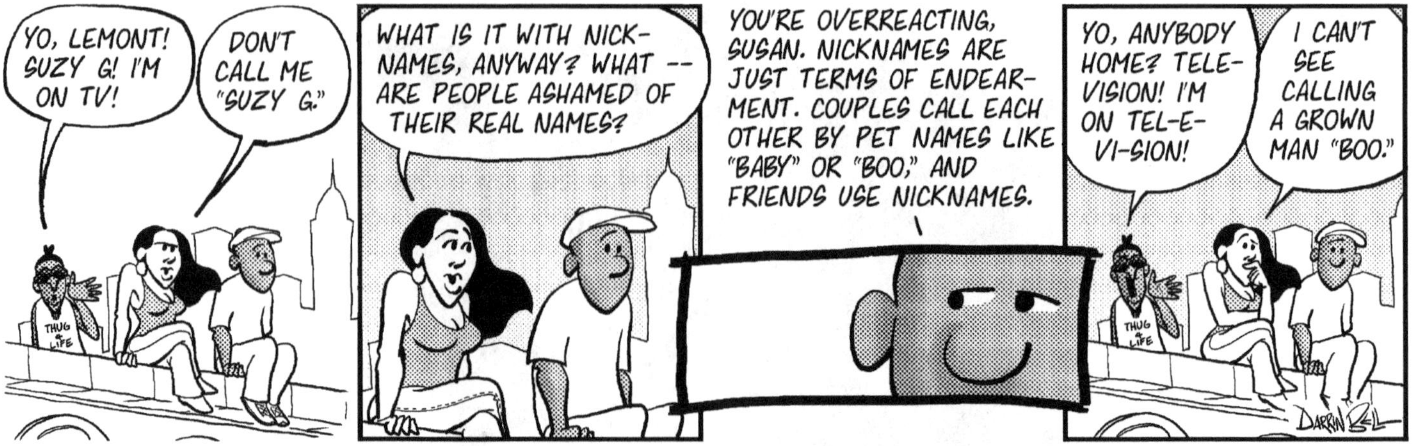
YO, LEMONT! SUZY G! I'M ON TV!
DON'T CALL ME "SUZY G."
WHAT IS IT WITH NICK-NAMES, ANYWAY? WHAT -- ARE PEOPLE ASHAMED OF THEIR REAL NAMES?
YOU'RE OVERREACTING, SUSAN. NICKNAMES ARE JUST TERMS OF ENDEAR-MENT. COUPLES CALL EACH OTHER BY PET NAMES LIKE "BABY" OR "BOO," AND FRIENDS USE NICKNAMES.
YO, ANYBODY HOME? TELE-VISION! I'M ON TEL-E-VI-SION!
I CAN'T SEE CALLING A GROWN MAN "BOO."
THUG LIFE
DARRIN BELL

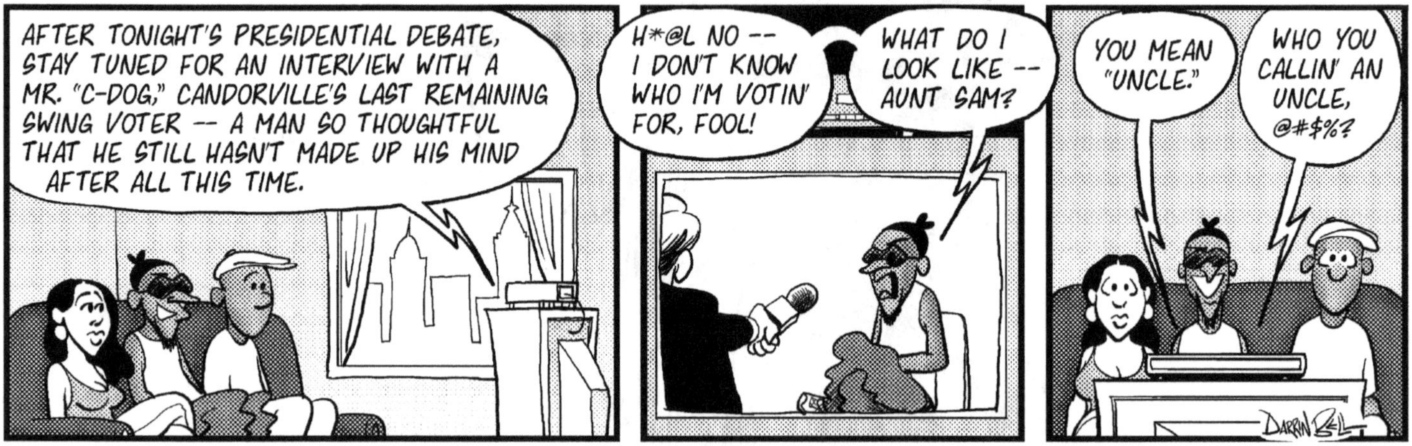
AFTER TONIGHT'S PRESIDENTIAL DEBATE, STAY TUNED FOR AN INTERVIEW WITH A MR. "C-DOG," CANDORVILLE'S LAST REMAINING SWING VOTER -- A MAN SO THOUGHTFUL THAT HE STILL HASN'T MADE UP HIS MIND AFTER ALL THIS TIME.
H*@L NO -- I DON'T KNOW WHO I'M VOTIN' FOR, FOOL!
WHAT DO I LOOK LIKE -- AUNT SAM?
YOU MEAN "UNCLE."
WHO YOU CALLIN' AN UNCLE, @#$%?
DARRIN BELL

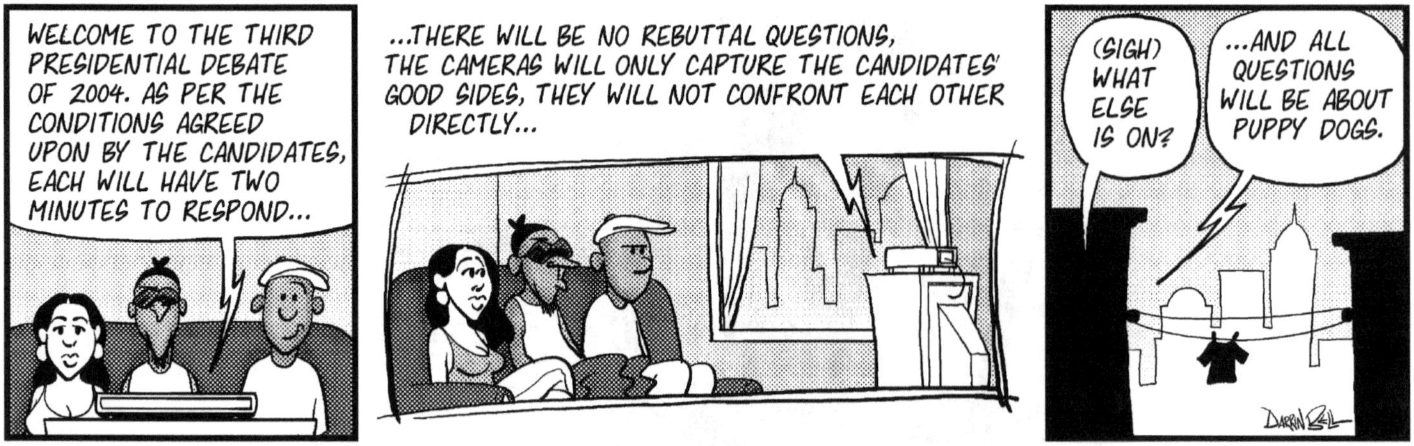
WELCOME TO THE THIRD PRESIDENTIAL DEBATE OF 2004. AS PER THE CONDITIONS AGREED UPON BY THE CANDIDATES, EACH WILL HAVE TWO MINUTES TO RESPOND...
...THERE WILL BE NO REBUTTAL QUESTIONS, THE CAMERAS WILL ONLY CAPTURE THE CANDIDATES' GOOD SIDES, THEY WILL NOT CONFRONT EACH OTHER DIRECTLY...
(SIGH) WHAT ELSE IS ON?
...AND ALL QUESTIONS WILL BE ABOUT PUPPY DOGS.
DARRIN BELL

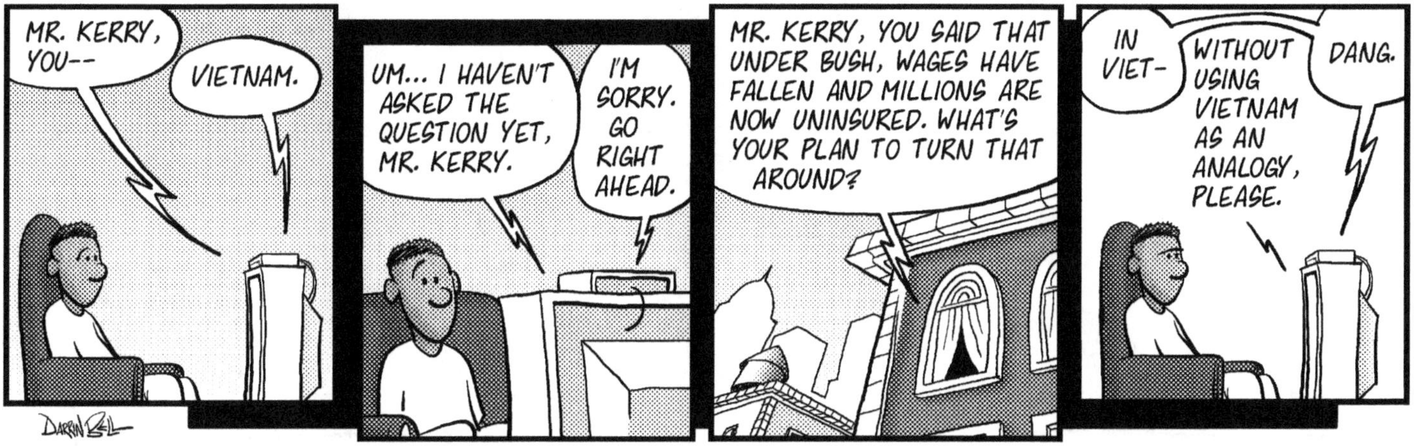
MR. KERRY, YOU--
VIETNAM.
UM... I HAVEN'T ASKED THE QUESTION YET, MR. KERRY.
I'M SORRY. GO RIGHT AHEAD.
MR. KERRY, YOU SAID THAT UNDER BUSH, WAGES HAVE FALLEN AND MILLIONS ARE NOW UNINSURED. WHAT'S YOUR PLAN TO TURN THAT AROUND?
IN VIET-
WITHOUT USING VIETNAM AS AN ANALOGY, PLEASE.
DANG.
DARRIN BELL

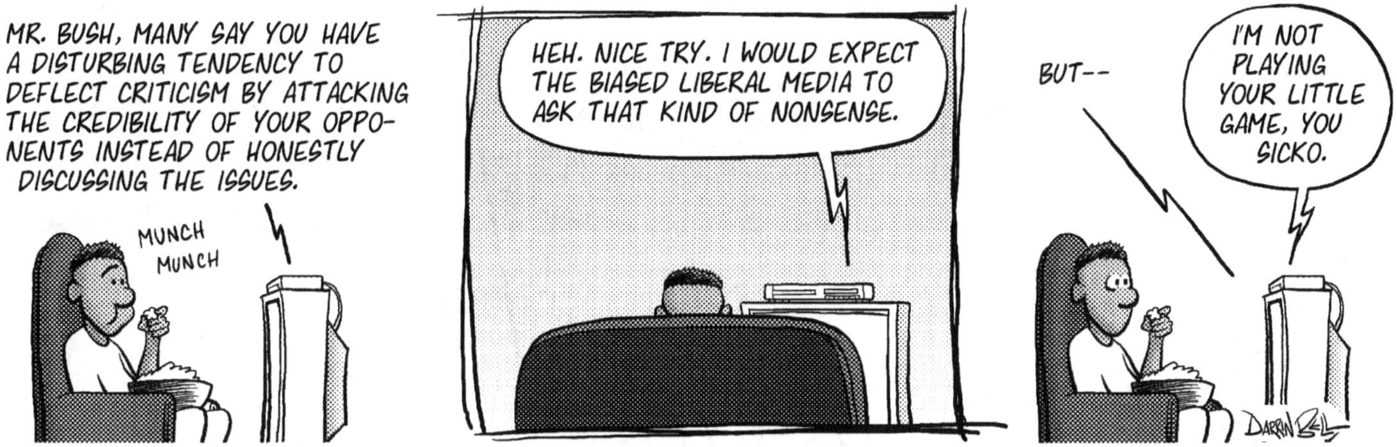
MR. BUSH, MANY SAY YOU HAVE A DISTURBING TENDENCY TO DEFLECT CRITICISM BY ATTACKING THE CREDIBILITY OF YOUR OPPONENTS INSTEAD OF HONESTLY DISCUSSING THE ISSUES.
MUNCH MUNCH
HEH. NICE TRY. I WOULD EXPECT THE BIASED LIBERAL MEDIA TO ASK THAT KIND OF NONSENSE.
BUT--
I'M NOT PLAYING YOUR LITTLE GAME, YOU SICKO.
DARRIN BELL

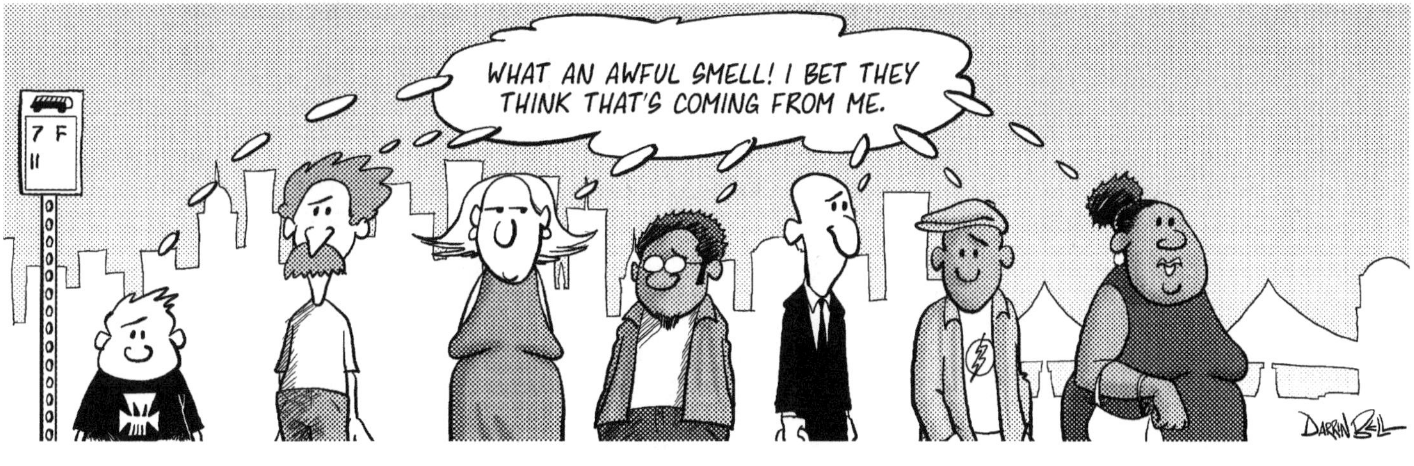
WHAT AN AWFUL SMELL! I BET THEY THINK THAT'S COMING FROM ME.
7 F
11
DARRIN BELL

HELLO, YOU'VE REACHED WELLS FRAGGO BANK. TO ACCESS YOUR ACCOUNT, PRESS ONE.

TO HEAR YOUR PATHETICALLY LOW ACCOUNT BALANCE, PRESS ONE AGAIN.

TO APPLY FOR A LOAN YOU HAVE NO HOPE OF QUALIFYING FOR, PRESS TWO.

TO SPEAK WITH A CUSTOMER REPRESENTATIVE WHO WILL DO HER BEST TO MAKE YOU FEEL LIKE A COMPLETE AND TOTAL IDIOT, PRESS THREE.

AT LEAST THEY'RE HONEST.

¡¡IDIOTA! PARA CONTINUAR EN ESPAÑOL, PULSE "CUATRO".

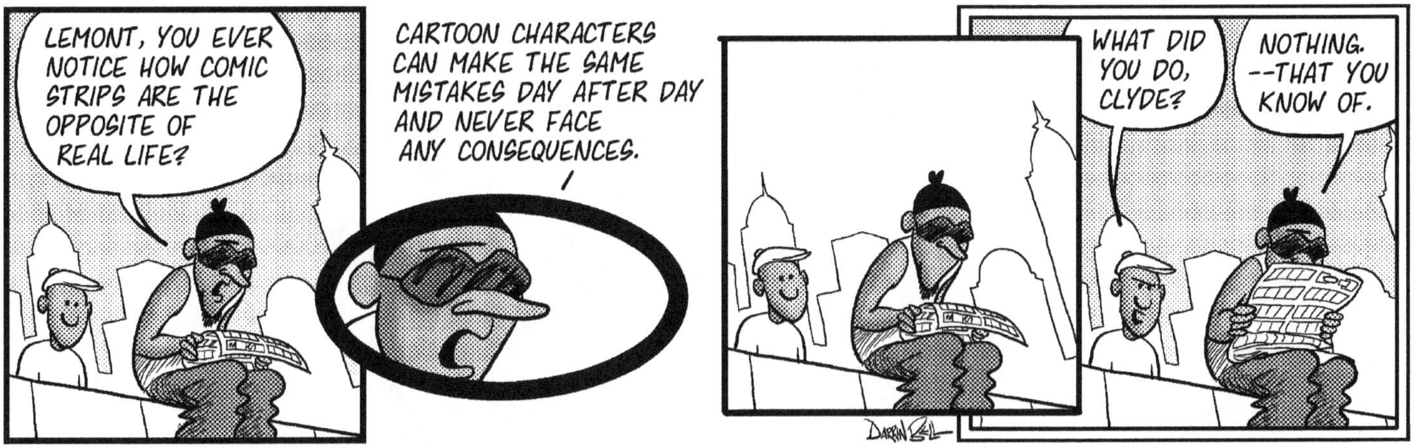
LEMONT, YOU EVER NOTICE HOW COMIC STRIPS ARE THE OPPOSITE OF REAL LIFE?
CARTOON CHARACTERS CAN MAKE THE SAME MISTAKES DAY AFTER DAY AND NEVER FACE ANY CONSEQUENCES.
WHAT DID YOU DO, CLYDE?
NOTHING. --THAT YOU KNOW OF.
DARRIN BELL

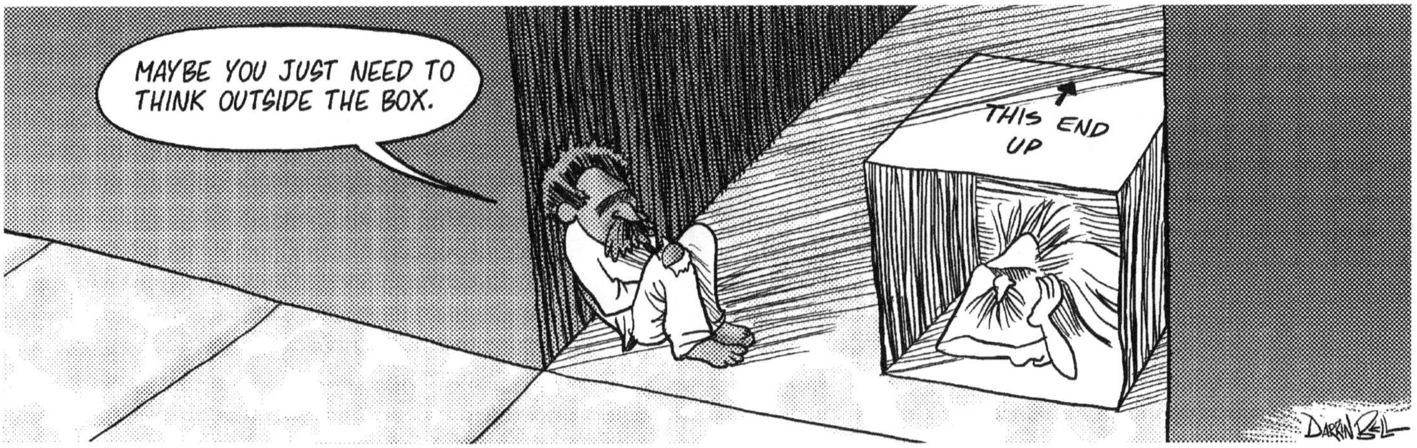
MAYBE YOU JUST NEED TO THINK OUTSIDE THE BOX.
THIS END UP
DARRIN BELL

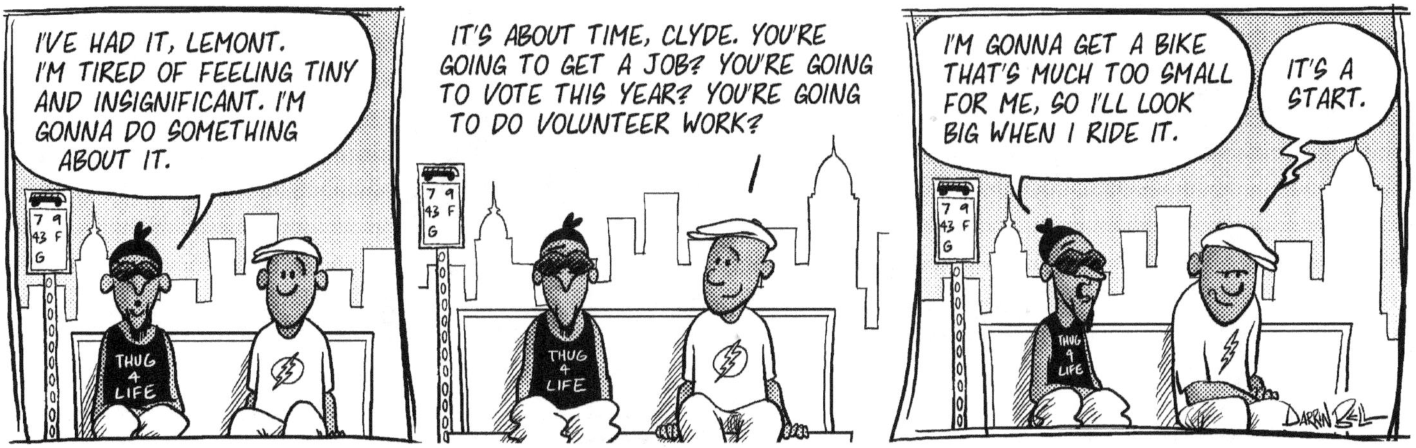
I'VE HAD IT, LEMONT. I'M TIRED OF FEELING TINY AND INSIGNIFICANT. I'M GONNA DO SOMETHING ABOUT IT.
IT'S ABOUT TIME, CLYDE. YOU'RE GOING TO GET A JOB? YOU'RE GOING TO VOTE THIS YEAR? YOU'RE GOING TO DO VOLUNTEER WORK?
I'M GONNA GET A BIKE THAT'S MUCH TOO SMALL FOR ME, SO I'LL LOOK BIG WHEN I RIDE IT.
IT'S A START.
THUG 4 LIFE
DARRIN BELL

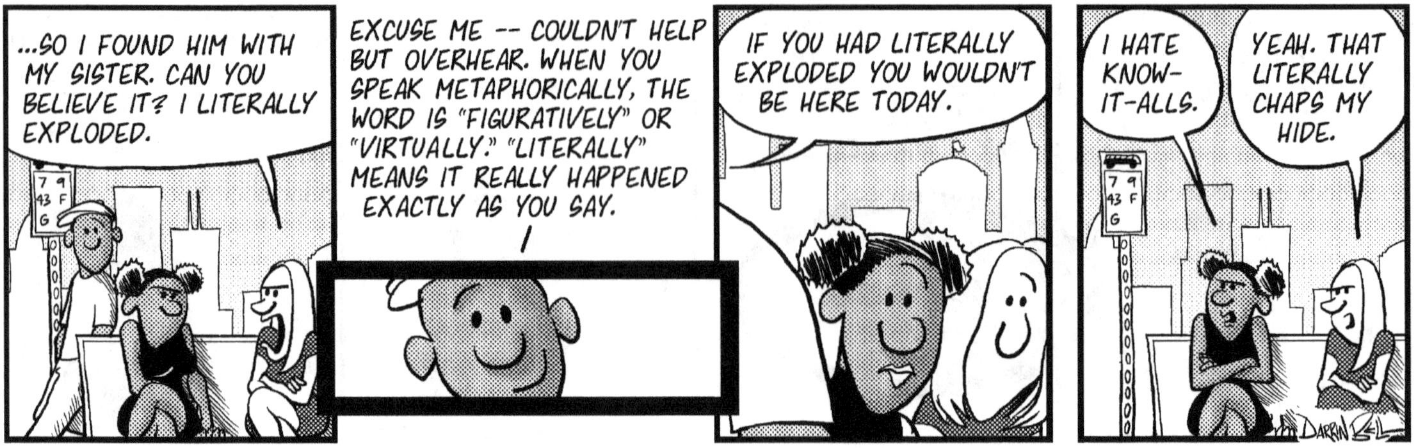
...SO I FOUND HIM WITH MY SISTER. CAN YOU BELIEVE IT? I LITERALLY EXPLODED.
EXCUSE ME -- COULDN'T HELP BUT OVERHEAR. WHEN YOU SPEAK METAPHORICALLY, THE WORD IS "FIGURATIVELY" OR "VIRTUALLY." "LITERALLY" MEANS IT REALLY HAPPENED EXACTLY AS YOU SAY.
IF YOU HAD LITERALLY EXPLODED YOU WOULDN'T BE HERE TODAY.
I HATE KNOW-IT-ALLS.
YEAH. THAT LITERALLY CHAPS MY HIDE.
DARRIN BELL

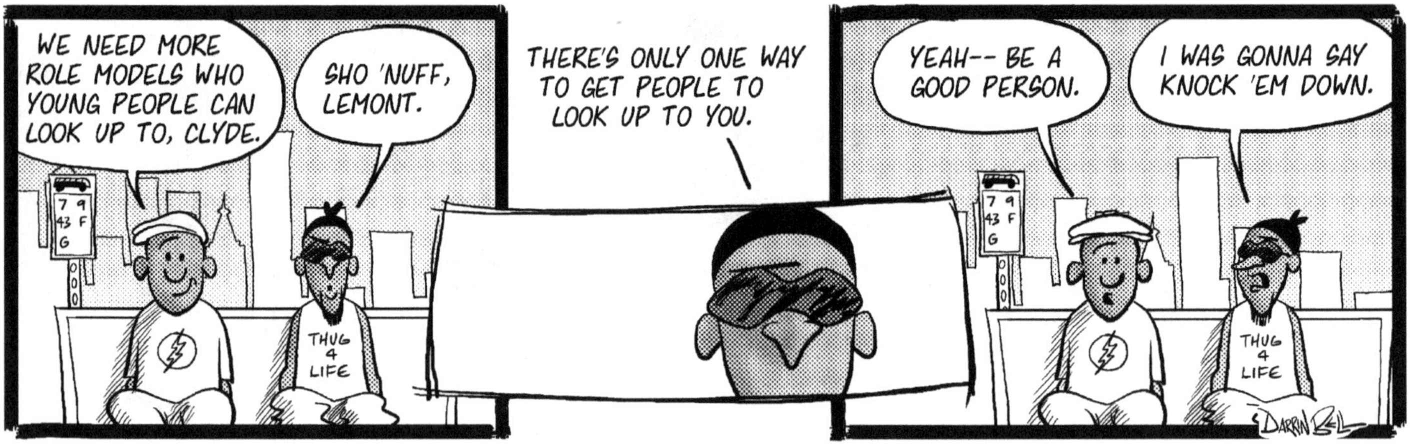
WE NEED MORE ROLE MODELS WHO YOUNG PEOPLE CAN LOOK UP TO, CLYDE.
SHO 'NUFF, LEMONT.
THUG 4 LIFE
THERE'S ONLY ONE WAY TO GET PEOPLE TO LOOK UP TO YOU.
YEAH-- BE A GOOD PERSON.
I WAS GONNA SAY KNOCK 'EM DOWN.
DARRIN BELL

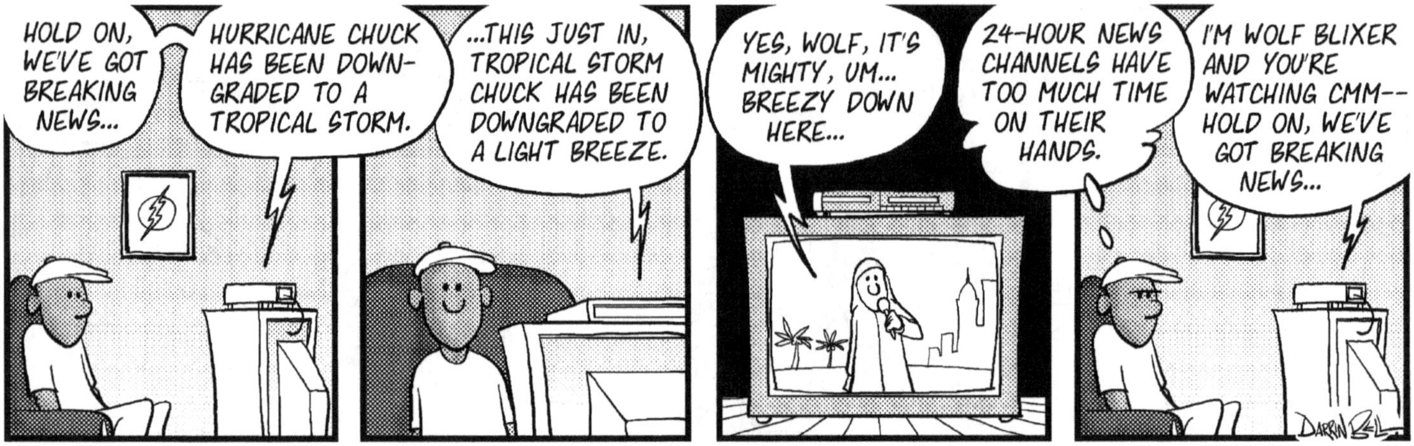
HOLD ON, WE'VE GOT BREAKING NEWS...
HURRICANE CHUCK HAS BEEN DOWN-GRADED TO A TROPICAL STORM.
...THIS JUST IN, TROPICAL STORM CHUCK HAS BEEN DOWNGRADED TO A LIGHT BREEZE.
YES, WOLF, IT'S MIGHTY, UM... BREEZY DOWN HERE...
24-HOUR NEWS CHANNELS HAVE TOO MUCH TIME ON THEIR HANDS.
I'M WOLF BLIXER AND YOU'RE WATCHING CMM-- HOLD ON, WE'VE GOT BREAKING NEWS...
DARRIN BELL

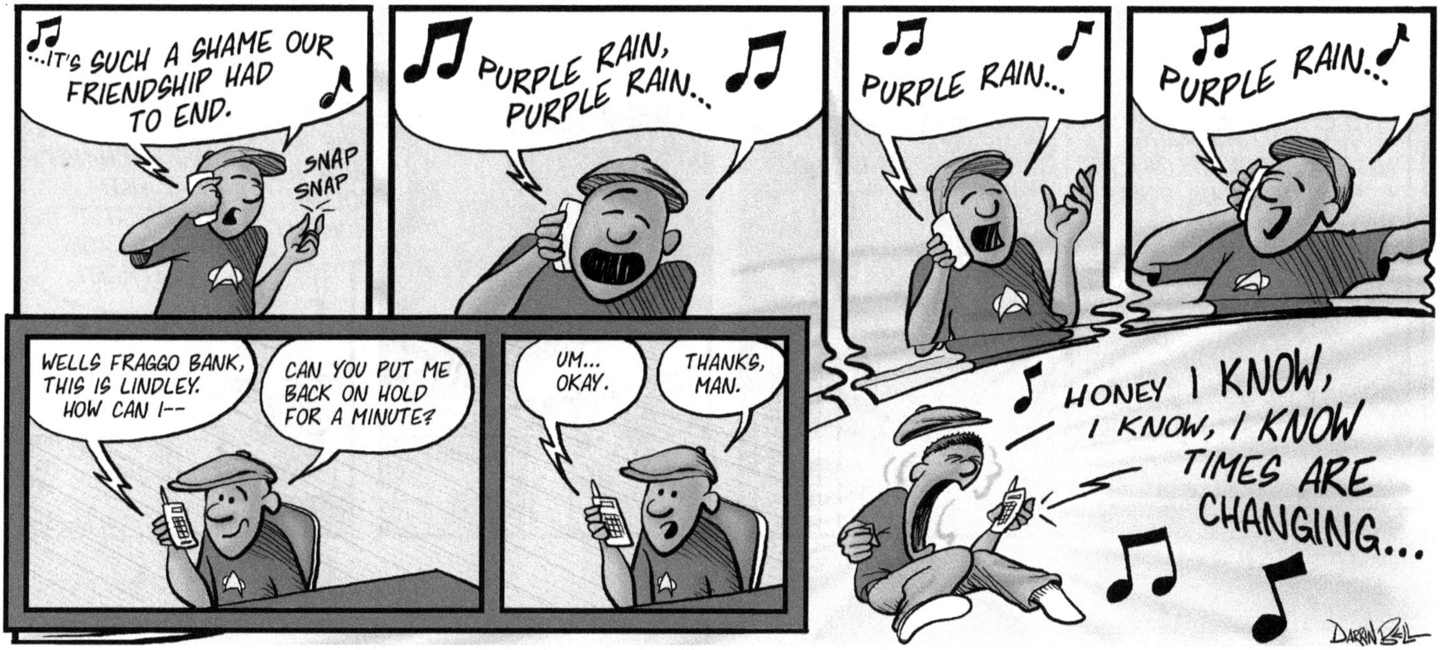
...IT'S SUCH A SHAME OUR FRIENDSHIP HAD TO END.
SNAP SNAP
PURPLE RAIN, PURPLE RAIN...
PURPLE RAIN...
PURPLE RAIN...
WELLS FRAGGO BANK, THIS IS LINDLEY. HOW CAN I--
CAN YOU PUT ME BACK ON HOLD FOR A MINUTE?
UM... OKAY.
THANKS, MAN.
HONEY I KNOW, I KNOW, I KNOW TIMES ARE CHANGING...
DARRIN BELL

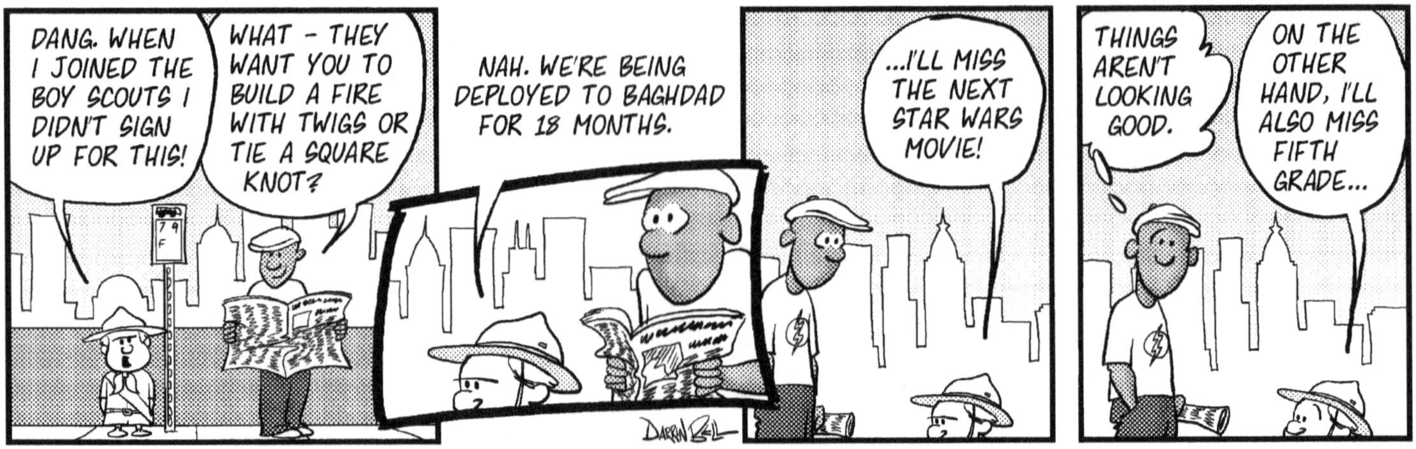
DANG. WHEN I JOINED THE BOY SCOUTS I DIDN'T SIGN UP FOR THIS!
WHAT - THEY WANT YOU TO BUILD A FIRE WITH TWIGS OR TIE A SQUARE KNOT?
NAH. WE'RE BEING DEPLOYED TO BAGHDAD FOR 18 MONTHS.
...I'LL MISS THE NEXT STAR WARS MOVIE!
THINGS AREN'T LOOKING GOOD.
ON THE OTHER HAND, I'LL ALSO MISS FIFTH GRADE...
DARRIN BELL

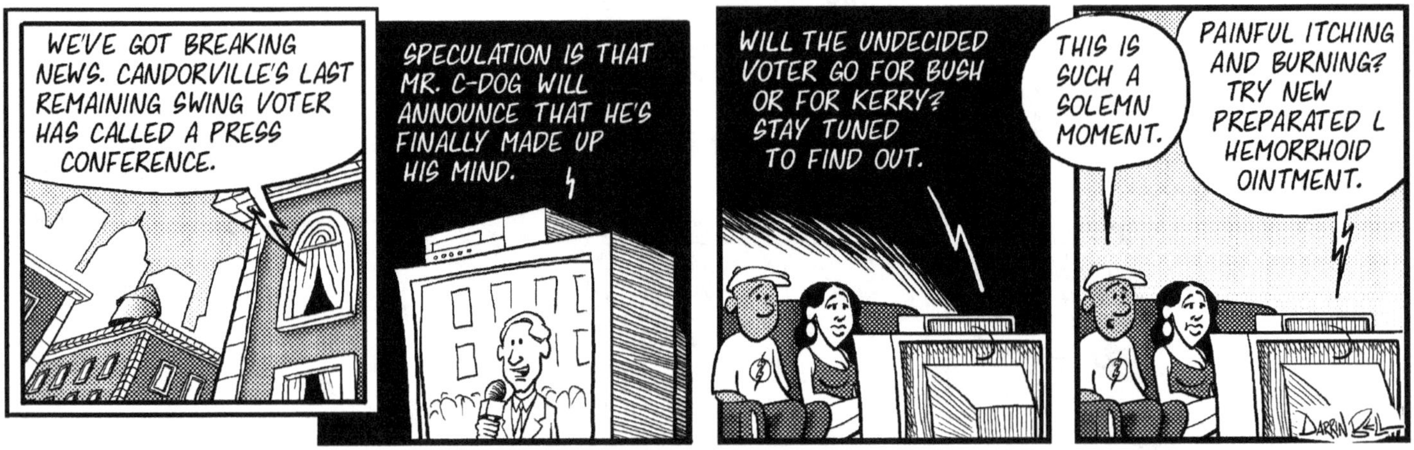
WE'VE GOT BREAKING NEWS. CANDORVILLE'S LAST REMAINING SWING VOTER HAS CALLED A PRESS CONFERENCE.
SPECULATION IS THAT MR. C-DOG WILL ANNOUNCE THAT HE'S FINALLY MADE UP HIS MIND.
WILL THE UNDECIDED VOTER GO FOR BUSH OR FOR KERRY? STAY TUNED TO FIND OUT.
THIS IS SUCH A SOLEMN MOMENT.
PAINFUL ITCHING AND BURNING? TRY NEW PREPARATED L HEMORRHOID OINTMENT.
DARRIN BELL

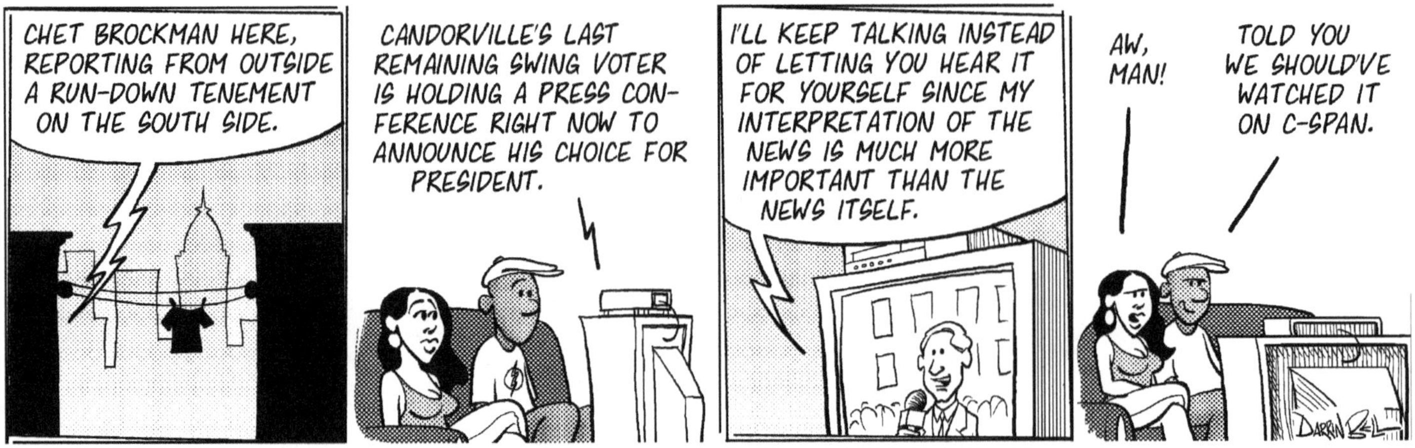
CHET BROCKMAN HERE, REPORTING FROM OUTSIDE A RUN-DOWN TENEMENT ON THE SOUTH SIDE.
CANDORVILLE'S LAST REMAINING SWING VOTER IS HOLDING A PRESS CONFERENCE RIGHT NOW TO ANNOUNCE HIS CHOICE FOR PRESIDENT.
I'LL KEEP TALKING INSTEAD OF LETTING YOU HEAR IT FOR YOURSELF SINCE MY INTERPRETATION OF THE NEWS IS MUCH MORE IMPORTANT THAN THE NEWS ITSELF.
AW, MAN!
TOLD YOU WE SHOULD'VE WATCHED IT ON C-SPAN.
DARRIN BELL

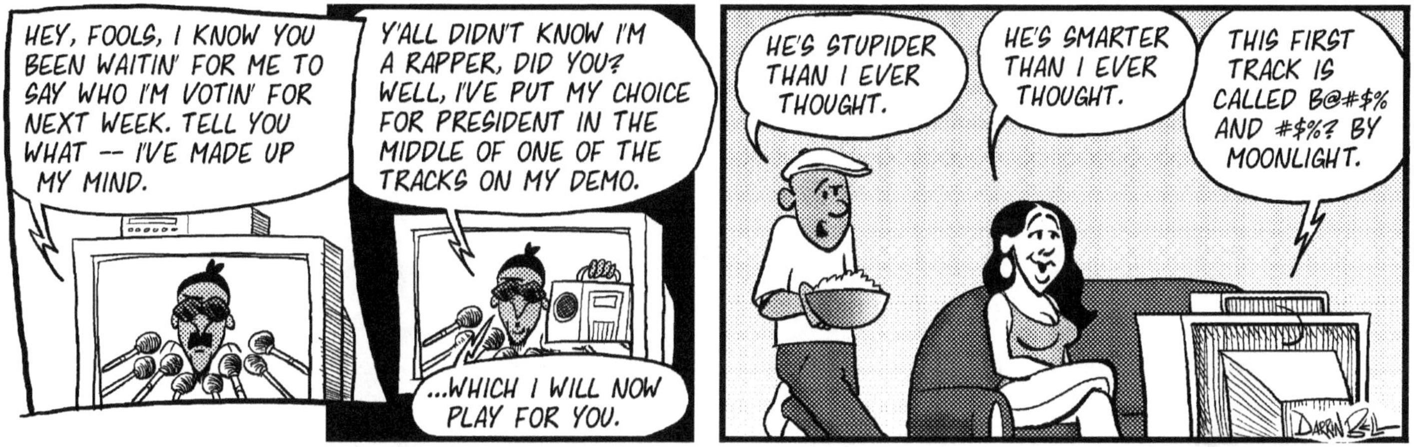
HEY, FOOLS, I KNOW YOU BEEN WAITIN' FOR ME TO SAY WHO I'M VOTIN' FOR NEXT WEEK. TELL YOU WHAT -- I'VE MADE UP MY MIND.
Y'ALL DIDN'T KNOW I'M A RAPPER, DID YOU? WELL, I'VE PUT MY CHOICE FOR PRESIDENT IN THE MIDDLE OF ONE OF THE TRACKS ON MY DEMO.
...WHICH I WILL NOW PLAY FOR YOU.
HE'S STUPIDER THAN I EVER THOUGHT.
HE'S SMARTER THAN I EVER THOUGHT.
THIS FIRST TRACK IS CALLED B@#$% AND #$%? BY MOONLIGHT.

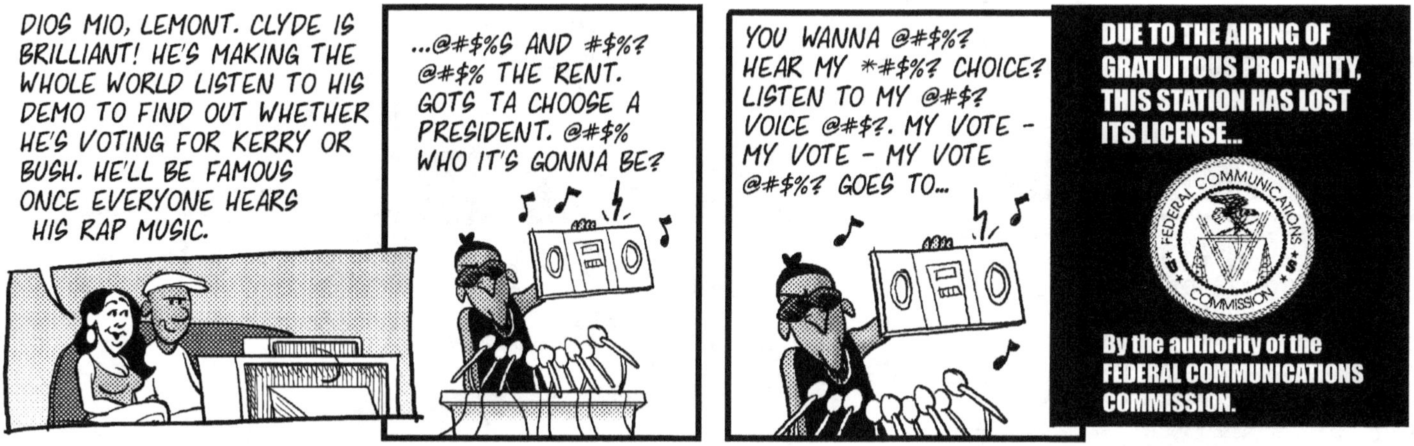
DIOS MIO, LEMONT. CLYDE IS BRILLIANT! HE'S MAKING THE WHOLE WORLD LISTEN TO HIS DEMO TO FIND OUT WHETHER HE'S VOTING FOR KERRY OR BUSH. HE'LL BE FAMOUS ONCE EVERYONE HEARS HIS RAP MUSIC.
...@#$%S AND #$%? @#$% THE RENT. GOTS TA CHOOSE A PRESIDENT. @#$% WHO IT'S GONNA BE?
YOU WANNA @#$%? HEAR MY *#$%? CHOICE? LISTEN TO MY @#$? VOICE @#$?. MY VOTE - MY VOTE - MY VOTE @#$%? GOES TO...
DUE TO THE AIRING OF GRATUITOUS PROFANITY, THIS STATION HAS LOST ITS LICENSE...
FEDERAL COMMUNICATIONS COMMISSION
By the authority of the FEDERAL COMMUNICATIONS COMMISSION.

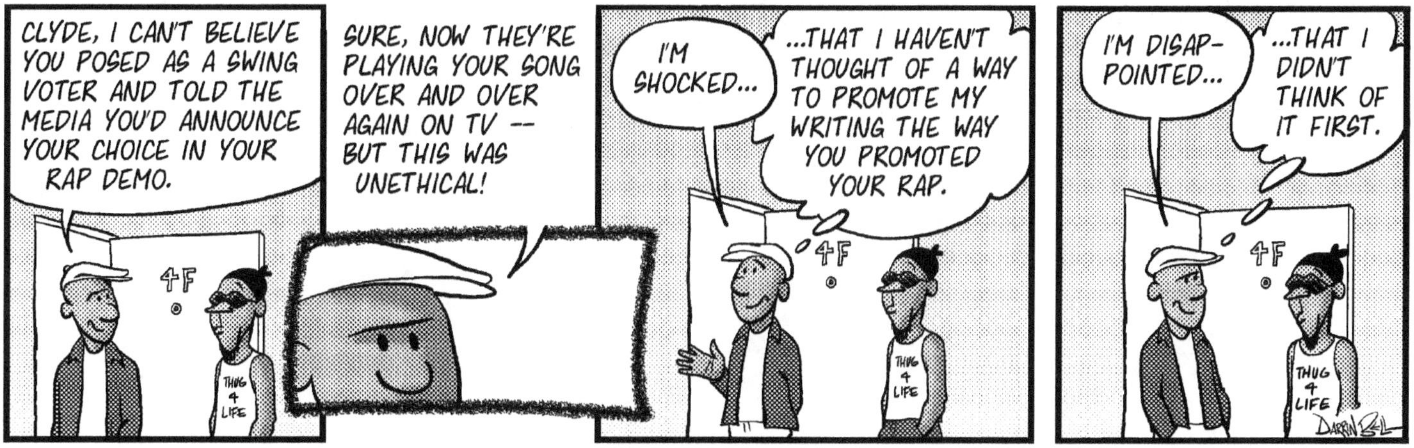
CLYDE, I CAN'T BELIEVE YOU POSED AS A SWING VOTER AND TOLD THE MEDIA YOU'D ANNOUNCE YOUR CHOICE IN YOUR RAP DEMO.
SURE, NOW THEY'RE PLAYING YOUR SONG OVER AND OVER AGAIN ON TV -- BUT THIS WAS UNETHICAL!
I'M SHOCKED...
...THAT I HAVEN'T THOUGHT OF A WAY TO PROMOTE MY WRITING THE WAY YOU PROMOTED YOUR RAP.
I'M DISAP-POINTED...
...THAT I DIDN'T THINK OF IT FIRST.

WELLS FRAGGO BANK. HOW MAY I HINDER YOU?
HI, I'M LEMONT BROWN. I'M CALLING TO APPLY FOR A $3000 SMALL BUSINESS LOAN.
YOU CAN USE MY WELLS FRAGGO IRA AS COLLATERAL. I HAVE $3300 IN THERE.
WOULD YOU HOLD ON FOR A MINUTE, SIR?
CERTAINLY.
I'M SORRY, SIR. YOUR APPLICATION HAS BEEN REJECTED. WE'RE NOT SURE YOU WOULD PAY THE LOAN BACK.
WHAT? ISN'T THAT WHAT COLLATERAL'S FOR? IF I DON'T PAY IT BACK, YOU CAN JUST TAKE THE MONEY FROM MY IRA.
UM, I MEANT TO SAY YOU WERE DENIED BECAUSE YOU'VE SPENT TOO LITTLE TIME AT YOUR CURRENT RESIDENCE.
I'VE BEEN HERE TEN YEARS!
DARRIN BELL
YOU PEOPLE ARE JUST REJECTING ME FOR THE HECK OF IT, AREN'T YOU? YOU GET SOME PERVERSE PLEASURE FROM SAYING NO TO YOUR CUSTOMERS.
...I MEANT YOU'VE SPENT TOO MUCH TIME AT YOUR CURRENT RESIDENCE.
YOU PEOPLE ARE SICK! SICK!

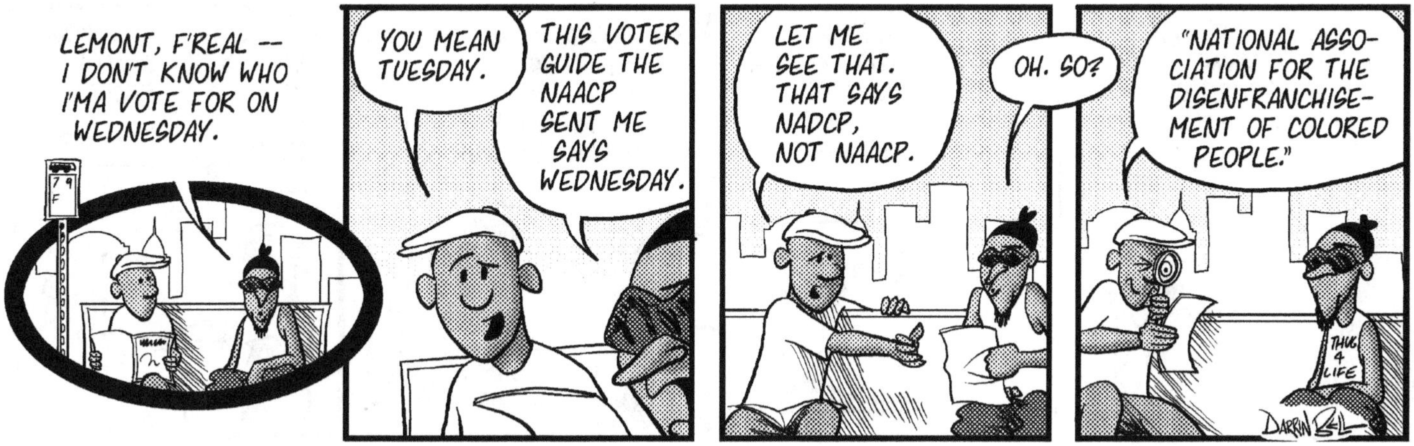
LEMONT, F'REAL -- I DON'T KNOW WHO I'MA VOTE FOR ON WEDNESDAY.
YOU MEAN TUESDAY.
THIS VOTER GUIDE THE NAACP SENT ME SAYS WEDNESDAY.
LET ME SEE THAT. THAT SAYS NADCP, NOT NAACP.
OH. SO?
"NATIONAL ASSOCIATION FOR THE DISENFRANCHISEMENT OF COLORED PEOPLE."
THUG 4 LIFE
DARRIN BELL

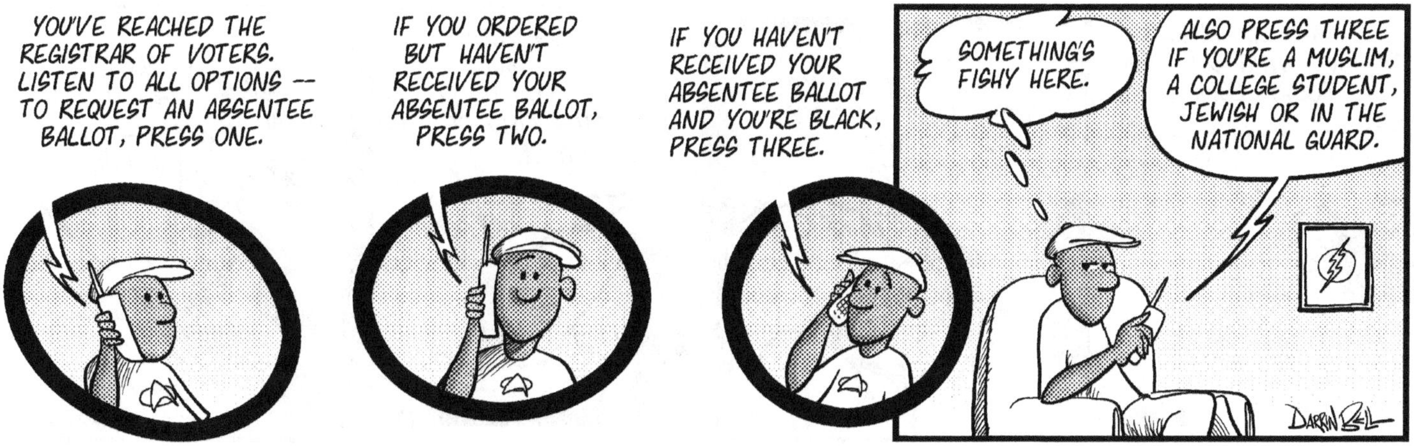
YOU'VE REACHED THE REGISTRAR OF VOTERS. LISTEN TO ALL OPTIONS -- TO REQUEST AN ABSENTEE BALLOT, PRESS ONE.
IF YOU ORDERED BUT HAVEN'T RECEIVED YOUR ABSENTEE BALLOT, PRESS TWO.
IF YOU HAVEN'T RECEIVED YOUR ABSENTEE BALLOT AND YOU'RE BLACK, PRESS THREE.
SOMETHING'S FISHY HERE.
ALSO PRESS THREE IF YOU'RE A MUSLIM, A COLLEGE STUDENT, JEWISH OR IN THE NATIONAL GUARD.
DARRIN BELL

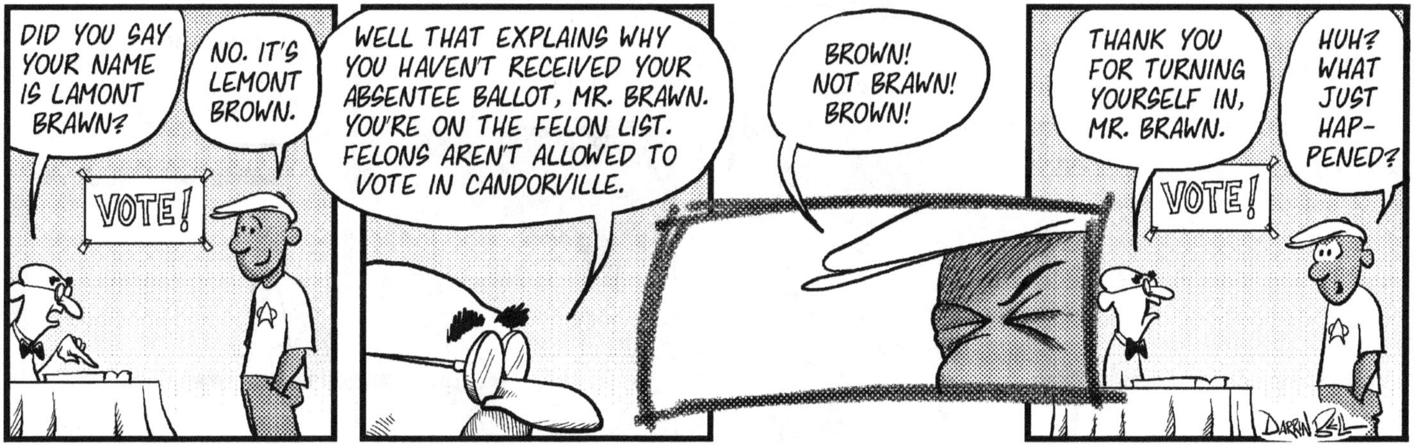
DID YOU SAY YOUR NAME IS LAMONT BRAWN?
NO. IT'S LEMONT BROWN.
VOTE!
WELL THAT EXPLAINS WHY YOU HAVEN'T RECEIVED YOUR ABSENTEE BALLOT, MR. BRAWN. YOU'RE ON THE FELON LIST. FELONS AREN'T ALLOWED TO VOTE IN CANDORVILLE.
BROWN! NOT BRAWN! BROWN!
THANK YOU FOR TURNING YOURSELF IN, MR. BRAWN.
HUH? WHAT JUST HAPPENED?
VOTE!
DARRIN BELL

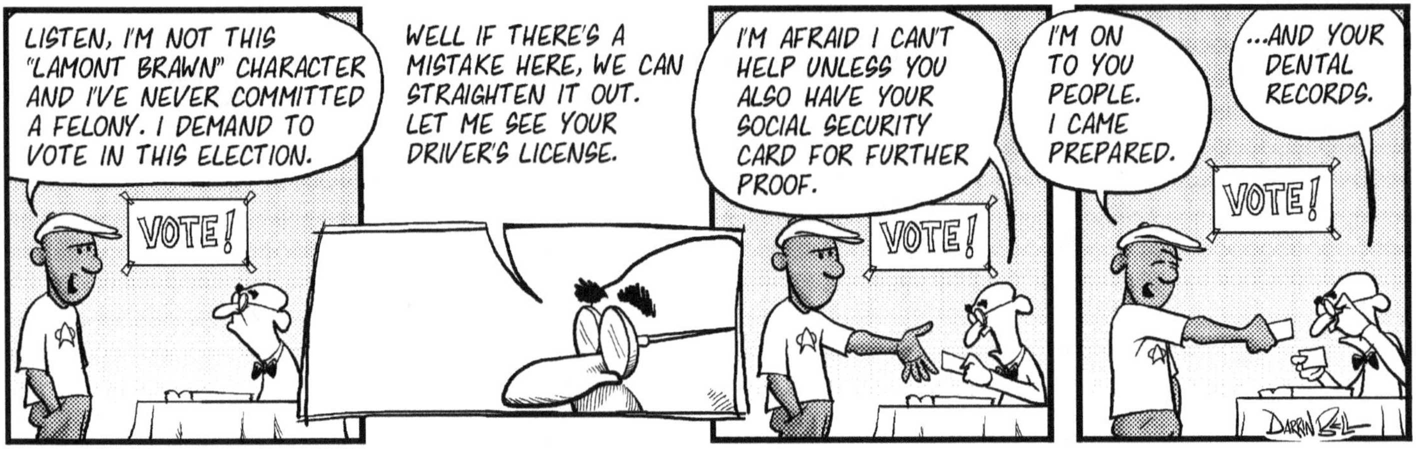
LISTEN, I'M NOT THIS "LAMONT BRAWN" CHARACTER AND I'VE NEVER COMMITTED A FELONY. I DEMAND TO VOTE IN THIS ELECTION.
VOTE!
WELL IF THERE'S A MISTAKE HERE, WE CAN STRAIGHTEN IT OUT. LET ME SEE YOUR DRIVER'S LICENSE.
I'M AFRAID I CAN'T HELP UNLESS YOU ALSO HAVE YOUR SOCIAL SECURITY CARD FOR FURTHER PROOF.
VOTE!
I'M ON TO YOU PEOPLE. I CAME PREPARED.
...AND YOUR DENTAL RECORDS.
VOTE!
DARRIN BELL

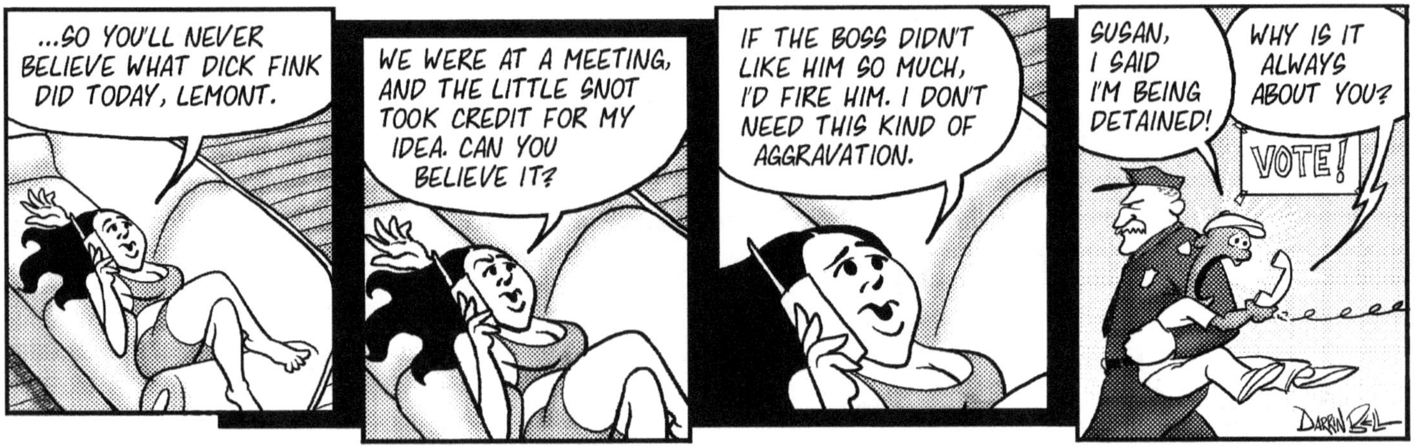
...SO YOU'LL NEVER BELIEVE WHAT DICK FINK DID TODAY, LEMONT.
WE WERE AT A MEETING, AND THE LITTLE SNOT TOOK CREDIT FOR MY IDEA. CAN YOU BELIEVE IT?
IF THE BOSS DIDN'T LIKE HIM SO MUCH, I'D FIRE HIM. I DON'T NEED THIS KIND OF AGGRAVATION.
SUSAN, I SAID I'M BEING DETAINED!
WHY IS IT ALWAYS ABOUT YOU?
VOTE!
DARRIN BELL

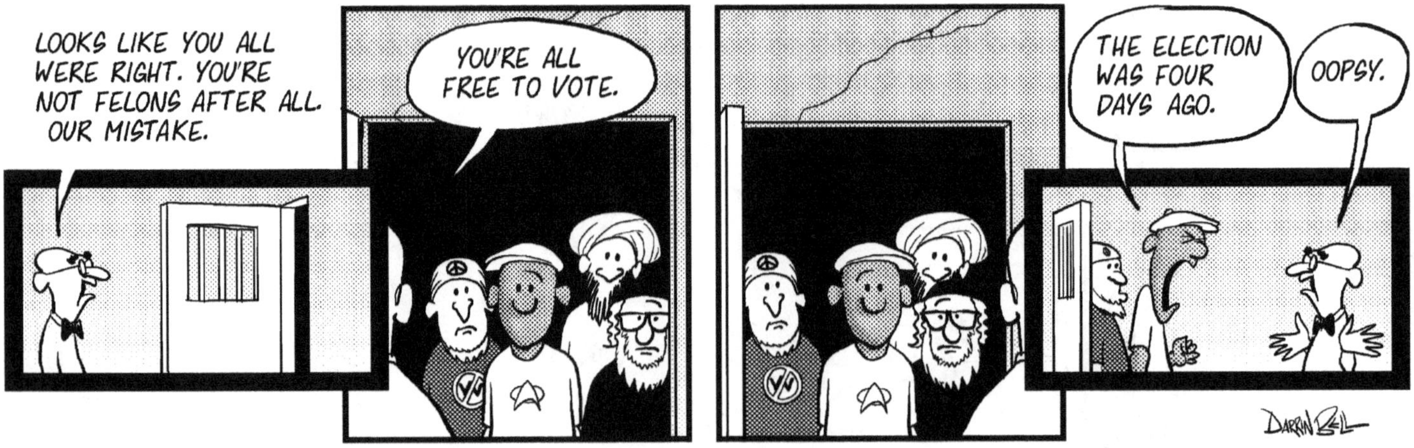
LOOKS LIKE YOU ALL WERE RIGHT. YOU'RE NOT FELONS AFTER ALL. OUR MISTAKE.
YOU'RE ALL FREE TO VOTE.
THE ELECTION WAS FOUR DAYS AGO.
OOPSY.
DARRIN BELL

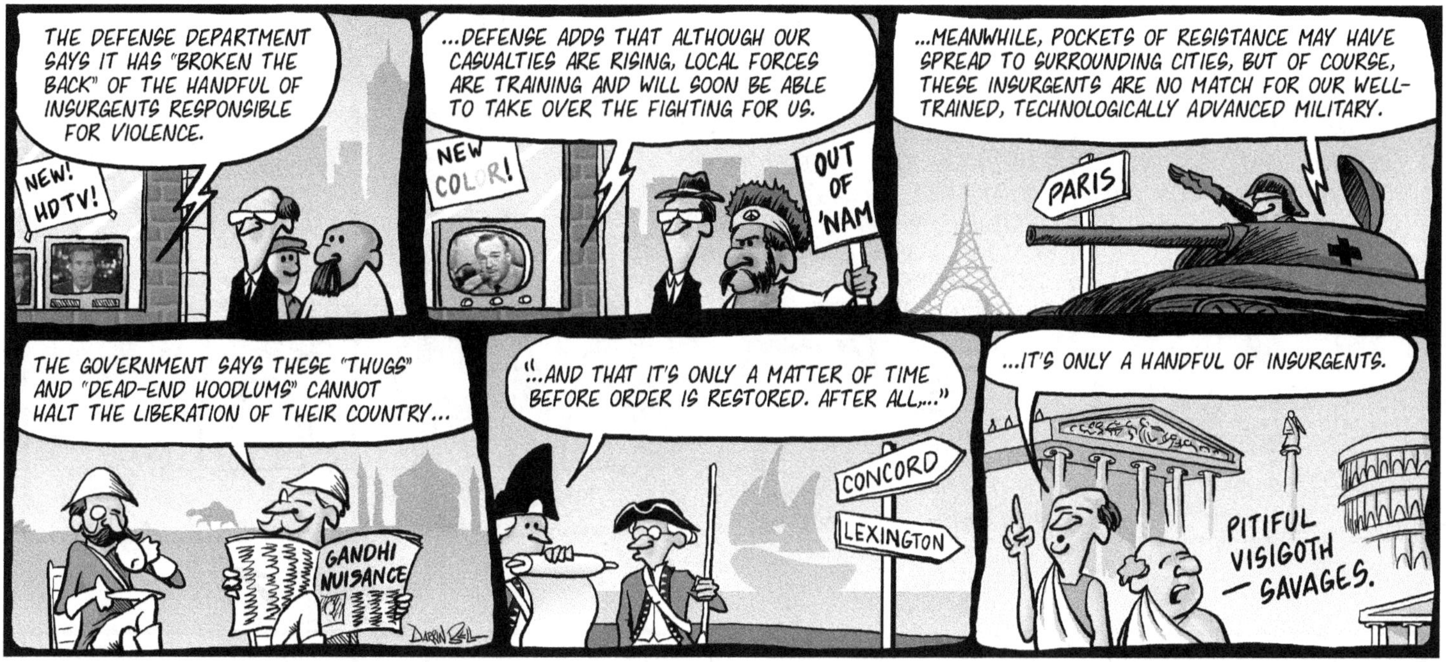
THE DEFENSE DEPARTMENT SAYS IT HAS "BROKEN THE BACK" OF THE HANDFUL OF INSURGENTS RESPONSIBLE FOR VIOLENCE.
NEW! HDTV!
...DEFENSE ADDS THAT ALTHOUGH OUR CASUALTIES ARE RISING, LOCAL FORCES ARE TRAINING AND WILL SOON BE ABLE TO TAKE OVER THE FIGHTING FOR US.
NEW COLOR!
OUT OF 'NAM
...MEANWHILE, POCKETS OF RESISTANCE MAY HAVE SPREAD TO SURROUNDING CITIES, BUT OF COURSE, THESE INSURGENTS ARE NO MATCH FOR OUR WELL-TRAINED, TECHNOLOGICALLY ADVANCED MILITARY.
PARIS
THE GOVERNMENT SAYS THESE "THUGS" AND "DEAD-END HOODLUMS" CANNOT HALT THE LIBERATION OF THEIR COUNTRY...
GANDHI NUISANCE
DARRIN BELL
"...AND THAT IT'S ONLY A MATTER OF TIME BEFORE ORDER IS RESTORED. AFTER ALL,..."
CONCORD
LEXINGTON
...IT'S ONLY A HANDFUL OF INSURGENTS.
PITIFUL VISIGOTH SAVAGES.

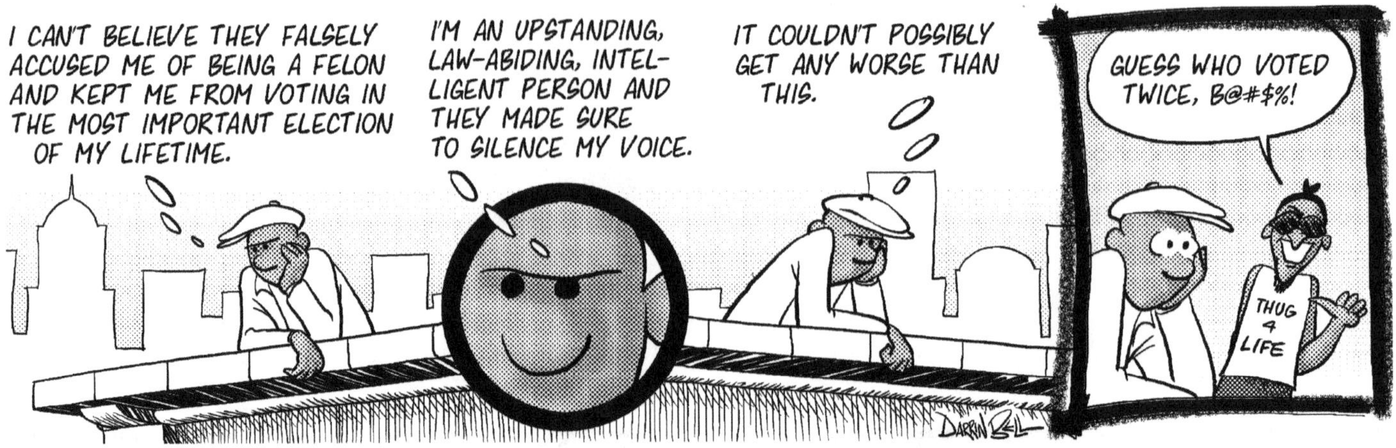
I CAN'T BELIEVE THEY FALSELY ACCUSED ME OF BEING A FELON AND KEPT ME FROM VOTING IN THE MOST IMPORTANT ELECTION OF MY LIFETIME.
I'M AN UPSTANDING, LAW-ABIDING, INTELLIGENT PERSON AND THEY MADE SURE TO SILENCE MY VOICE.
IT COULDN'T POSSIBLY GET ANY WORSE THAN THIS.
GUESS WHO VOTED TWICE, B@#$%!
THUG 4 LIFE
DARRIN BELL

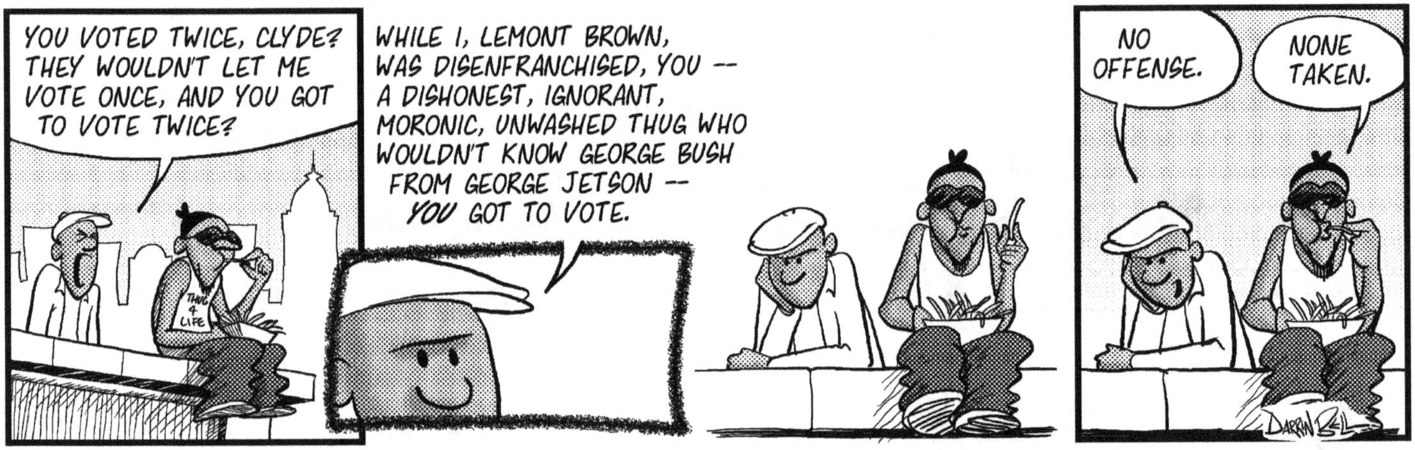
YOU VOTED TWICE, CLYDE? THEY WOULDN'T LET ME VOTE ONCE, AND YOU GOT TO VOTE TWICE?
THUG 4 LIFE
WHILE I, LEMONT BROWN, WAS DISENFRANCHISED, YOU -- A DISHONEST, IGNORANT, MORONIC, UNWASHED THUG WHO WOULDN'T KNOW GEORGE BUSH FROM GEORGE JETSON -- YOU GOT TO VOTE.
NO OFFENSE.
NONE TAKEN.
DARRIN BELL

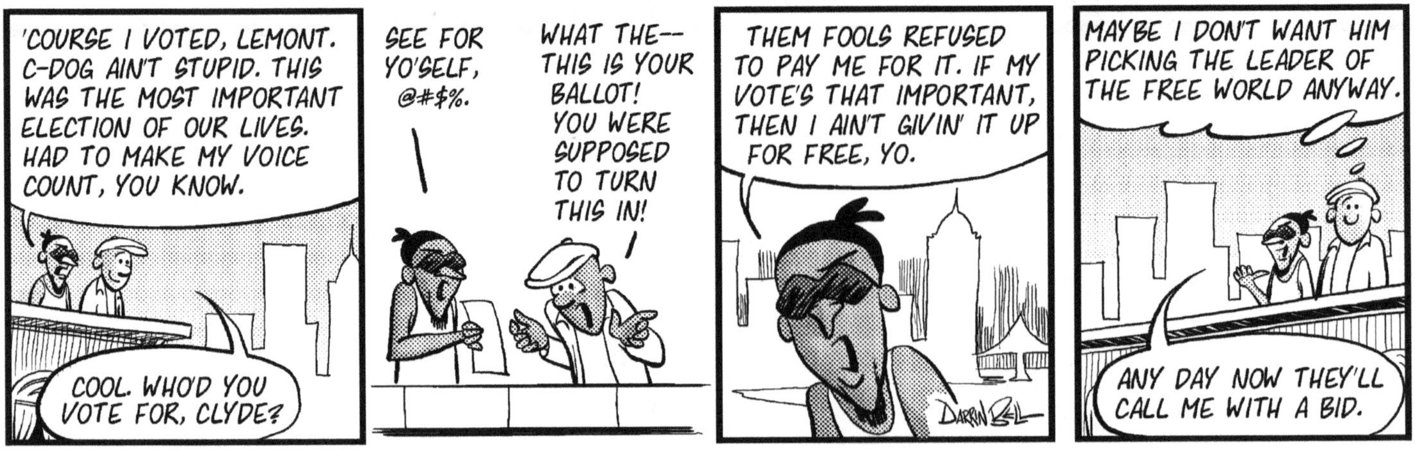
'COURSE I VOTED, LEMONT. C-DOG AIN'T STUPID. THIS WAS THE MOST IMPORTANT ELECTION OF OUR LIVES. HAD TO MAKE MY VOICE COUNT, YOU KNOW.
COOL. WHO'D YOU VOTE FOR, CLYDE?
SEE FOR YO'SELF, @#$%.
WHAT THE-- THIS IS YOUR BALLOT! YOU WERE SUPPOSED TO TURN THIS IN!
THEM FOOLS REFUSED TO PAY ME FOR IT. IF MY VOTE'S THAT IMPORTANT, THEN I AIN'T GIVIN' IT UP FOR FREE, YO.
DARRIN BELL
MAYBE I DON'T WANT HIM PICKING THE LEADER OF THE FREE WORLD ANYWAY.
ANY DAY NOW THEY'LL CALL ME WITH A BID.

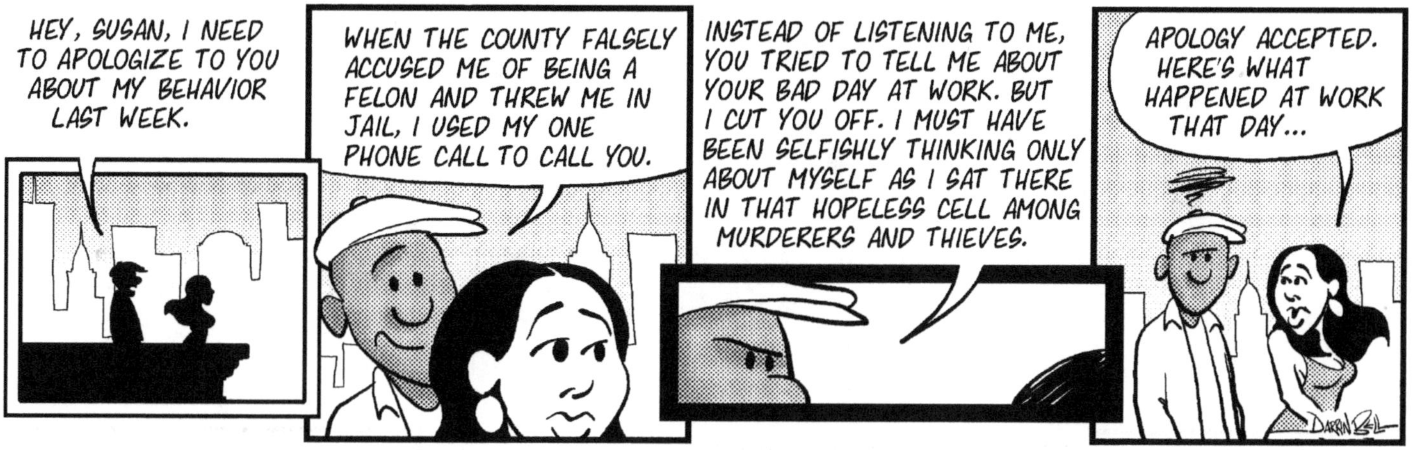
HEY, SUSAN, I NEED TO APOLOGIZE TO YOU ABOUT MY BEHAVIOR LAST WEEK.
WHEN THE COUNTY FALSELY ACCUSED ME OF BEING A FELON AND THREW ME IN JAIL, I USED MY ONE PHONE CALL TO CALL YOU.
INSTEAD OF LISTENING TO ME, YOU TRIED TO TELL ME ABOUT YOUR BAD DAY AT WORK. BUT I CUT YOU OFF. I MUST HAVE BEEN SELFISHLY THINKING ONLY ABOUT MYSELF AS I SAT THERE IN THAT HOPELESS CELL AMONG MURDERERS AND THIEVES.
APOLOGY ACCEPTED. HERE'S WHAT HAPPENED AT WORK THAT DAY...
DARRIN BELL

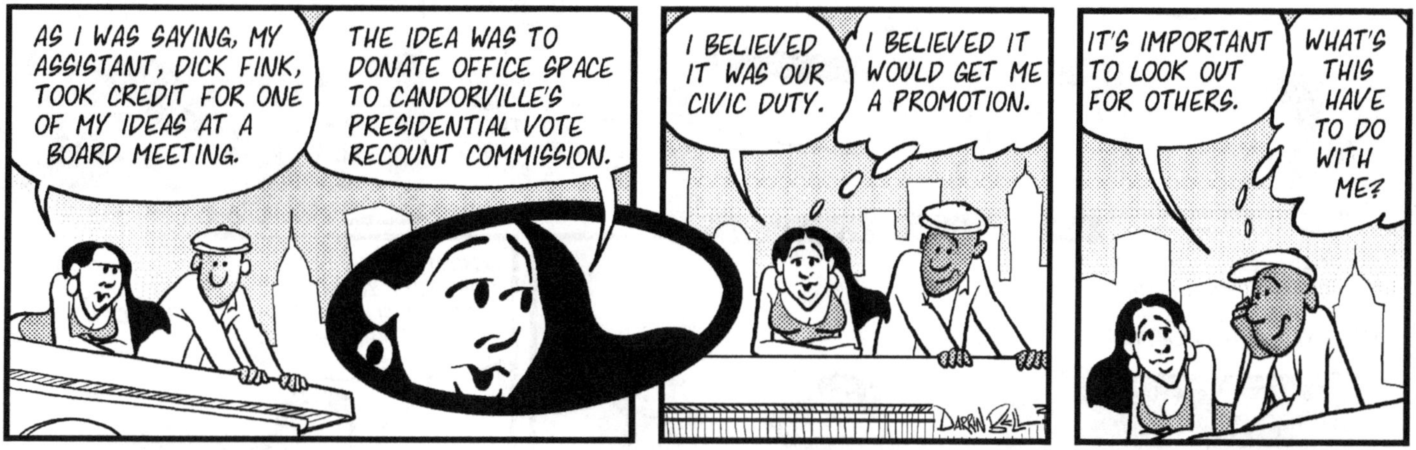
AS I WAS SAYING, MY ASSISTANT, DICK FINK, TOOK CREDIT FOR ONE OF MY IDEAS AT A BOARD MEETING.
THE IDEA WAS TO DONATE OFFICE SPACE TO CANDORVILLE'S PRESIDENTIAL VOTE RECOUNT COMMISSION.
I BELIEVED IT WAS OUR CIVIC DUTY.
I BELIEVED IT WOULD GET ME A PROMOTION.
IT'S IMPORTANT TO LOOK OUT FOR OTHERS.
WHAT'S THIS HAVE TO DO WITH ME?
DARRIN BELL

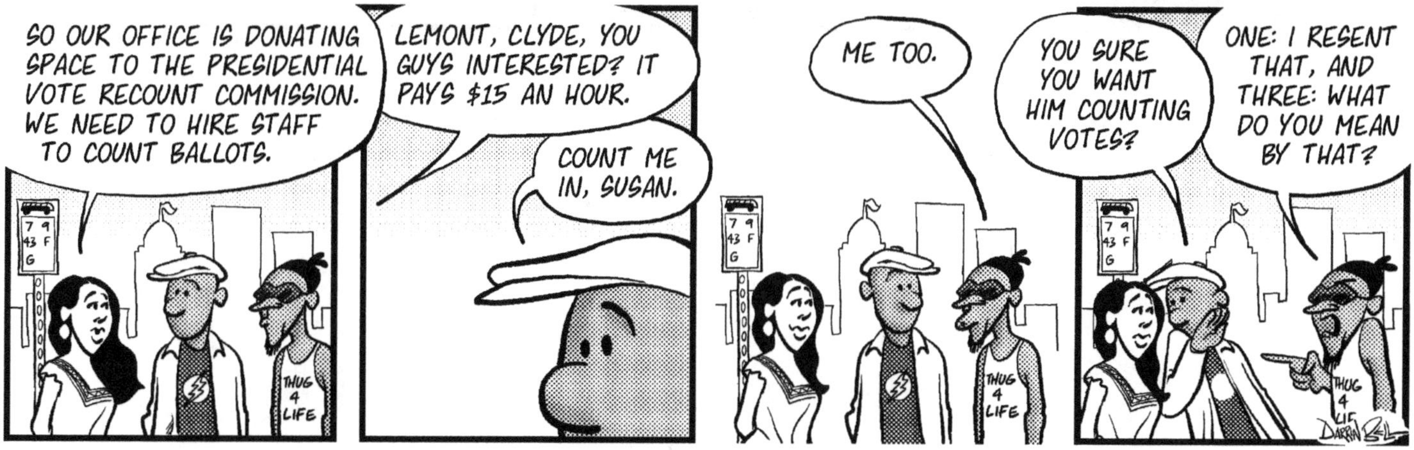
SO OUR OFFICE IS DONATING SPACE TO THE PRESIDENTIAL VOTE RECOUNT COMMISSION. WE NEED TO HIRE STAFF TO COUNT BALLOTS.
THUG 4 LIFE
LEMONT, CLYDE, YOU GUYS INTERESTED? IT PAYS $15 AN HOUR.
COUNT ME IN, SUSAN.
ME TOO.
YOU SURE YOU WANT HIM COUNTING VOTES?
ONE: I RESENT THAT, AND THREE: WHAT DO YOU MEAN BY THAT?
DARRIN BELL

SUSAN, HAVE YOU EVER HEARD OF A CONTROVERSIAL THEORY CALLED "MORPHIC RESONANCE"?

WHEN ONE ANIMAL THINKS OF SOMETHING THAT NO OTHERS IN HIS SPECIES HAVE EVER THOUGHT OF BEFORE, SUDDENLY OTHERS IN HIS SPECIES THINK OF THE SAME EXACT THING.

FOR EXAMPLE, A FEW BIRDS IN ENGLAND FIGURED OUT HOW TO OPEN MILK BOTTLES. ALL OF A SUDDEN, A HUGE NUMBER OF BIRDS IN OTHER PARTS OF THE COUNTRY FIGURED OUT THE SAME THING.

FOR CENTURIES, ASTRONOMERS TRIED TO FIND PLANETS OUTSIDE OUR SOLAR SYSTEM AND THEY ALWAYS FAILED. BUT A FEW YEARS AGO ONE TEAM FIGURED OUT A WAY TO DO IT.

NEARLY SIMULTANEOUSLY, OTHER ASTRONOMERS WORKING INDEPENDENTLY IN OTHER PARTS OF THE WORLD ALSO DISCOVERED EXTRASOLAR PLANETS.

LEMONT, I STILL THINK THIS STORY YOU WROTE IS TOO MUCH LIKE SOMETHING I'VE READ BEFORE.

YOU HAVE NO APPRECIATION FOR THE SCIENCES.

DARRIN BELL

54

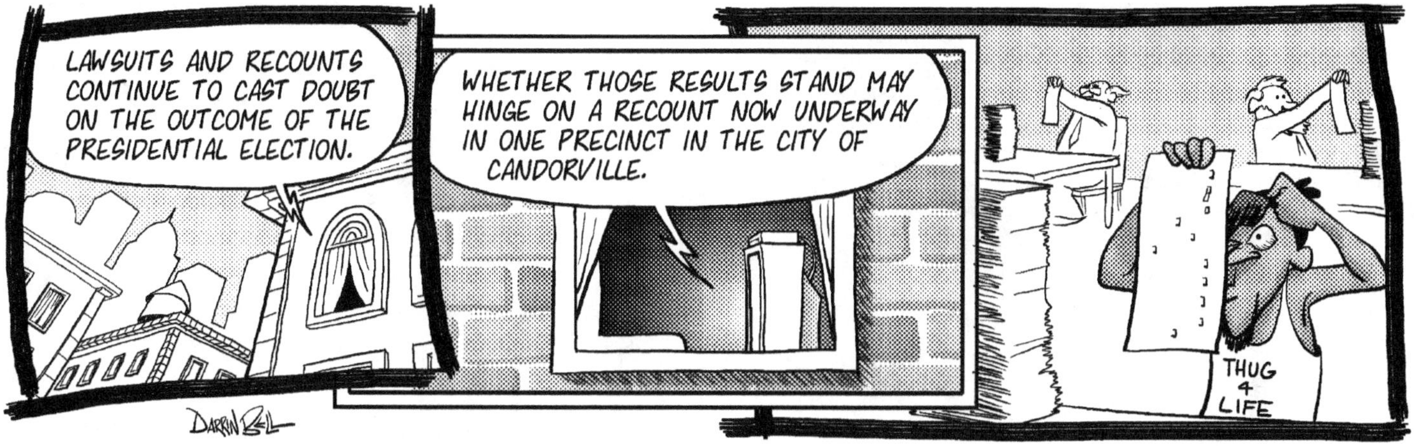
LAWSUITS AND RECOUNTS CONTINUE TO CAST DOUBT ON THE OUTCOME OF THE PRESIDENTIAL ELECTION.
WHETHER THOSE RESULTS STAND MAY HINGE ON A RECOUNT NOW UNDERWAY IN ONE PRECINCT IN THE CITY OF CANDORVILLE.
THUG 4 LIFE
DARRIN BELL

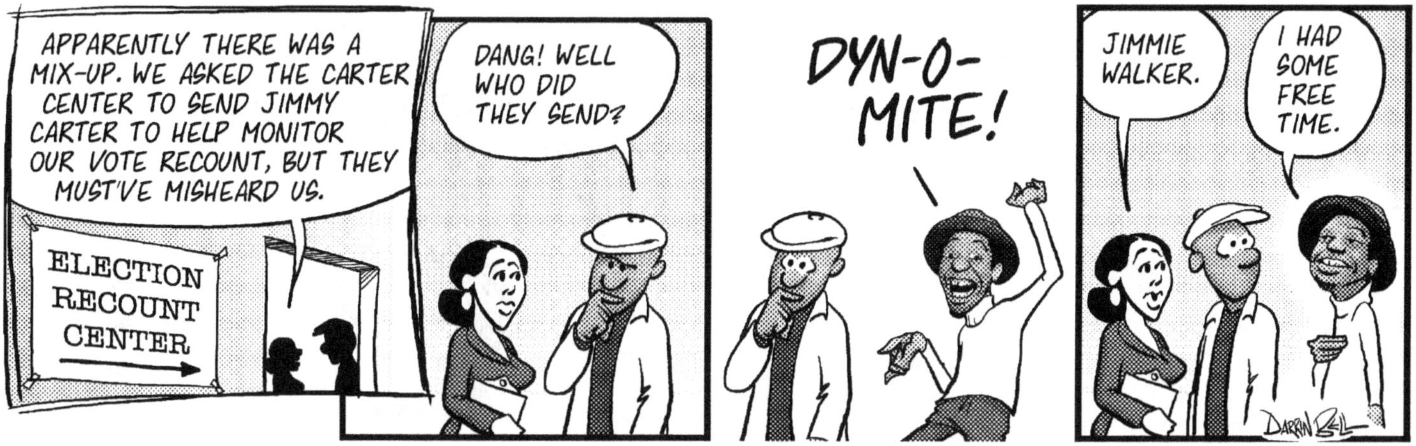
APPARENTLY THERE WAS A MIX-UP. WE ASKED THE CARTER CENTER TO SEND JIMMY CARTER TO HELP MONITOR OUR VOTE RECOUNT, BUT THEY MUST'VE MISHEARD US.
ELECTION RECOUNT CENTER
DANG! WELL WHO DID THEY SEND?
DYN-O-MITE!
JIMMIE WALKER.
I HAD SOME FREE TIME.
DARRIN BELL

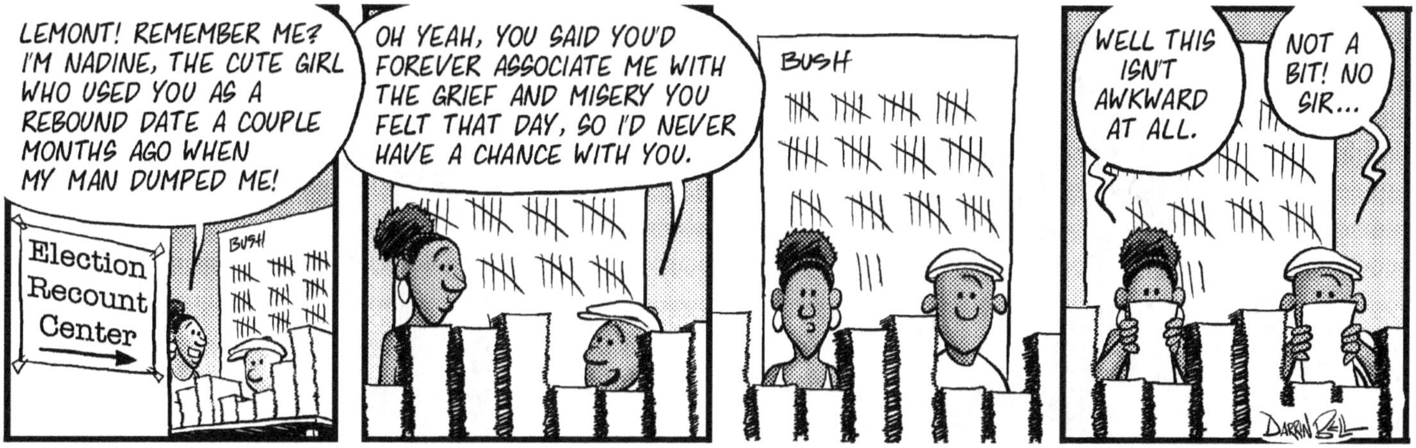
LEMONT! REMEMBER ME? I'M NADINE, THE CUTE GIRL WHO USED YOU AS A REBOUND DATE A COUPLE MONTHS AGO WHEN MY MAN DUMPED ME!
Election Recount Center
BUSH
OH YEAH, YOU SAID YOU'D FOREVER ASSOCIATE ME WITH THE GRIEF AND MISERY YOU FELT THAT DAY, SO I'D NEVER HAVE A CHANCE WITH YOU.
BUSH
WELL THIS ISN'T AWKWARD AT ALL.
NOT A BIT! NO SIR...
DARRIN BELL

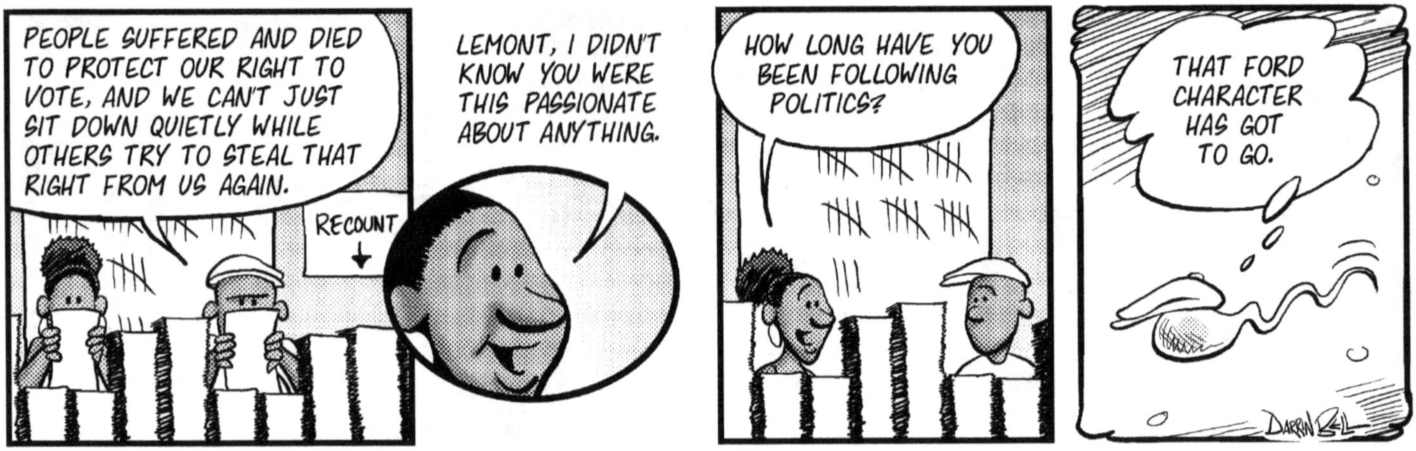
PEOPLE SUFFERED AND DIED TO PROTECT OUR RIGHT TO VOTE, AND WE CAN'T JUST SIT DOWN QUIETLY WHILE OTHERS TRY TO STEAL THAT RIGHT FROM US AGAIN.
RECOUNT
LEMONT, I DIDN'T KNOW YOU WERE THIS PASSIONATE ABOUT ANYTHING.
HOW LONG HAVE YOU BEEN FOLLOWING POLITICS?
THAT FORD CHARACTER HAS GOT TO GO.
DARRIN BELL

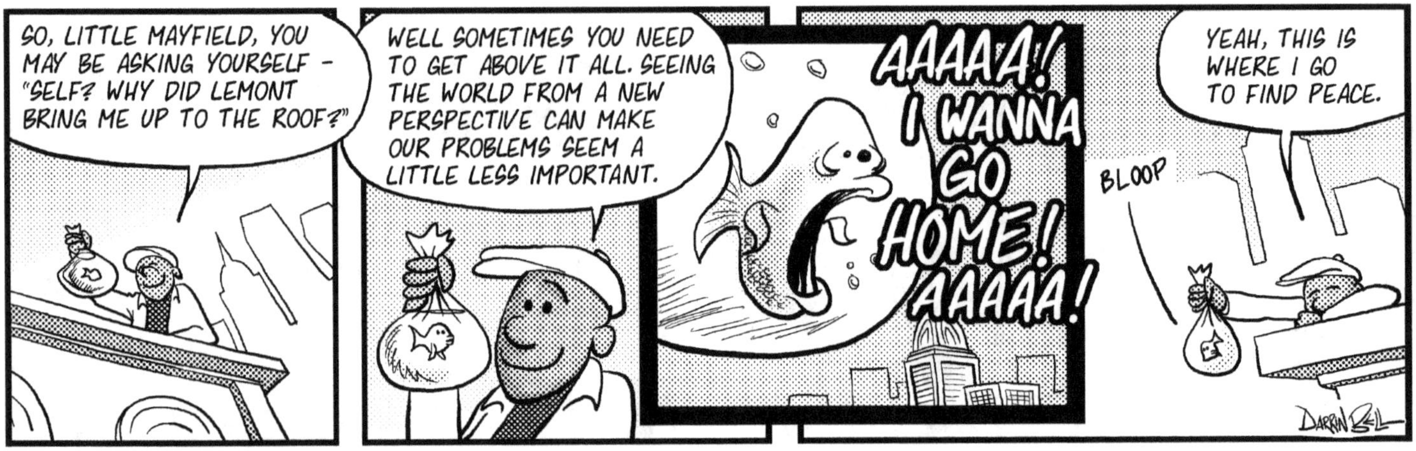
SO, LITTLE MAYFIELD, YOU MAY BE ASKING YOURSELF - "SELF? WHY DID LEMONT BRING ME UP TO THE ROOF?"
WELL SOMETIMES YOU NEED TO GET ABOVE IT ALL. SEEING THE WORLD FROM A NEW PERSPECTIVE CAN MAKE OUR PROBLEMS SEEM A LITTLE LESS IMPORTANT.
AAAAA! I WANNA GO HOME! AAAAA!
BLOOP
YEAH, THIS IS WHERE I GO TO FIND PEACE.
DARRIN BELL

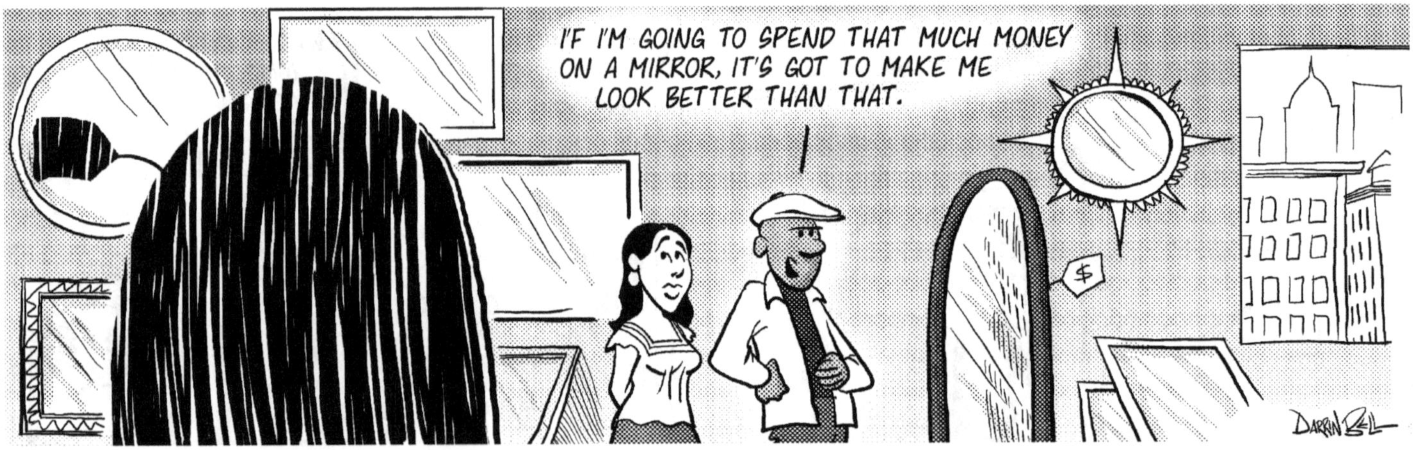
IF I'M GOING TO SPEND THAT MUCH MONEY ON A MIRROR, IT'S GOT TO MAKE ME LOOK BETTER THAN THAT.
$
DARRIN BELL

HELLO, WASHINGTON, D.C.? I WANT TO THANK YOU FOR THE TAX CUT YOU GAVE ME IN 2002.
I HAD A GREAT TIME WITH THE $300 YOU SENT. I BOUGHT AN X-BOX AND SOME GAMES, AND HAD A NICE DINNER.
BUT I HAVE A QUESTION.
I NOTICED THAT MY PELL GRANT HAS BEEN ELIMINATED, SO I NOW HAVE TO PAY $5000 MORE PER SEMESTER FOR COLLEGE.
ALSO, MY LOCAL BUS COSTS TWICE AS MUCH TO RIDE AS IT USED TO, SO I PAY AN EXTRA $300 PER YEAR TO GET TO SCHOOL.
AND MY BROTHER'S NATIONAL GUARD UNIT COULDN'T AFFORD ARMOR, SO HE WAS KILLED BY A ROADSIDE BOMB LAST WEEK.
SO MY QUESTION IS...
IF I GIVE BACK THE $300, CAN YOU GIVE ME BACK MY CHEAP COLLEGE EDUCATION, MY AFFORDABLE PUBLIC TRANSPORTATION AND MY BROTHER?
DARRIN BELL

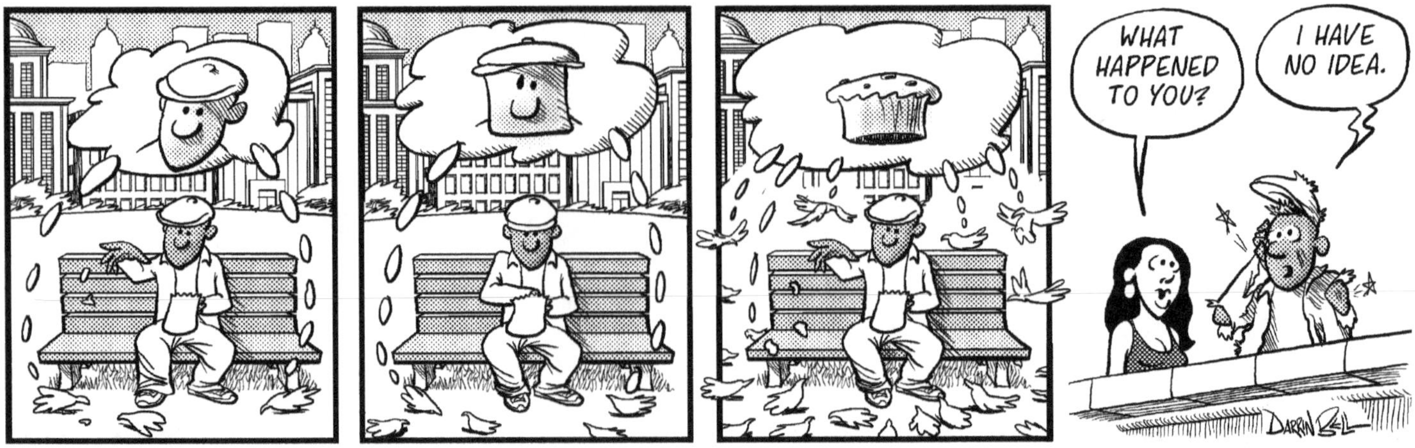
WHAT HAPPENED TO YOU?
I HAVE NO IDEA.
DARRIN BELL

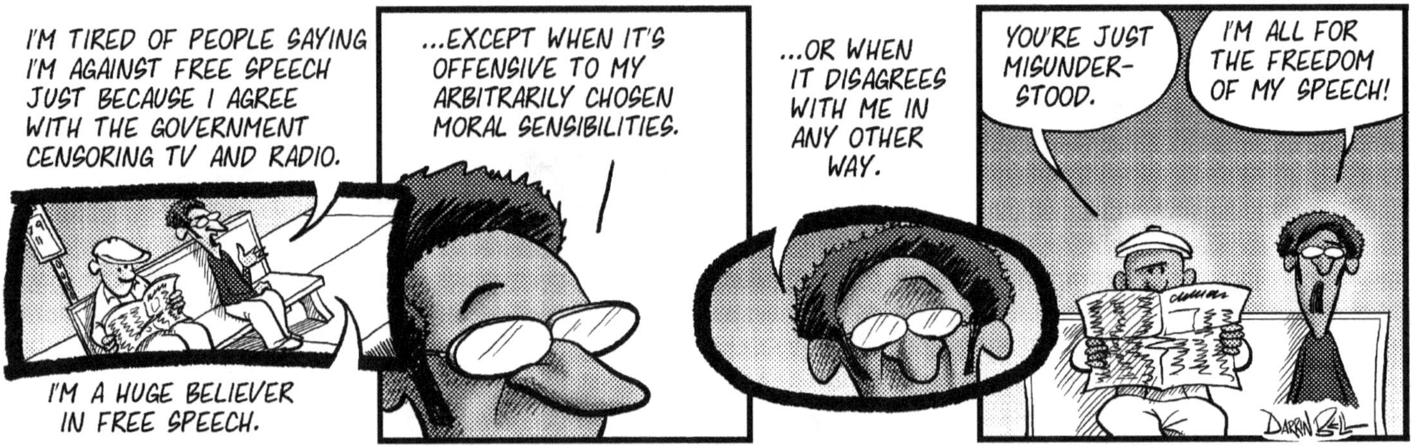
I'M TIRED OF PEOPLE SAYING I'M AGAINST FREE SPEECH JUST BECAUSE I AGREE WITH THE GOVERNMENT CENSORING TV AND RADIO.
I'M A HUGE BELIEVER IN FREE SPEECH.
...EXCEPT WHEN IT'S OFFENSIVE TO MY ARBITRARILY CHOSEN MORAL SENSIBILITIES.
...OR WHEN IT DISAGREES WITH ME IN ANY OTHER WAY.
YOU'RE JUST MISUNDER-STOOD.
I'M ALL FOR THE FREEDOM OF MY SPEECH!
DARRIN BELL

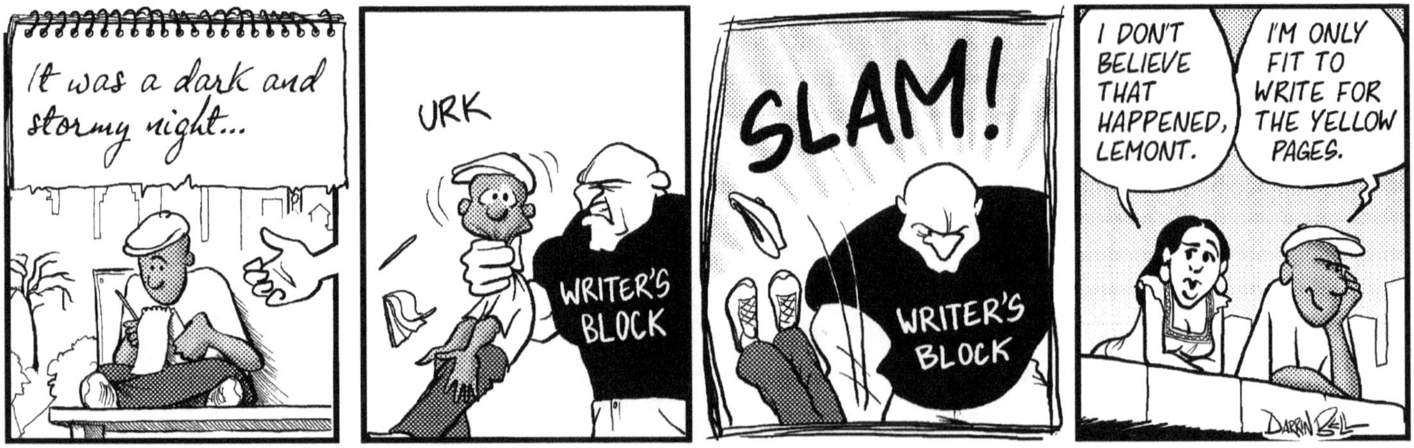
It was a dark and stormy night...
URK
WRITER'S BLOCK
SLAM!
WRITER'S BLOCK
I DON'T BELIEVE THAT HAPPENED, LEMONT.
I'M ONLY FIT TO WRITE FOR THE YELLOW PAGES.
DARRIN BELL

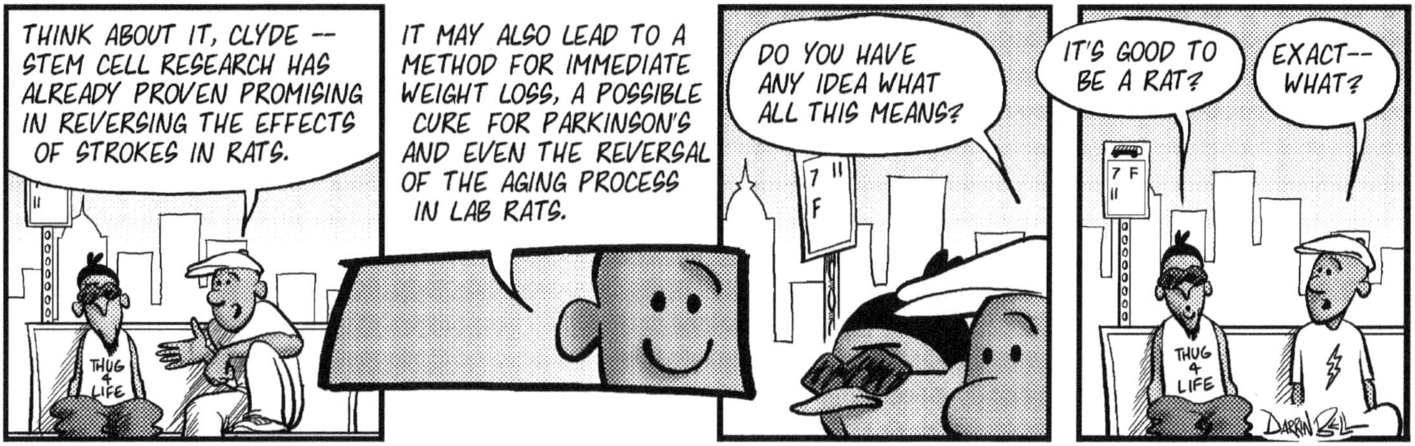
THINK ABOUT IT, CLYDE -- STEM CELL RESEARCH HAS ALREADY PROVEN PROMISING IN REVERSING THE EFFECTS OF STROKES IN RATS.
THUG 4 LIFE
IT MAY ALSO LEAD TO A METHOD FOR IMMEDIATE WEIGHT LOSS, A POSSIBLE CURE FOR PARKINSON'S AND EVEN THE REVERSAL OF THE AGING PROCESS IN LAB RATS.
DO YOU HAVE ANY IDEA WHAT ALL THIS MEANS?
IT'S GOOD TO BE A RAT?
EXACT-- WHAT?
DARRIN BELL

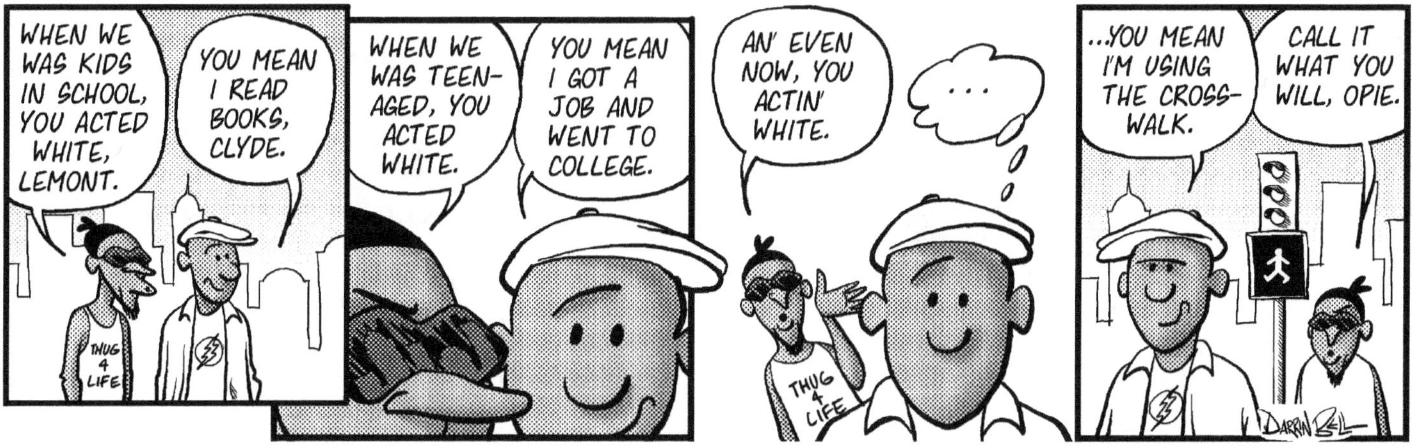
WHEN WE WAS KIDS IN SCHOOL, YOU ACTED WHITE, LEMONT.
YOU MEAN I READ BOOKS, CLYDE.
WHEN WE WAS TEEN-AGED, YOU ACTED WHITE.
YOU MEAN I GOT A JOB AND WENT TO COLLEGE.
AN' EVEN NOW, YOU ACTIN' WHITE.
. . .
...YOU MEAN I'M USING THE CROSS-WALK.
CALL IT WHAT YOU WILL, OPIE.
DARRIN BELL

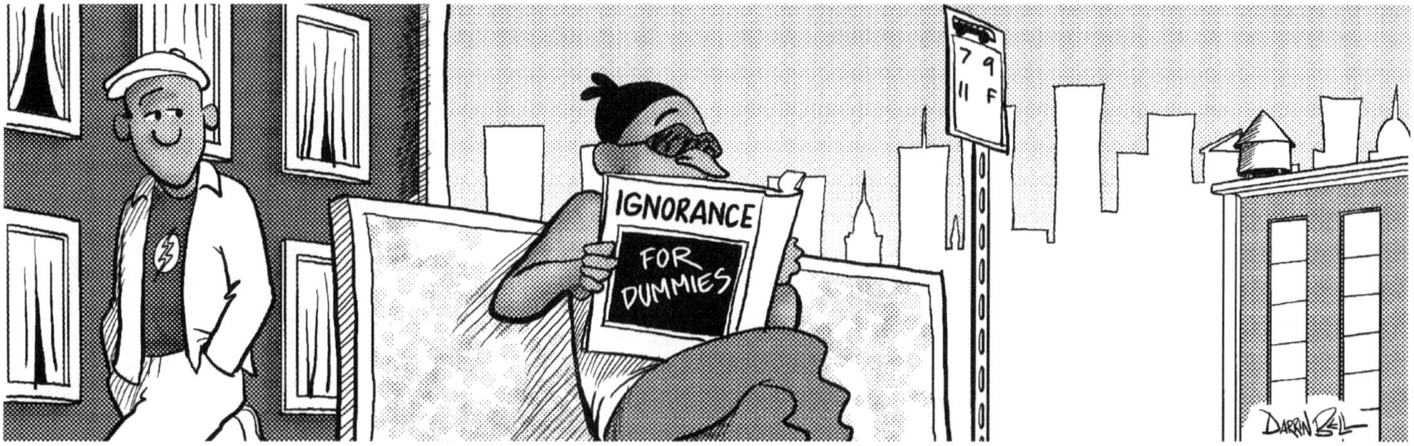
IGNORANCE
FOR DUMMIES
DARRIN BELL

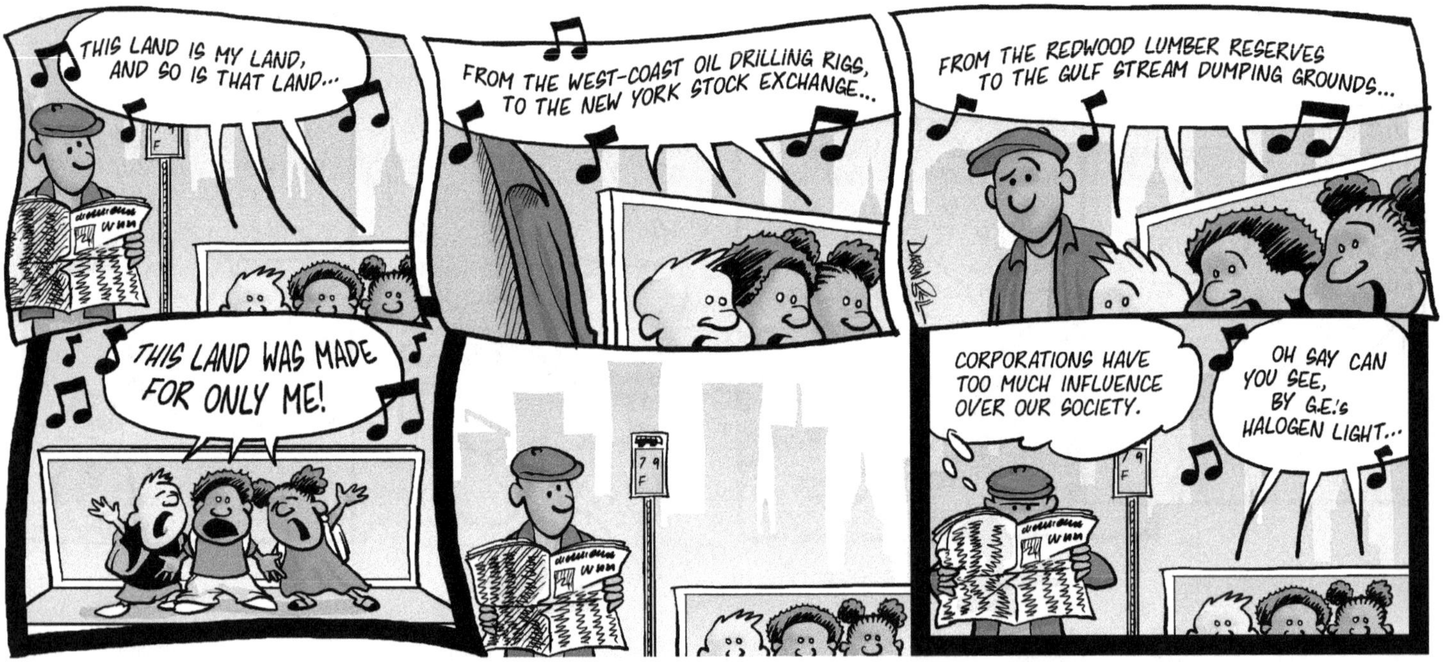
THIS LAND IS MY LAND,
AND SO IS THAT LAND...
FROM THE WEST-COAST OIL DRILLING RIGS,
TO THE NEW YORK STOCK EXCHANGE...
FROM THE REDWOOD LUMBER RESERVES
TO THE GULF STREAM DUMPING GROUNDS...
THIS LAND WAS MADE FOR ONLY ME!
CORPORATIONS HAVE TOO MUCH INFLUENCE OVER OUR SOCIETY.
OH SAY CAN YOU SEE, BY G.E.'s HALOGEN LIGHT...

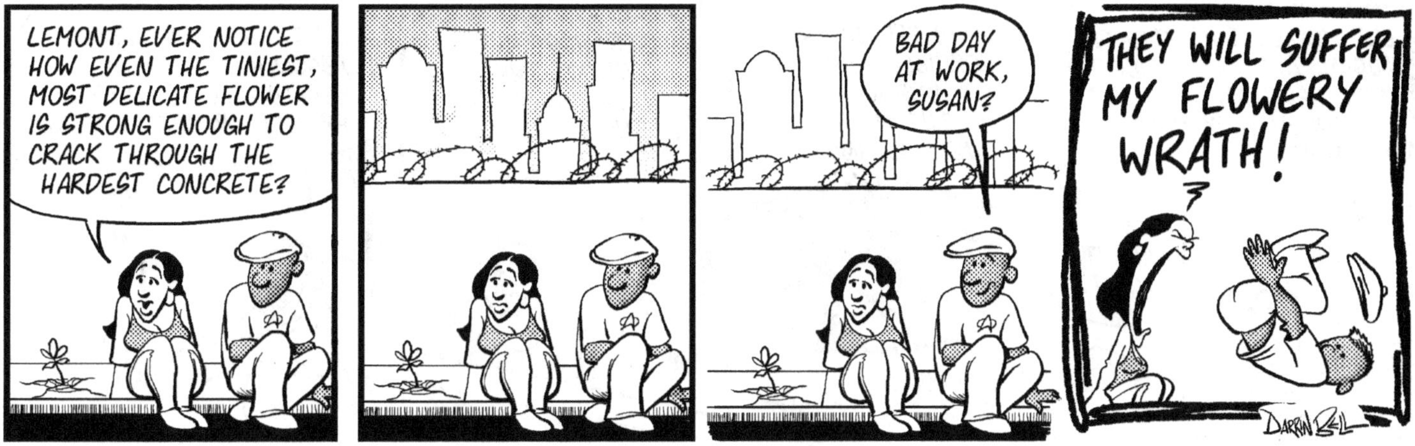
LEMONT, EVER NOTICE HOW EVEN THE TINIEST, MOST DELICATE FLOWER IS STRONG ENOUGH TO CRACK THROUGH THE HARDEST CONCRETE?
BAD DAY AT WORK, SUSAN?
THEY WILL SUFFER MY FLOWERY WRATH!
DARRIN BELL

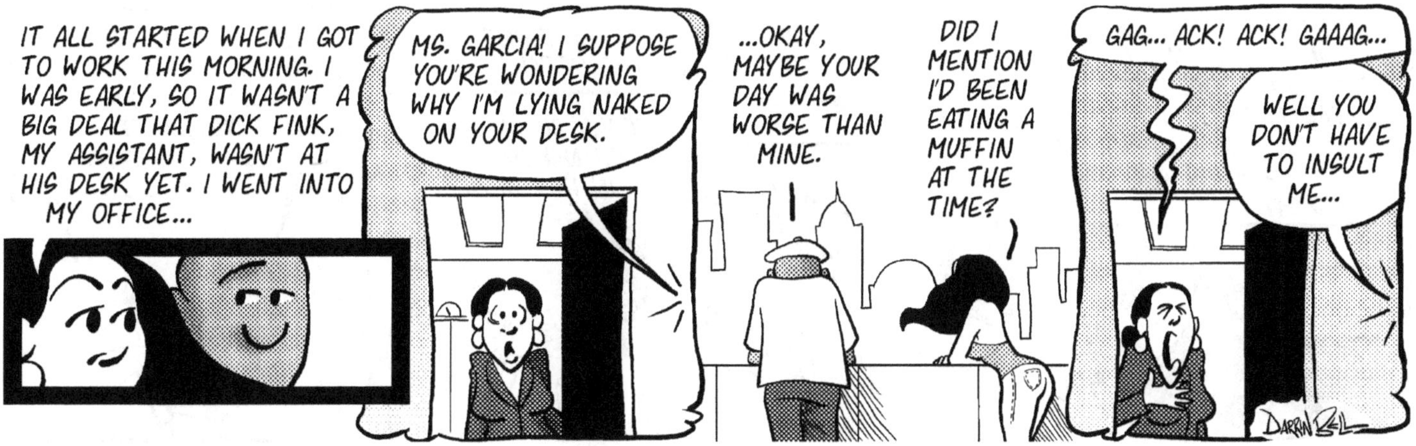
IT ALL STARTED WHEN I GOT TO WORK THIS MORNING. I WAS EARLY, SO IT WASN'T A BIG DEAL THAT DICK FINK, MY ASSISTANT, WASN'T AT HIS DESK YET. I WENT INTO MY OFFICE...
MS. GARCIA! I SUPPOSE YOU'RE WONDERING WHY I'M LYING NAKED ON YOUR DESK.
...OKAY, MAYBE YOUR DAY WAS WORSE THAN MINE.
DID I MENTION I'D BEEN EATING A MUFFIN AT THE TIME?
GAG... ACK! ACK! GAAAG...
WELL YOU DON'T HAVE TO INSULT ME...
DARRIN BELL

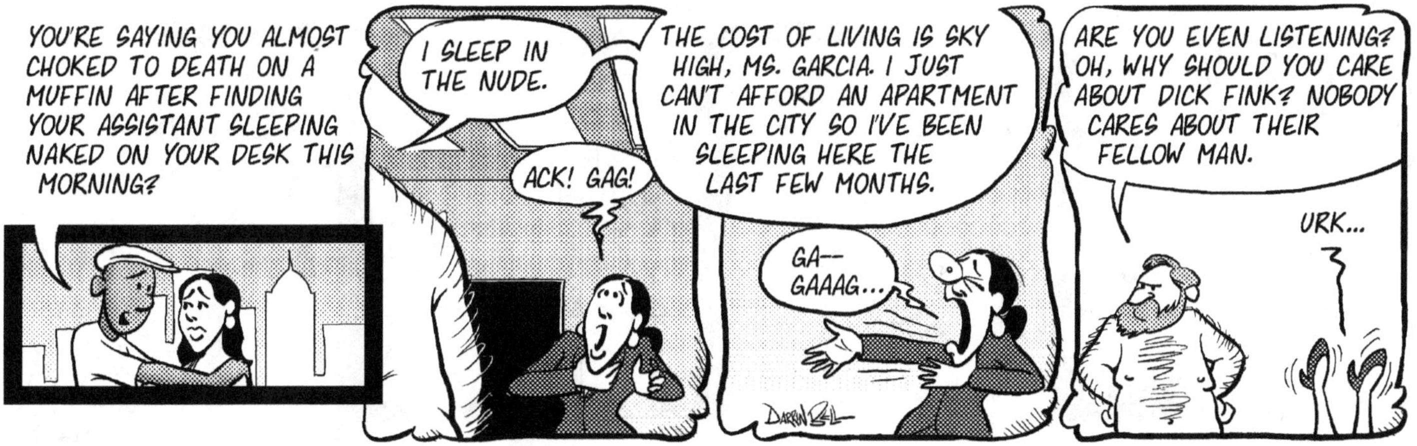
YOU'RE SAYING YOU ALMOST CHOKED TO DEATH ON A MUFFIN AFTER FINDING YOUR ASSISTANT SLEEPING NAKED ON YOUR DESK THIS MORNING?
I SLEEP IN THE NUDE.
ACK! GAG!
THE COST OF LIVING IS SKY HIGH, MS. GARCIA. I JUST CAN'T AFFORD AN APARTMENT IN THE CITY SO I'VE BEEN SLEEPING HERE THE LAST FEW MONTHS.
GA— GAAAG...
DARRIN BELL
ARE YOU EVEN LISTENING? OH, WHY SHOULD YOU CARE ABOUT DICK FINK? NOBODY CARES ABOUT THEIR FELLOW MAN.
URK...

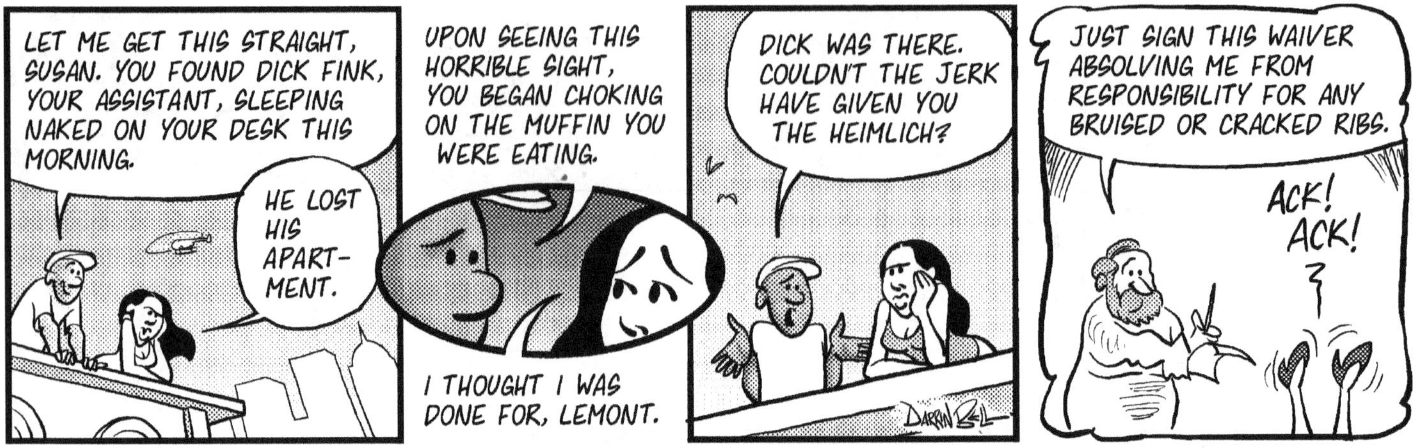
LET ME GET THIS STRAIGHT, SUSAN. YOU FOUND DICK FINK, YOUR ASSISTANT, SLEEPING NAKED ON YOUR DESK THIS MORNING.
HE LOST HIS APART-MENT.
UPON SEEING THIS HORRIBLE SIGHT, YOU BEGAN CHOKING ON THE MUFFIN YOU WERE EATING.
I THOUGHT I WAS DONE FOR, LEMONT.
DICK WAS THERE. COULDN'T THE JERK HAVE GIVEN YOU THE HEIMLICH?
JUST SIGN THIS WAIVER ABSOLVING ME FROM RESPONSIBILITY FOR ANY BRUISED OR CRACKED RIBS.
ACK! ACK!
DARRIN BELL

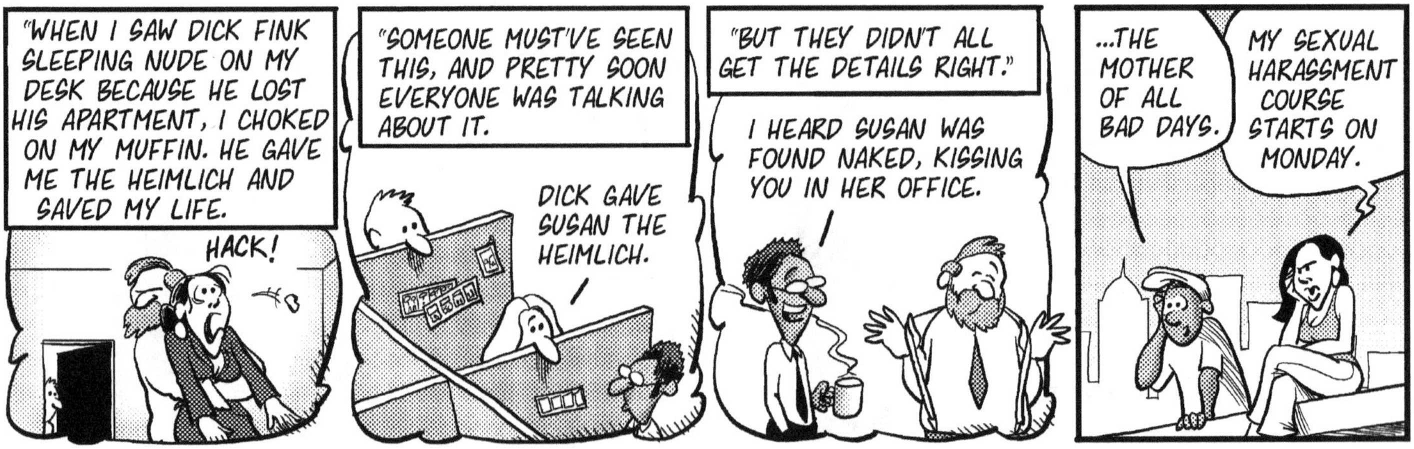
"WHEN I SAW DICK FINK SLEEPING NUDE ON MY DESK BECAUSE HE LOST HIS APARTMENT, I CHOKED ON MY MUFFIN. HE GAVE ME THE HEIMLICH AND SAVED MY LIFE.
HACK!
"SOMEONE MUST'VE SEEN THIS, AND PRETTY SOON EVERYONE WAS TALKING ABOUT IT.
DICK GAVE SUSAN THE HEIMLICH.
"BUT THEY DIDN'T ALL GET THE DETAILS RIGHT."
I HEARD SUSAN WAS FOUND NAKED, KISSING YOU IN HER OFFICE.
...THE MOTHER OF ALL BAD DAYS.
MY SEXUAL HARASSMENT COURSE STARTS ON MONDAY.

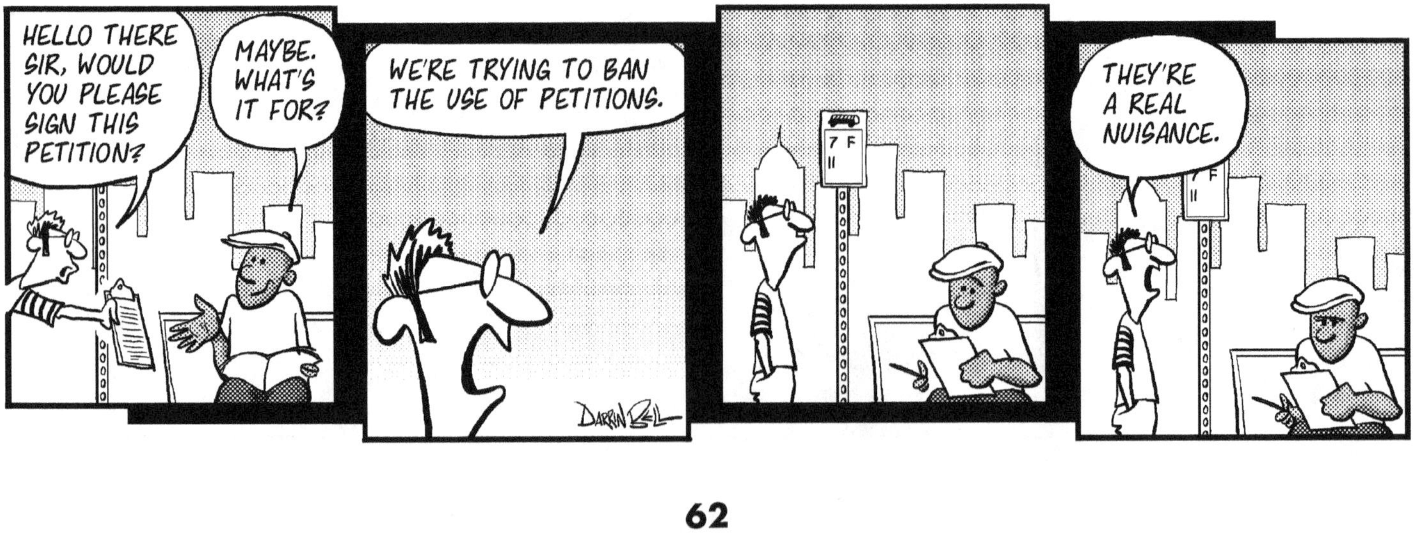
HELLO THERE SIR, WOULD YOU PLEASE SIGN THIS PETITION?
MAYBE. WHAT'S IT FOR?
WE'RE TRYING TO BAN THE USE OF PETITIONS.
DARRIN BELL
THEY'RE A REAL NUISANCE.

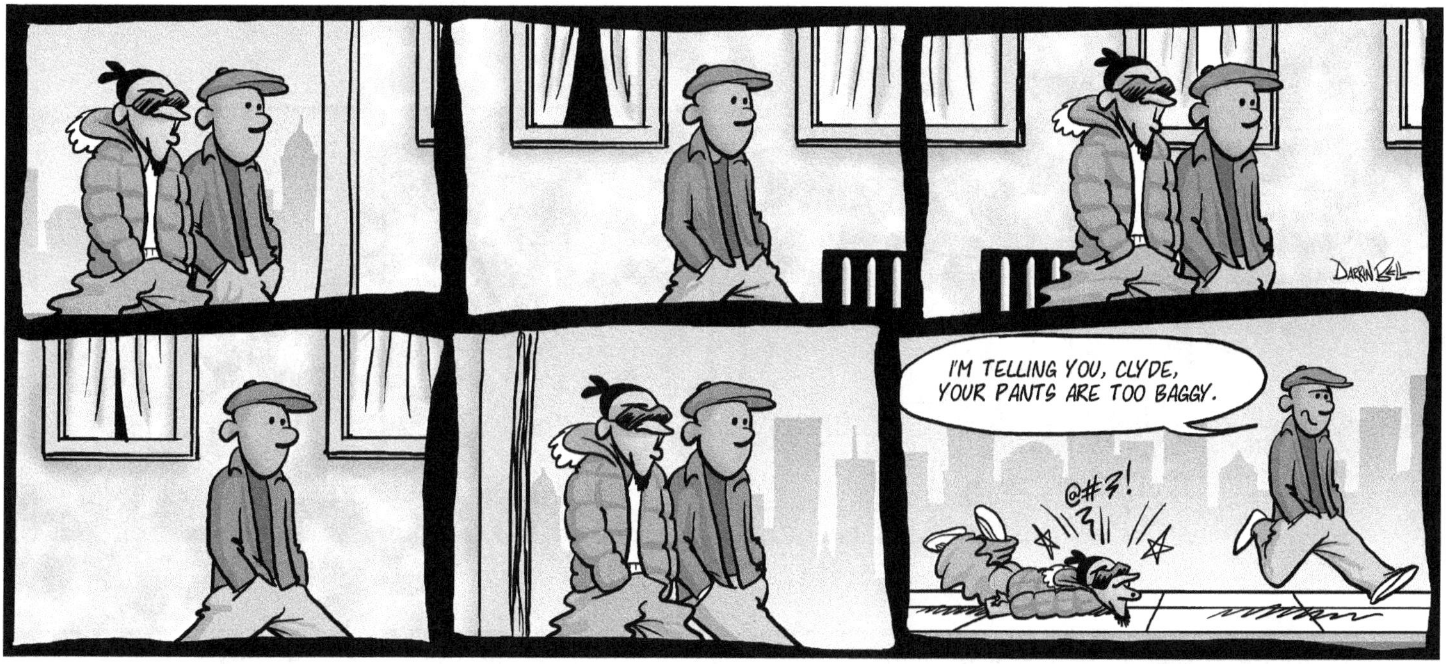
DARRIN BELL
I'M TELLING YOU, CLYDE, YOUR PANTS ARE TOO BAGGY.
@#Ƨ!

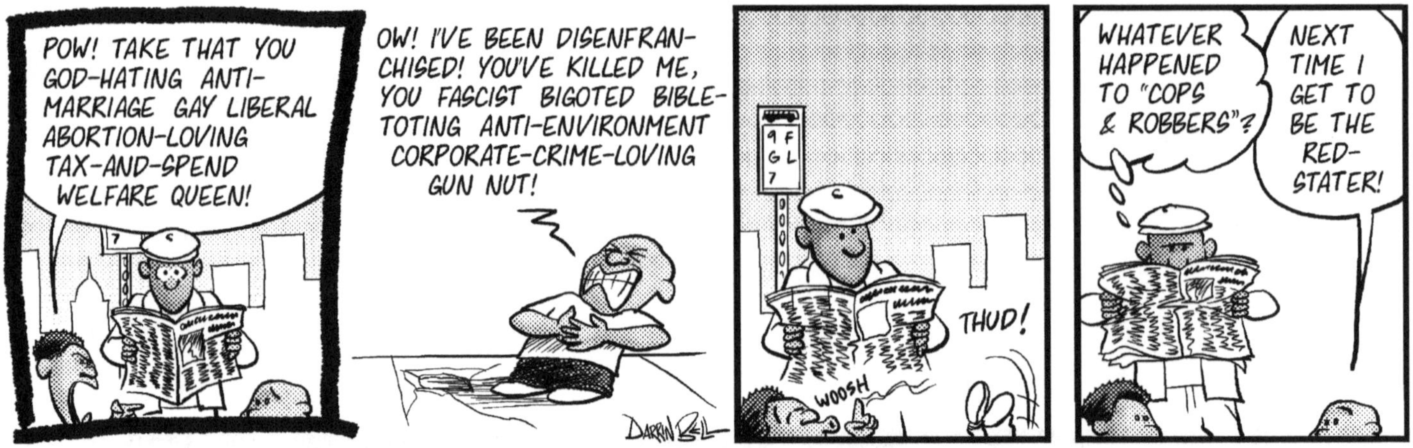
POW! TAKE THAT YOU GOD-HATING ANTI-MARRIAGE GAY LIBERAL ABORTION-LOVING TAX-AND-SPEND WELFARE QUEEN!
OW! I'VE BEEN DISENFRANCHISED! YOU'VE KILLED ME, YOU FASCIST BIGOTED BIBLE-TOTING ANTI-ENVIRONMENT CORPORATE-CRIME-LOVING GUN NUT!
DARRIN BELL
WOOSH
THUD!
WHATEVER HAPPENED TO "COPS & ROBBERS"?
NEXT TIME I GET TO BE THE RED-STATER!

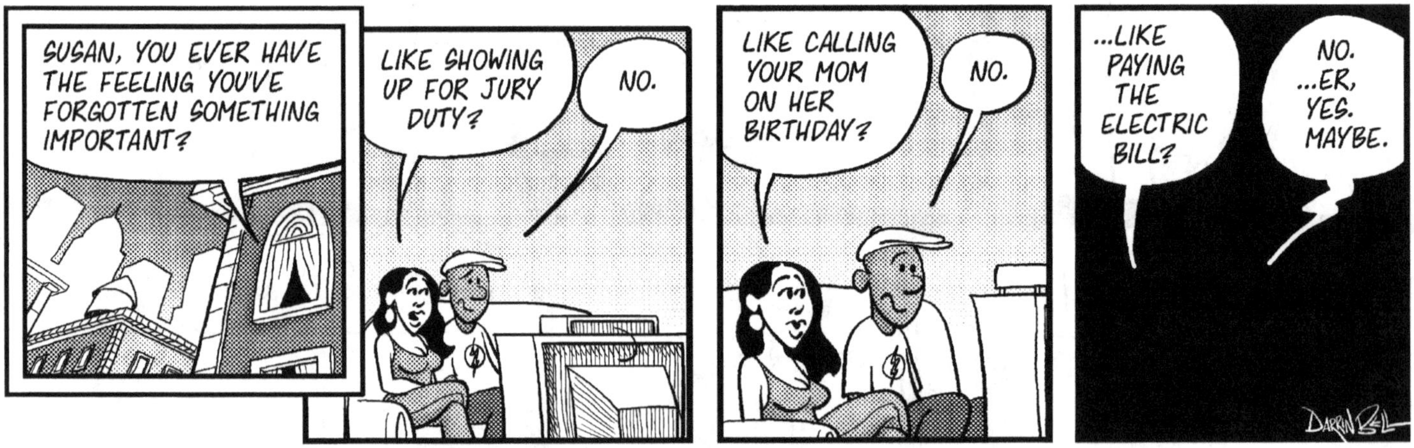
SUSAN, YOU EVER HAVE THE FEELING YOU'VE FORGOTTEN SOMETHING IMPORTANT?
LIKE SHOWING UP FOR JURY DUTY?
NO.
LIKE CALLING YOUR MOM ON HER BIRTHDAY?
NO.
...LIKE PAYING THE ELECTRIC BILL?
NO. ...ER, YES. MAYBE.
DARRIN BELL

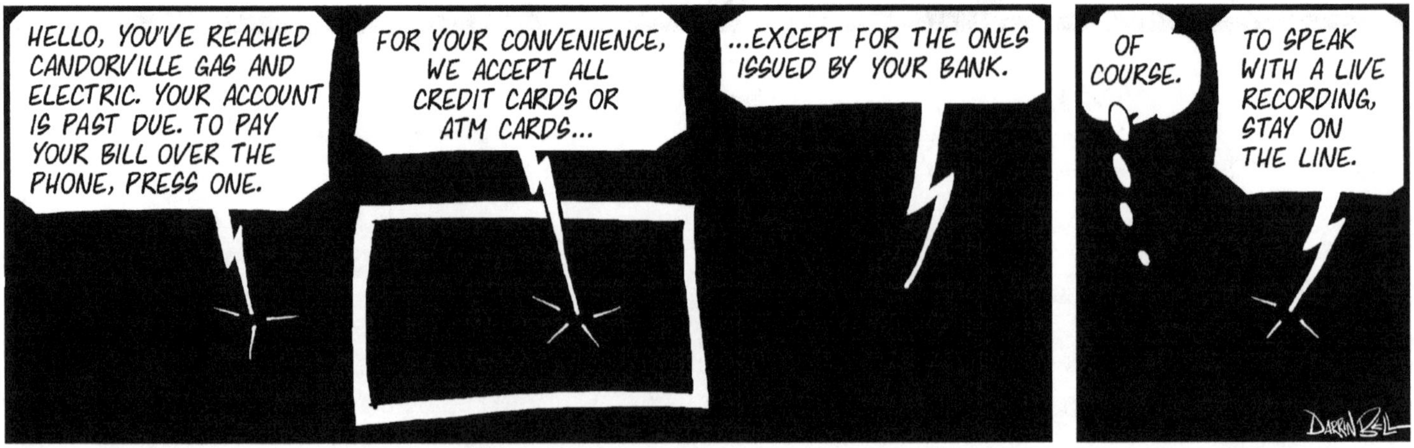
HELLO, YOU'VE REACHED CANDORVILLE GAS AND ELECTRIC. YOUR ACCOUNT IS PAST DUE. TO PAY YOUR BILL OVER THE PHONE, PRESS ONE.
FOR YOUR CONVENIENCE, WE ACCEPT ALL CREDIT CARDS OR ATM CARDS...
...EXCEPT FOR THE ONES ISSUED BY YOUR BANK.
OF COURSE.
TO SPEAK WITH A LIVE RECORDING, STAY ON THE LINE.
DARRIN BELL

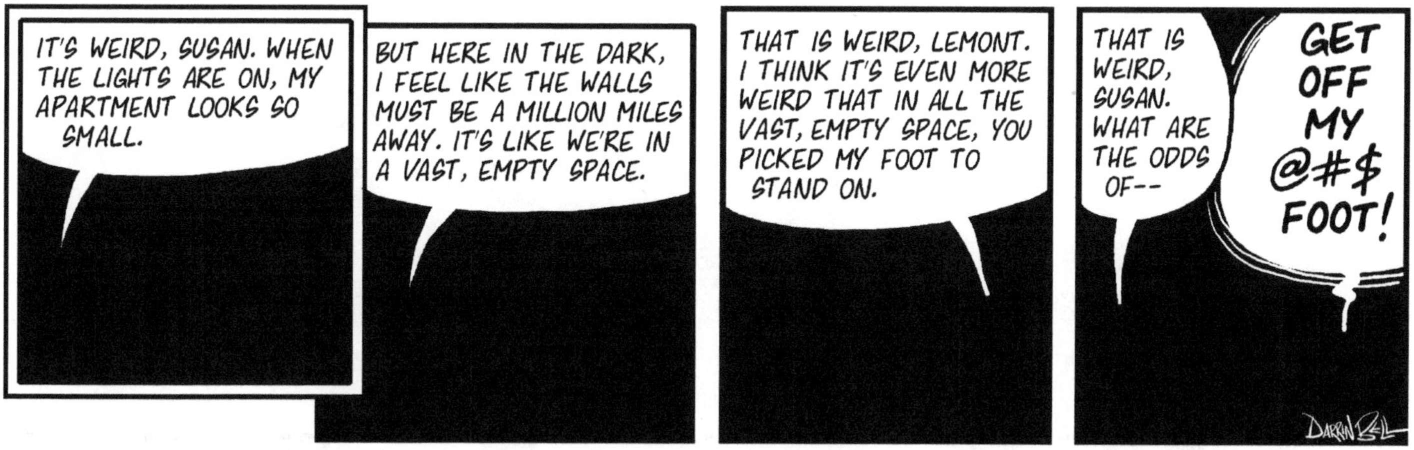
IT'S WEIRD, SUSAN. WHEN THE LIGHTS ARE ON, MY APARTMENT LOOKS SO SMALL.
BUT HERE IN THE DARK, I FEEL LIKE THE WALLS MUST BE A MILLION MILES AWAY. IT'S LIKE WE'RE IN A VAST, EMPTY SPACE.
THAT IS WEIRD, LEMONT. I THINK IT'S EVEN MORE WEIRD THAT IN ALL THE VAST, EMPTY SPACE, YOU PICKED MY FOOT TO STAND ON.
THAT IS WEIRD, SUSAN. WHAT ARE THE ODDS OF--
GET OFF MY @#$ FOOT!
DARRIN BELL

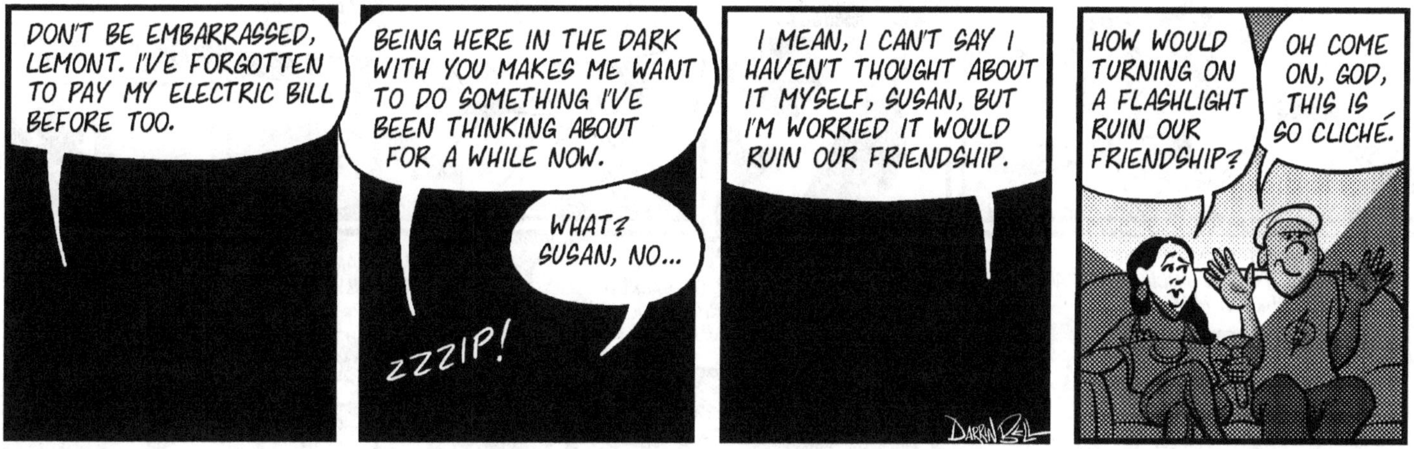
DON'T BE EMBARRASSED, LEMONT. I'VE FORGOTTEN TO PAY MY ELECTRIC BILL BEFORE TOO.
BEING HERE IN THE DARK WITH YOU MAKES ME WANT TO DO SOMETHING I'VE BEEN THINKING ABOUT FOR A WHILE NOW.
ZZZIP!
WHAT? SUSAN, NO...
I MEAN, I CAN'T SAY I HAVEN'T THOUGHT ABOUT IT MYSELF, SUSAN, BUT I'M WORRIED IT WOULD RUIN OUR FRIENDSHIP.
DARRIN BELL
HOW WOULD TURNING ON A FLASHLIGHT RUIN OUR FRIENDSHIP?
OH COME ON, GOD, THIS IS SO CLICHÉ.

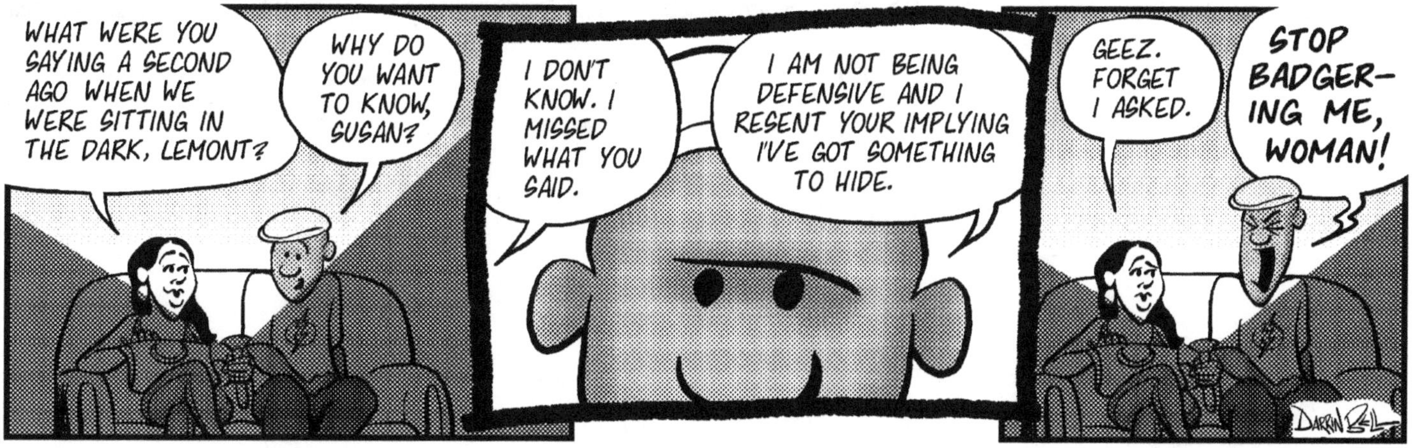
WHAT WERE YOU SAYING A SECOND AGO WHEN WE WERE SITTING IN THE DARK, LEMONT?
WHY DO YOU WANT TO KNOW, SUSAN?
I DON'T KNOW. I MISSED WHAT YOU SAID.
I AM NOT BEING DEFENSIVE AND I RESENT YOUR IMPLYING I'VE GOT SOMETHING TO HIDE.
GEEZ. FORGET I ASKED.
STOP BADGERING ME, WOMAN!
DARRIN BELL

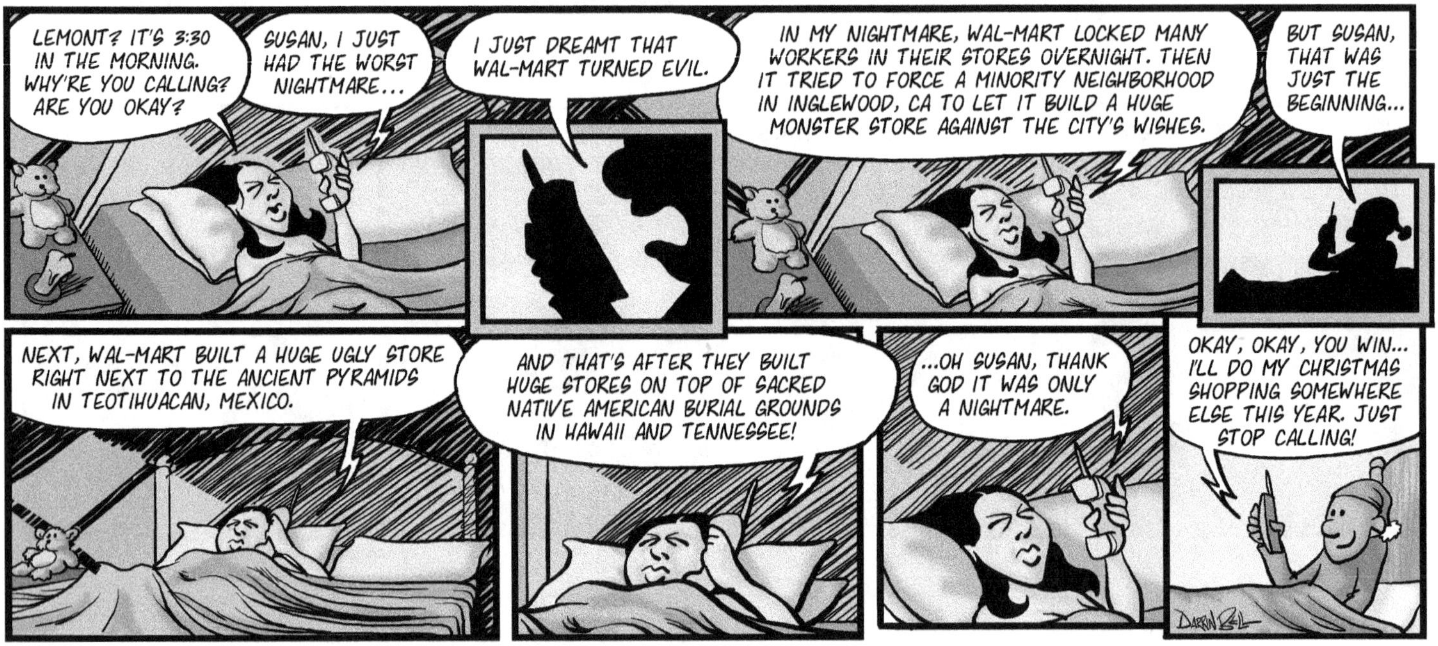
LEMONT? IT'S 3:30 IN THE MORNING. WHY'RE YOU CALLING? ARE YOU OKAY?
SUSAN, I JUST HAD THE WORST NIGHTMARE...
I JUST DREAMT THAT WAL-MART TURNED EVIL.
IN MY NIGHTMARE, WAL-MART LOCKED MANY WORKERS IN THEIR STORES OVERNIGHT. THEN IT TRIED TO FORCE A MINORITY NEIGHBORHOOD IN INGLEWOOD, CA TO LET IT BUILD A HUGE MONSTER STORE AGAINST THE CITY'S WISHES.
BUT SUSAN, THAT WAS JUST THE BEGINNING...
NEXT, WAL-MART BUILT A HUGE UGLY STORE RIGHT NEXT TO THE ANCIENT PYRAMIDS IN TEOTIHUACAN, MEXICO.
AND THAT'S AFTER THEY BUILT HUGE STORES ON TOP OF SACRED NATIVE AMERICAN BURIAL GROUNDS IN HAWAII AND TENNESSEE!
...OH SUSAN, THANK GOD IT WAS ONLY A NIGHTMARE.
OKAY, OKAY, YOU WIN... I'LL DO MY CHRISTMAS SHOPPING SOMEWHERE ELSE THIS YEAR. JUST STOP CALLING!
DARRIN BELL

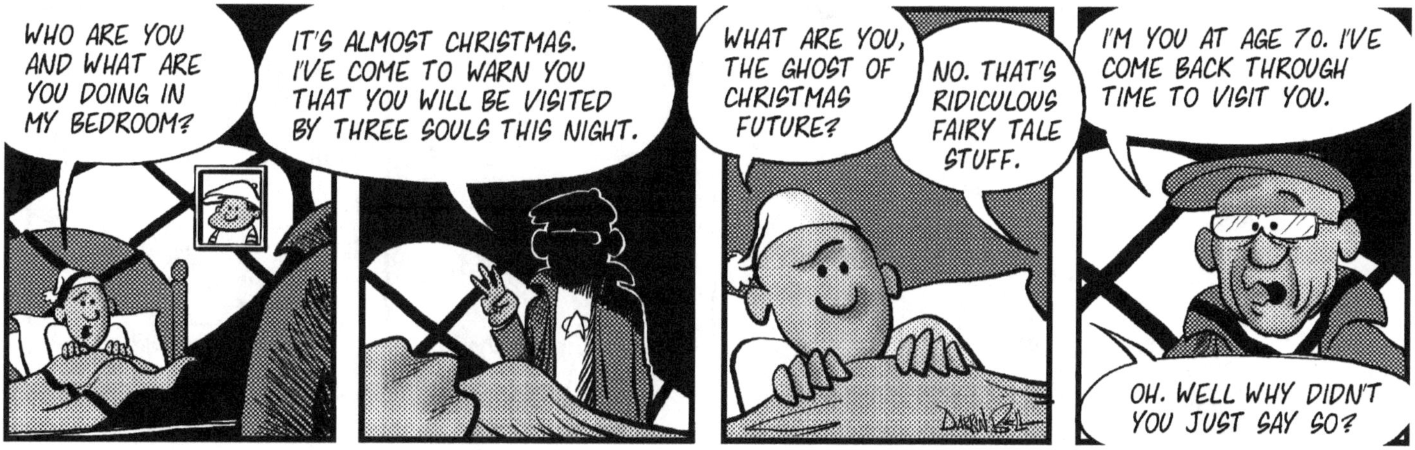
WHO ARE YOU AND WHAT ARE YOU DOING IN MY BEDROOM?
IT'S ALMOST CHRISTMAS. I'VE COME TO WARN YOU THAT YOU WILL BE VISITED BY THREE SOULS THIS NIGHT.
WHAT ARE YOU, THE GHOST OF CHRISTMAS FUTURE?
NO. THAT'S RIDICULOUS FAIRY TALE STUFF.
I'M YOU AT AGE 70. I'VE COME BACK THROUGH TIME TO VISIT YOU.
OH. WELL WHY DIDN'T YOU JUST SAY SO?
DARRIN BELL

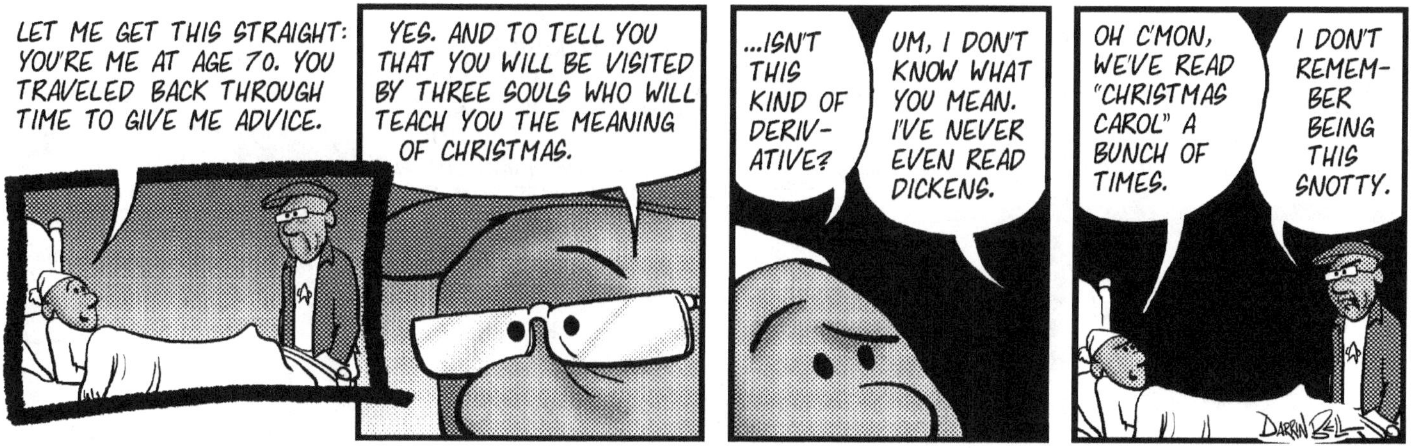
LET ME GET THIS STRAIGHT: YOU'RE ME AT AGE 70. YOU TRAVELED BACK THROUGH TIME TO GIVE ME ADVICE.
YES. AND TO TELL YOU THAT YOU WILL BE VISITED BY THREE SOULS WHO WILL TEACH YOU THE MEANING OF CHRISTMAS.
...ISN'T THIS KIND OF DERIV-ATIVE?
UM, I DON'T KNOW WHAT YOU MEAN. I'VE NEVER EVEN READ DICKENS.
OH C'MON, WE'VE READ "CHRISTMAS CAROL" A BUNCH OF TIMES.
I DON'T REMEM-BER BEING THIS SNOTTY.
DARRIN BELL

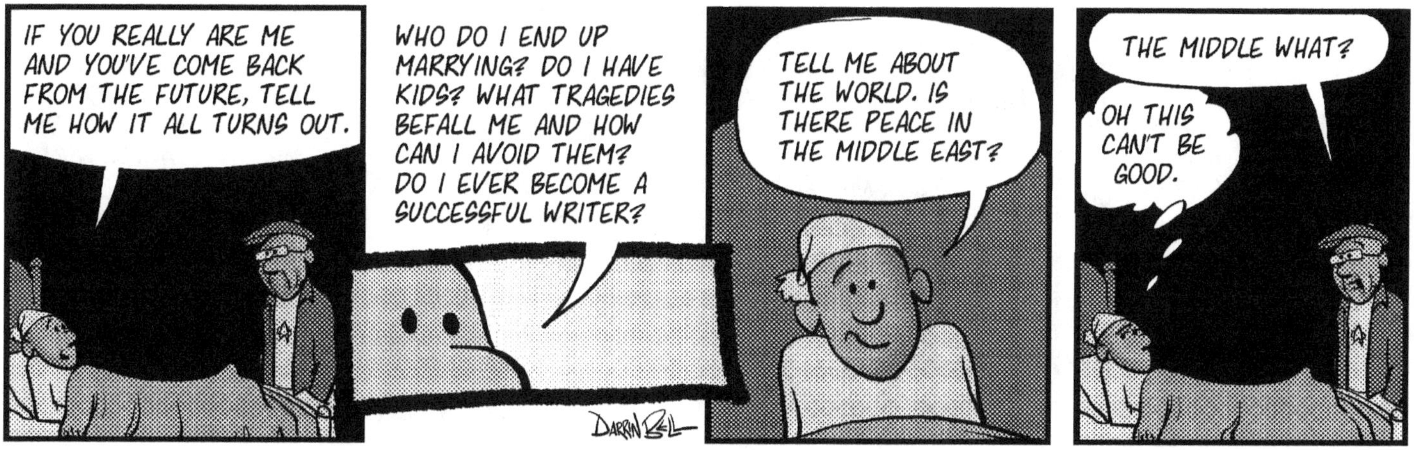
IF YOU REALLY ARE ME AND YOU'VE COME BACK FROM THE FUTURE, TELL ME HOW IT ALL TURNS OUT.
WHO DO I END UP MARRYING? DO I HAVE KIDS? WHAT TRAGEDIES BEFALL ME AND HOW CAN I AVOID THEM? DO I EVER BECOME A SUCCESSFUL WRITER?
DARRIN BELL
TELL ME ABOUT THE WORLD. IS THERE PEACE IN THE MIDDLE EAST?
THE MIDDLE WHAT?
OH THIS CAN'T BE GOOD.

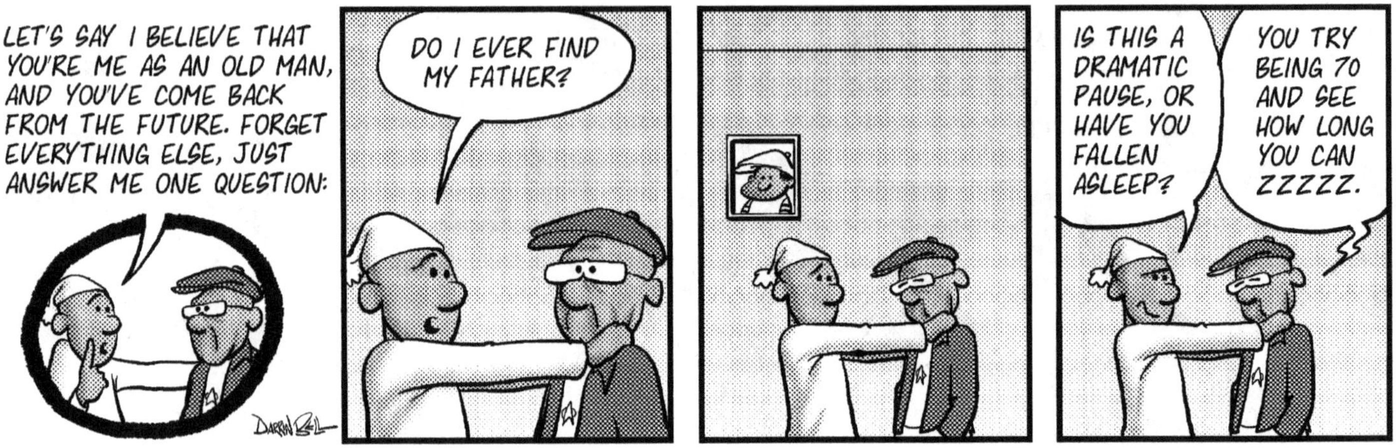
LET'S SAY I BELIEVE THAT YOU'RE ME AS AN OLD MAN, AND YOU'VE COME BACK FROM THE FUTURE. FORGET EVERYTHING ELSE, JUST ANSWER ME ONE QUESTION:
DO I EVER FIND MY FATHER?
IS THIS A DRAMATIC PAUSE, OR HAVE YOU FALLEN ASLEEP?
YOU TRY BEING 70 AND SEE HOW LONG YOU CAN ZZZZZ.
DARRIN BELL

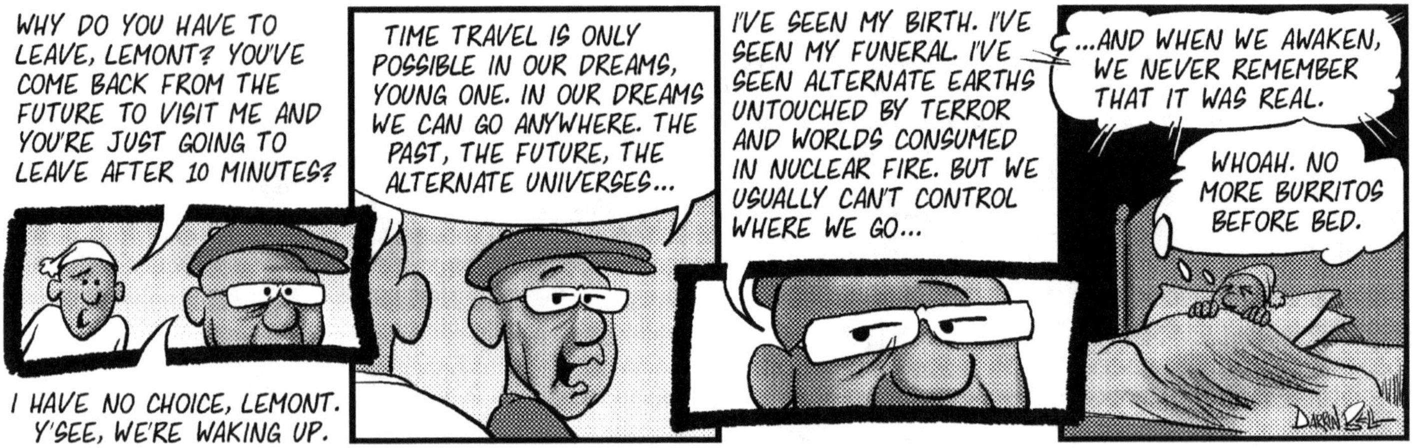
WHY DO YOU HAVE TO LEAVE, LEMONT? YOU'VE COME BACK FROM THE FUTURE TO VISIT ME AND YOU'RE JUST GOING TO LEAVE AFTER 10 MINUTES?
I HAVE NO CHOICE, LEMONT. Y'SEE, WE'RE WAKING UP.
TIME TRAVEL IS ONLY POSSIBLE IN OUR DREAMS, YOUNG ONE. IN OUR DREAMS WE CAN GO ANYWHERE. THE PAST, THE FUTURE, THE ALTERNATE UNIVERSES...
I'VE SEEN MY BIRTH. I'VE SEEN MY FUNERAL. I'VE SEEN ALTERNATE EARTHS UNTOUCHED BY TERROR AND WORLDS CONSUMED IN NUCLEAR FIRE. BUT WE USUALLY CAN'T CONTROL WHERE WE GO...
...AND WHEN WE AWAKEN, WE NEVER REMEMBER THAT IT WAS REAL.
WHOAH. NO MORE BURRITOS BEFORE BED.
DARRIN BELL

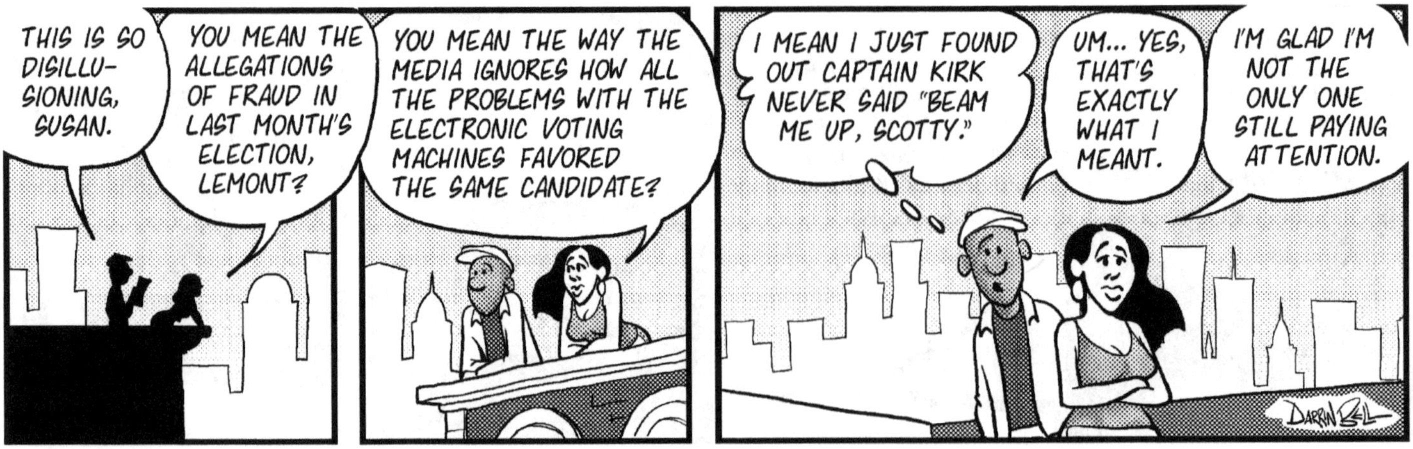
THIS IS SO DISILLU-SIONING, SUSAN.
YOU MEAN THE ALLEGATIONS OF FRAUD IN LAST MONTH'S ELECTION, LEMONT?
YOU MEAN THE WAY THE MEDIA IGNORES HOW ALL THE PROBLEMS WITH THE ELECTRONIC VOTING MACHINES FAVORED THE SAME CANDIDATE?
I MEAN I JUST FOUND OUT CAPTAIN KIRK NEVER SAID "BEAM ME UP, SCOTTY."
UM... YES, THAT'S EXACTLY WHAT I MEANT.
I'M GLAD I'M NOT THE ONLY ONE STILL PAYING ATTENTION.
DARRIN BELL

YOU'RE A RAPPER, CLYDE — WHY DON'T YOU GIVE ME YOUR EXPERT OPINION ABOUT THIS NEW POEM I'VE WRITTEN.

SURE THING, LEMONT.

"TWAS THE WEEK BEFORE CHRISTMAS, AND ALL THROUGH THE HOOD NOT A BURGLAR WAS STEALING AND IT WAS ALL GOOD.

"THE HOMELESS WERE NESTLED ALL SNUG IN THE STREET ENVISIONING FOOD, OR SHOES FOR THEIR FEET.

"MY GOLDFISH IN ITS BOWL, AND I IN MY CAP, HAD JUST SETTLED DOWN FOR A HOLIDAY NAP.

"WHEN DOWN ON THE STOOP THERE AROSE SUCH A CLATTER, I SPRANG FROM THE BED TO SEE WHAT WAS THE MATTER.

"AWAY TO MY WINDOW I FLEW LIKE A FLASH, AND DOWN BY THE STREET, LIKE A CAN FULL OF TRASH...

"I SAW CLYDE, WITH MY WALLET, SPENDING ALL OF MY CASH!"

WELL FIRST OF ALL IT COULD USE SOME PROFANITY...

GIVE ME BACK MY @#@$! WALLET!

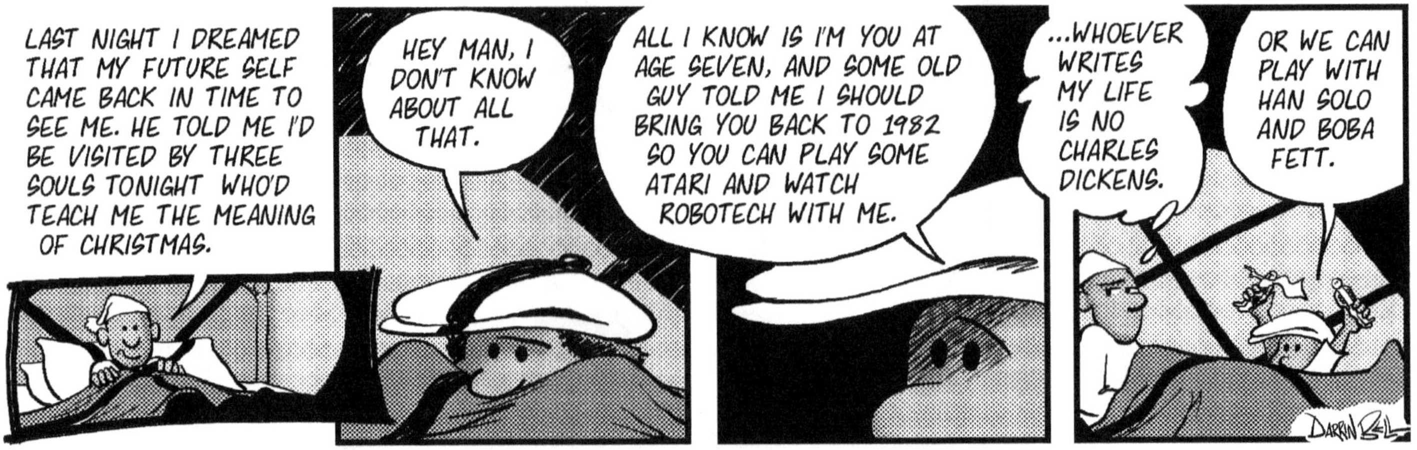
LAST NIGHT I DREAMED THAT MY FUTURE SELF CAME BACK IN TIME TO SEE ME. HE TOLD ME I'D BE VISITED BY THREE SOULS TONIGHT WHO'D TEACH ME THE MEANING OF CHRISTMAS.
HEY MAN, I DON'T KNOW ABOUT ALL THAT.
ALL I KNOW IS I'M YOU AT AGE SEVEN, AND SOME OLD GUY TOLD ME I SHOULD BRING YOU BACK TO 1982 SO YOU CAN PLAY SOME ATARI AND WATCH ROBOTECH WITH ME.
...WHOEVER WRITES MY LIFE IS NO CHARLES DICKENS.
OR WE CAN PLAY WITH HAN SOLO AND BOBA FETT.
DARRIN BELL

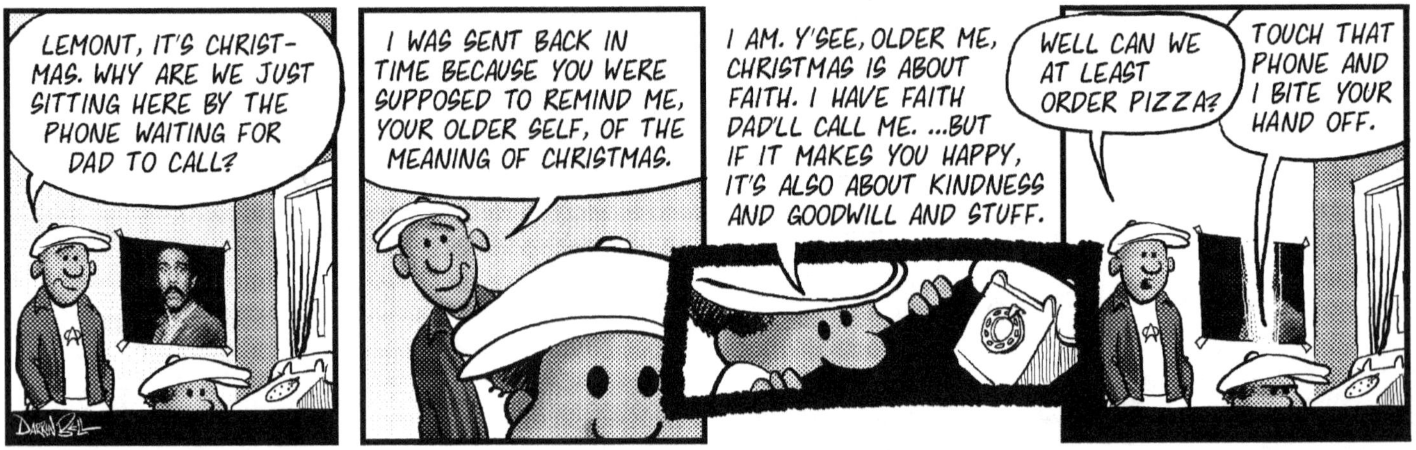
LEMONT, IT'S CHRIST-MAS. WHY ARE WE JUST SITTING HERE BY THE PHONE WAITING FOR DAD TO CALL?
DARRIN BELL
I WAS SENT BACK IN TIME BECAUSE YOU WERE SUPPOSED TO REMIND ME, YOUR OLDER SELF, OF THE MEANING OF CHRISTMAS.
I AM. Y'SEE, OLDER ME, CHRISTMAS IS ABOUT FAITH. I HAVE FAITH DAD'LL CALL ME. ...BUT IF IT MAKES YOU HAPPY, IT'S ALSO ABOUT KINDNESS AND GOODWILL AND STUFF.
WELL CAN WE AT LEAST ORDER PIZZA?
TOUCH THAT PHONE AND I BITE YOUR HAND OFF.

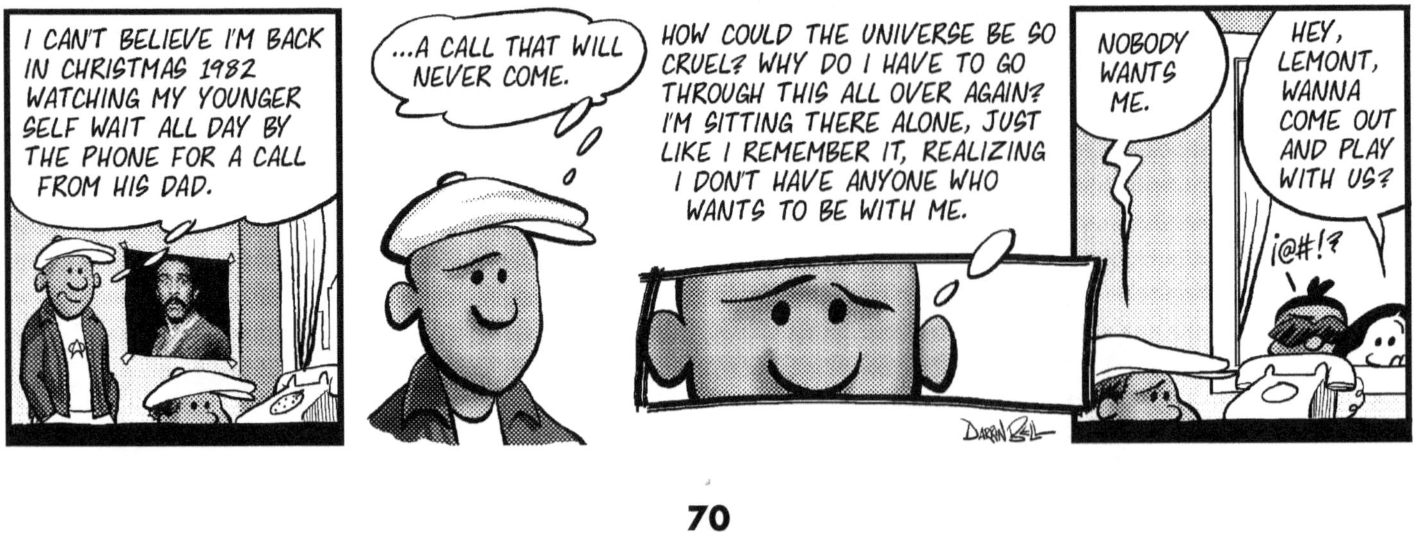
I CAN'T BELIEVE I'M BACK IN CHRISTMAS 1982 WATCHING MY YOUNGER SELF WAIT ALL DAY BY THE PHONE FOR A CALL FROM HIS DAD.
...A CALL THAT WILL NEVER COME.
HOW COULD THE UNIVERSE BE SO CRUEL? WHY DO I HAVE TO GO THROUGH THIS ALL OVER AGAIN? I'M SITTING THERE ALONE, JUST LIKE I REMEMBER IT, REALIZING I DON'T HAVE ANYONE WHO WANTS TO BE WITH ME.
DARRIN BELL
NOBODY WANTS ME.
HEY, LEMONT, WANNA COME OUT AND PLAY WITH US?
¡@#!?

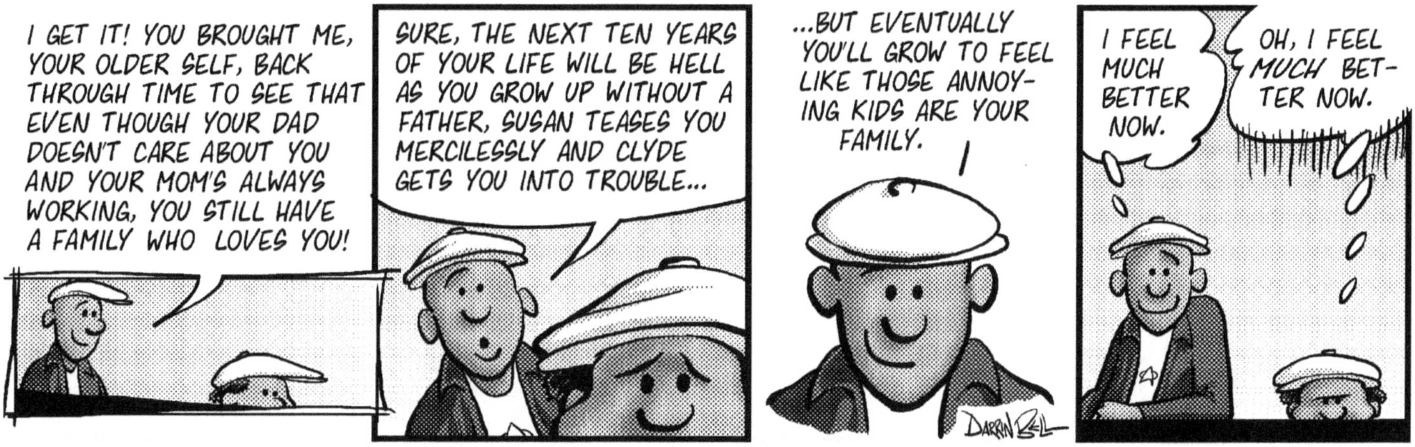
I GET IT! YOU BROUGHT ME, YOUR OLDER SELF, BACK THROUGH TIME TO SEE THAT EVEN THOUGH YOUR DAD DOESN'T CARE ABOUT YOU AND YOUR MOM'S ALWAYS WORKING, YOU STILL HAVE A FAMILY WHO LOVES YOU!
SURE, THE NEXT TEN YEARS OF YOUR LIFE WILL BE HELL AS YOU GROW UP WITHOUT A FATHER, SUSAN TEASES YOU MERCILESSLY AND CLYDE GETS YOU INTO TROUBLE...
...BUT EVENTUALLY YOU'LL GROW TO FEEL LIKE THOSE ANNOY-ING KIDS ARE YOUR FAMILY.
DARRIN BELL
I FEEL MUCH BETTER NOW.
OH, I FEEL *MUCH* BET-TER NOW.

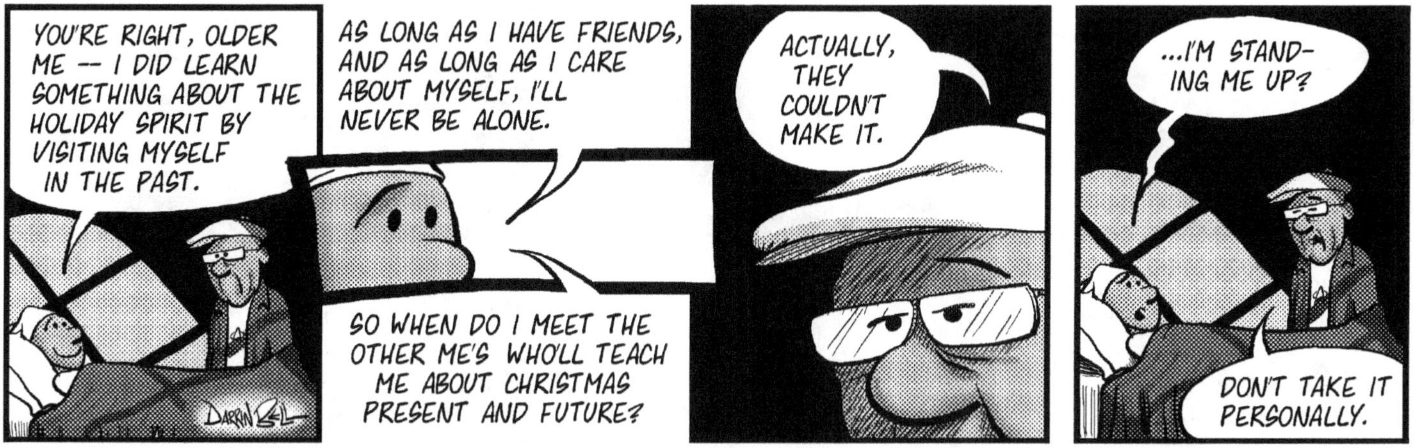
YOU'RE RIGHT, OLDER ME -- I DID LEARN SOMETHING ABOUT THE HOLIDAY SPIRIT BY VISITING MYSELF IN THE PAST.
DARRIN BELL
AS LONG AS I HAVE FRIENDS, AND AS LONG AS I CARE ABOUT MYSELF, I'LL NEVER BE ALONE.
SO WHEN DO I MEET THE OTHER ME'S WHO'LL TEACH ME ABOUT CHRISTMAS PRESENT AND FUTURE?
ACTUALLY, THEY COULDN'T MAKE IT.
...I'M STAND-ING ME UP?
DON'T TAKE IT PERSONALLY.

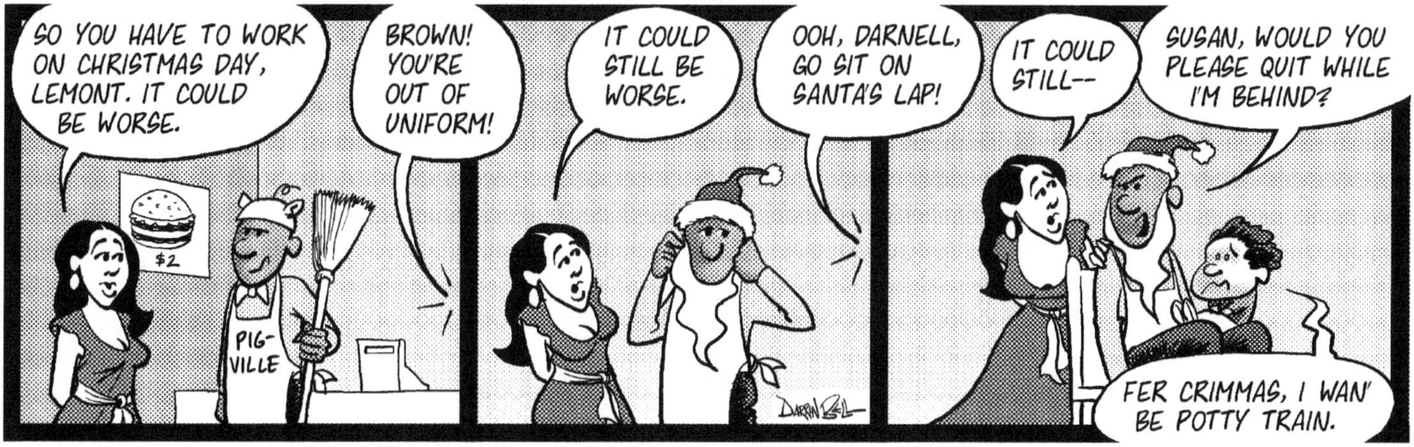
SO YOU HAVE TO WORK ON CHRISTMAS DAY, LEMONT. IT COULD BE WORSE.
$2
PIG-VILLE
BROWN! YOU'RE OUT OF UNIFORM!
IT COULD STILL BE WORSE.
OOH, DARNELL, GO SIT ON SANTA'S LAP!
DARRIN BELL
IT COULD STILL--
SUSAN, WOULD YOU PLEASE QUIT WHILE I'M BEHIND?
FER CRIMMAS, I WAN' BE POTTY TRAIN.

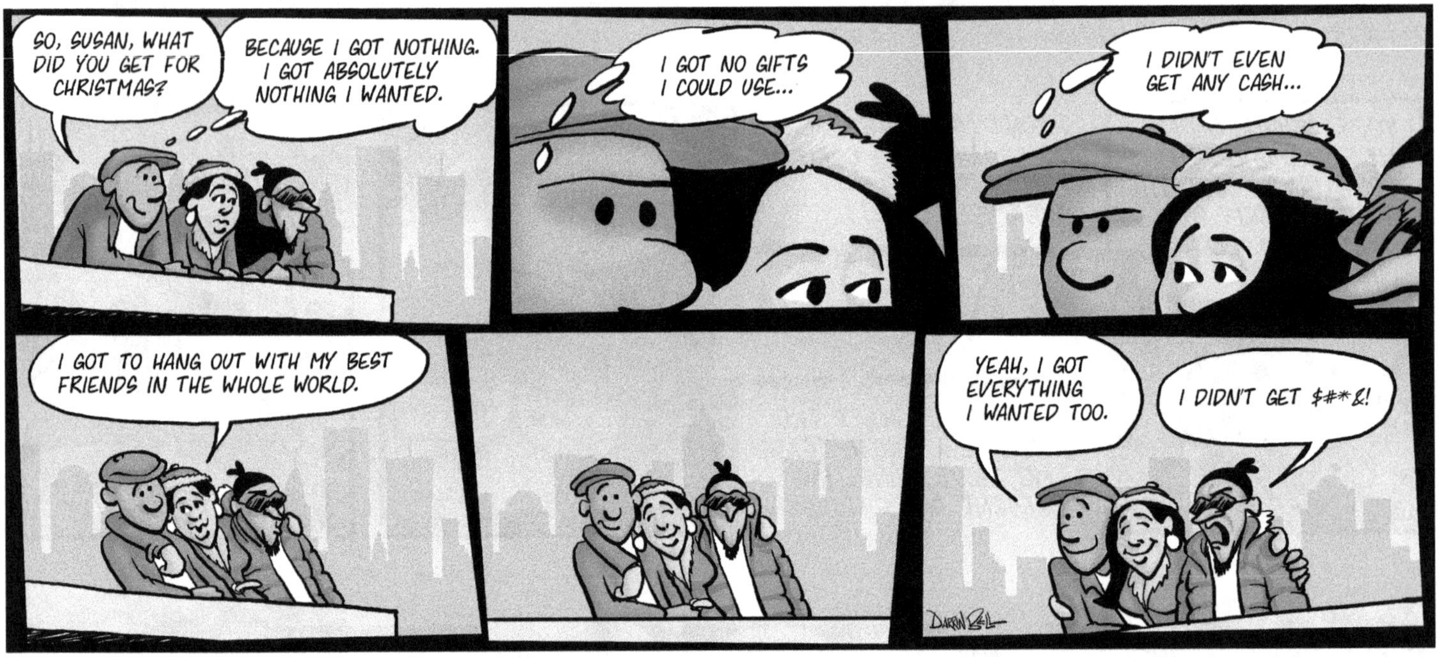

SO, SUSAN, WHAT DID YOU GET FOR CHRISTMAS?
BECAUSE I GOT NOTHING. I GOT ABSOLUTELY NOTHING I WANTED.
I GOT NO GIFTS I COULD USE...
I DIDN'T EVEN GET ANY CASH...
I GOT TO HANG OUT WITH MY BEST FRIENDS IN THE WHOLE WORLD.
YEAH, I GOT EVERYTHING I WANTED TOO.
I DIDN'T GET $#*&!
DARRIN BELL

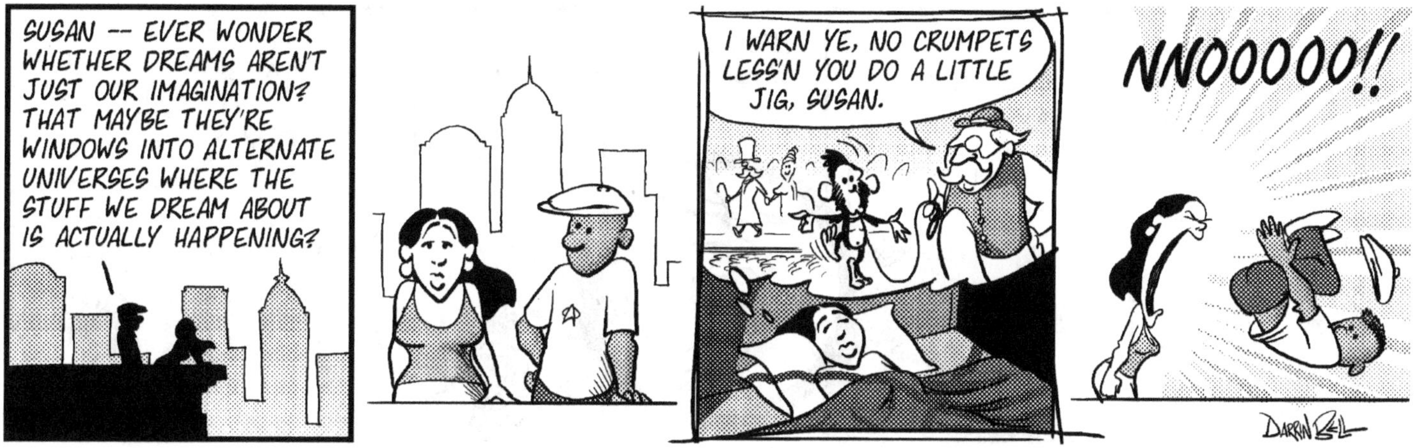
SUSAN -- EVER WONDER WHETHER DREAMS AREN'T JUST OUR IMAGINATION? THAT MAYBE THEY'RE WINDOWS INTO ALTERNATE UNIVERSES WHERE THE STUFF WE DREAM ABOUT IS ACTUALLY HAPPENING?
I WARN YE, NO CRUMPETS LESS'N YOU DO A LITTLE JIG, SUSAN.
NNOOOOO!!
DARRIN BELL

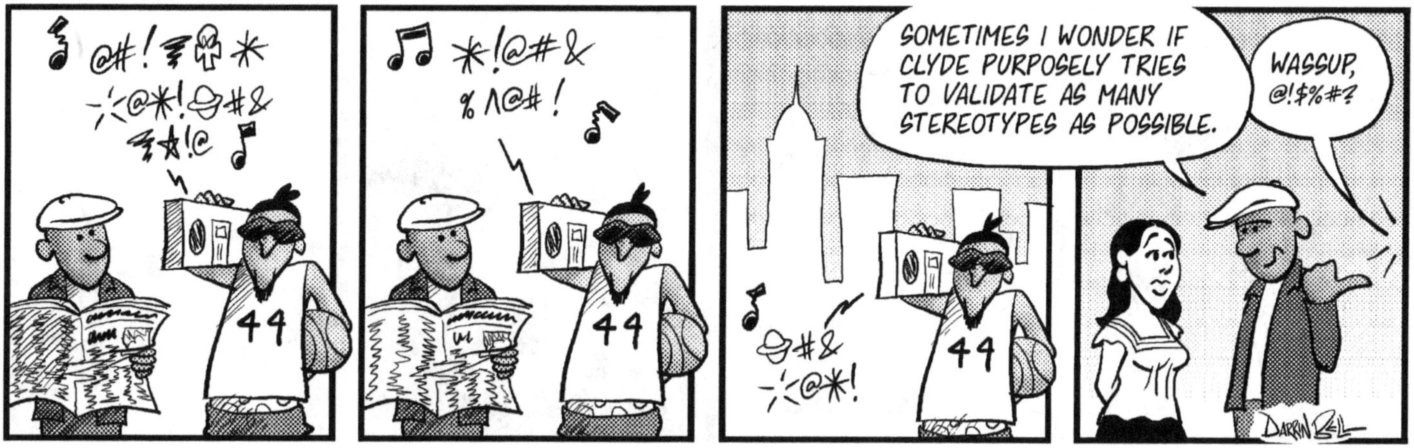
44
SOMETIMES I WONDER IF CLYDE PURPOSELY TRIES TO VALIDATE AS MANY STEREOTYPES AS POSSIBLE.
WASSUP, @!$%#?
DARRIN BELL

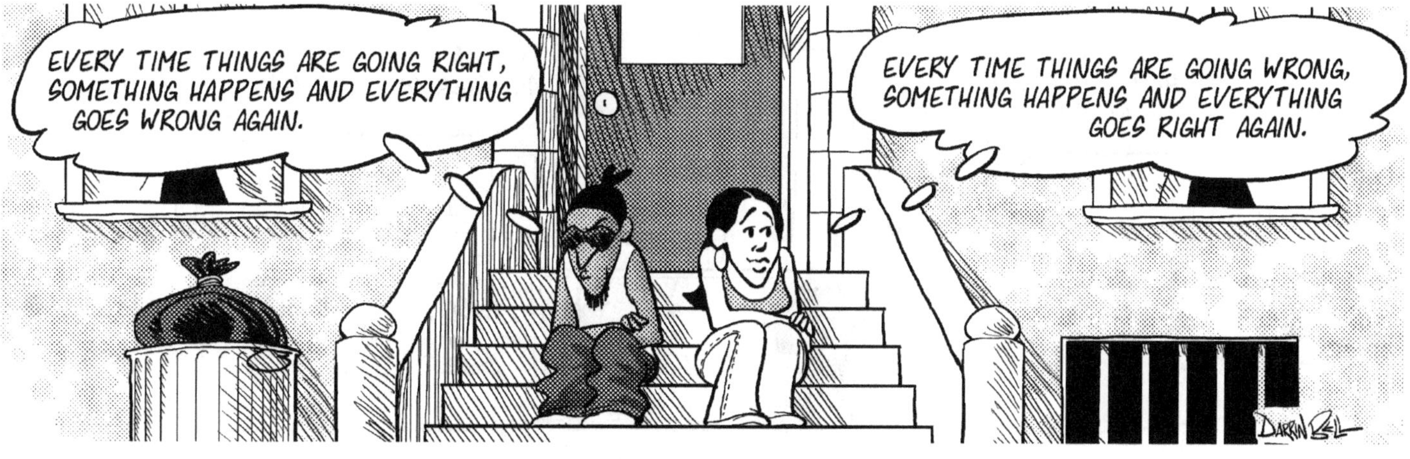
EVERY TIME THINGS ARE GOING RIGHT, SOMETHING HAPPENS AND EVERYTHING GOES WRONG AGAIN.
EVERY TIME THINGS ARE GOING WRONG, SOMETHING HAPPENS AND EVERYTHING GOES RIGHT AGAIN.
DARRIN BELL

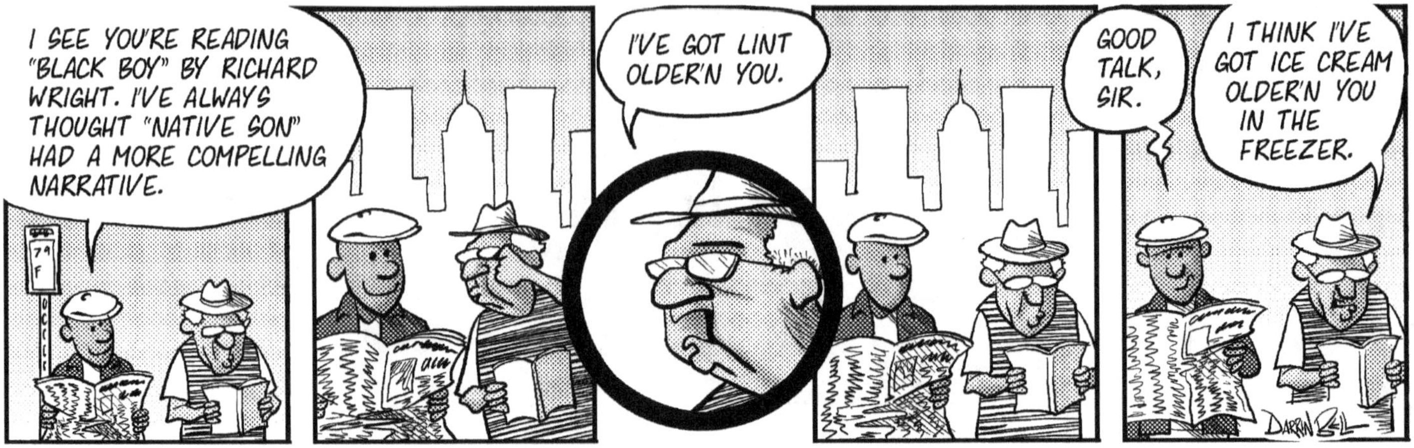
I SEE YOU'RE READING "BLACK BOY" BY RICHARD WRIGHT. I'VE ALWAYS THOUGHT "NATIVE SON" HAD A MORE COMPELLING NARRATIVE.
I'VE GOT LINT OLDER'N YOU.
GOOD TALK, SIR.
I THINK I'VE GOT ICE CREAM OLDER'N YOU IN THE FREEZER.
DARRIN BELL

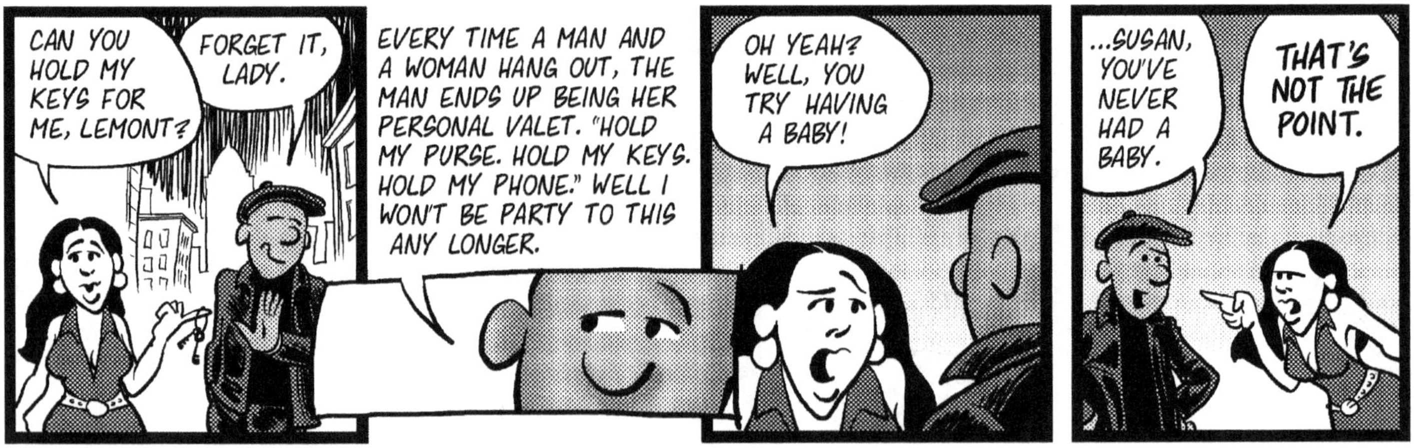
CAN YOU HOLD MY KEYS FOR ME, LEMONT?
FORGET IT, LADY.
EVERY TIME A MAN AND A WOMAN HANG OUT, THE MAN ENDS UP BEING HER PERSONAL VALET. "HOLD MY PURSE. HOLD MY KEYS. HOLD MY PHONE." WELL I WON'T BE PARTY TO THIS ANY LONGER.
OH YEAH? WELL, YOU TRY HAVING A BABY!
...SUSAN, YOU'VE NEVER HAD A BABY.
THAT'S NOT THE POINT.

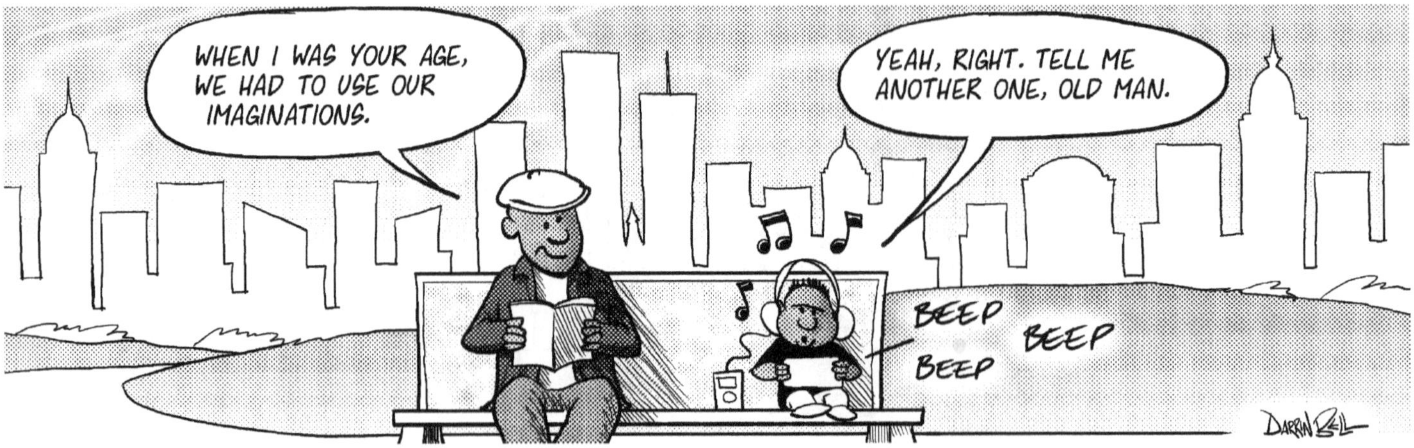
WHEN I WAS YOUR AGE, WE HAD TO USE OUR IMAGINATIONS.
YEAH, RIGHT. TELL ME ANOTHER ONE, OLD MAN.
BEEP
BEEP
BEEP
DARRIN BELL

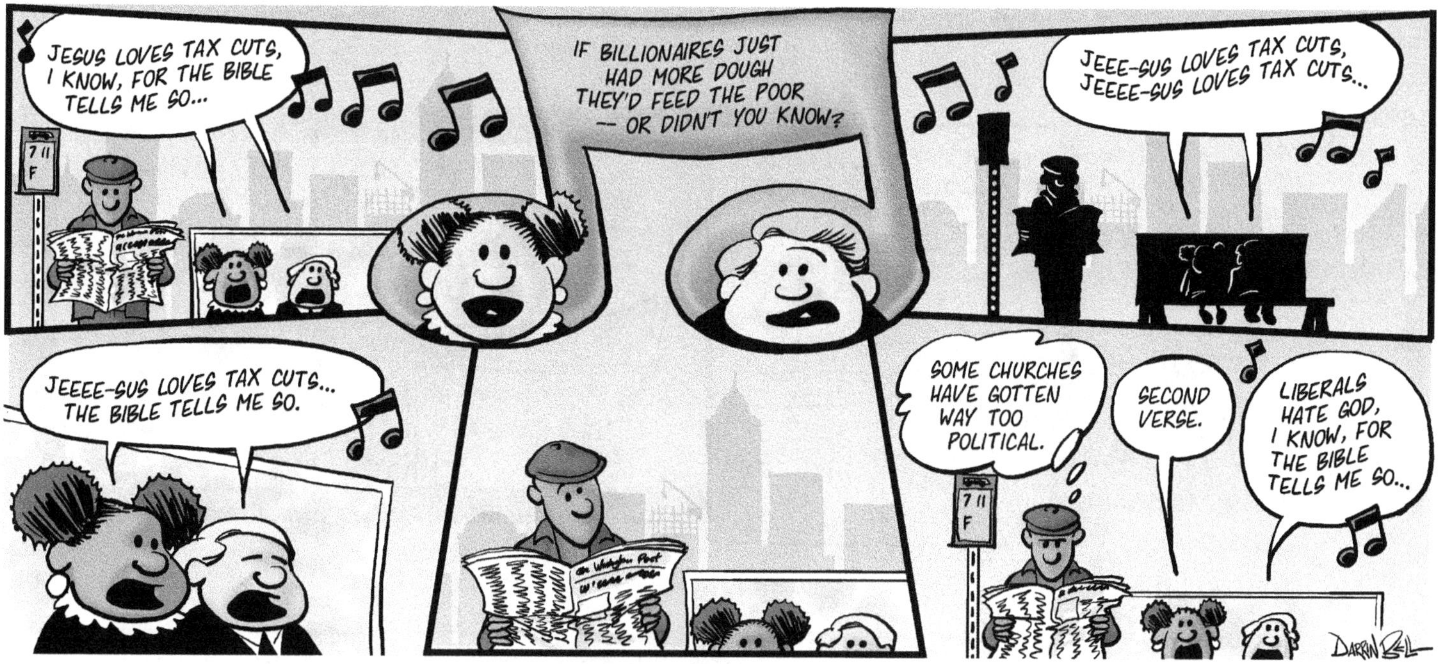
JESUS LOVES TAX CUTS, I KNOW, FOR THE BIBLE TELLS ME SO...
IF BILLIONAIRES JUST HAD MORE DOUGH THEY'D FEED THE POOR — OR DIDN'T YOU KNOW?
JEEE-SUS LOVES TAX CUTS, JEEEE-SUS LOVES TAX CUTS...
JEEEE-SUS LOVES TAX CUTS... THE BIBLE TELLS ME SO.
SOME CHURCHES HAVE GOTTEN WAY TOO POLITICAL.
SECOND VERSE.
LIBERALS HATE GOD, I KNOW, FOR THE BIBLE TELLS ME SO...
7 11
F
DARRIN BELL

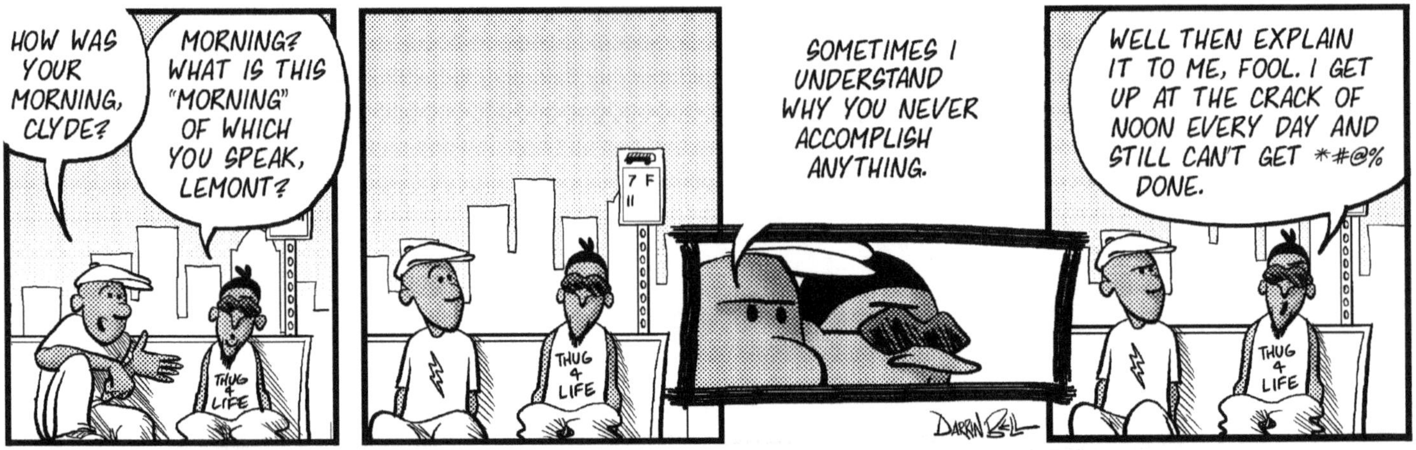
HOW WAS YOUR MORNING, CLYDE?
MORNING? WHAT IS THIS "MORNING" OF WHICH YOU SPEAK, LEMONT?
THUG 4 LIFE
SOMETIMES I UNDERSTAND WHY YOU NEVER ACCOMPLISH ANYTHING.
WELL THEN EXPLAIN IT TO ME, FOOL. I GET UP AT THE CRACK OF NOON EVERY DAY AND STILL CAN'T GET *#@% DONE.
DARRIN BELL

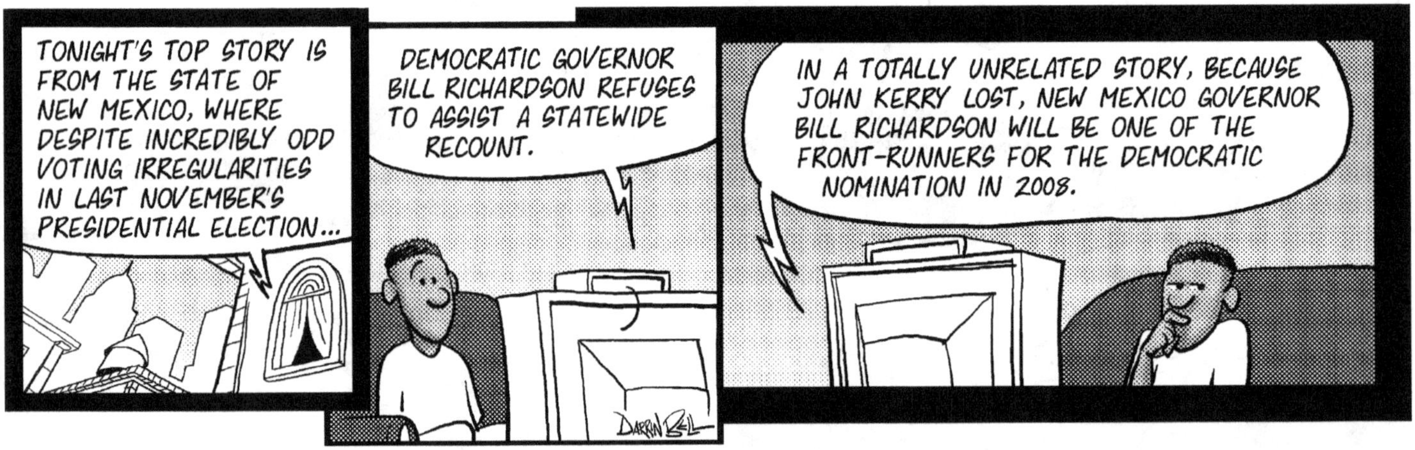
TONIGHT'S TOP STORY IS FROM THE STATE OF NEW MEXICO, WHERE DESPITE INCREDIBLY ODD VOTING IRREGULARITIES IN LAST NOVEMBER'S PRESIDENTIAL ELECTION...
DEMOCRATIC GOVERNOR BILL RICHARDSON REFUSES TO ASSIST A STATEWIDE RECOUNT.
IN A TOTALLY UNRELATED STORY, BECAUSE JOHN KERRY LOST, NEW MEXICO GOVERNOR BILL RICHARDSON WILL BE ONE OF THE FRONT-RUNNERS FOR THE DEMOCRATIC NOMINATION IN 2008.
DARRIN BELL

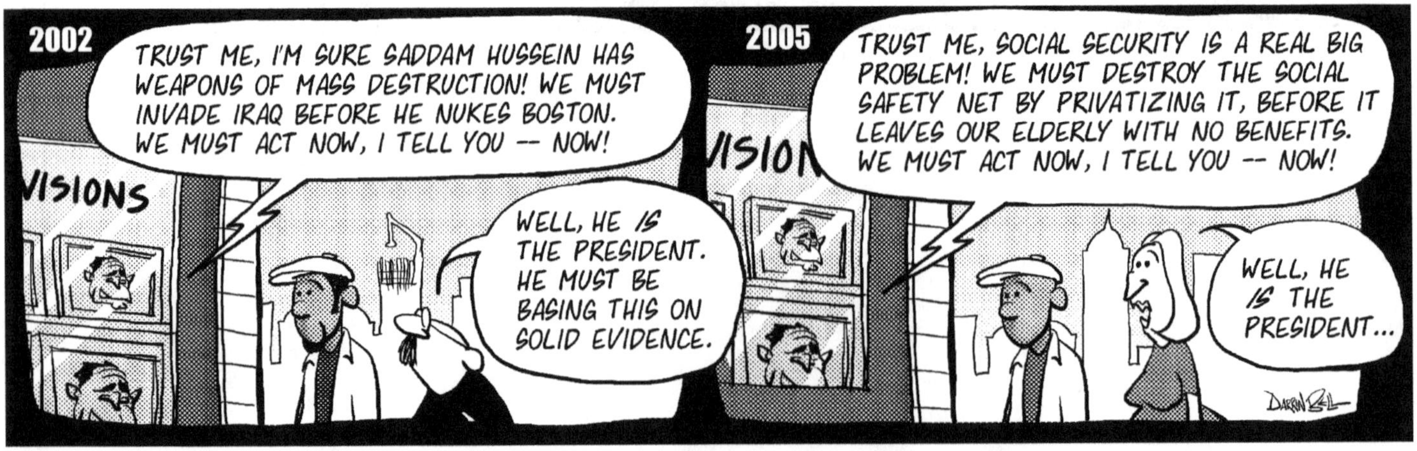
2002
TRUST ME, I'M SURE SADDAM HUSSEIN HAS WEAPONS OF MASS DESTRUCTION! WE MUST INVADE IRAQ BEFORE HE NUKES BOSTON. WE MUST ACT NOW, I TELL YOU -- NOW!
VISIONS
WELL, HE IS THE PRESIDENT. HE MUST BE BASING THIS ON SOLID EVIDENCE.
2005
TRUST ME, SOCIAL SECURITY IS A REAL BIG PROBLEM! WE MUST DESTROY THE SOCIAL SAFETY NET BY PRIVATIZING IT, BEFORE IT LEAVES OUR ELDERLY WITH NO BENEFITS. WE MUST ACT NOW, I TELL YOU -- NOW!
WELL, HE IS THE PRESIDENT...
DARRIN BELL

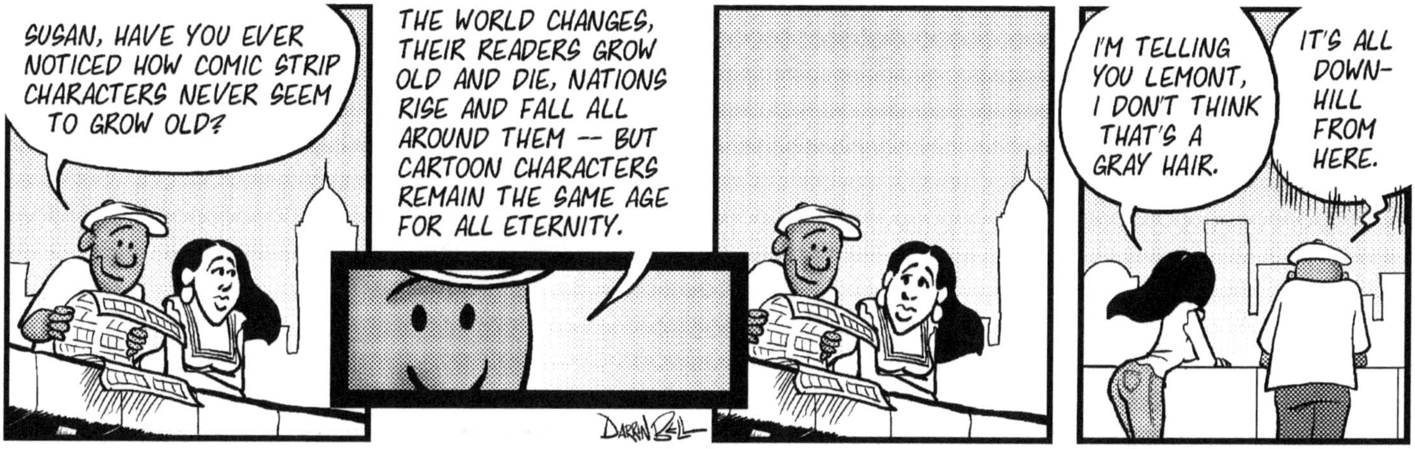
SUSAN, HAVE YOU EVER NOTICED HOW COMIC STRIP CHARACTERS NEVER SEEM TO GROW OLD?
THE WORLD CHANGES, THEIR READERS GROW OLD AND DIE, NATIONS RISE AND FALL ALL AROUND THEM -- BUT CARTOON CHARACTERS REMAIN THE SAME AGE FOR ALL ETERNITY.
I'M TELLING YOU LEMONT, I DON'T THINK THAT'S A GRAY HAIR.
IT'S ALL DOWN-HILL FROM HERE.
DARRIN BELL

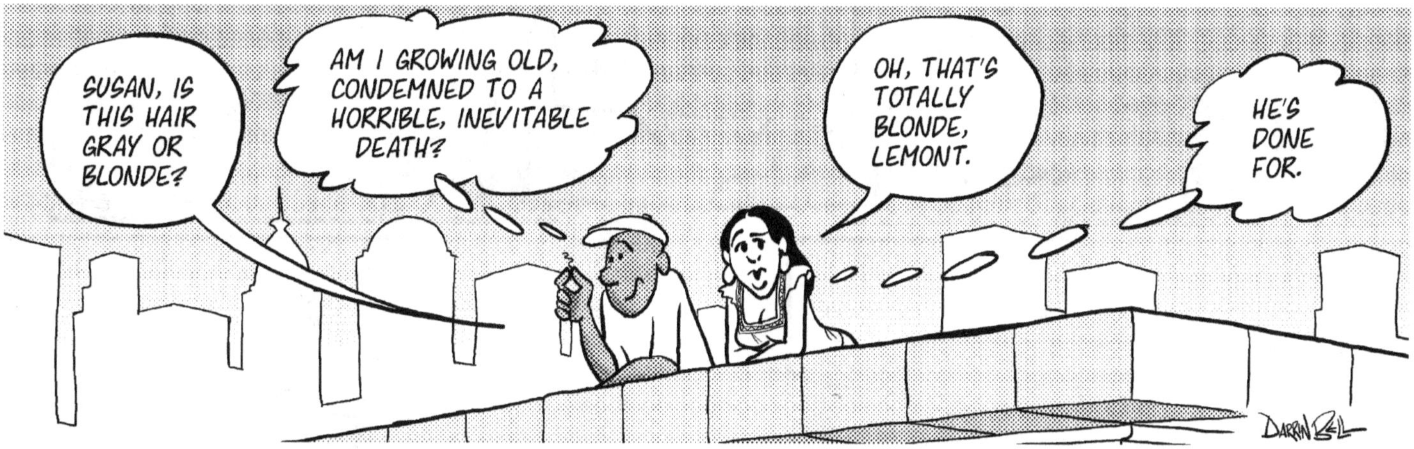
SUSAN, IS THIS HAIR GRAY OR BLONDE?
AM I GROWING OLD, CONDEMNED TO A HORRIBLE, INEVITABLE DEATH?
OH, THAT'S TOTALLY BLONDE, LEMONT.
HE'S DONE FOR.
DARRIN BELL

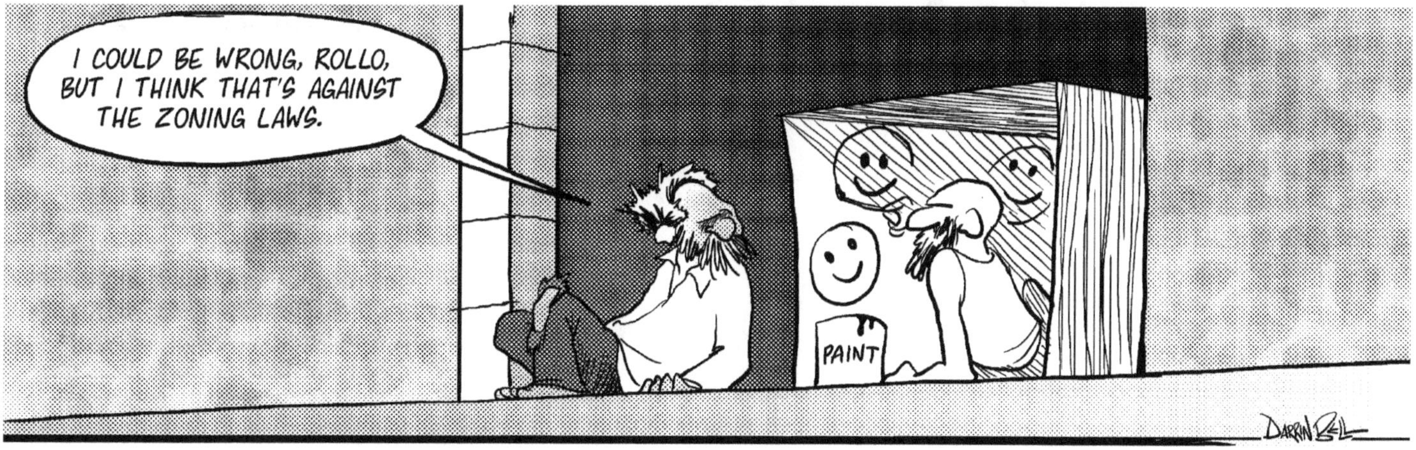
I COULD BE WRONG, ROLLO, BUT I THINK THAT'S AGAINST THE ZONING LAWS.
PAINT
DARRIN BELL

MISTER, WHO WON THE CIVIL WAR?

THAT WOULD BE THE NORTH, KID.

THAT'S WHAT MY TEACHER SAID. BUT I'M CONFUSED.

WHEN THE NORTH WON, BLACK PEOPLE WERE ELECTED TO CONGRESS. BUT THEN THE SOUTH KICKED THEM OUT AGAIN AND DIDN'T LET THEM EVEN VOTE FOR 100 YEARS.

NOW WE HAVE A PRESIDENT WHO WAS FIRST ELECTED BECAUSE BLACKS IN FLORIDA WEREN'T ALLOWED TO VOTE AND WAS RE-ELECTED BECAUSE OHIO, FLORIDA AND NEW MEXICO DIDN'T LET BLACKS AND OTHER MINORITIES HAVE ENOUGH VOTING MACHINES.

AND YOU CAN'T EVEN BE THE PRESIDENT ANYWAY UNLESS THE SOUTH LIKES YOU. THE REST OF THE COUNTRY DOESN'T EVEN SEEM TO MATTER.

RELIGION'S IN AND SCIENCE IS OUT — AND NOW EVERYONE'S SAYING THE VALUES OF THE SOUTH ARE THE NEW VALUES OF AMERICA.

DARRIN BELL

I DON'T THINK I LIKE WHERE THIS IS GOING.

ARE YOU SURE THE NORTH WON THE CIVIL WAR?

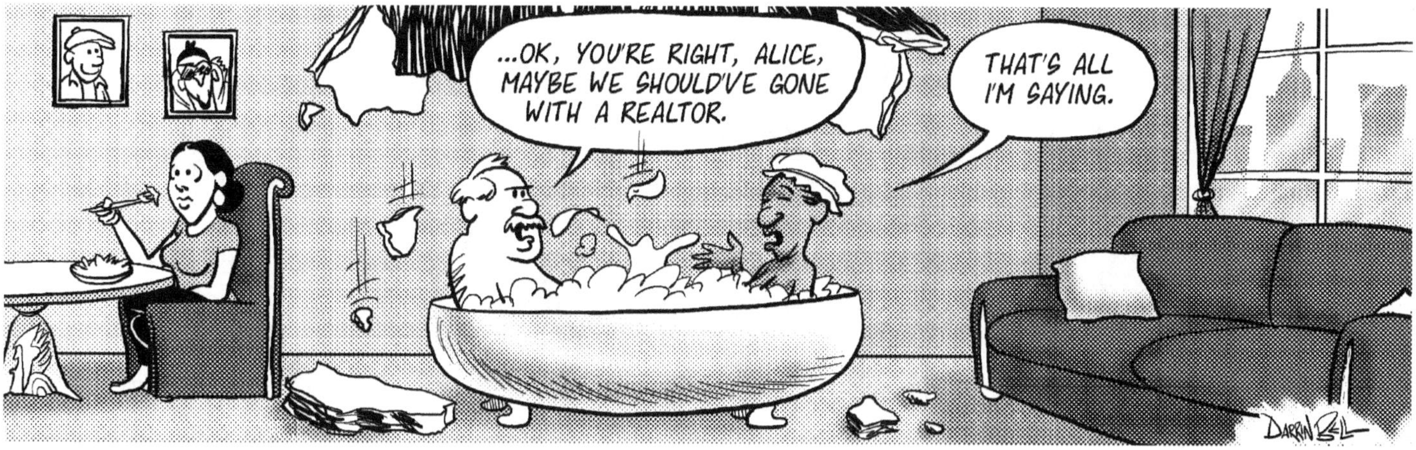
...OK, YOU'RE RIGHT, ALICE, MAYBE WE SHOULD'VE GONE WITH A REALTOR.
THAT'S ALL I'M SAYING.
DARRIN BELL

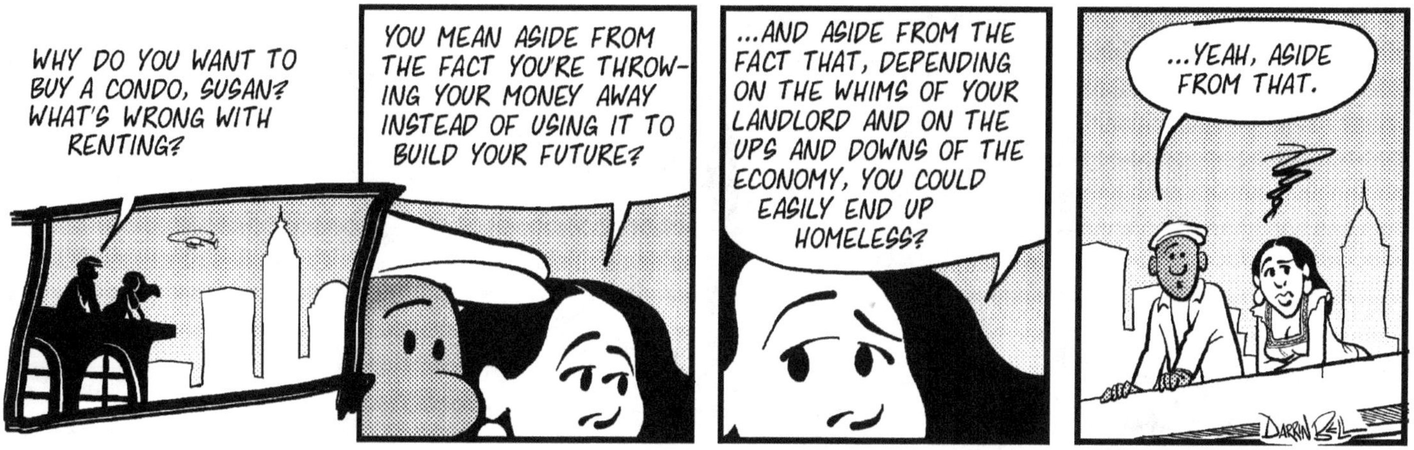
WHY DO YOU WANT TO BUY A CONDO, SUSAN? WHAT'S WRONG WITH RENTING?
YOU MEAN ASIDE FROM THE FACT YOU'RE THROWING YOUR MONEY AWAY INSTEAD OF USING IT TO BUILD YOUR FUTURE?
...AND ASIDE FROM THE FACT THAT, DEPENDING ON THE WHIMS OF YOUR LANDLORD AND ON THE UPS AND DOWNS OF THE ECONOMY, YOU COULD EASILY END UP HOMELESS?
...YEAH, ASIDE FROM THAT.
DARRIN BELL

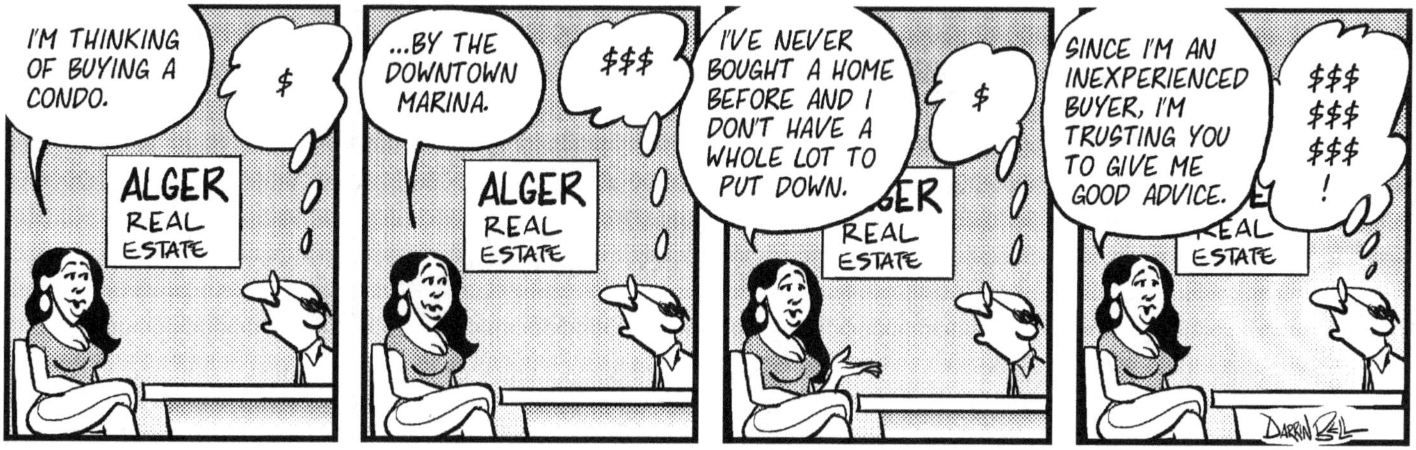
I'M THINKING OF BUYING A CONDO.
$
ALGER REAL ESTATE
...BY THE DOWNTOWN MARINA.
$$$
ALGER REAL ESTATE
I'VE NEVER BOUGHT A HOME BEFORE AND I DON'T HAVE A WHOLE LOT TO PUT DOWN.
$
SINCE I'M AN INEXPERIENCED BUYER, I'M TRUSTING YOU TO GIVE ME GOOD ADVICE.
$$$ $$$ $$$!
DARRIN BELL

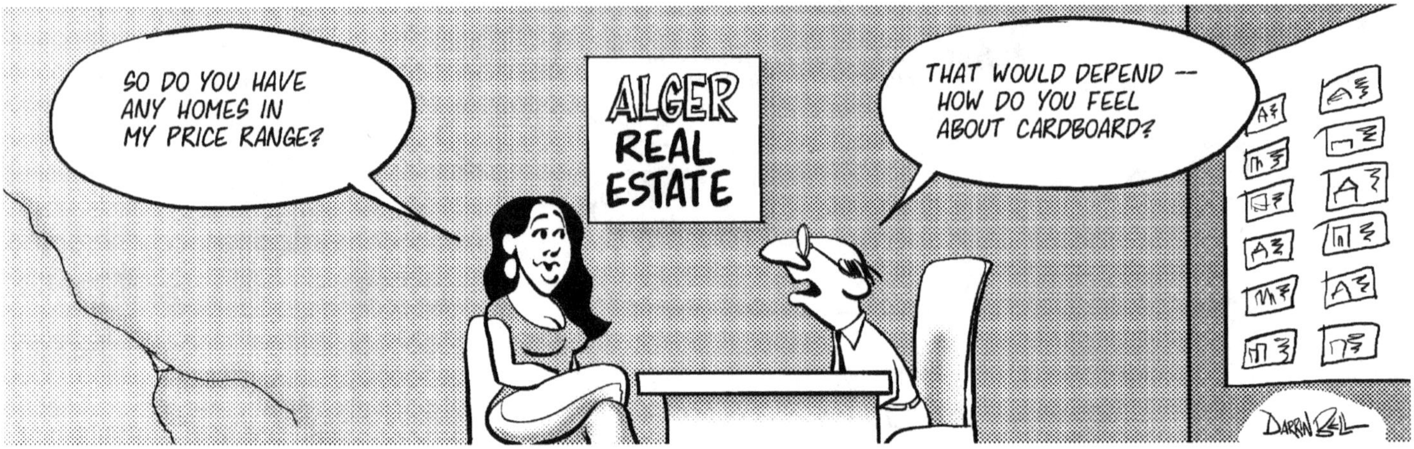
SO DO YOU HAVE ANY HOMES IN MY PRICE RANGE?
ALGER REAL ESTATE
THAT WOULD DEPEND -- HOW DO YOU FEEL ABOUT CARDBOARD?
DARRIN BELL

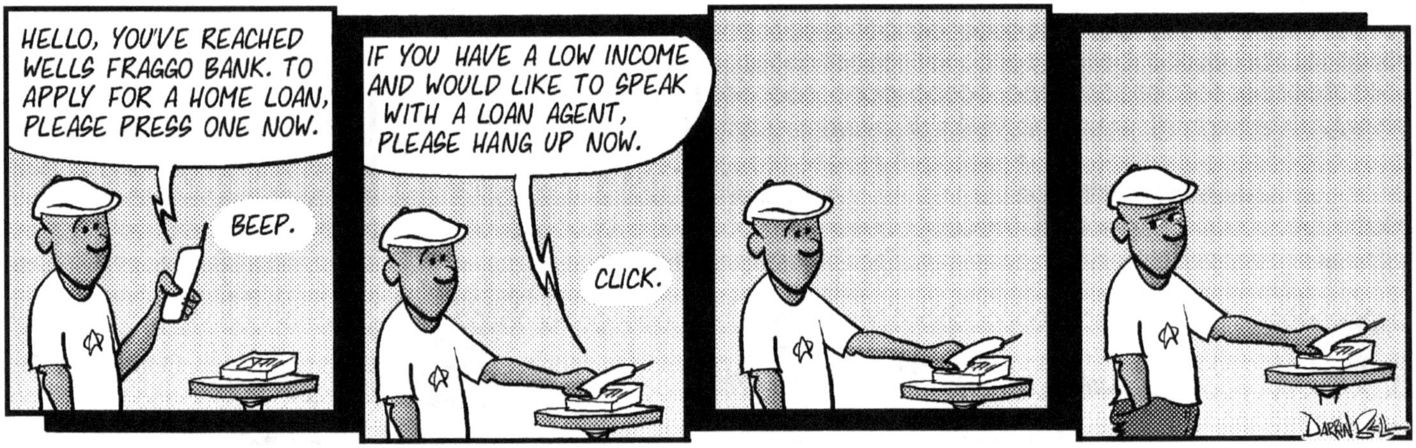
HELLO, YOU'VE REACHED WELLS FRAGGO BANK. TO APPLY FOR A HOME LOAN, PLEASE PRESS ONE NOW.
BEEP.
IF YOU HAVE A LOW INCOME AND WOULD LIKE TO SPEAK WITH A LOAN AGENT, PLEASE HANG UP NOW.
CLICK.
DARRIN BELL

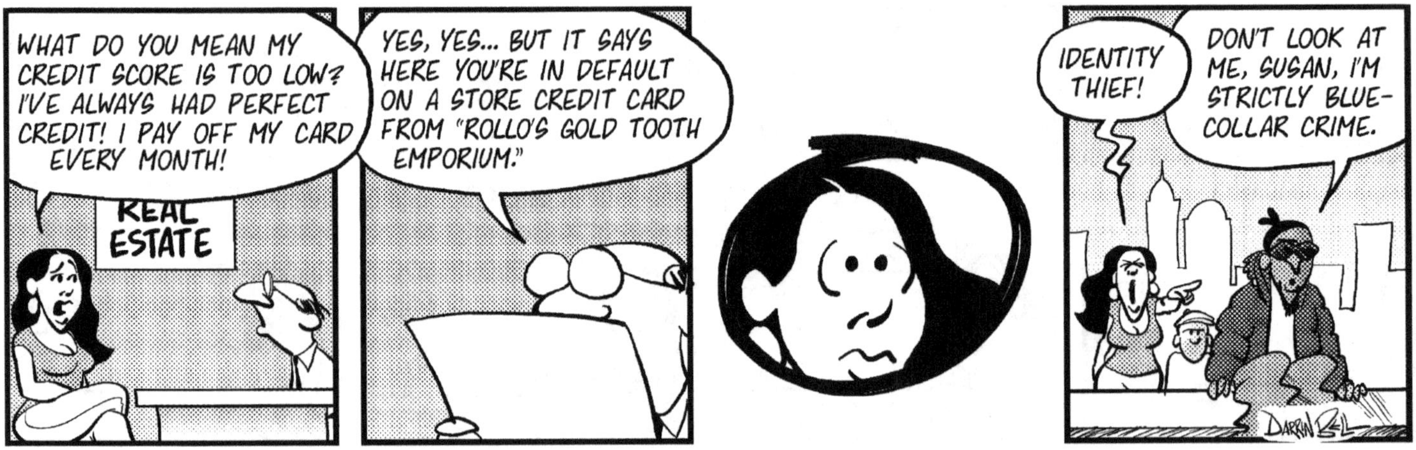
WHAT DO YOU MEAN MY CREDIT SCORE IS TOO LOW? I'VE ALWAYS HAD PERFECT CREDIT! I PAY OFF MY CARD EVERY MONTH!
REAL ESTATE
YES, YES... BUT IT SAYS HERE YOU'RE IN DEFAULT ON A STORE CREDIT CARD FROM "ROLLO'S GOLD TOOTH EMPORIUM."
IDENTITY THIEF!
DON'T LOOK AT ME, SUSAN, I'M STRICTLY BLUE-COLLAR CRIME.
DARRIN BELL

WELCOME TO THE SUNDAY MORNING POLITICAL SHOW, WHERE ALL PERSPECTIVES ARE GIVEN EQUAL TIME. I'M YOUR HOST, BOB ROBERTS.

THIS WEEK'S HOT TOPIC -- THE PRESIDENT'S PLAN TO PRIVATIZE SOCIAL SECURITY. REPRESENTING THE RIGHT, WE HAVE A MEMBER OF THE PRESIDENT'S CABINET, WHO WILL REPEAT THE PARTY LINE OVER AND OVER AGAIN NO MATTER WHAT I ASK.

ALSO REPRESENTING THE RIGHT WILL BE TWO CONGRESSIONAL REPUBLICANS, A REPUBLICAN SENATOR AND RUDY GIULIANI.

Sunday Morning Political Show

REPRESENTING THE LEFT, WE HAVE SOME INARTICULATE PSYCHO WE FOUND LIVING AT THE LOCAL YMCA.

WHATEVER HAPPENED TO THE "LIBERAL" MEDIA?

THE PRESIDENT'S RIGHT, BOB.

WE DISAGREE, BOB. THE PRESIDENT'S RIGHT, BUT IT'S MORE IMPORTANT TO NOTE THAT ANYONE WHO DOESN'T AGREE IS CRAZY.

EXCUSE ME, THEY TOLD ME AT THE YMCA THERE WOULD BE SANDWICHES.

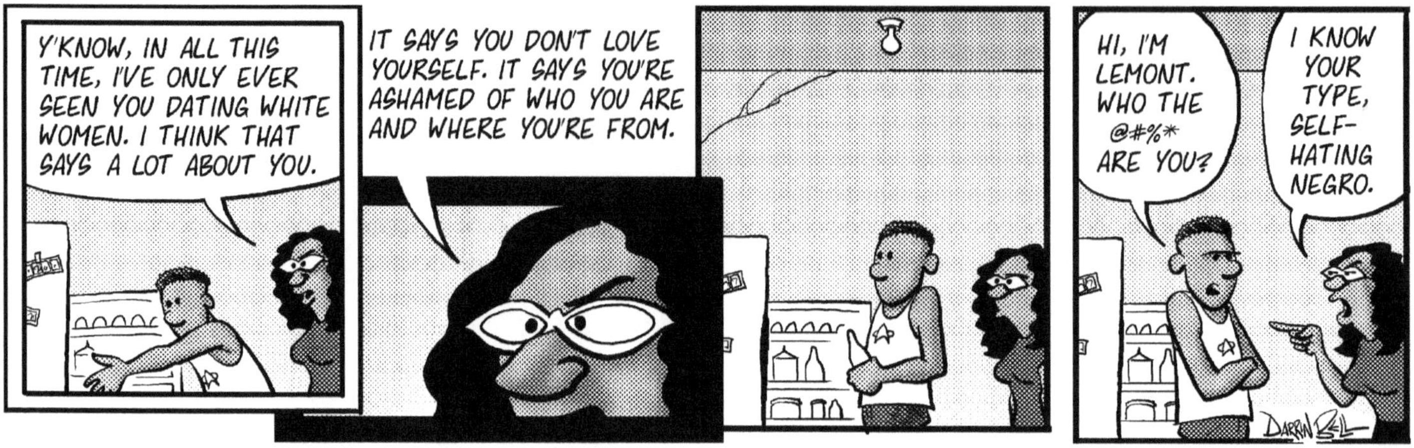
Y'KNOW, IN ALL THIS TIME, I'VE ONLY EVER SEEN YOU DATING WHITE WOMEN. I THINK THAT SAYS A LOT ABOUT YOU.
IT SAYS YOU DON'T LOVE YOURSELF. IT SAYS YOU'RE ASHAMED OF WHO YOU ARE AND WHERE YOU'RE FROM.
HI, I'M LEMONT. WHO THE @#%* ARE YOU?
I KNOW YOUR TYPE, SELF-HATING NEGRO.
DARRIN BELL

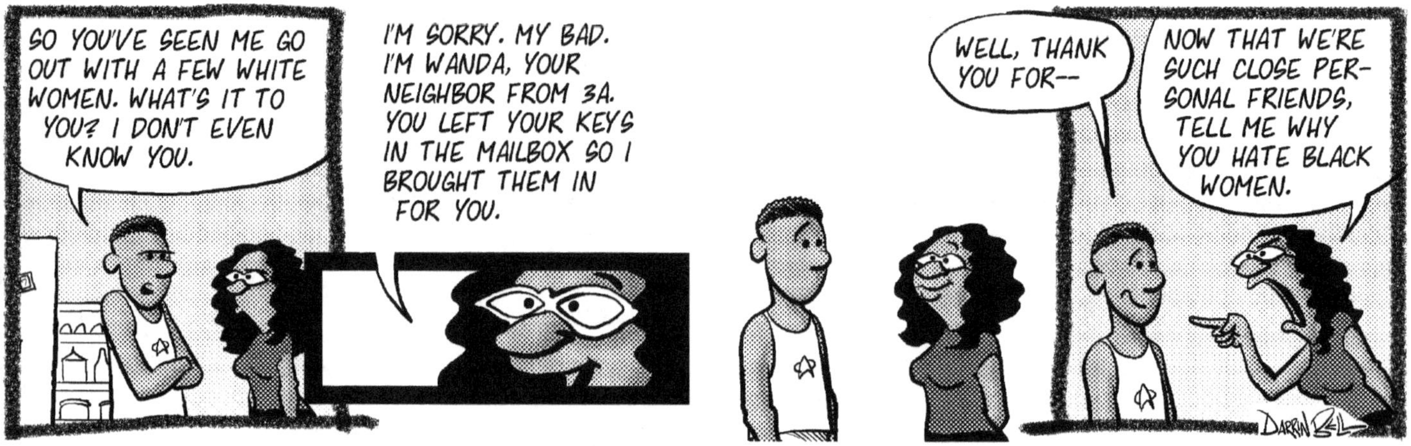
SO YOU'VE SEEN ME GO OUT WITH A FEW WHITE WOMEN. WHAT'S IT TO YOU? I DON'T EVEN KNOW YOU.
I'M SORRY. MY BAD. I'M WANDA, YOUR NEIGHBOR FROM 3A. YOU LEFT YOUR KEYS IN THE MAILBOX SO I BROUGHT THEM IN FOR YOU.
WELL, THANK YOU FOR--
NOW THAT WE'RE SUCH CLOSE PERSONAL FRIENDS, TELL ME WHY YOU HATE BLACK WOMEN.
DARRIN BELL

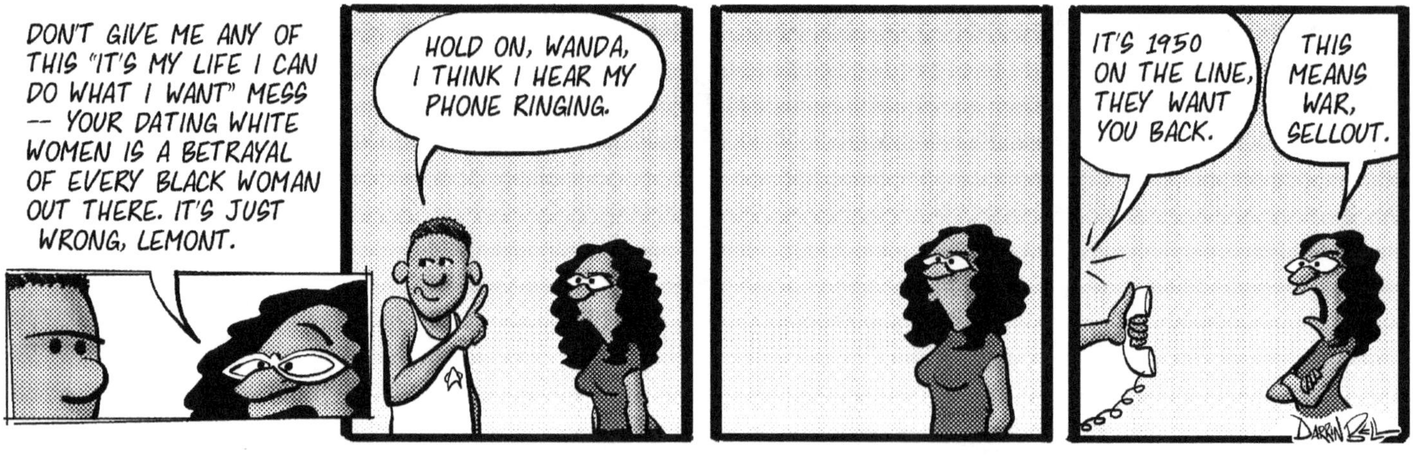
DON'T GIVE ME ANY OF THIS "IT'S MY LIFE I CAN DO WHAT I WANT" MESS -- YOUR DATING WHITE WOMEN IS A BETRAYAL OF EVERY BLACK WOMAN OUT THERE. IT'S JUST WRONG, LEMONT.
HOLD ON, WANDA, I THINK I HEAR MY PHONE RINGING.
IT'S 1950 ON THE LINE, THEY WANT YOU BACK.
THIS MEANS WAR, SELLOUT.
DARRIN BELL

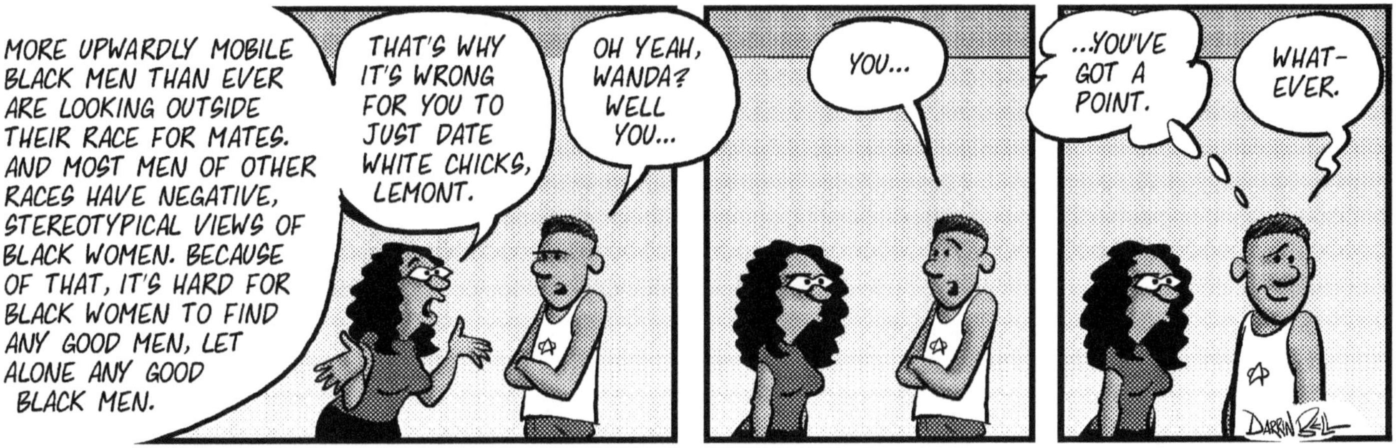
MORE UPWARDLY MOBILE BLACK MEN THAN EVER ARE LOOKING OUTSIDE THEIR RACE FOR MATES. AND MOST MEN OF OTHER RACES HAVE NEGATIVE, STEREOTYPICAL VIEWS OF BLACK WOMEN. BECAUSE OF THAT, IT'S HARD FOR BLACK WOMEN TO FIND ANY GOOD MEN, LET ALONE ANY GOOD BLACK MEN.
THAT'S WHY IT'S WRONG FOR YOU TO JUST DATE WHITE CHICKS, LEMONT.
OH YEAH, WANDA? WELL YOU...
YOU...
...YOU'VE GOT A POINT.
WHAT-EVER.
DARRIN BELL

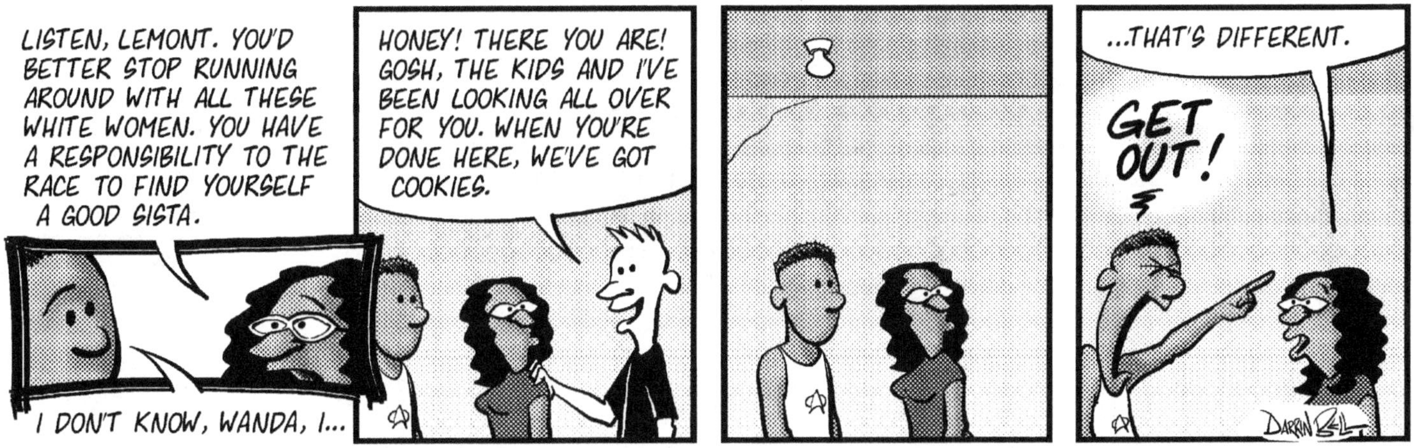
LISTEN, LEMONT. YOU'D BETTER STOP RUNNING AROUND WITH ALL THESE WHITE WOMEN. YOU HAVE A RESPONSIBILITY TO THE RACE TO FIND YOURSELF A GOOD SISTA.
I DON'T KNOW, WANDA, I...
HONEY! THERE YOU ARE! GOSH, THE KIDS AND I'VE BEEN LOOKING ALL OVER FOR YOU. WHEN YOU'RE DONE HERE, WE'VE GOT COOKIES.
...THAT'S DIFFERENT.
GET OUT!
DARRIN BELL

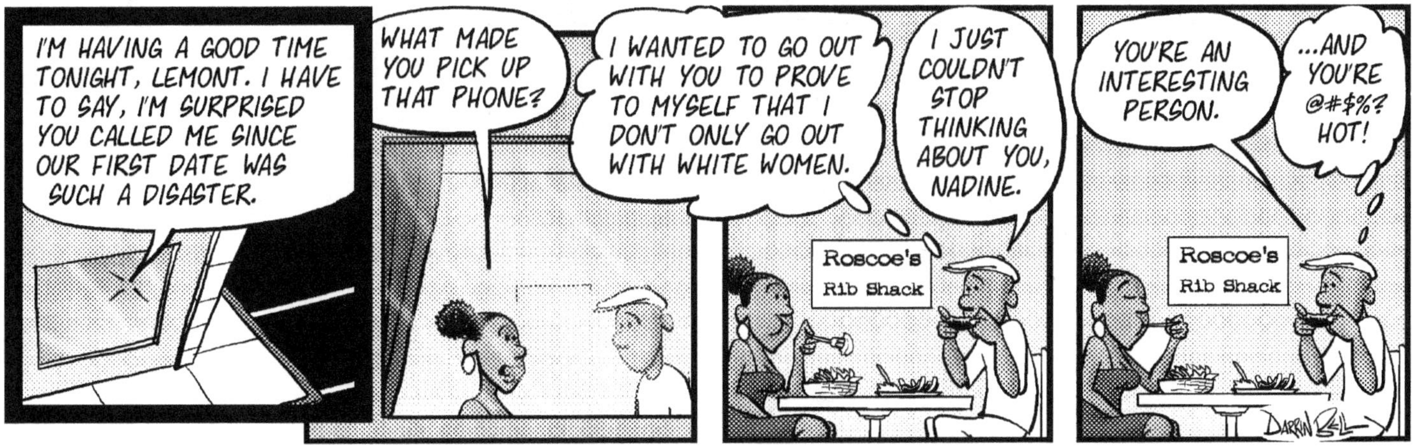
I'M HAVING A GOOD TIME TONIGHT, LEMONT. I HAVE TO SAY, I'M SURPRISED YOU CALLED ME SINCE OUR FIRST DATE WAS SUCH A DISASTER.
WHAT MADE YOU PICK UP THAT PHONE?
I WANTED TO GO OUT WITH YOU TO PROVE TO MYSELF THAT I DON'T ONLY GO OUT WITH WHITE WOMEN.
I JUST COULDN'T STOP THINKING ABOUT YOU, NADINE.
Roscoe's Rib Shack
YOU'RE AN INTERESTING PERSON.
...AND YOU'RE @#$%? HOT!
Roscoe's Rib Shack
DARRIN BELL

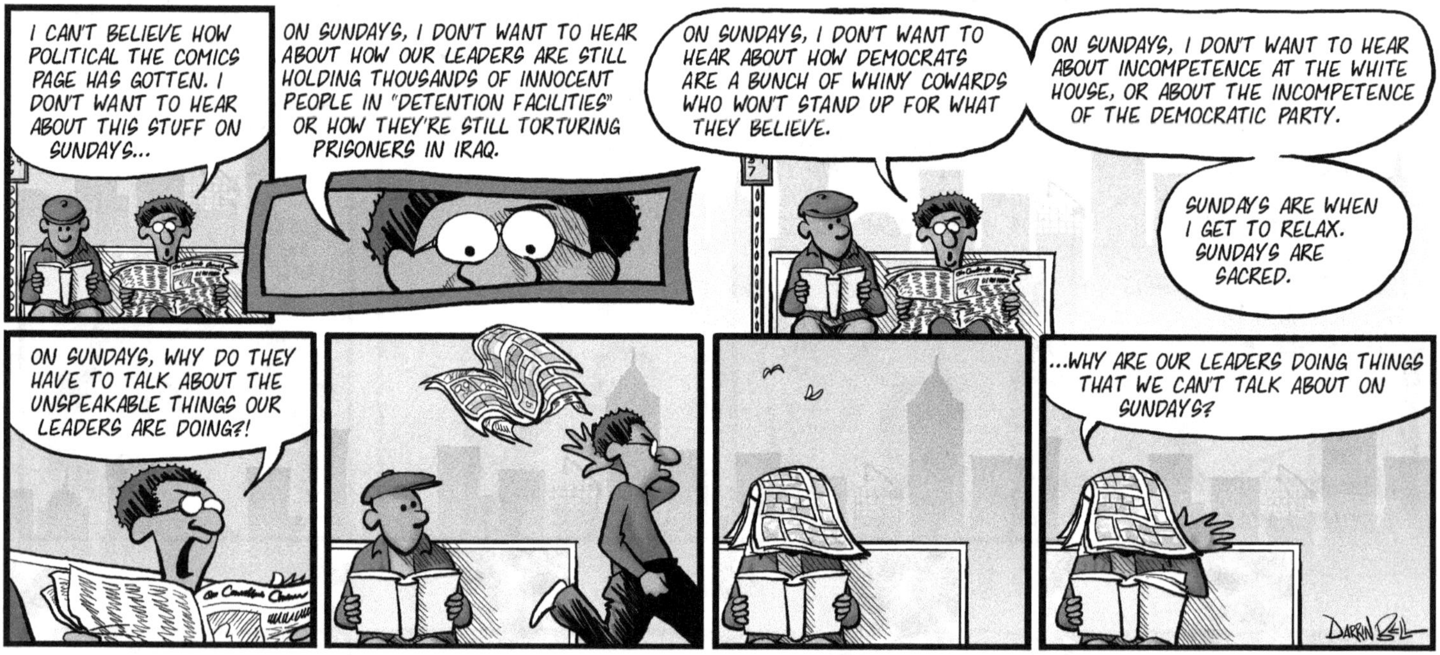

I CAN'T BELIEVE HOW POLITICAL THE COMICS PAGE HAS GOTTEN. I DON'T WANT TO HEAR ABOUT THIS STUFF ON SUNDAYS...
ON SUNDAYS, I DON'T WANT TO HEAR ABOUT HOW OUR LEADERS ARE STILL HOLDING THOUSANDS OF INNOCENT PEOPLE IN "DETENTION FACILITIES" OR HOW THEY'RE STILL TORTURING PRISONERS IN IRAQ.
ON SUNDAYS, I DON'T WANT TO HEAR ABOUT HOW DEMOCRATS ARE A BUNCH OF WHINY COWARDS WHO WON'T STAND UP FOR WHAT THEY BELIEVE.
ON SUNDAYS, I DON'T WANT TO HEAR ABOUT INCOMPETENCE AT THE WHITE HOUSE, OR ABOUT THE INCOMPETENCE OF THE DEMOCRATIC PARTY.
SUNDAYS ARE WHEN I GET TO RELAX. SUNDAYS ARE SACRED.
ON SUNDAYS, WHY DO THEY HAVE TO TALK ABOUT THE UNSPEAKABLE THINGS OUR LEADERS ARE DOING?!
...WHY ARE OUR LEADERS DOING THINGS THAT WE CAN'T TALK ABOUT ON SUNDAYS?
DARRIN BELL

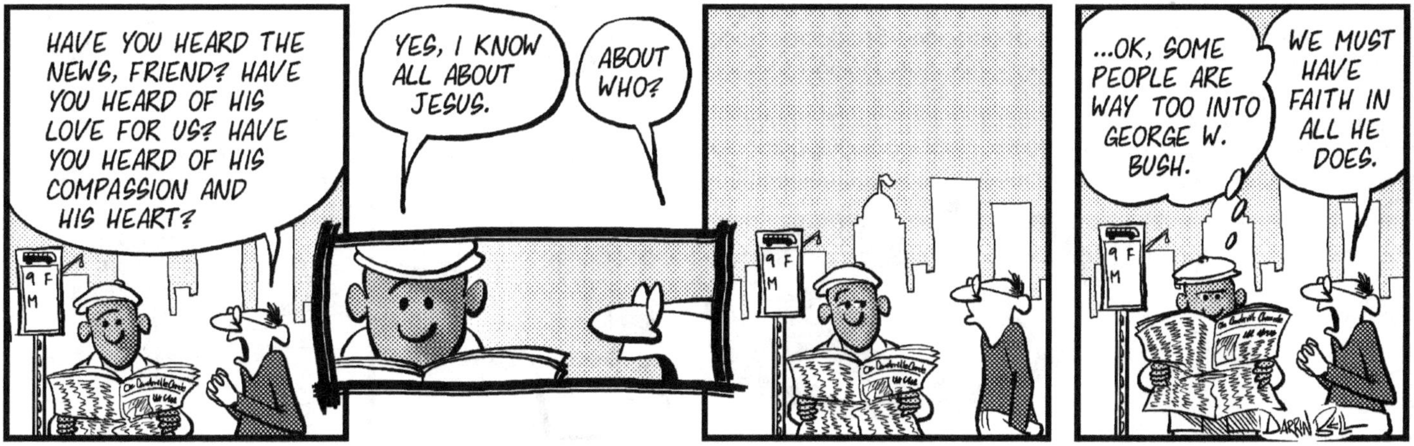

HAVE YOU HEARD THE NEWS, FRIEND? HAVE YOU HEARD OF HIS LOVE FOR US? HAVE YOU HEARD OF HIS COMPASSION AND HIS HEART?
YES, I KNOW ALL ABOUT JESUS.
ABOUT WHO?
...OK, SOME PEOPLE ARE WAY TOO INTO GEORGE W. BUSH.
WE MUST HAVE FAITH IN ALL HE DOES.
DARRIN BELL

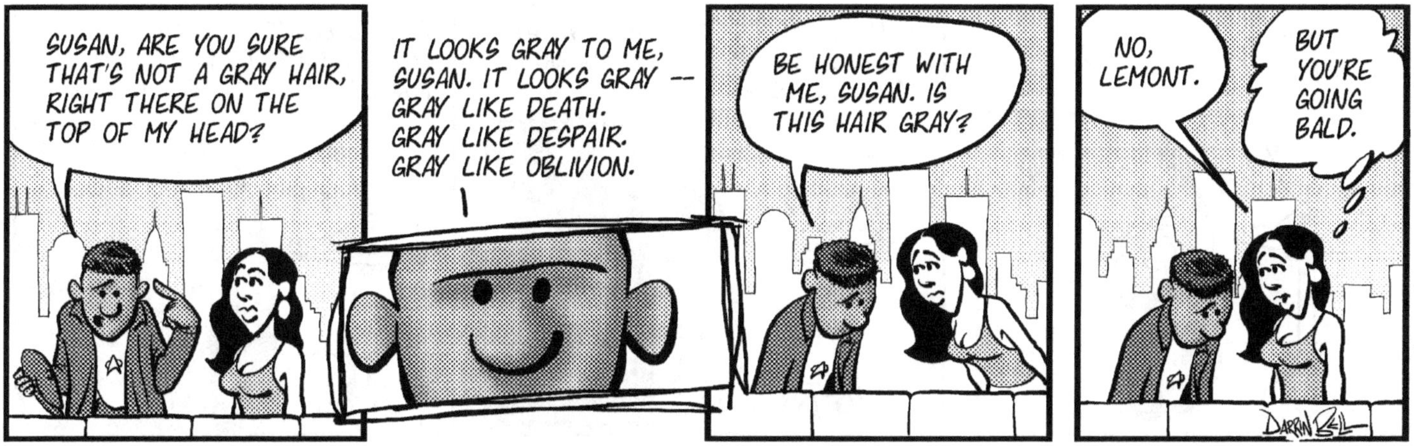

SUSAN, ARE YOU SURE THAT'S NOT A GRAY HAIR, RIGHT THERE ON THE TOP OF MY HEAD?
IT LOOKS GRAY TO ME, SUSAN. IT LOOKS GRAY -- GRAY LIKE DEATH. GRAY LIKE DESPAIR. GRAY LIKE OBLIVION.
BE HONEST WITH ME, SUSAN. IS THIS HAIR GRAY?
NO, LEMONT.
BUT YOU'RE GOING BALD.
DARRIN BELL

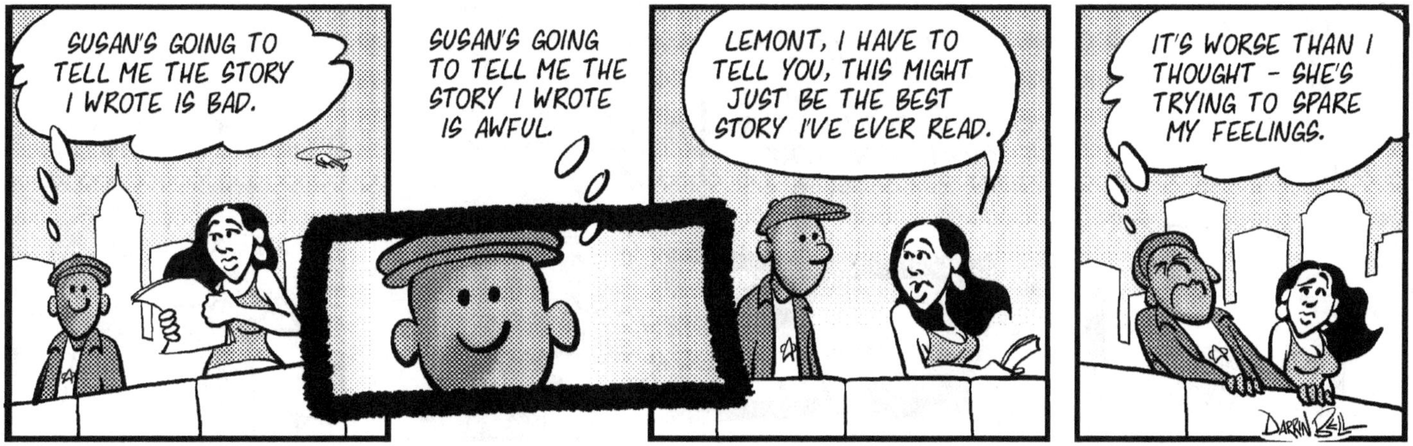

SUSAN'S GOING TO TELL ME THE STORY I WROTE IS BAD.
SUSAN'S GOING TO TELL ME THE STORY I WROTE IS AWFUL.
LEMONT, I HAVE TO TELL YOU, THIS MIGHT JUST BE THE BEST STORY I'VE EVER READ.
IT'S WORSE THAN I THOUGHT - SHE'S TRYING TO SPARE MY FEELINGS.
DARRIN BELL

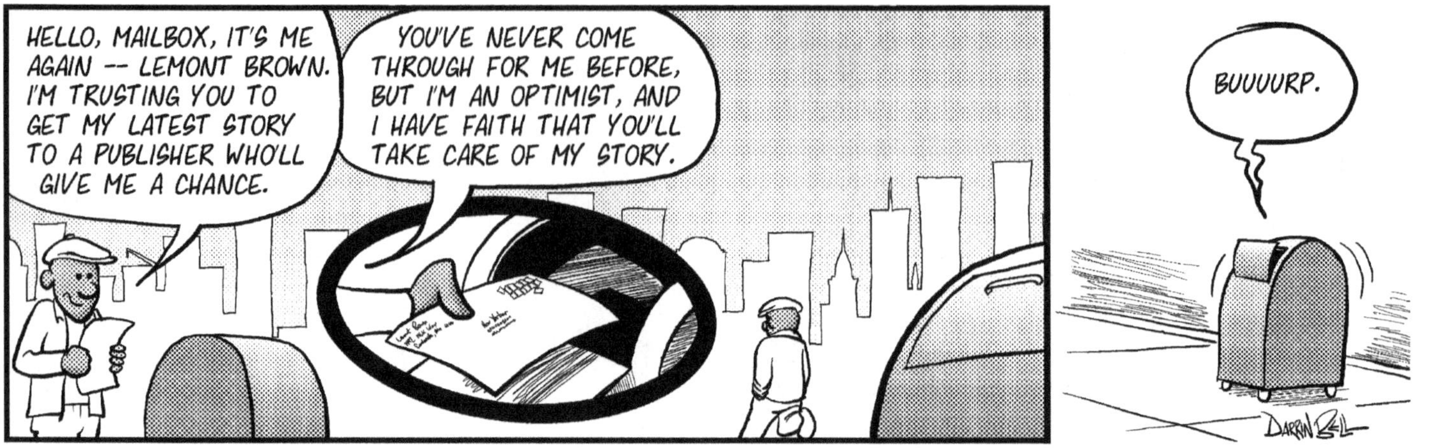
HELLO, MAILBOX, IT'S ME AGAIN -- LEMONT BROWN. I'M TRUSTING YOU TO GET MY LATEST STORY TO A PUBLISHER WHO'LL GIVE ME A CHANCE.
YOU'VE NEVER COME THROUGH FOR ME BEFORE, BUT I'M AN OPTIMIST, AND I HAVE FAITH THAT YOU'LL TAKE CARE OF MY STORY.
BUUUURP.
DARRIN BELL

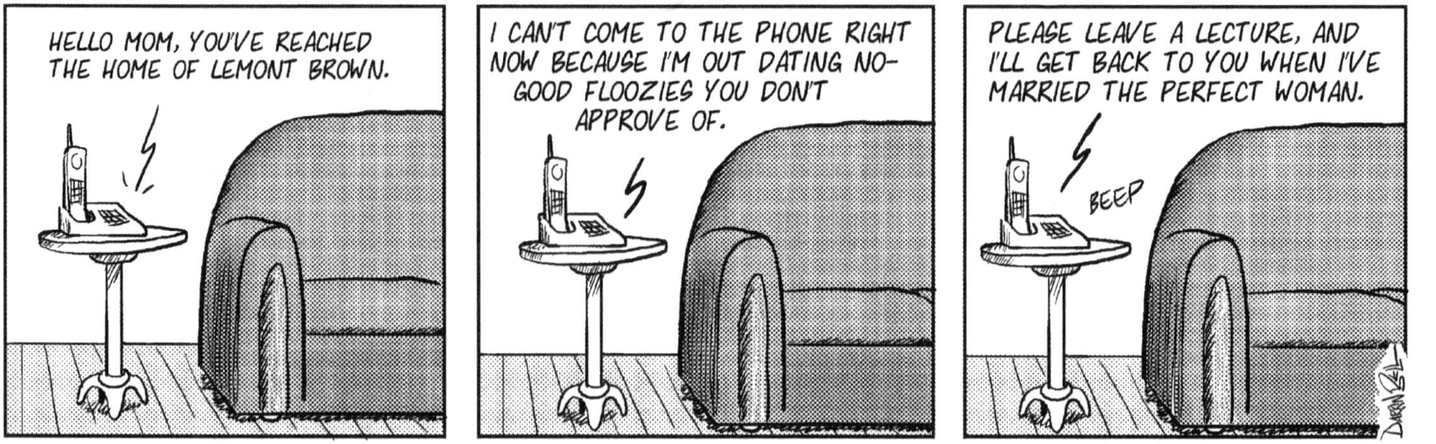
HELLO MOM, YOU'VE REACHED THE HOME OF LEMONT BROWN.
I CAN'T COME TO THE PHONE RIGHT NOW BECAUSE I'M OUT DATING NO-GOOD FLOOZIES YOU DON'T APPROVE OF.
PLEASE LEAVE A LECTURE, AND I'LL GET BACK TO YOU WHEN I'VE MARRIED THE PERFECT WOMAN.
BEEP

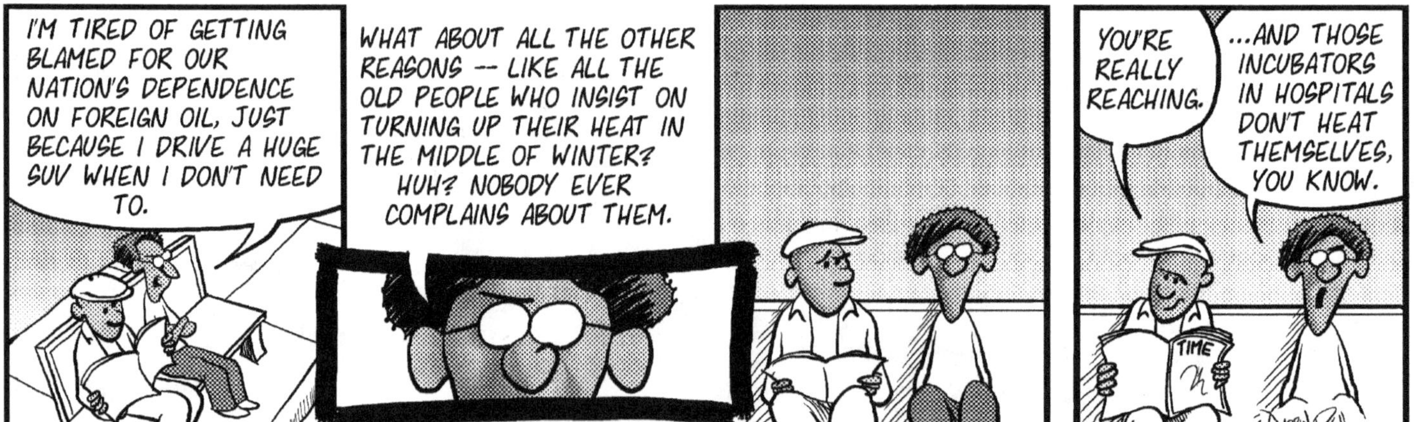
I'M TIRED OF GETTING BLAMED FOR OUR NATION'S DEPENDENCE ON FOREIGN OIL, JUST BECAUSE I DRIVE A HUGE SUV WHEN I DON'T NEED TO.
WHAT ABOUT ALL THE OTHER REASONS -- LIKE ALL THE OLD PEOPLE WHO INSIST ON TURNING UP THEIR HEAT IN THE MIDDLE OF WINTER? HUH? NOBODY EVER COMPLAINS ABOUT THEM.
YOU'RE REALLY REACHING.
...AND THOSE INCUBATORS IN HOSPITALS DON'T HEAT THEMSELVES, YOU KNOW.
TIME
DARRIN BELL

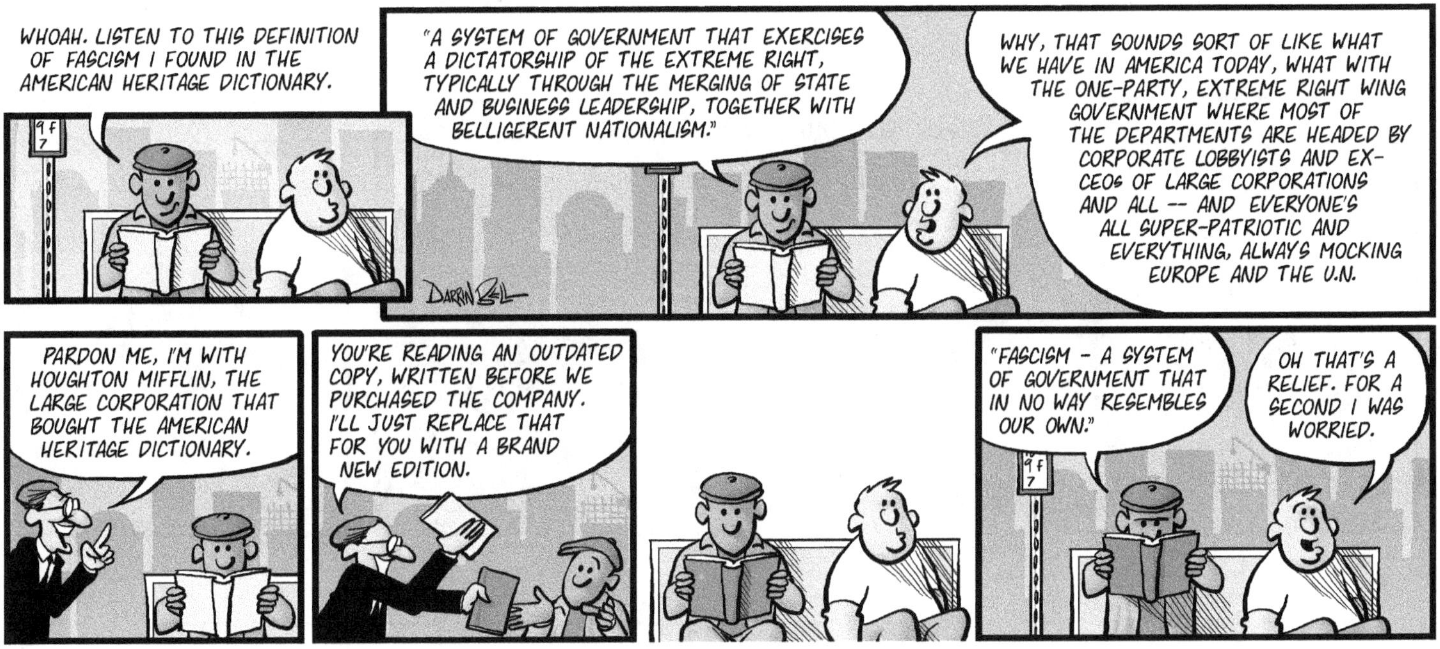
WHOAH. LISTEN TO THIS DEFINITION OF FASCISM I FOUND IN THE AMERICAN HERITAGE DICTIONARY.
"A SYSTEM OF GOVERNMENT THAT EXERCISES A DICTATORSHIP OF THE EXTREME RIGHT, TYPICALLY THROUGH THE MERGING OF STATE AND BUSINESS LEADERSHIP, TOGETHER WITH BELLIGERENT NATIONALISM."
WHY, THAT SOUNDS SORT OF LIKE WHAT WE HAVE IN AMERICA TODAY, WHAT WITH THE ONE-PARTY, EXTREME RIGHT WING GOVERNMENT WHERE MOST OF THE DEPARTMENTS ARE HEADED BY CORPORATE LOBBYISTS AND EX-CEOS OF LARGE CORPORATIONS AND ALL -- AND EVERYONE'S ALL SUPER-PATRIOTIC AND EVERYTHING, ALWAYS MOCKING EUROPE AND THE U.N.
DARRIN BELL
PARDON ME, I'M WITH HOUGHTON MIFFLIN, THE LARGE CORPORATION THAT BOUGHT THE AMERICAN HERITAGE DICTIONARY.
YOU'RE READING AN OUTDATED COPY, WRITTEN BEFORE WE PURCHASED THE COMPANY. I'LL JUST REPLACE THAT FOR YOU WITH A BRAND NEW EDITION.
"FASCISM - A SYSTEM OF GOVERNMENT THAT IN NO WAY RESEMBLES OUR OWN."
OH THAT'S A RELIEF. FOR A SECOND I WAS WORRIED.

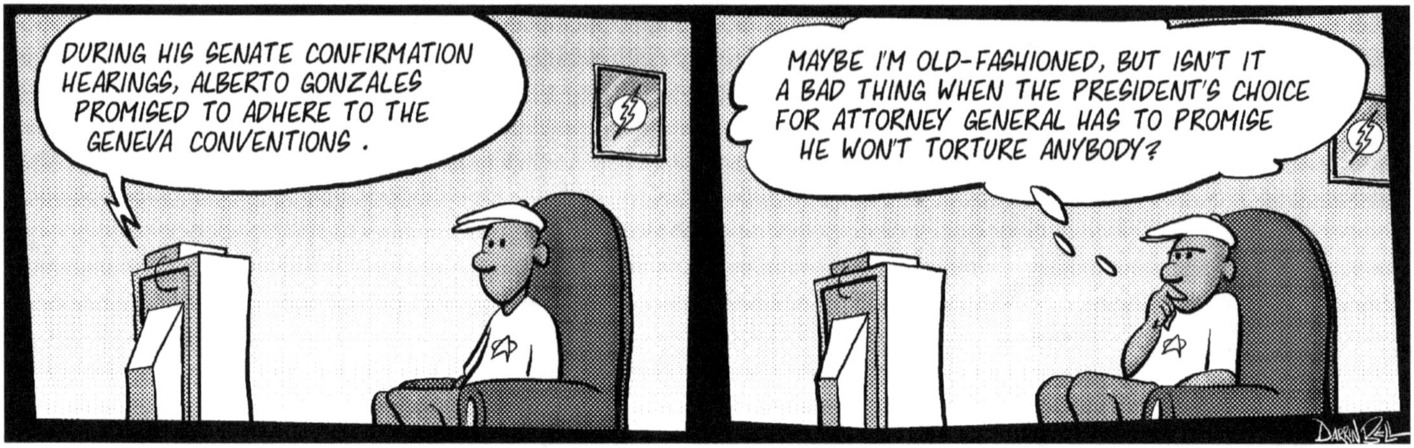
DURING HIS SENATE CONFIRMATION HEARINGS, ALBERTO GONZALES PROMISED TO ADHERE TO THE GENEVA CONVENTIONS.
MAYBE I'M OLD-FASHIONED, BUT ISN'T IT A BAD THING WHEN THE PRESIDENT'S CHOICE FOR ATTORNEY GENERAL HAS TO PROMISE HE WON'T TORTURE ANYBODY?
DARRIN BELL

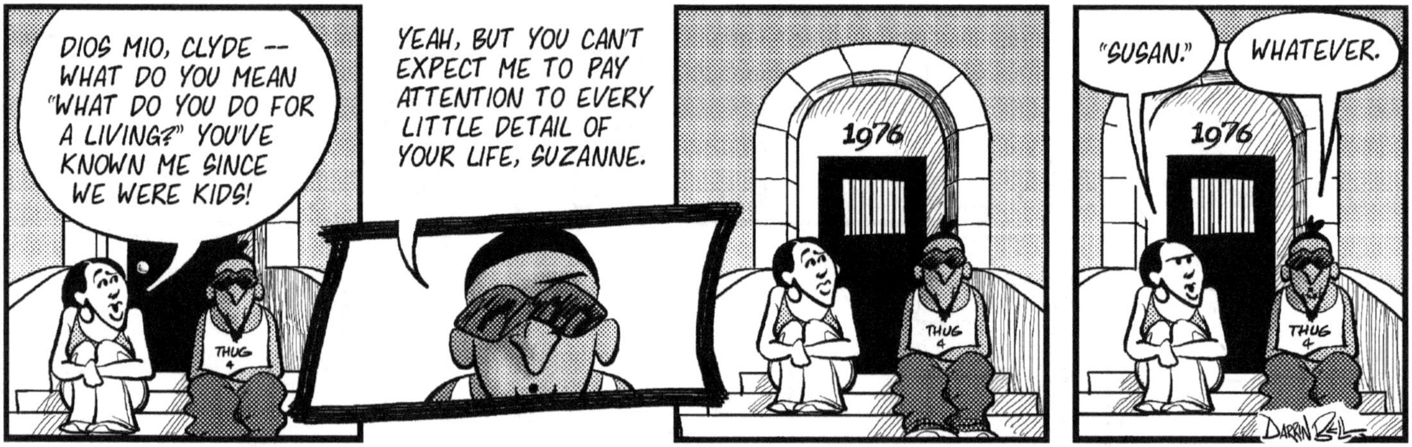
DIOS MIO, CLYDE -- WHAT DO YOU MEAN "WHAT DO YOU DO FOR A LIVING?" YOU'VE KNOWN ME SINCE WE WERE KIDS!
THUG 4
YEAH, BUT YOU CAN'T EXPECT ME TO PAY ATTENTION TO EVERY LITTLE DETAIL OF YOUR LIFE, SUZANNE.
1976
"SUSAN."
WHATEVER.
DARRIN BELL

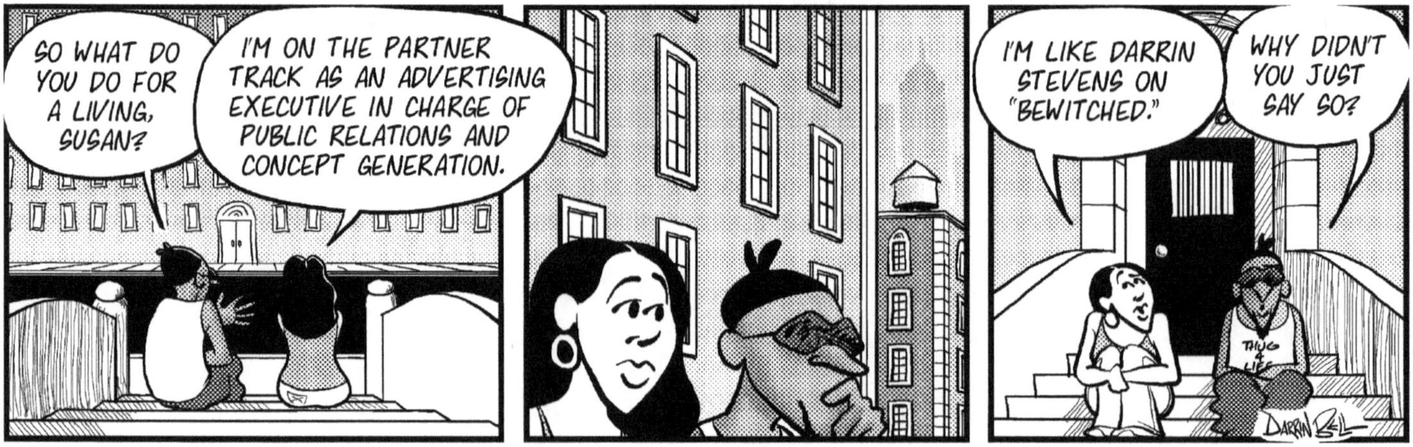
SO WHAT DO YOU DO FOR A LIVING, SUSAN?
I'M ON THE PARTNER TRACK AS AN ADVERTISING EXECUTIVE IN CHARGE OF PUBLIC RELATIONS AND CONCEPT GENERATION.
I'M LIKE DARRIN STEVENS ON "BEWITCHED."
WHY DIDN'T YOU JUST SAY SO?
DARRIN BELL

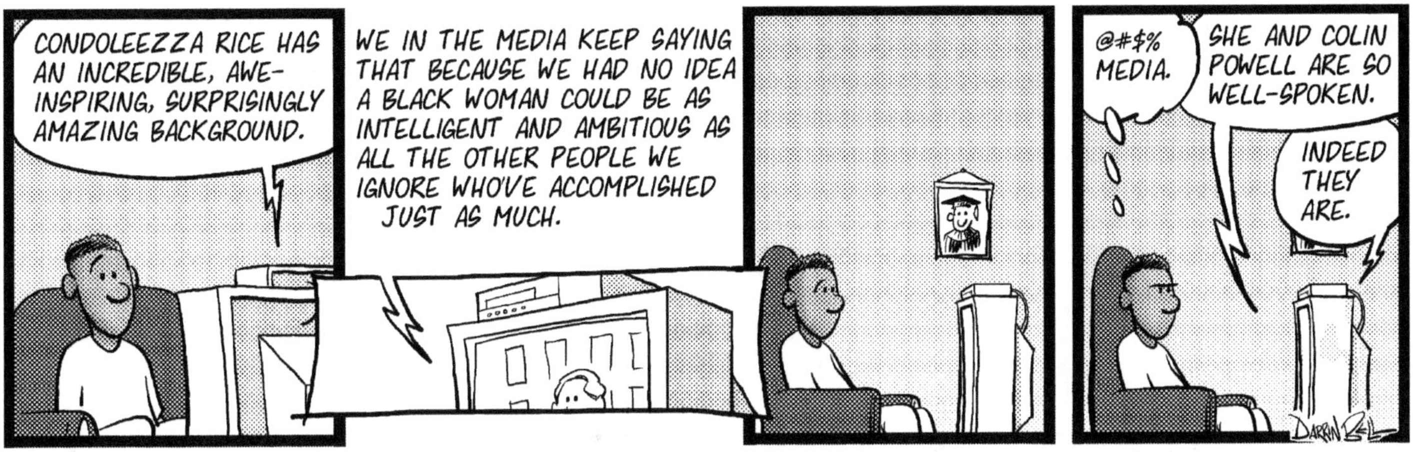
CONDOLEEZZA RICE HAS AN INCREDIBLE, AWE-INSPIRING, SURPRISINGLY AMAZING BACKGROUND.
WE IN THE MEDIA KEEP SAYING THAT BECAUSE WE HAD NO IDEA A BLACK WOMAN COULD BE AS INTELLIGENT AND AMBITIOUS AS ALL THE OTHER PEOPLE WE IGNORE WHO'VE ACCOMPLISHED JUST AS MUCH.
@#$% MEDIA.
SHE AND COLIN POWELL ARE SO WELL-SPOKEN.
INDEED THEY ARE.
DARRIN BELL

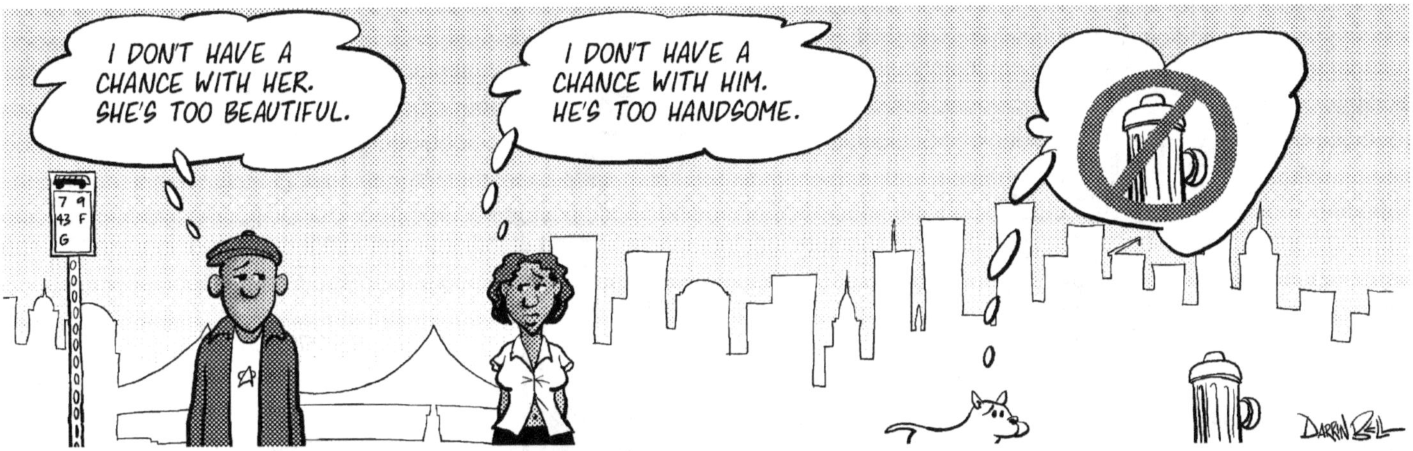
I DON'T HAVE A CHANCE WITH HER. SHE'S TOO BEAUTIFUL.
I DON'T HAVE A CHANCE WITH HIM. HE'S TOO HANDSOME.
7 9
43 F
G
DARRIN BELL

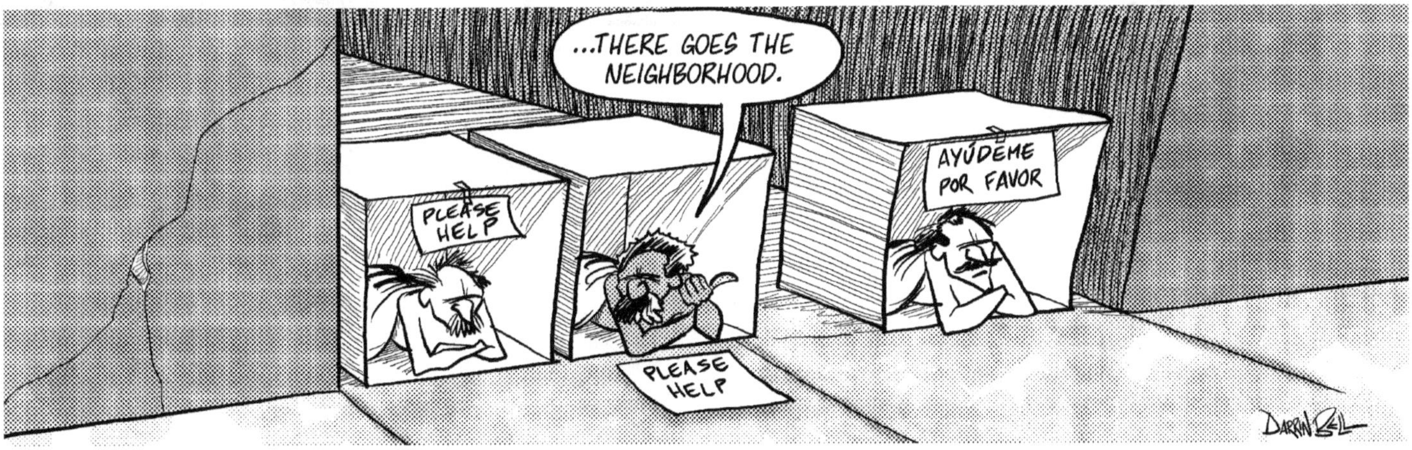
...THERE GOES THE NEIGHBORHOOD.
PLEASE HELP
AYÚDEME POR FAVOR
PLEASE HELP
DARRIN BELL

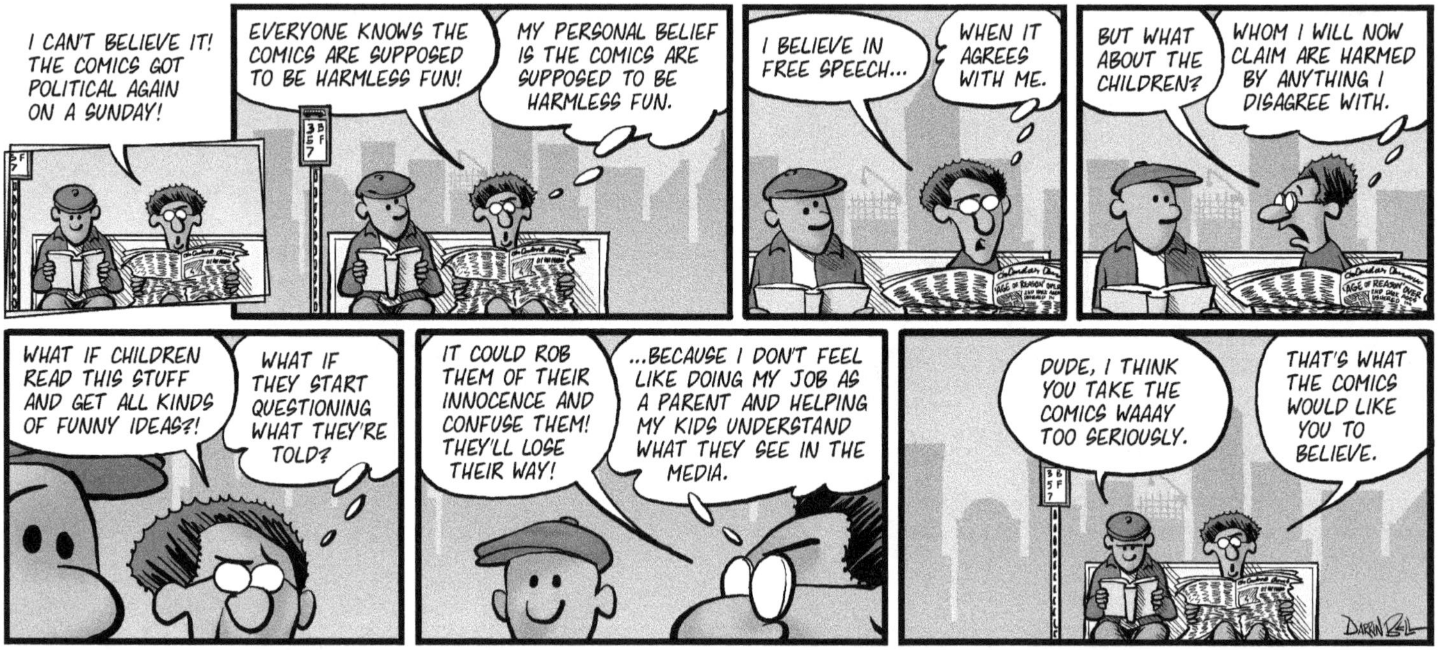
I CAN'T BELIEVE IT! THE COMICS GOT POLITICAL AGAIN ON A SUNDAY!
EVERYONE KNOWS THE COMICS ARE SUPPOSED TO BE HARMLESS FUN!
MY PERSONAL BELIEF IS THE COMICS ARE SUPPOSED TO BE HARMLESS FUN.
I BELIEVE IN FREE SPEECH...
WHEN IT AGREES WITH ME.
BUT WHAT ABOUT THE CHILDREN?
WHOM I WILL NOW CLAIM ARE HARMED BY ANYTHING I DISAGREE WITH.
WHAT IF CHILDREN READ THIS STUFF AND GET ALL KINDS OF FUNNY IDEAS?!
WHAT IF THEY START QUESTIONING WHAT THEY'RE TOLD?
IT COULD ROB THEM OF THEIR INNOCENCE AND CONFUSE THEM! THEY'LL LOSE THEIR WAY!
...BECAUSE I DON'T FEEL LIKE DOING MY JOB AS A PARENT AND HELPING MY KIDS UNDERSTAND WHAT THEY SEE IN THE MEDIA.
DUDE, I THINK YOU TAKE THE COMICS WAAAY TOO SERIOUSLY.
THAT'S WHAT THE COMICS WOULD LIKE YOU TO BELIEVE.
DARRIN BELL

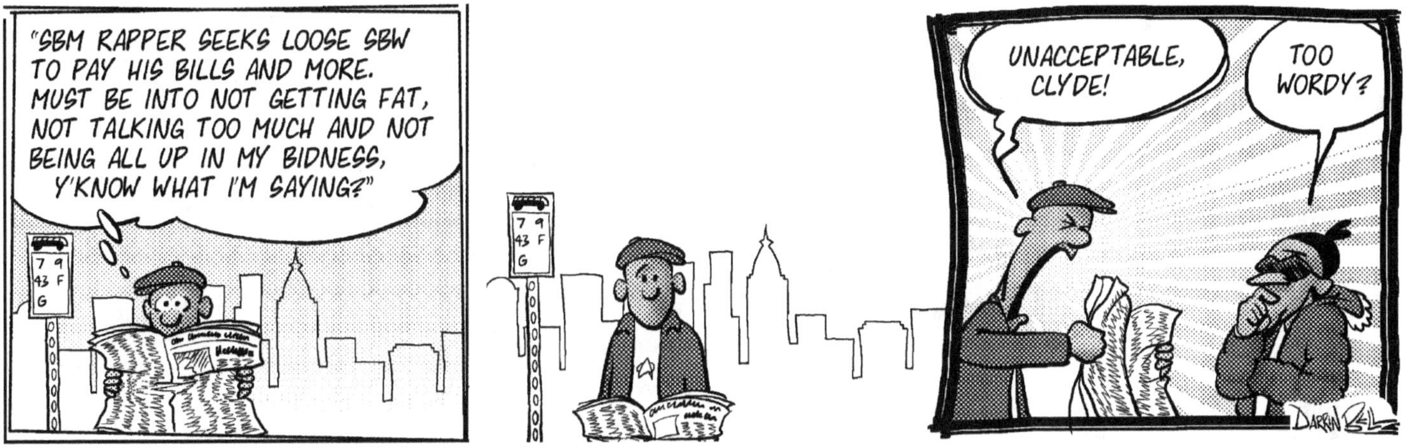
"SBM RAPPER SEEKS LOOSE SBW TO PAY HIS BILLS AND MORE. MUST BE INTO NOT GETTING FAT, NOT TALKING TOO MUCH AND NOT BEING ALL UP IN MY BIDNESS, Y'KNOW WHAT I'M SAYING?"
7 9 43 F G
UNACCEPTABLE, CLYDE!
TOO WORDY?
DARRIN BELL

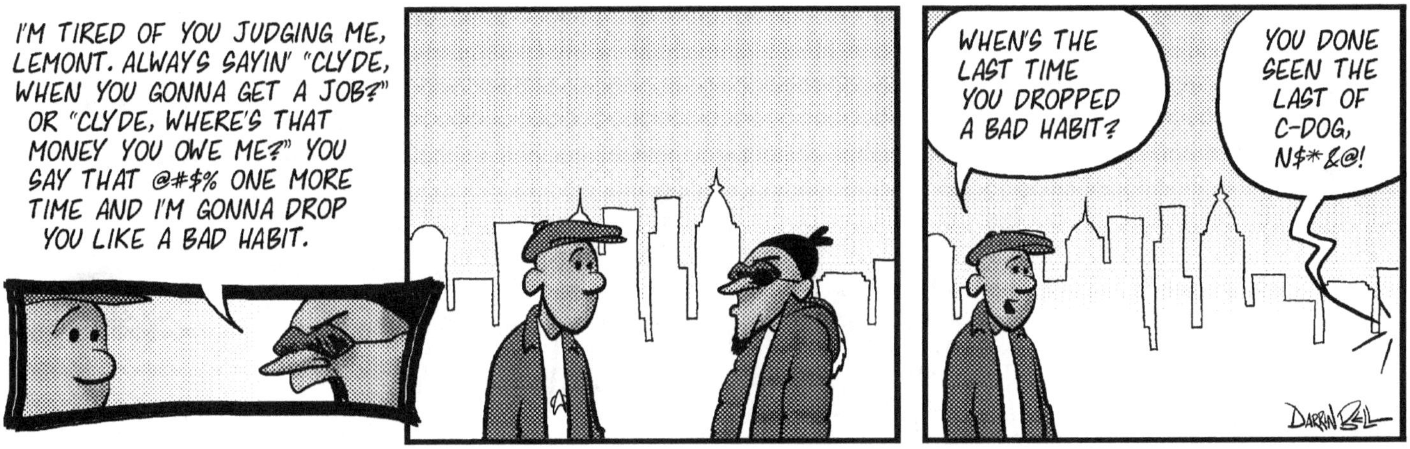
I'M TIRED OF YOU JUDGING ME, LEMONT. ALWAYS SAYIN' "CLYDE, WHEN YOU GONNA GET A JOB?" OR "CLYDE, WHERE'S THAT MONEY YOU OWE ME?" YOU SAY THAT @#$% ONE MORE TIME AND I'M GONNA DROP YOU LIKE A BAD HABIT.
WHEN'S THE LAST TIME YOU DROPPED A BAD HABIT?
YOU DONE SEEN THE LAST OF C-DOG, N$*&@!
DARRIN BELL

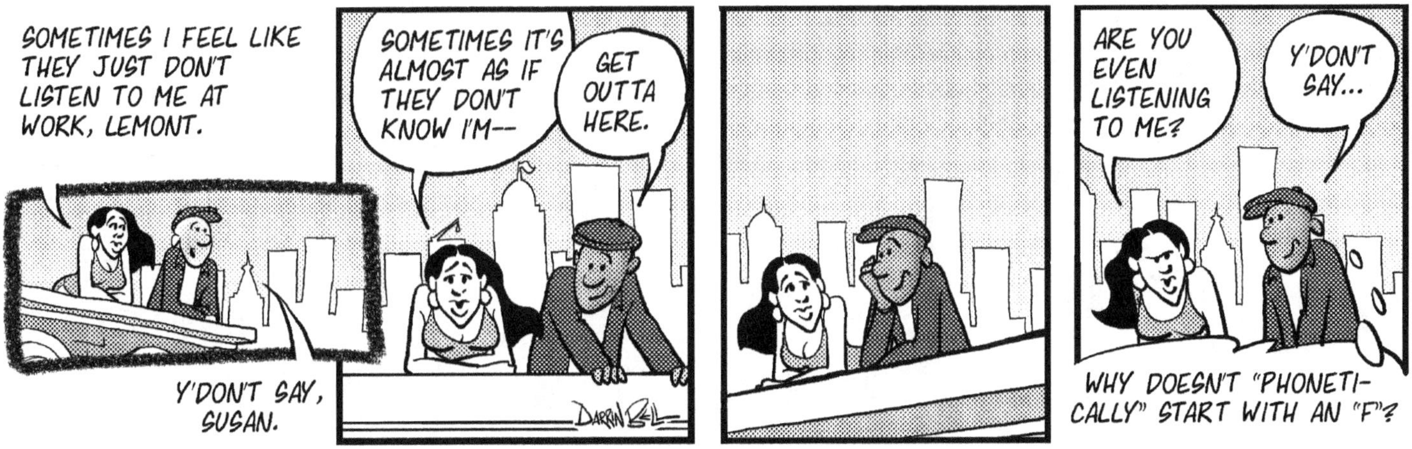
SOMETIMES I FEEL LIKE THEY JUST DON'T LISTEN TO ME AT WORK, LEMONT.
Y'DON'T SAY, SUSAN.
SOMETIMES IT'S ALMOST AS IF THEY DON'T KNOW I'M--
GET OUTTA HERE.
DARRIN BELL
ARE YOU EVEN LISTENING TO ME?
Y'DON'T SAY...
WHY DOESN'T "PHONETICALLY" START WITH AN "F"?

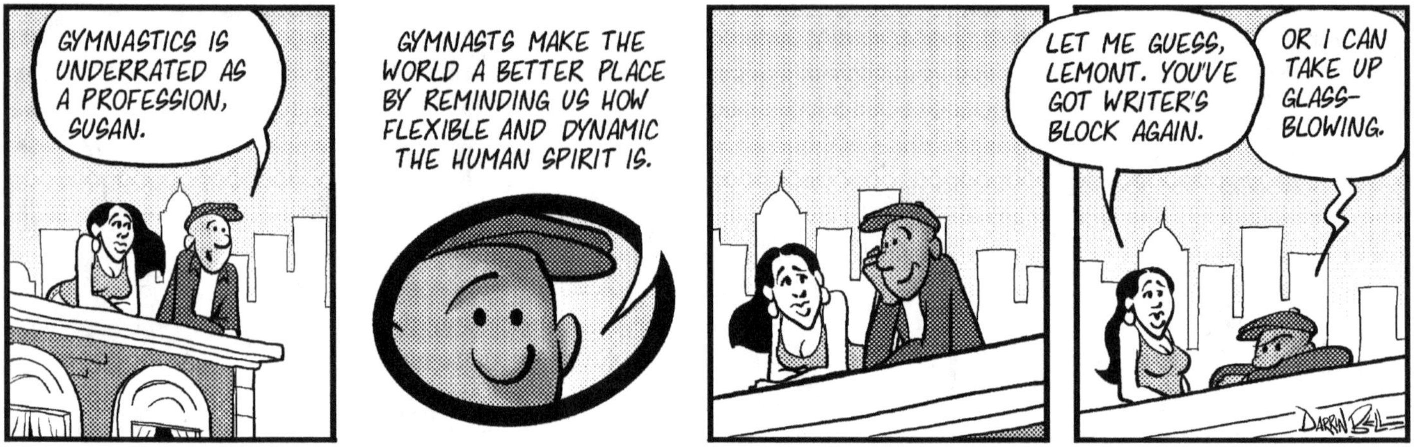
GYMNASTICS IS UNDERRATED AS A PROFESSION, SUSAN.
GYMNASTS MAKE THE WORLD A BETTER PLACE BY REMINDING US HOW FLEXIBLE AND DYNAMIC THE HUMAN SPIRIT IS.
LET ME GUESS, LEMONT. YOU'VE GOT WRITER'S BLOCK AGAIN.
OR I CAN TAKE UP GLASS-BLOWING.
DARRIN BELL

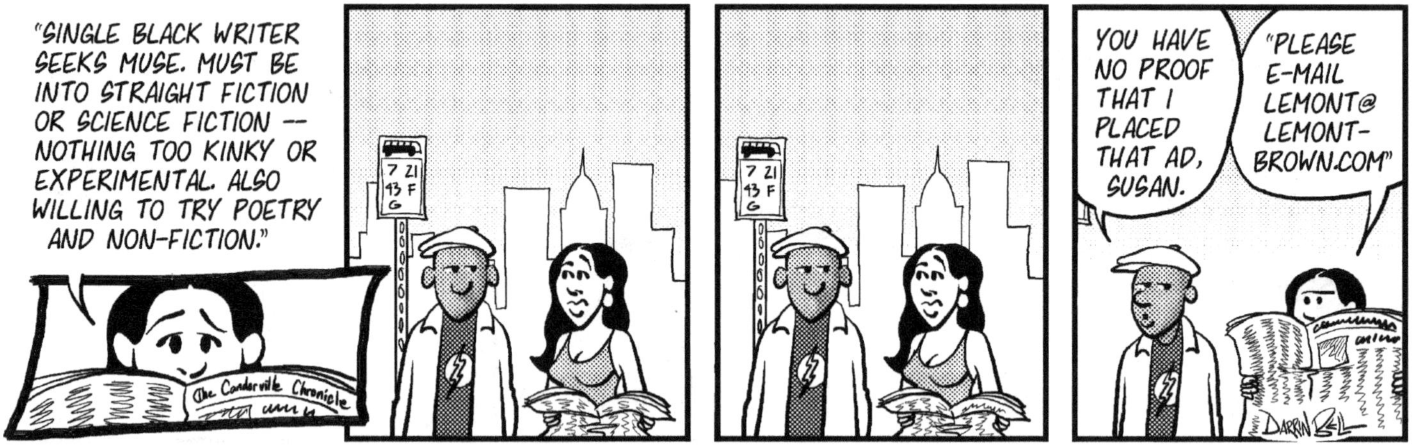
"SINGLE BLACK WRITER SEEKS MUSE. MUST BE INTO STRAIGHT FICTION OR SCIENCE FICTION -- NOTHING TOO KINKY OR EXPERIMENTAL. ALSO WILLING TO TRY POETRY AND NON-FICTION."
YOU HAVE NO PROOF THAT I PLACED THAT AD, SUSAN.
"PLEASE E-MAIL LEMONT@LEMONT-BROWN.COM"
DARRIN BELL

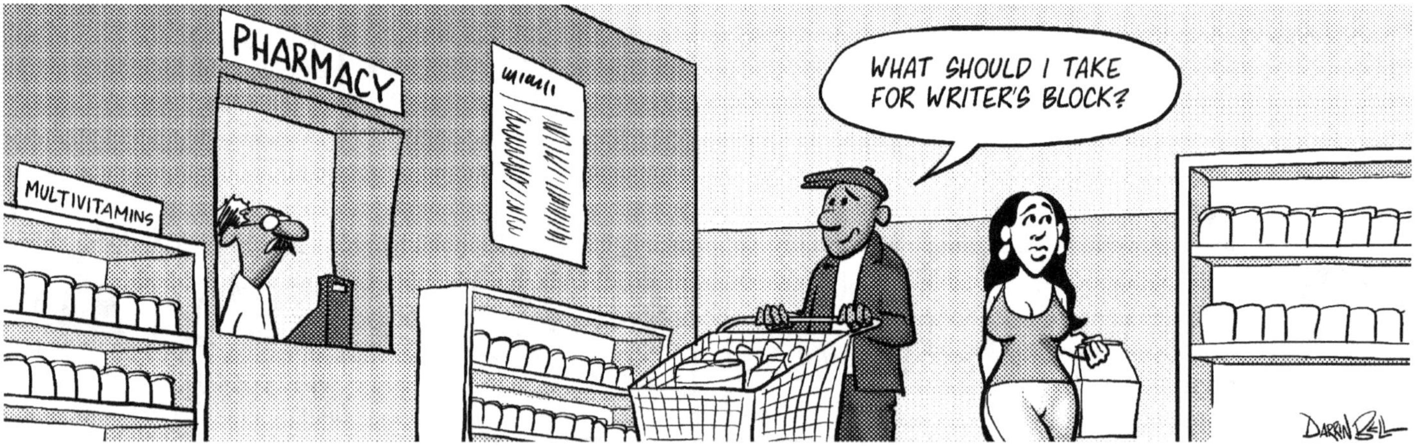
PHARMACY
MULTIVITAMINS
WHAT SHOULD I TAKE FOR WRITER'S BLOCK?
DARRIN BELL

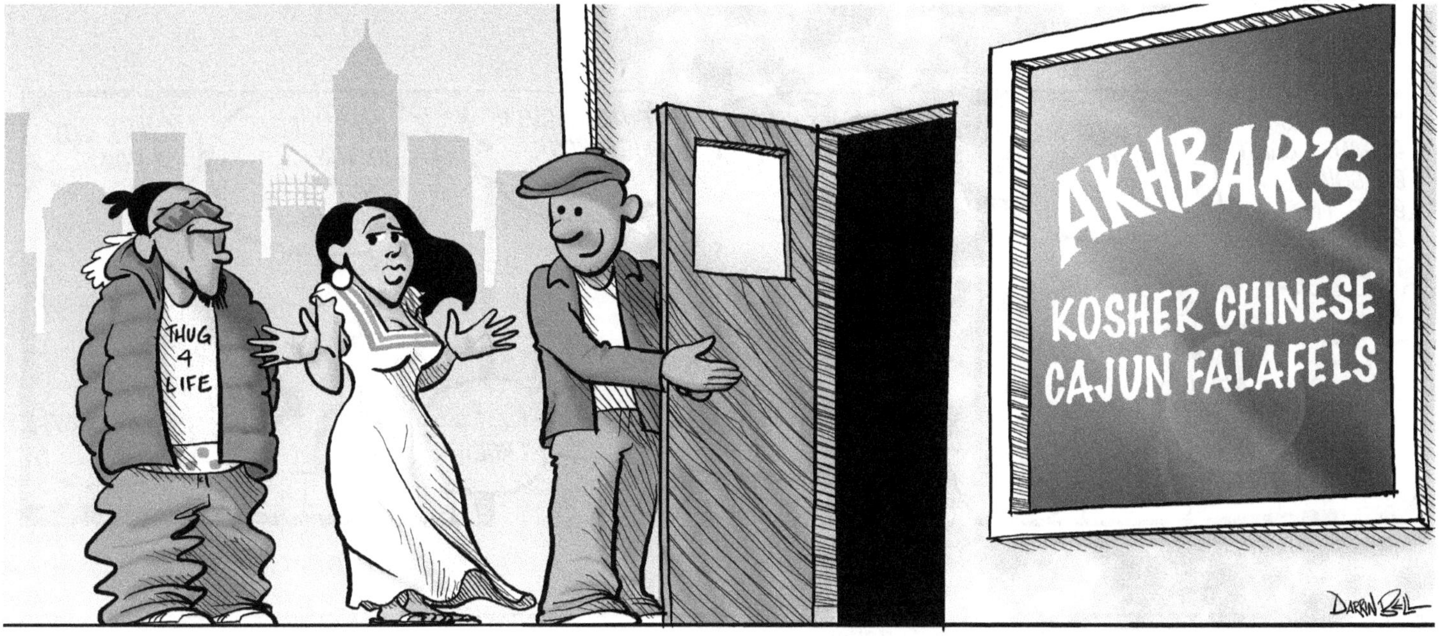
THUG
4
LIFE
AKHBAR'S
KOSHER CHINESE
CAJUN FALAFELS
DARRIN BELL

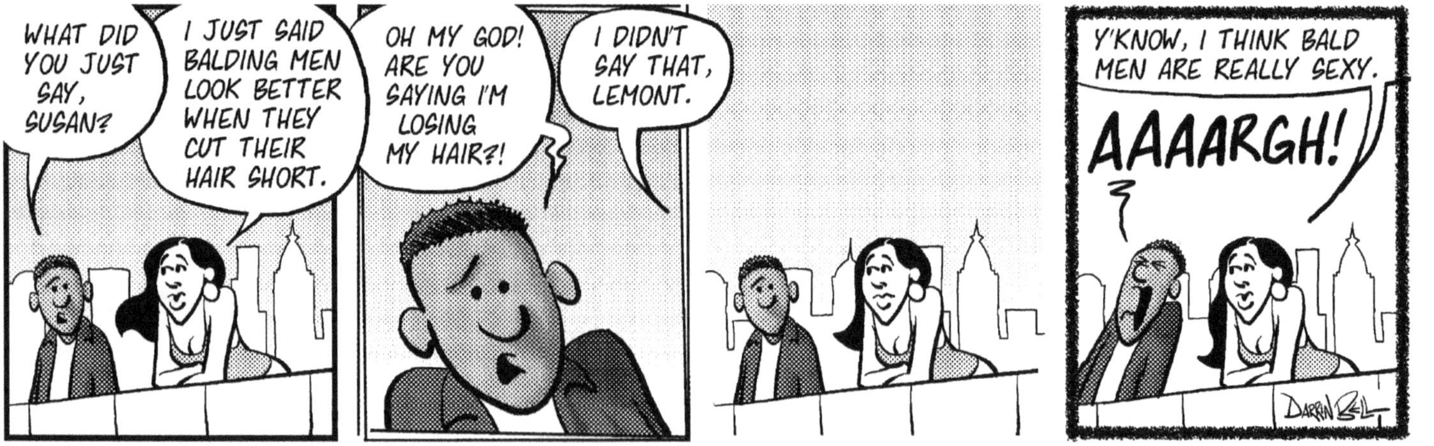
WHAT DID YOU JUST SAY, SUSAN?
I JUST SAID BALDING MEN LOOK BETTER WHEN THEY CUT THEIR HAIR SHORT.
OH MY GOD! ARE YOU SAYING I'M LOSING MY HAIR?!
I DIDN'T SAY THAT, LEMONT.
Y'KNOW, I THINK BALD MEN ARE REALLY SEXY.
AAAARGH!
DARRIN BELL

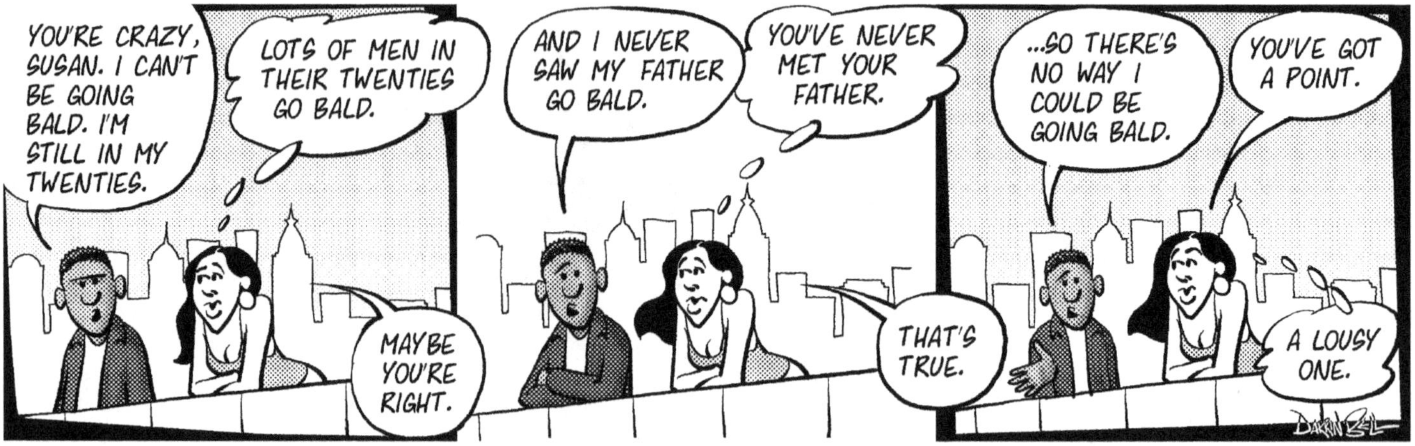
YOU'RE CRAZY, SUSAN. I CAN'T BE GOING BALD. I'M STILL IN MY TWENTIES.
LOTS OF MEN IN THEIR TWENTIES GO BALD.
MAYBE YOU'RE RIGHT.
AND I NEVER SAW MY FATHER GO BALD.
YOU'VE NEVER MET YOUR FATHER.
THAT'S TRUE.
...SO THERE'S NO WAY I COULD BE GOING BALD.
YOU'VE GOT A POINT.
A LOUSY ONE.
DARRIN BELL

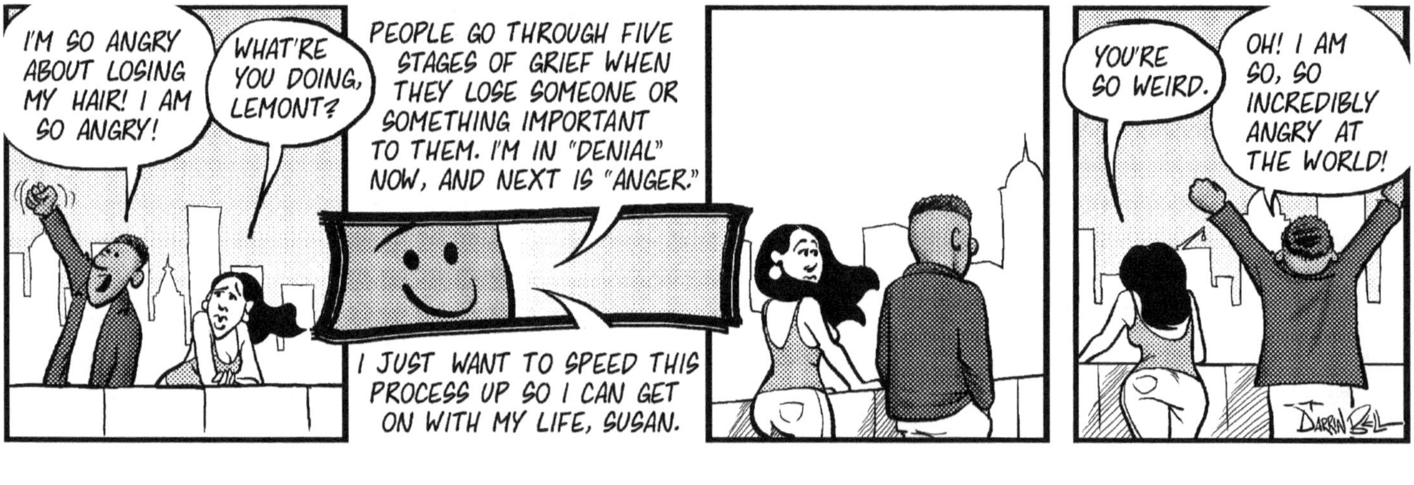
I'M SO ANGRY ABOUT LOSING MY HAIR! I AM SO ANGRY!
WHAT'RE YOU DOING, LEMONT?
PEOPLE GO THROUGH FIVE STAGES OF GRIEF WHEN THEY LOSE SOMEONE OR SOMETHING IMPORTANT TO THEM. I'M IN "DENIAL" NOW, AND NEXT IS "ANGER."
I JUST WANT TO SPEED THIS PROCESS UP SO I CAN GET ON WITH MY LIFE, SUSAN.
YOU'RE SO WEIRD.
OH! I AM SO, SO INCREDIBLY ANGRY AT THE WORLD!
DARRIN BELL

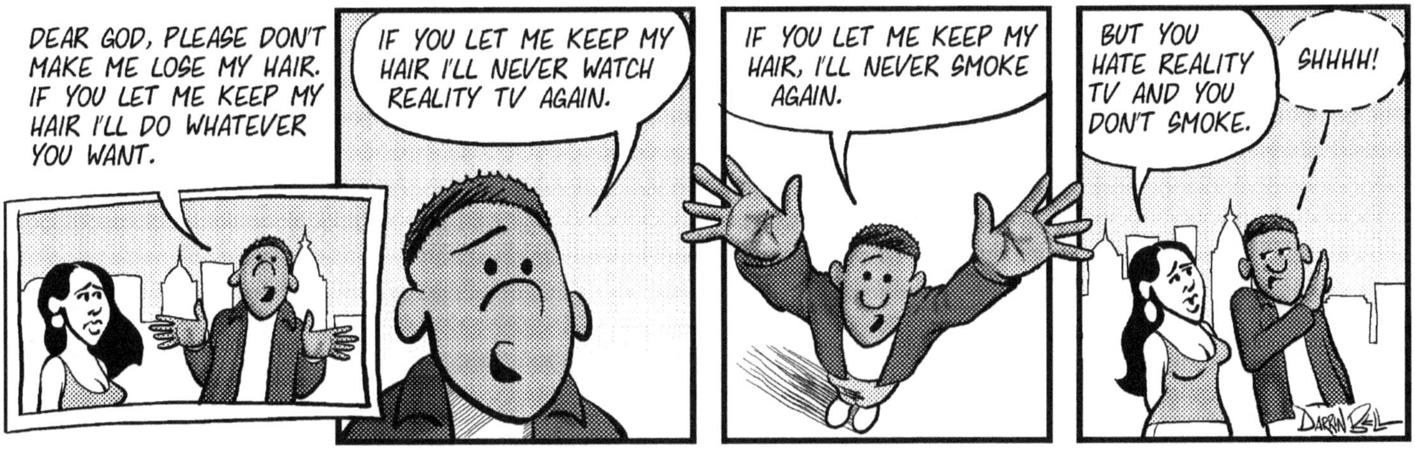
DEAR GOD, PLEASE DON'T MAKE ME LOSE MY HAIR. IF YOU LET ME KEEP MY HAIR I'LL DO WHATEVER YOU WANT.
IF YOU LET ME KEEP MY HAIR I'LL NEVER WATCH REALITY TV AGAIN.
IF YOU LET ME KEEP MY HAIR, I'LL NEVER SMOKE AGAIN.
BUT YOU HATE REALITY TV AND YOU DON'T SMOKE.
SHHHH!
DARRIN BELL

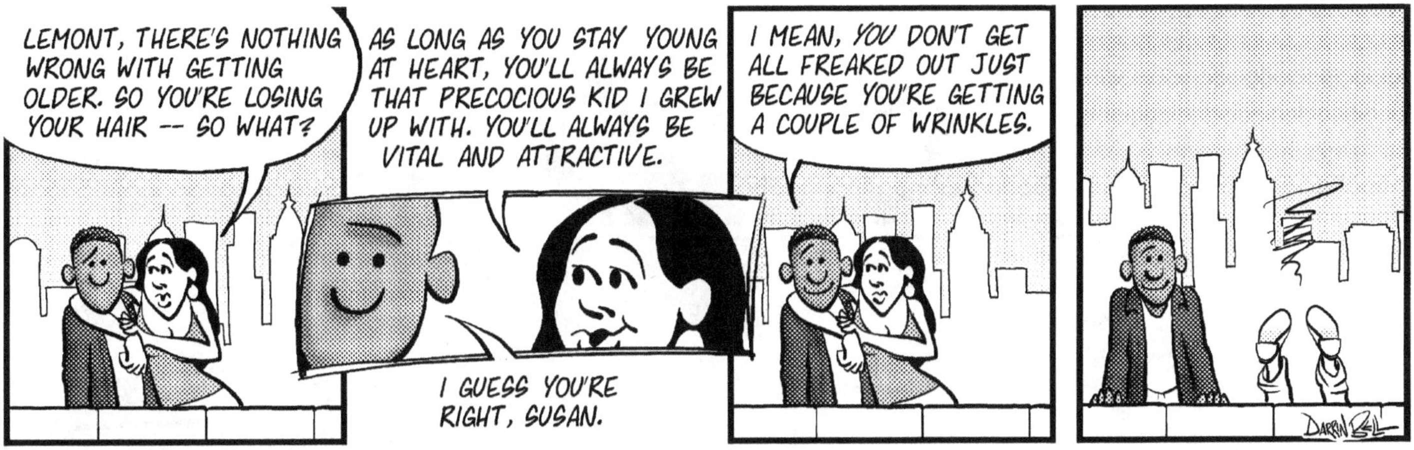
LEMONT, THERE'S NOTHING WRONG WITH GETTING OLDER. SO YOU'RE LOSING YOUR HAIR -- SO WHAT?
AS LONG AS YOU STAY YOUNG AT HEART, YOU'LL ALWAYS BE THAT PRECOCIOUS KID I GREW UP WITH. YOU'LL ALWAYS BE VITAL AND ATTRACTIVE.
I GUESS YOU'RE RIGHT, SUSAN.
I MEAN, YOU DON'T GET ALL FREAKED OUT JUST BECAUSE YOU'RE GETTING A COUPLE OF WRINKLES.
DARRIN BELL

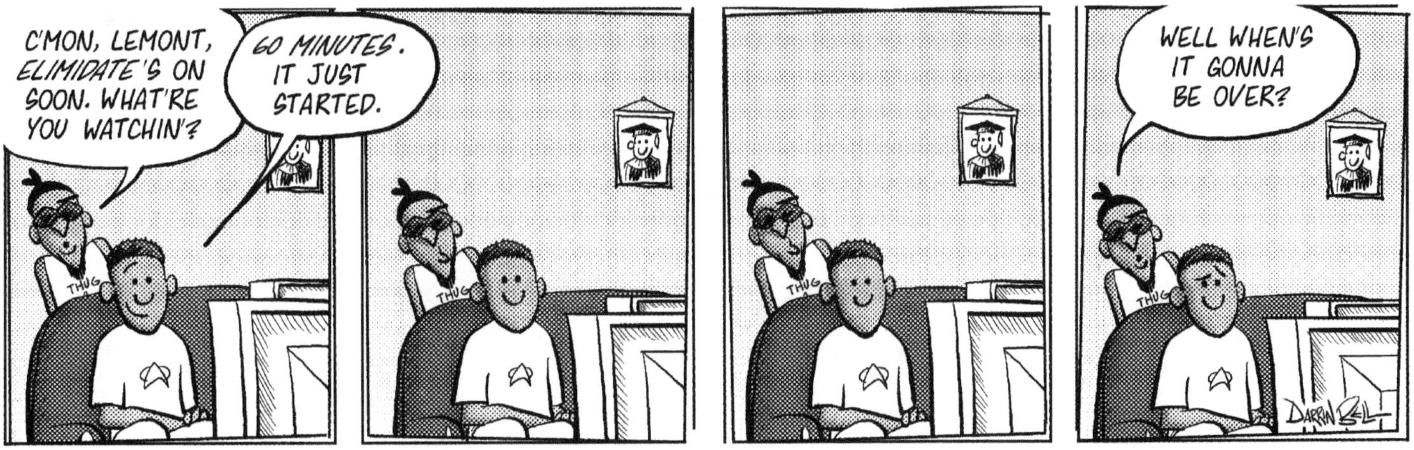
C'MON, LEMONT, ELIMIDATE'S ON SOON. WHAT'RE YOU WATCHIN'?
60 MINUTES. IT JUST STARTED.
THUG
WELL WHEN'S IT GONNA BE OVER?
DARRIN BELL

LEMONT? IT'S 3:30 IN THE MORNING. WHY ARE YOU CALLING? YOU OK?
SUSAN, EVER SINCE YOU TOLD ME I'M GOING BALD I HAVEN'T BEEN ABLE TO SLEEP.
I LIE AWAKE ALL NIGHT WORRYING THAT I WON'T BE ATTRACTIVE ANYMORE.
I LIE AWAKE ALL NIGHT WORRYING THAT I'M GETTING OLDER, THAT MY BEST YEARS ARE BEHIND ME AND THAT BEFORE I KNOW IT, I'LL BE BREATHING MY LAST BREATH, SEEING MY LAST SUNRISE, FEELING MY LAST RAINDROP -- I'M GOING TO DIE, SUSAN.
DARRIN BELL
DIOS MIO... TRY COUNTING SHEEP, YOU NUTJOB. GOOD NIGHT.
WAIT!
CLICK

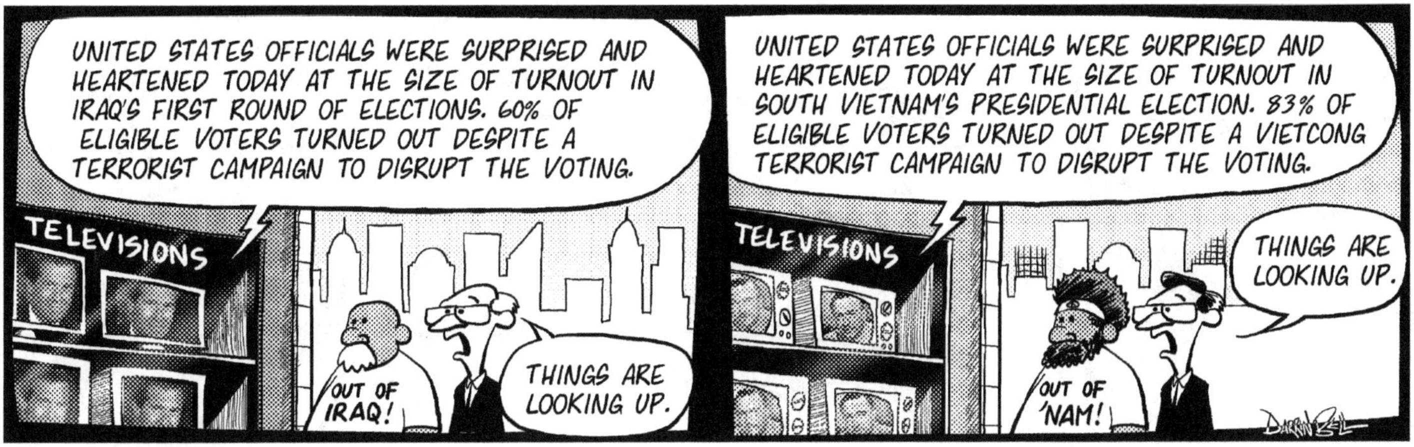
UNITED STATES OFFICIALS WERE SURPRISED AND HEARTENED TODAY AT THE SIZE OF TURNOUT IN IRAQ'S FIRST ROUND OF ELECTIONS. 60% OF ELIGIBLE VOTERS TURNED OUT DESPITE A TERRORIST CAMPAIGN TO DISRUPT THE VOTING.
TELEVISIONS
OUT OF IRAQ!
THINGS ARE LOOKING UP.
UNITED STATES OFFICIALS WERE SURPRISED AND HEARTENED TODAY AT THE SIZE OF TURNOUT IN SOUTH VIETNAM'S PRESIDENTIAL ELECTION. 83% OF ELIGIBLE VOTERS TURNED OUT DESPITE A VIETCONG TERRORIST CAMPAIGN TO DISRUPT THE VOTING.
TELEVISIONS
THINGS ARE LOOKING UP.
OUT OF 'NAM!

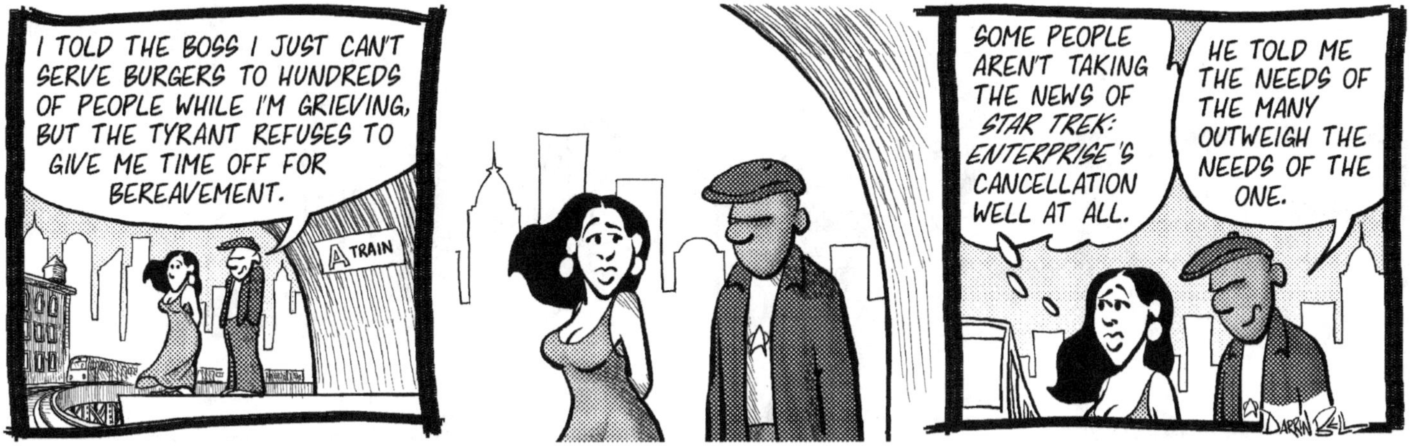
I TOLD THE BOSS I JUST CAN'T SERVE BURGERS TO HUNDREDS OF PEOPLE WHILE I'M GRIEVING, BUT THE TYRANT REFUSES TO GIVE ME TIME OFF FOR BEREAVEMENT.
A TRAIN
SOME PEOPLE AREN'T TAKING THE NEWS OF STAR TREK: ENTERPRISE'S CANCELLATION WELL AT ALL.
HE TOLD ME THE NEEDS OF THE MANY OUTWEIGH THE NEEDS OF THE ONE.

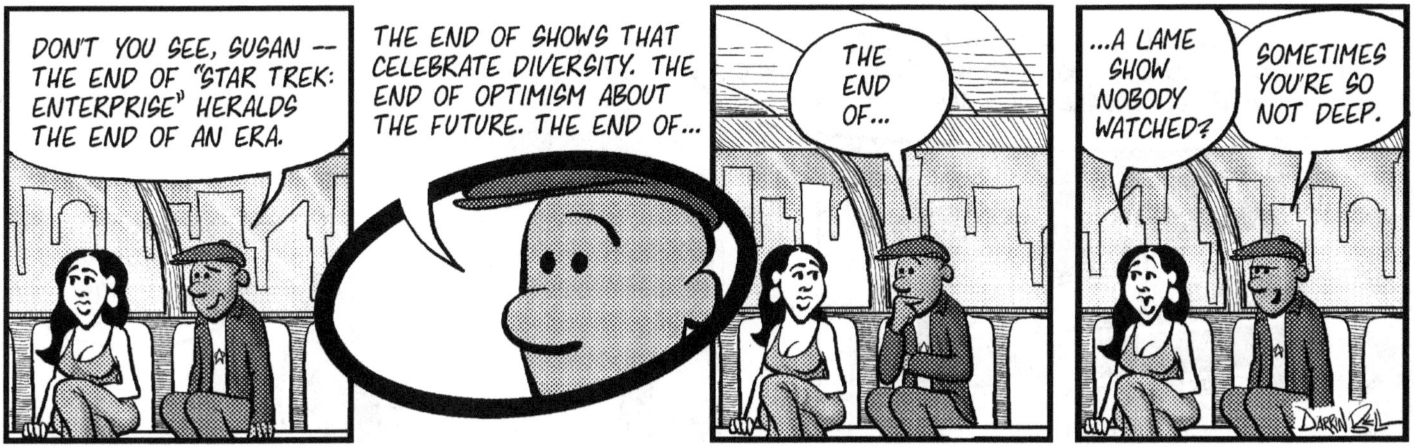
DON'T YOU SEE, SUSAN -- THE END OF "STAR TREK: ENTERPRISE" HERALDS THE END OF AN ERA.
THE END OF SHOWS THAT CELEBRATE DIVERSITY. THE END OF OPTIMISM ABOUT THE FUTURE. THE END OF...
THE END OF...
...A LAME SHOW NOBODY WATCHED?
SOMETIMES YOU'RE SO NOT DEEP.

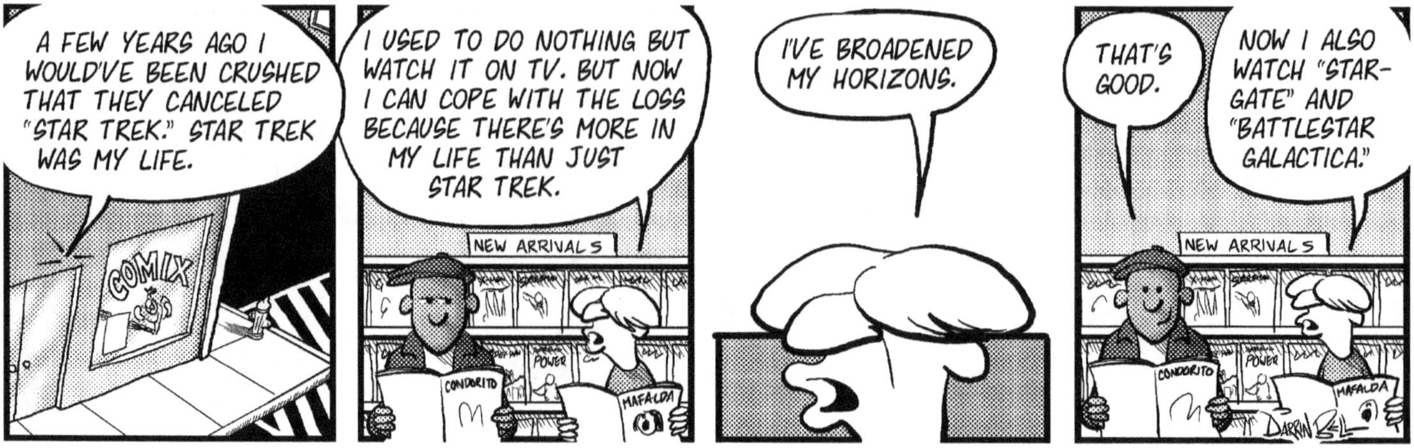
A FEW YEARS AGO I WOULD'VE BEEN CRUSHED THAT THEY CANCELED "STAR TREK." STAR TREK WAS MY LIFE.
COMIX
I USED TO DO NOTHING BUT WATCH IT ON TV. BUT NOW I CAN COPE WITH THE LOSS BECAUSE THERE'S MORE IN MY LIFE THAN JUST STAR TREK.
NEW ARRIVALS
CONDORITO
MAFALDA
I'VE BROADENED MY HORIZONS.
THAT'S GOOD.
NOW I ALSO WATCH "STAR-GATE" AND "BATTLESTAR GALACTICA."
NEW ARRIVALS
CONDORITO
MAFALDA
DARRIN BELL

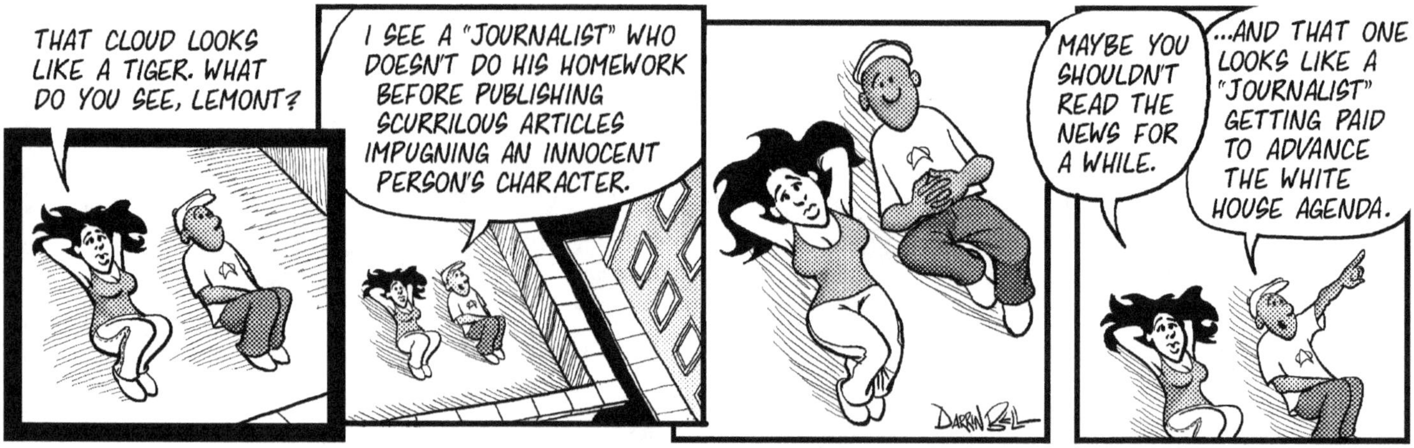
THAT CLOUD LOOKS LIKE A TIGER. WHAT DO YOU SEE, LEMONT?
I SEE A "JOURNALIST" WHO DOESN'T DO HIS HOMEWORK BEFORE PUBLISHING SCURRILOUS ARTICLES IMPUGNING AN INNOCENT PERSON'S CHARACTER.
DARRIN BELL
MAYBE YOU SHOULDN'T READ THE NEWS FOR A WHILE.
...AND THAT ONE LOOKS LIKE A "JOURNALIST" GETTING PAID TO ADVANCE THE WHITE HOUSE AGENDA.

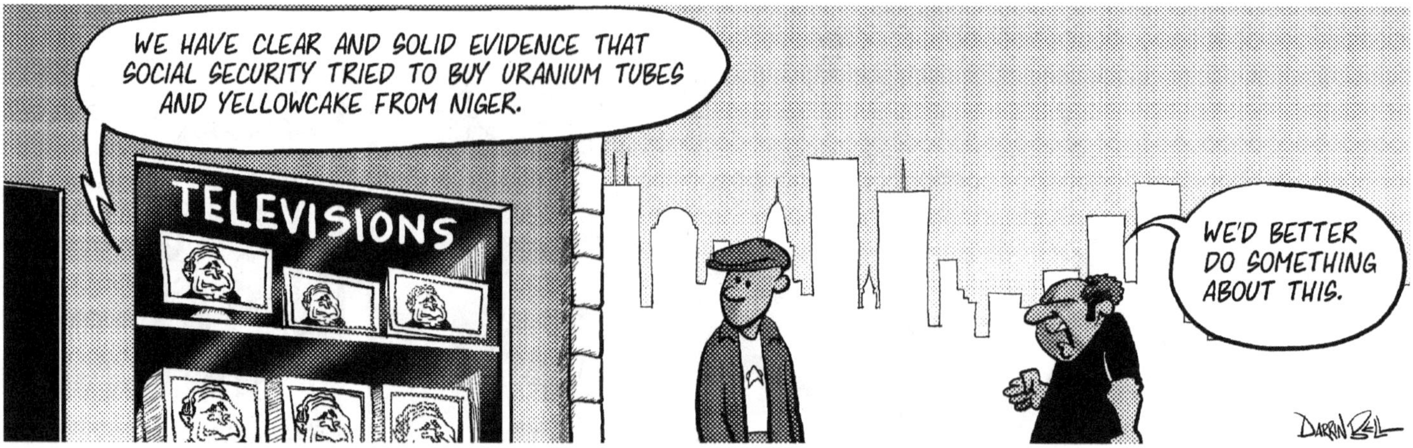
WE HAVE CLEAR AND SOLID EVIDENCE THAT SOCIAL SECURITY TRIED TO BUY URANIUM TUBES AND YELLOWCAKE FROM NIGER.
TELEVISIONS
WE'D BETTER DO SOMETHING ABOUT THIS.
DARRIN BELL

SUSAN, I THINK I MIGHT OWE MY BUDDY AL $40.

"MIGHT"?

YEAH. REMEMBER WHEN WE HUNG OUT WITH AL AND MARI A COUPLE MONTHS BACK? THEY PAID FOR THE DRINKS. THAT WAS PROBABLY AROUND $10.

"THEN AL LOANED ME $40. AT THE MOVIES I BOUGHT THE POPCORN AND DRINKS FOR $10, BUT HE BOUGHT THE NACHOS FOR $5.

"I PAID FOR DINNER WITH MY CITTOBANK VISTA CARD. THAT WAS $60. I ALSO PAID $20 FOR THE MARIACHI, BUT THEN HE PUT IN $15 FOR THE TIP."

SO DO I OWE HIM $40?

FIRST OF ALL, LEMONT YOUR MATH'S ALL WRONG. SECONDLY, THIS IS A FRIEND YOU'RE TALKING ABOUT. WHY WORRY ABOUT NICKELS AND DIMES?

YOU'RE RIGHT -- FRIENDS SHOULDN'T WORRY ABOUT MONEY. BESIDES, I WAS THERE FOR HIM A FEW YEARS AGO WHEN HE NEEDED MORAL SUPPORT. THAT KIND OF COUNSELING COULD GO FOR UP TO $300 ON THE OPEN MARKET.

DIOS MIO... I HAVE SUCH A HEADACHE.

THAT JERK OWES ME $260!

99

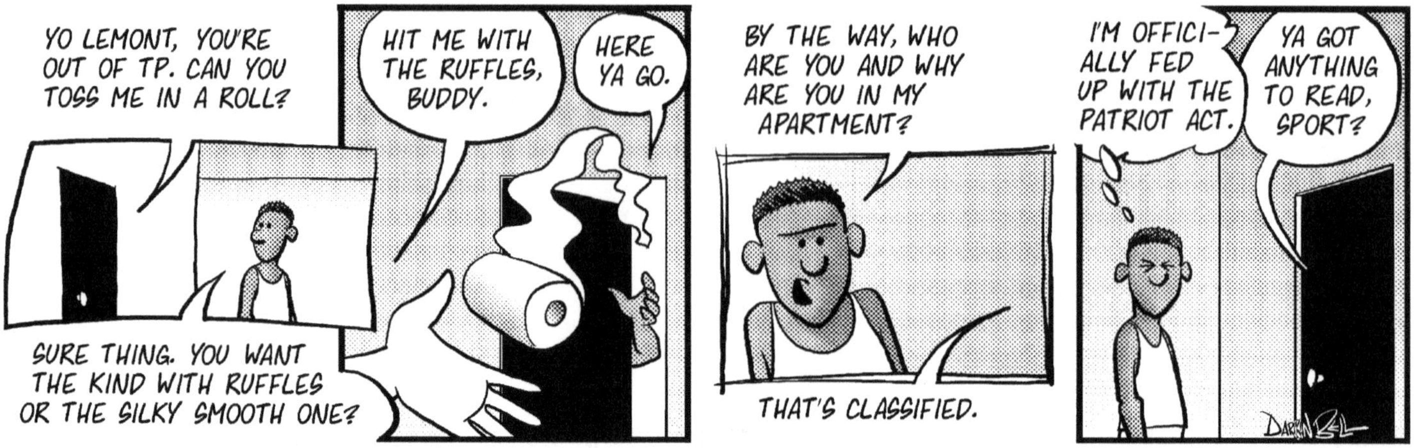
YO LEMONT, YOU'RE OUT OF TP. CAN YOU TOSS ME IN A ROLL?
SURE THING. YOU WANT THE KIND WITH RUFFLES OR THE SILKY SMOOTH ONE?
HIT ME WITH THE RUFFLES, BUDDY.
HERE YA GO.
BY THE WAY, WHO ARE YOU AND WHY ARE YOU IN MY APARTMENT?
THAT'S CLASSIFIED.
I'M OFFICIALLY FED UP WITH THE PATRIOT ACT.
YA GOT ANYTHING TO READ, SPORT?
DARRIN BELL

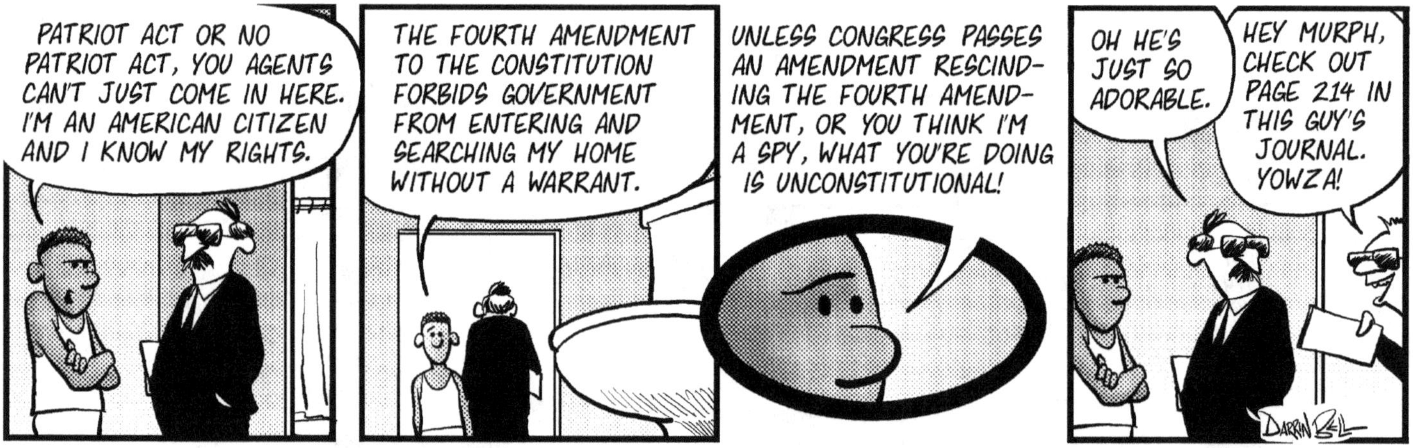
PATRIOT ACT OR NO PATRIOT ACT, YOU AGENTS CAN'T JUST COME IN HERE. I'M AN AMERICAN CITIZEN AND I KNOW MY RIGHTS.
THE FOURTH AMENDMENT TO THE CONSTITUTION FORBIDS GOVERNMENT FROM ENTERING AND SEARCHING MY HOME WITHOUT A WARRANT.
UNLESS CONGRESS PASSES AN AMENDMENT RESCINDING THE FOURTH AMENDMENT, OR YOU THINK I'M A SPY, WHAT YOU'RE DOING IS UNCONSTITUTIONAL!
OH HE'S JUST SO ADORABLE.
HEY MURPH, CHECK OUT PAGE 214 IN THIS GUY'S JOURNAL. YOWZA!
DARRIN BELL

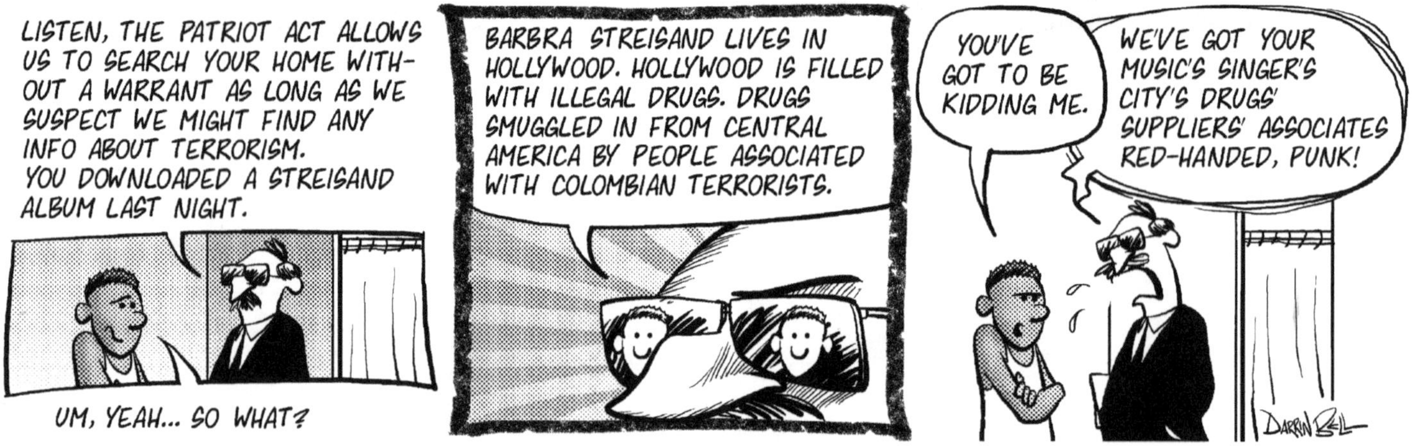
LISTEN, THE PATRIOT ACT ALLOWS US TO SEARCH YOUR HOME WITHOUT A WARRANT AS LONG AS WE SUSPECT WE MIGHT FIND ANY INFO ABOUT TERRORISM. YOU DOWNLOADED A STREISAND ALBUM LAST NIGHT.
UM, YEAH... SO WHAT?
BARBRA STREISAND LIVES IN HOLLYWOOD. HOLLYWOOD IS FILLED WITH ILLEGAL DRUGS. DRUGS SMUGGLED IN FROM CENTRAL AMERICA BY PEOPLE ASSOCIATED WITH COLOMBIAN TERRORISTS.
YOU'VE GOT TO BE KIDDING ME.
WE'VE GOT YOUR MUSIC'S SINGER'S CITY'S DRUGS' SUPPLIERS' ASSOCIATES RED-HANDED, PUNK!
DARRIN BELL

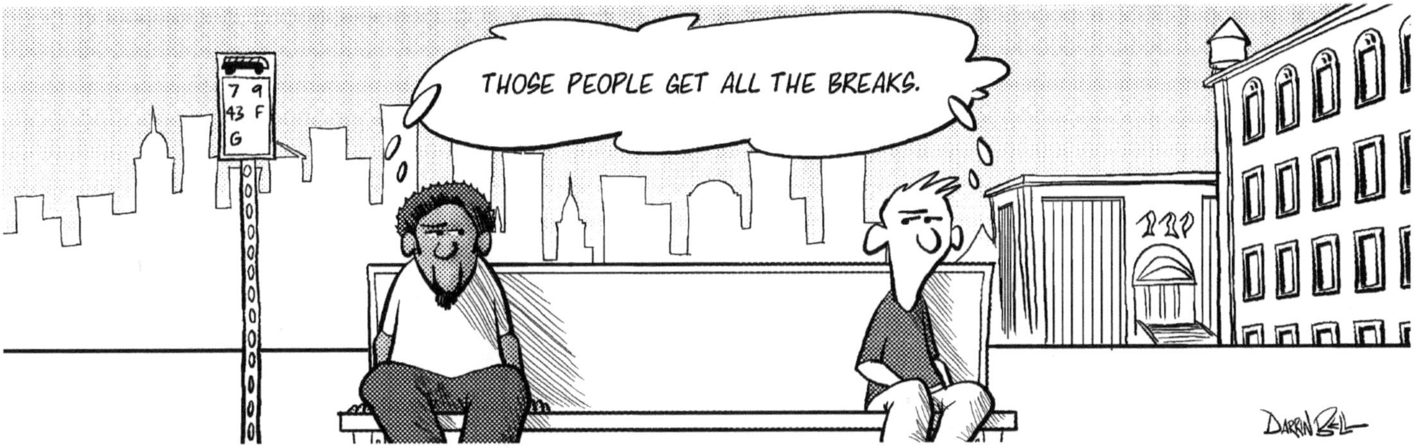
7 9
43 F
G
THOSE PEOPLE GET ALL THE BREAKS.
DARRIN BELL

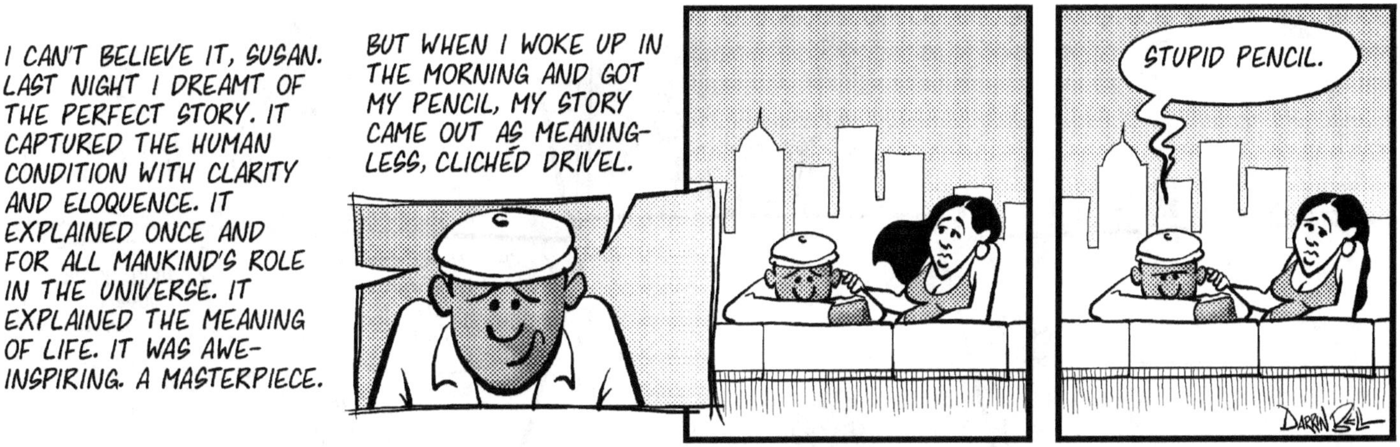
I CAN'T BELIEVE IT, SUSAN. LAST NIGHT I DREAMT OF THE PERFECT STORY. IT CAPTURED THE HUMAN CONDITION WITH CLARITY AND ELOQUENCE. IT EXPLAINED ONCE AND FOR ALL MANKIND'S ROLE IN THE UNIVERSE. IT EXPLAINED THE MEANING OF LIFE. IT WAS AWE-INSPIRING. A MASTERPIECE.
BUT WHEN I WOKE UP IN THE MORNING AND GOT MY PENCIL, MY STORY CAME OUT AS MEANING-LESS, CLICHÉD DRIVEL.
STUPID PENCIL.
DARRIN BELL

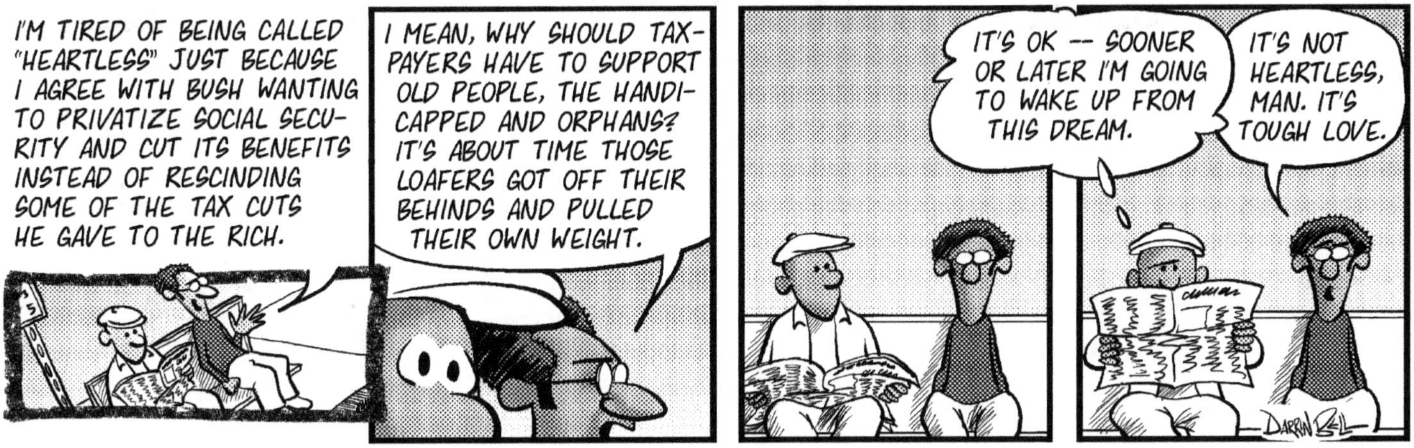
I'M TIRED OF BEING CALLED "HEARTLESS" JUST BECAUSE I AGREE WITH BUSH WANTING TO PRIVATIZE SOCIAL SECU-RITY AND CUT ITS BENEFITS INSTEAD OF RESCINDING SOME OF THE TAX CUTS HE GAVE TO THE RICH.
I MEAN, WHY SHOULD TAX-PAYERS HAVE TO SUPPORT OLD PEOPLE, THE HANDI-CAPPED AND ORPHANS? IT'S ABOUT TIME THOSE LOAFERS GOT OFF THEIR BEHINDS AND PULLED THEIR OWN WEIGHT.
IT'S OK -- SOONER OR LATER I'M GOING TO WAKE UP FROM THIS DREAM.
IT'S NOT HEARTLESS, MAN. IT'S TOUGH LOVE.
DARRIN BELL

AIN'T N-NO #$%@# W-W-WEATHER GONNA T-T-T-TELL C-DOG WHAT TA DO.
HERE, YOUR NOSE IS RUNNING.

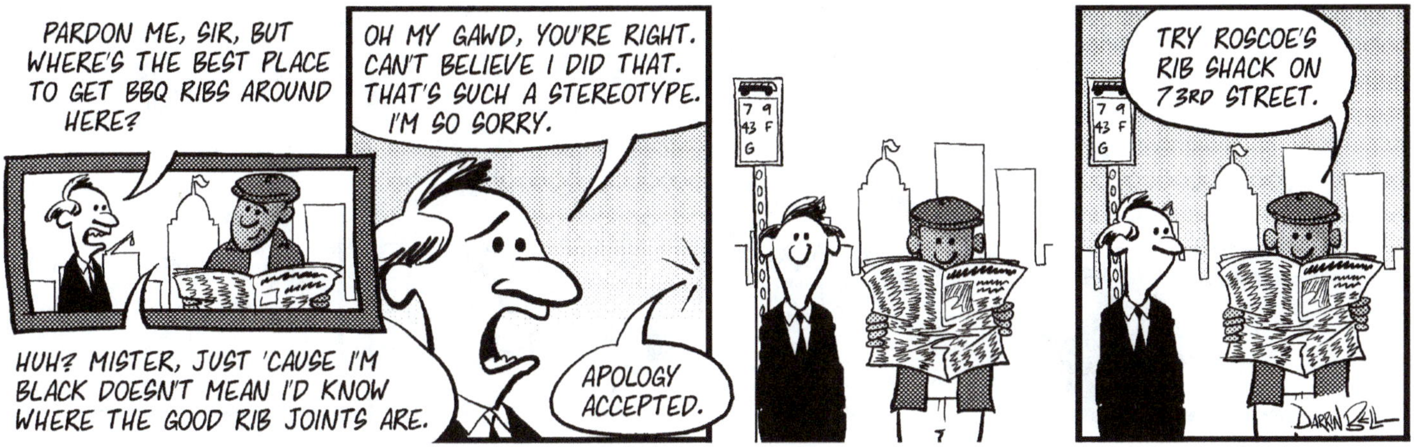
PARDON ME, SIR, BUT WHERE'S THE BEST PLACE TO GET BBQ RIBS AROUND HERE?
HUH? MISTER, JUST 'CAUSE I'M BLACK DOESN'T MEAN I'D KNOW WHERE THE GOOD RIB JOINTS ARE.
OH MY GAWD, YOU'RE RIGHT. CAN'T BELIEVE I DID THAT. THAT'S SUCH A STEREOTYPE. I'M SO SORRY.
APOLOGY ACCEPTED.
TRY ROSCOE'S RIB SHACK ON 73RD STREET.

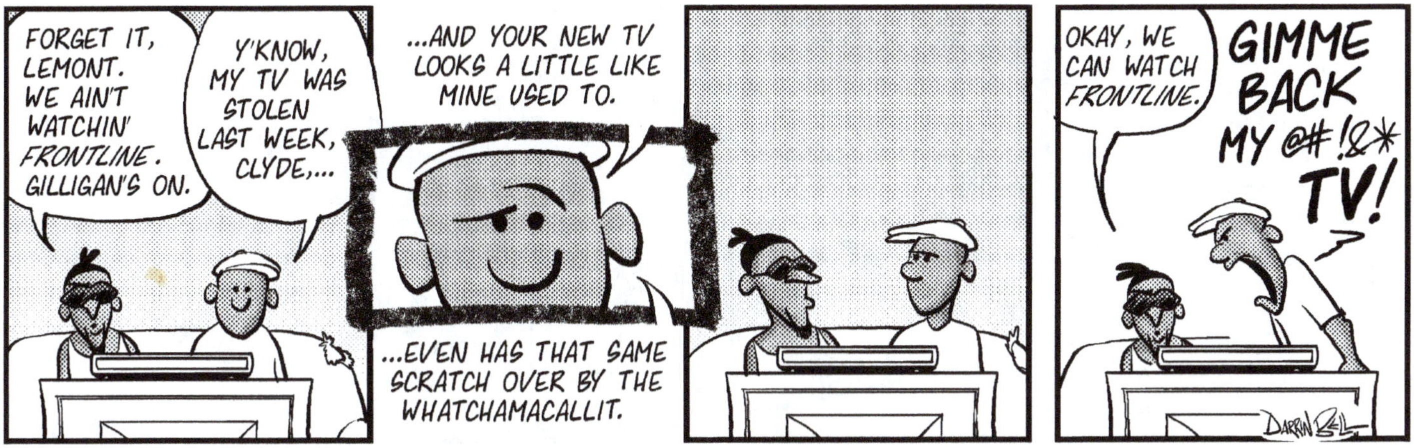
FORGET IT, LEMONT. WE AIN'T WATCHIN' *FRONTLINE*. GILLIGAN'S ON.
Y'KNOW, MY TV WAS STOLEN LAST WEEK, CLYDE,...
...AND YOUR NEW TV LOOKS A LITTLE LIKE MINE USED TO.
...EVEN HAS THAT SAME SCRATCH OVER BY THE WHATCHAMACALLIT.
OKAY, WE CAN WATCH *FRONTLINE*.
GIMME BACK MY @#!&* TV!

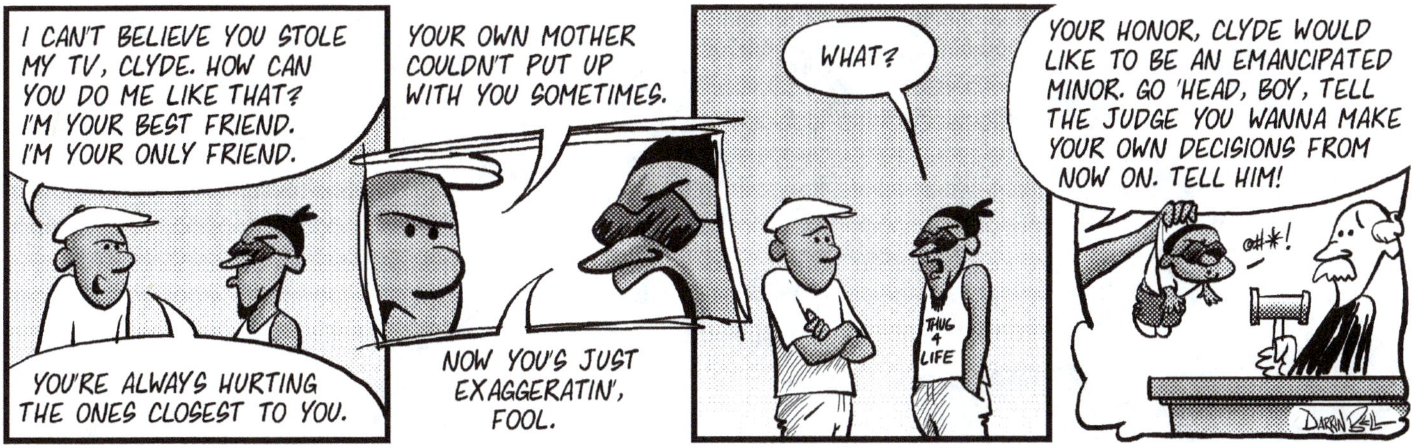
I CAN'T BELIEVE YOU STOLE MY TV, CLYDE. HOW CAN YOU DO ME LIKE THAT? I'M YOUR BEST FRIEND. I'M YOUR ONLY FRIEND.
YOU'RE ALWAYS HURTING THE ONES CLOSEST TO YOU.
YOUR OWN MOTHER COULDN'T PUT UP WITH YOU SOMETIMES.
NOW YOU'S JUST EXAGGERATIN', FOOL.
WHAT?
THUG 4 LIFE
YOUR HONOR, CLYDE WOULD LIKE TO BE AN EMANCIPATED MINOR. GO 'HEAD, BOY, TELL THE JUDGE YOU WANNA MAKE YOUR OWN DECISIONS FROM NOW ON. TELL HIM!
@#*!

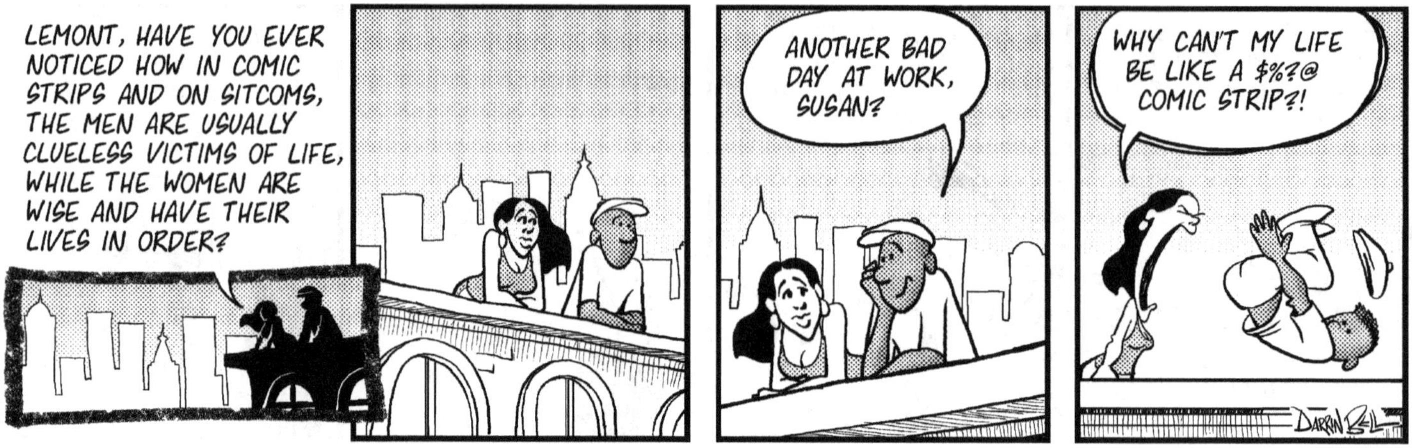
LEMONT, HAVE YOU EVER NOTICED HOW IN COMIC STRIPS AND ON SITCOMS, THE MEN ARE USUALLY CLUELESS VICTIMS OF LIFE, WHILE THE WOMEN ARE WISE AND HAVE THEIR LIVES IN ORDER?
ANOTHER BAD DAY AT WORK, SUSAN?
WHY CAN'T MY LIFE BE LIKE A $%?@ COMIC STRIP?!
DARRIN BELL

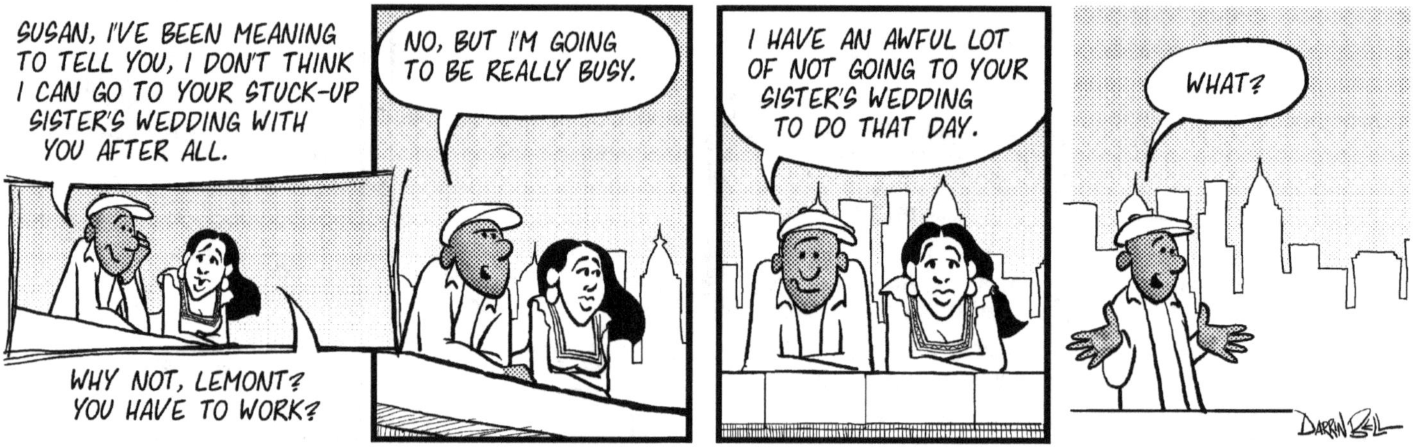
SUSAN, I'VE BEEN MEANING TO TELL YOU, I DON'T THINK I CAN GO TO YOUR STUCK-UP SISTER'S WEDDING WITH YOU AFTER ALL.
WHY NOT, LEMONT? YOU HAVE TO WORK?
NO, BUT I'M GOING TO BE REALLY BUSY.
I HAVE AN AWFUL LOT OF NOT GOING TO YOUR SISTER'S WEDDING TO DO THAT DAY.
WHAT?
DARRIN BELL

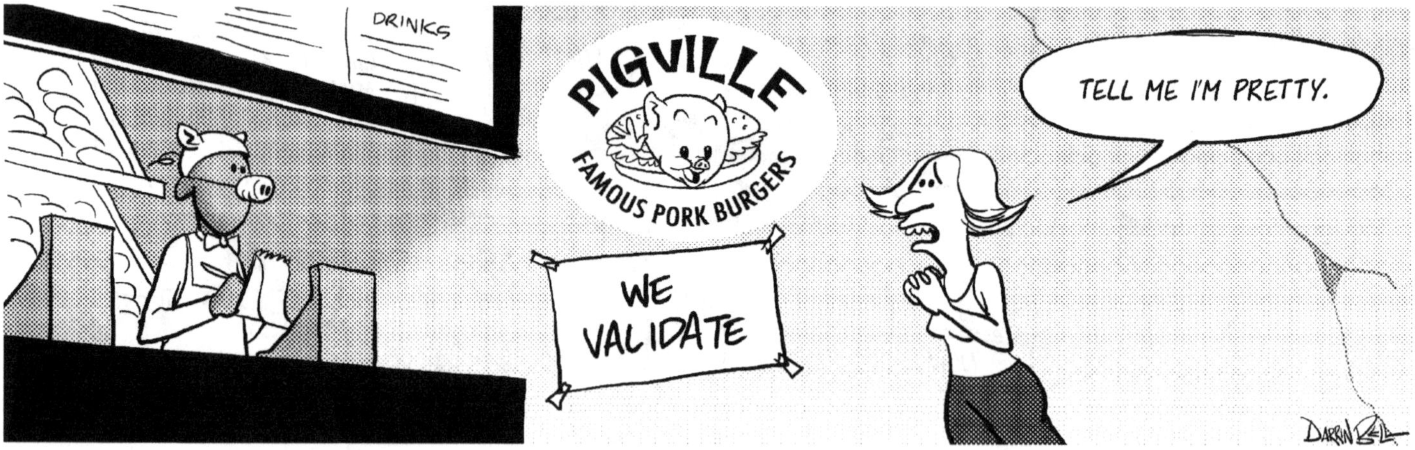
DRINKS
PIGVILLE
FAMOUS PORK BURGERS
WE VALIDATE
TELL ME I'M PRETTY.
DARRIN BELL

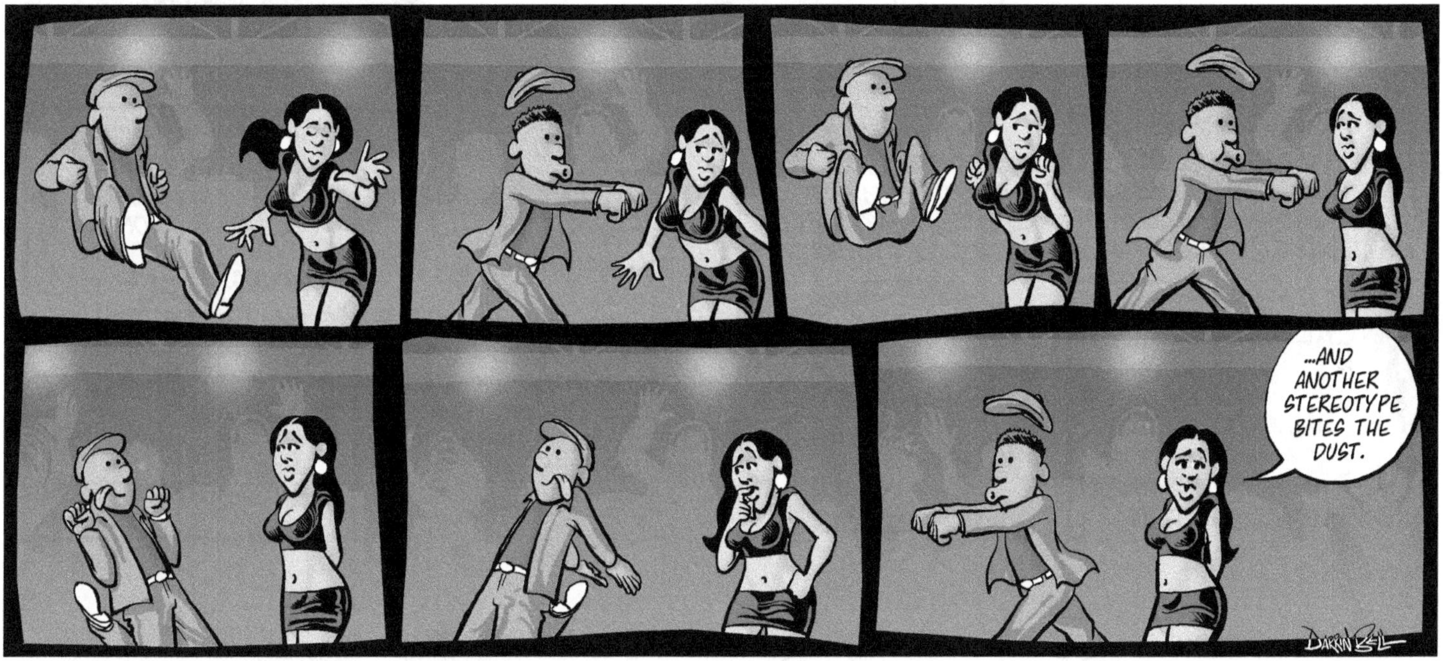
...AND ANOTHER STEREOTYPE BITES THE DUST.
DARRIN BELL

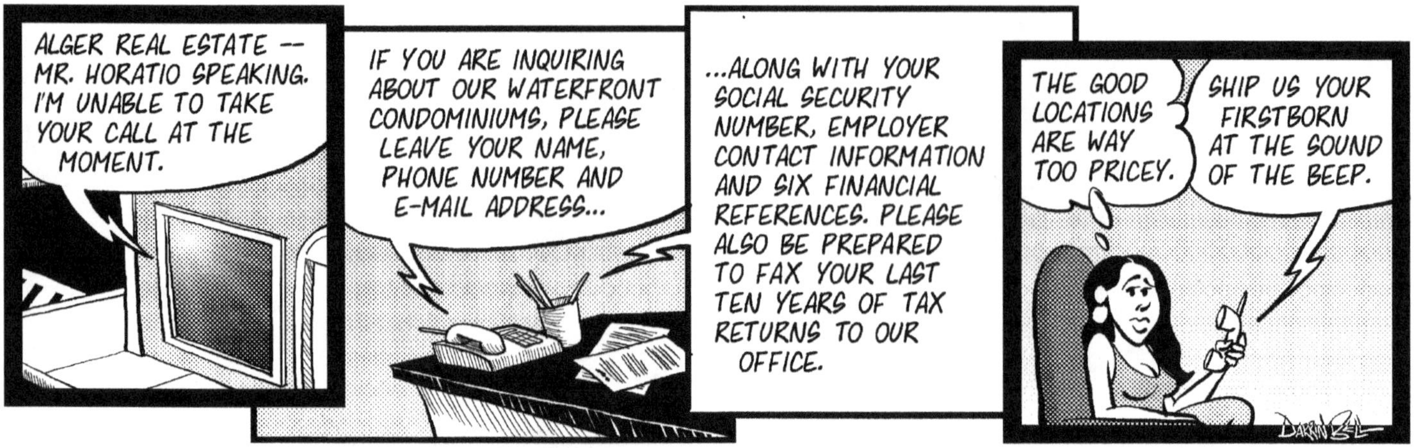
ALGER REAL ESTATE -- MR. HORATIO SPEAKING. I'M UNABLE TO TAKE YOUR CALL AT THE MOMENT.
IF YOU ARE INQUIRING ABOUT OUR WATERFRONT CONDOMINIUMS, PLEASE LEAVE YOUR NAME, PHONE NUMBER AND E-MAIL ADDRESS...
...ALONG WITH YOUR SOCIAL SECURITY NUMBER, EMPLOYER CONTACT INFORMATION AND SIX FINANCIAL REFERENCES. PLEASE ALSO BE PREPARED TO FAX YOUR LAST TEN YEARS OF TAX RETURNS TO OUR OFFICE.
THE GOOD LOCATIONS ARE WAY TOO PRICEY.
SHIP US YOUR FIRSTBORN AT THE SOUND OF THE BEEP.
DARRIN BELL

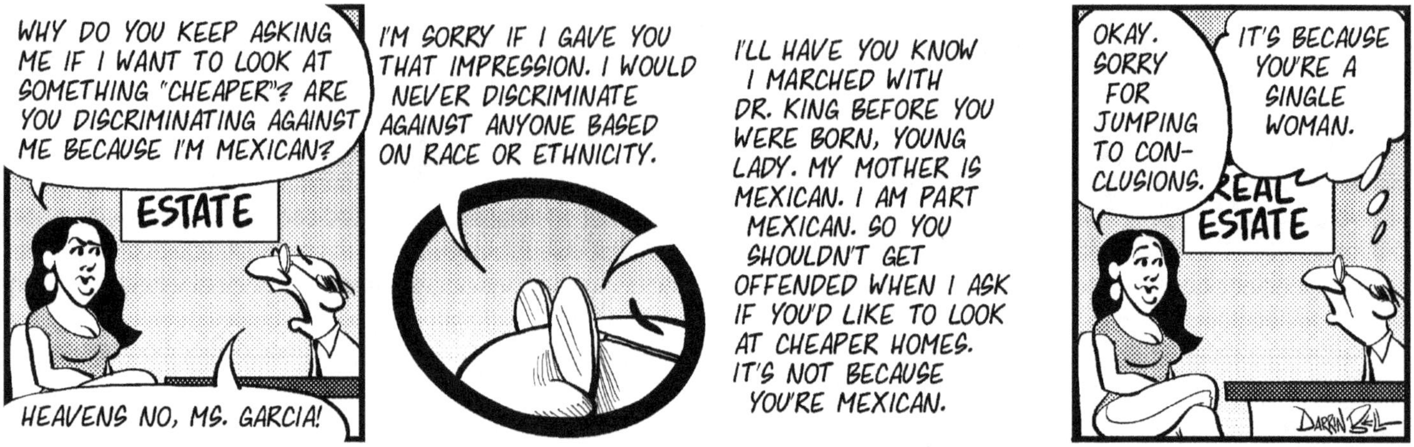
WHY DO YOU KEEP ASKING ME IF I WANT TO LOOK AT SOMETHING "CHEAPER"? ARE YOU DISCRIMINATING AGAINST ME BECAUSE I'M MEXICAN?
ESTATE
HEAVENS NO, MS. GARCIA!
I'M SORRY IF I GAVE YOU THAT IMPRESSION. I WOULD NEVER DISCRIMINATE AGAINST ANYONE BASED ON RACE OR ETHNICITY.
I'LL HAVE YOU KNOW I MARCHED WITH DR. KING BEFORE YOU WERE BORN, YOUNG LADY. MY MOTHER IS MEXICAN. I AM PART MEXICAN. SO YOU SHOULDN'T GET OFFENDED WHEN I ASK IF YOU'D LIKE TO LOOK AT CHEAPER HOMES. IT'S NOT BECAUSE YOU'RE MEXICAN.
OKAY. SORRY FOR JUMPING TO CONCLUSIONS.
IT'S BECAUSE YOU'RE A SINGLE WOMAN.
REAL ESTATE
DARRIN BELL

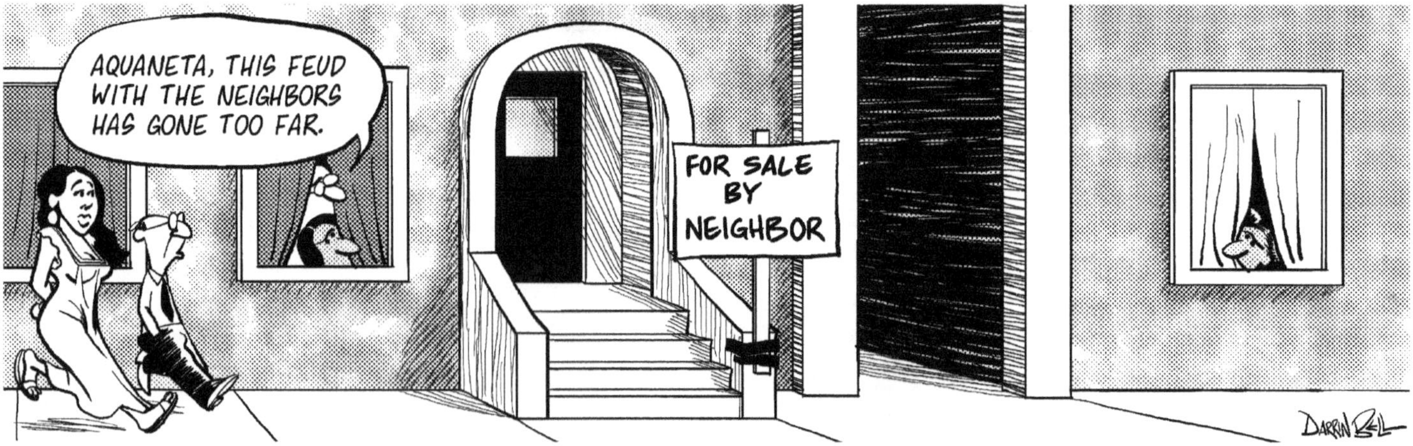
AQUANETA, THIS FEUD WITH THE NEIGHBORS HAS GONE TOO FAR.
FOR SALE BY NEIGHBOR
DARRIN BELL

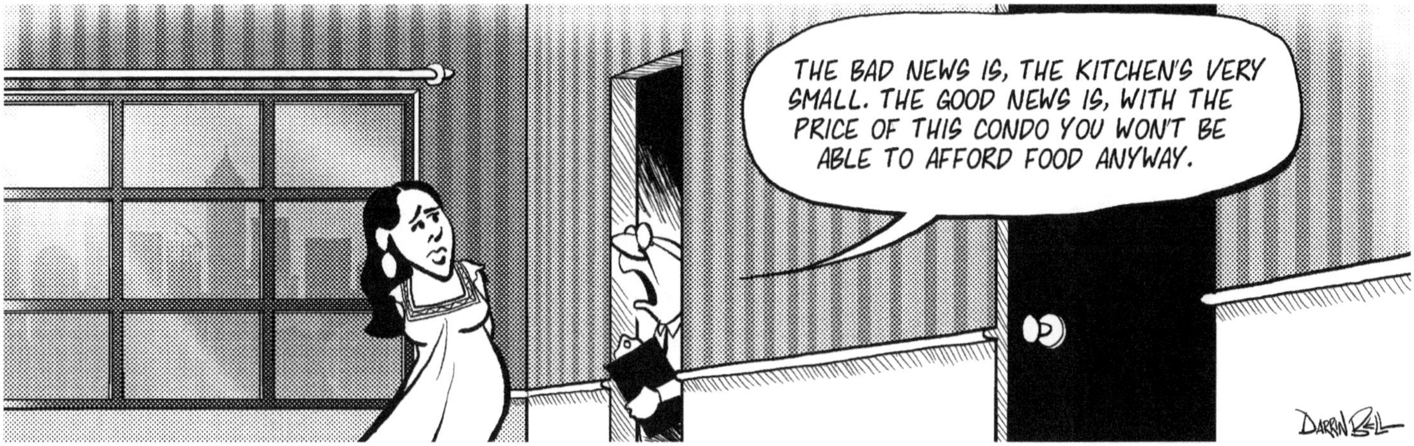
THE BAD NEWS IS, THE KITCHEN'S VERY SMALL. THE GOOD NEWS IS, WITH THE PRICE OF THIS CONDO YOU WON'T BE ABLE TO AFFORD FOOD ANYWAY.
DARRIN BELL

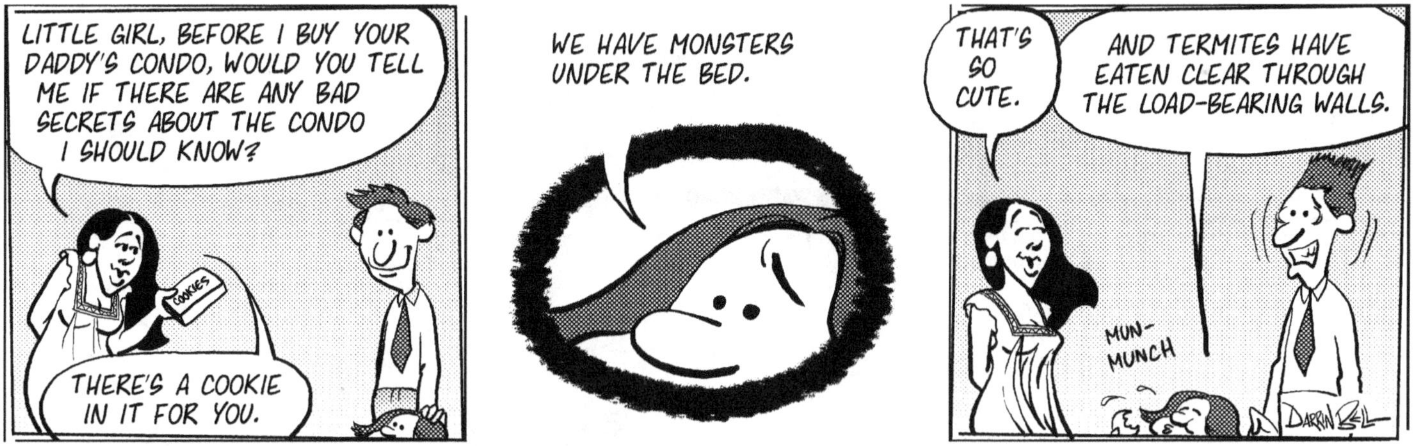
LITTLE GIRL, BEFORE I BUY YOUR DADDY'S CONDO, WOULD YOU TELL ME IF THERE ARE ANY BAD SECRETS ABOUT THE CONDO I SHOULD KNOW?
COOKIES
THERE'S A COOKIE IN IT FOR YOU.
WE HAVE MONSTERS UNDER THE BED.
THAT'S SO CUTE.
AND TERMITES HAVE EATEN CLEAR THROUGH THE LOAD-BEARING WALLS.
MUN-MUNCH
DARRIN BELL

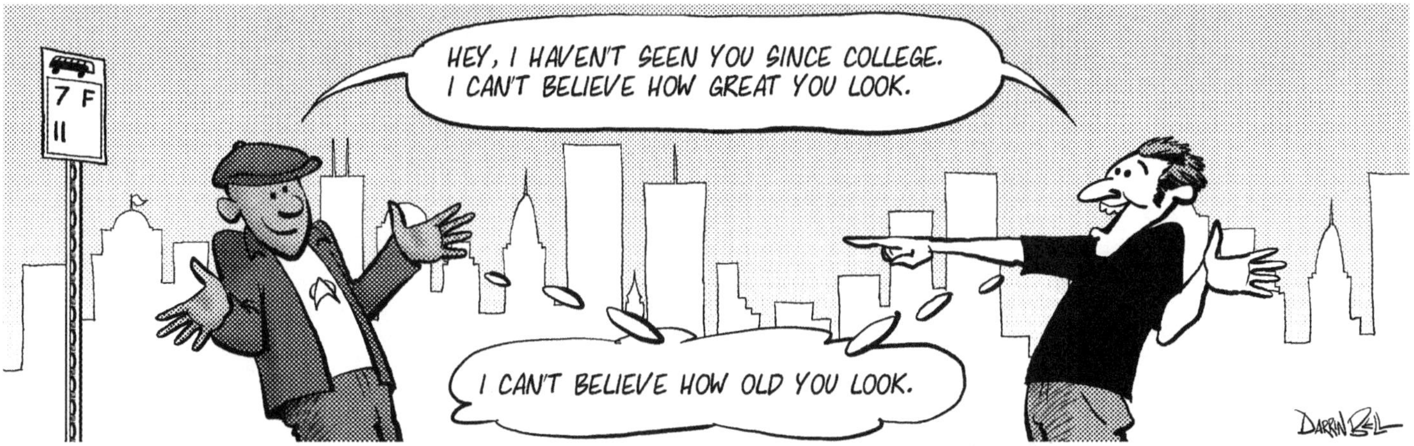
7 F
11
HEY, I HAVEN'T SEEN YOU SINCE COLLEGE. I CAN'T BELIEVE HOW GREAT YOU LOOK.
I CAN'T BELIEVE HOW OLD YOU LOOK.
DARRIN BELL

WHY SUSAN, YOU'VE DYED YOUR HAIR BLONDE.
THAT'S RIGHT, LEMONT. AND IF YOU DON'T LIKE IT YOU CAN BLAME SOCIETY.
BLONDES DON'T JUST HAVE MORE FUN -- THEY ALSO MAKE MORE MONEY, THEY GET MORE ATTENTION, MORE RESPECT AND GENERALLY LEAD HAPPIER, MORE SUCCESSFUL LIVES.
IF YOU'RE A WOMAN WITH GOLDEN HAIR, PEOPLE WILL THINK YOU'RE BEAUTIFUL EVEN IF YOU'VE GOT THE FACE OF A DERANGED MIDDLE-AGED COCKER SPANIEL.
IF YOU'RE A MEDIOCRE POP SINGER, YOU'D BETTER BE BLONDE OR PEOPLE WILL NOTICE YOU SOUND LIKE A FLATULENT MOOSE.
IT'S NOT FAIR! IS THIS WHAT IT'S GOING TO TAKE TO GET AHEAD IN THE WORLD?
Y'KNOW, I NEVER NOTICED HOW HOT YOU ARE.
@#$%? SOCIETY!
DARRIN BELL

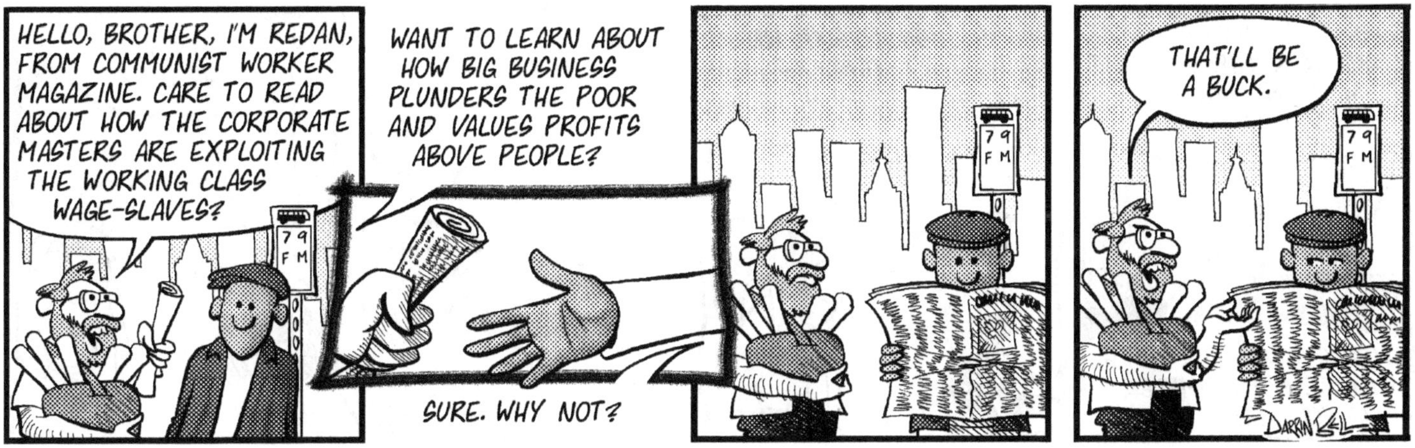
HELLO, BROTHER, I'M REDAN, FROM COMMUNIST WORKER MAGAZINE. CARE TO READ ABOUT HOW THE CORPORATE MASTERS ARE EXPLOITING THE WORKING CLASS WAGE-SLAVES?
WANT TO LEARN ABOUT HOW BIG BUSINESS PLUNDERS THE POOR AND VALUES PROFITS ABOVE PEOPLE?
SURE. WHY NOT?
THAT'LL BE A BUCK.
DARRIN BELL

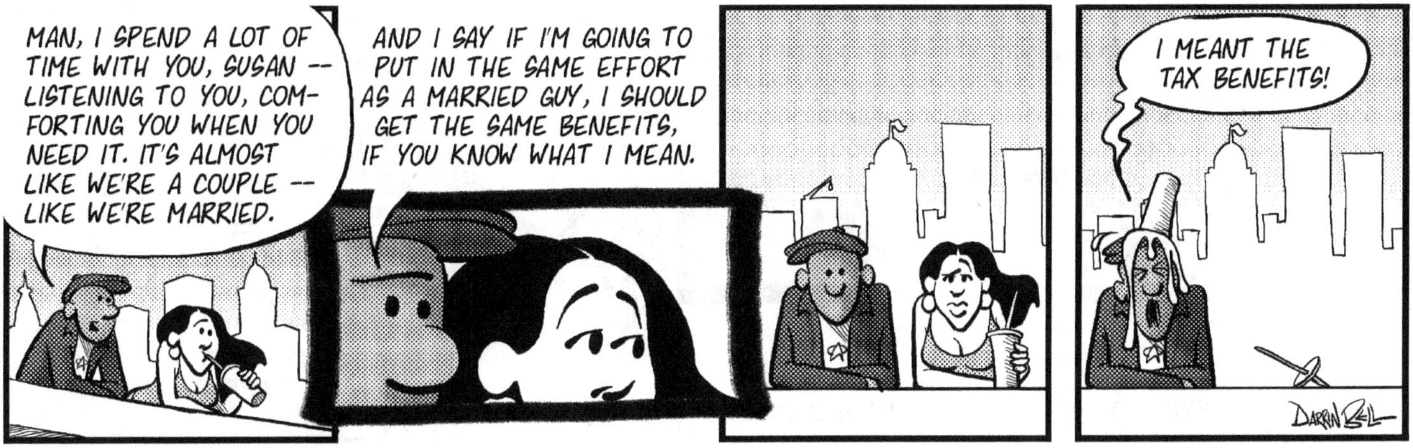
MAN, I SPEND A LOT OF TIME WITH YOU, SUSAN -- LISTENING TO YOU, COMFORTING YOU WHEN YOU NEED IT. IT'S ALMOST LIKE WE'RE A COUPLE -- LIKE WE'RE MARRIED.
AND I SAY IF I'M GOING TO PUT IN THE SAME EFFORT AS A MARRIED GUY, I SHOULD GET THE SAME BENEFITS, IF YOU KNOW WHAT I MEAN.
I MEANT THE TAX BENEFITS!
DARRIN BELL

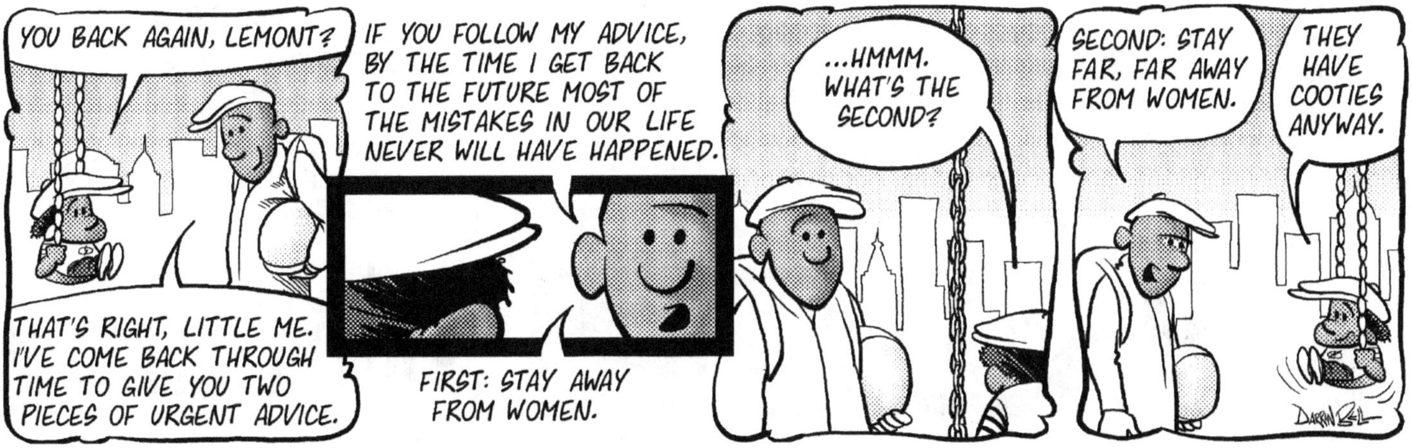
YOU BACK AGAIN, LEMONT?
THAT'S RIGHT, LITTLE ME. I'VE COME BACK THROUGH TIME TO GIVE YOU TWO PIECES OF URGENT ADVICE.
IF YOU FOLLOW MY ADVICE, BY THE TIME I GET BACK TO THE FUTURE MOST OF THE MISTAKES IN OUR LIFE NEVER WILL HAVE HAPPENED.
FIRST: STAY AWAY FROM WOMEN.
...HMMM. WHAT'S THE SECOND?
SECOND: STAY FAR, FAR AWAY FROM WOMEN.
THEY HAVE COOTIES ANYWAY.
DARRIN BELL

...SO YOU'RE SAYING YOU'VE COME BACK THROUGH TIME TO WARN ME NOT TO GET INVOLVED WITH WOMEN.
THAT'S RIGHT. OUR LIVES WILL BE MUCH SIMPLER IF YOU DON'T.
HMMM... HOW TO EXPLAIN THIS TO A 7-YEAR-OLD... BACK WHEN I WAS HIM, CHILDREN WERE MORE INNOCENT THAN THEY ARE TODAY.
KIDS WERE SO INNOCENT BACK THEN THAT HE PROBABLY WON'T EVEN KNOW WHAT I'M TALKING ABOUT.
WHY? ARE WE GAY?

YO, FUTURE ME, I SAID: DO I TURN OUT TO BE GAY?
NOW HOLD ON A MINUTE, LEMONT. THIS IS ALL WRONG.
YOU'RE ME AT AGE SEVEN. I DON'T REMEMBER EVEN KNOWING WHAT "GAY" MEANT WHEN I WAS SEVEN. WHEN I WAS A KID, KIDS WERE INNOCENT AND PURE.
WE DIDN'T KNOW ABOUT SEXUAL ORIENTATION - OR EVEN SEX, FOR THAT MATTER, UNTIL WE WERE MUCH OLDER.
NOTE TO SELF: DON'T REPRESS MEMORIES.
I DON'T REMEMBER KNOWING WHAT "REPRESSED MEMORIES" MEANT.

DO YOU REMEMBER DEION SANDERS AND BO JACKSON? THEY PLAYED BOTH MAJOR LEAGUE FOOTBALL AND MAJOR LEAGUE BASEBALL.
THEY PROVED THAT THE HUMAN SPIRIT NEEDN'T BE LIMITED TO ONE PATH -- THAT IF THEY HAD FAITH IN THEMSELVES THEY COULD BECOME MASTERS OF NOT ONE, BUT TWO WALKS OF LIFE!
...LEMONT, I STILL DON'T THINK YOU'RE ACCOMPLISHING MUCH BY WORKING AT BOTH PIGVILLE AND BURGER QUEEN.
YOU'RE SO LIMITED, SUSAN.

I THINK I MAY HAVE RUINED SUSAN'S LIFE, CLYDE.

WUZZAT, LEMONT?

"LAST WEEK SHE DYED HER HAIR BLONDE. I THOUGHT IT LOOKED AWFUL, BUT I WAS IN SHOCK AND DIDN'T WANT TO HURT HER FEELINGS -- SO I LIED AND SAID IT LOOKED GREAT."

BECAUSE I SAID IT LOOKED GREAT, SHE'S PROBABLY GOING TO KEEP DYING IT BLONDE FROM NOW ON. SINCE IT LOOKS BAD, SHE'LL BECOME THE BUTT OF JOKES AT THE OFFICE. SHE'LL LOSE THEIR RESPECT AND WON'T GET THAT PROMOTION SHE'S AFTER.

...AND SHE PROBABLY WON'T ATTRACT A MAN, EITHER.

SHE'LL FAIL AT WORK, SHE WON'T FIND THE MAN OF HER DREAMS AND SHE'LL DIE MISERABLE, POOR AND ALONE -- ALL BECAUSE I LIED AND SAID HER BAD DYE JOB LOOKS GOOD.

WHAT DO YOU THINK, CLYDE?

I THINK YOU HAVE A PRETTY BIG OPINION OF YOUR OWN OPINION.

OH DEAR GOD -- BECAUSE OF ME, HER CHILDREN WILL NEVER BE BORN.

DARRIN BELL

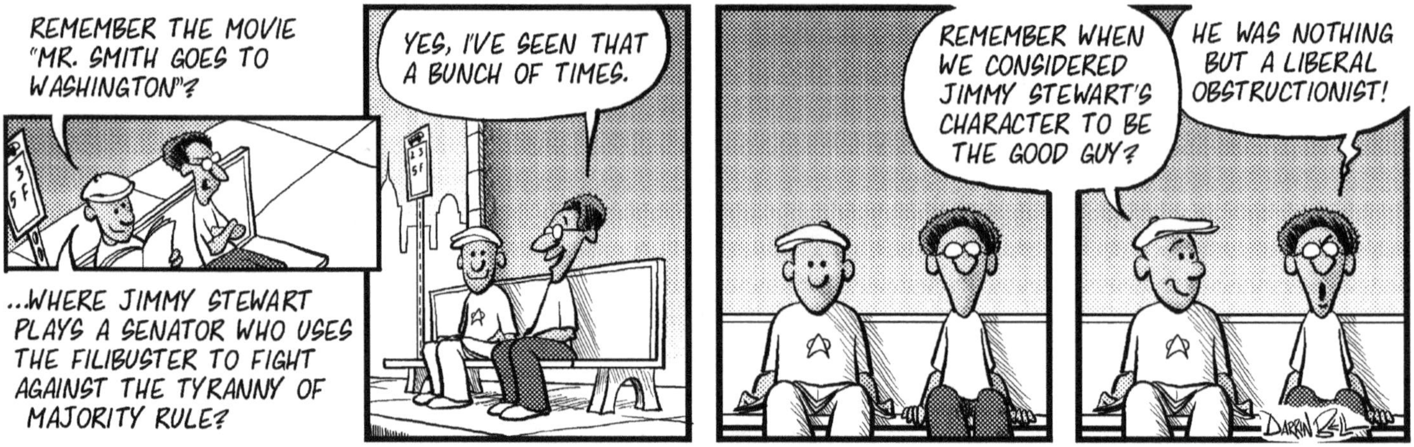
REMEMBER THE MOVIE "MR. SMITH GOES TO WASHINGTON"?
...WHERE JIMMY STEWART PLAYS A SENATOR WHO USES THE FILIBUSTER TO FIGHT AGAINST THE TYRANNY OF MAJORITY RULE?
YES, I'VE SEEN THAT A BUNCH OF TIMES.
REMEMBER WHEN WE CONSIDERED JIMMY STEWART'S CHARACTER TO BE THE GOOD GUY?
HE WAS NOTHING BUT A LIBERAL OBSTRUCTIONIST!
DARRIN BELL

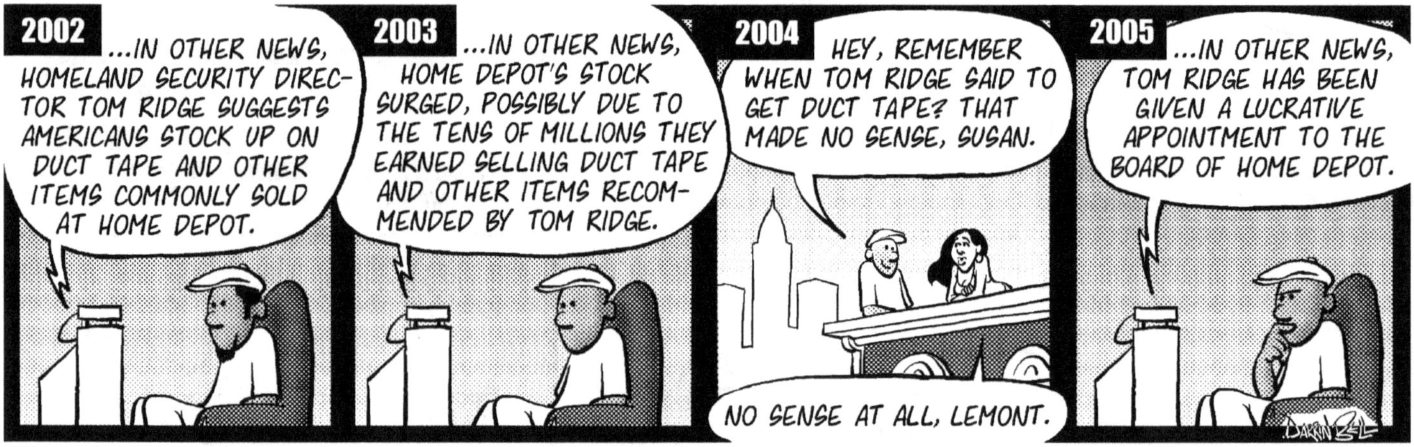
2002
...IN OTHER NEWS, HOMELAND SECURITY DIRECTOR TOM RIDGE SUGGESTS AMERICANS STOCK UP ON DUCT TAPE AND OTHER ITEMS COMMONLY SOLD AT HOME DEPOT.
2003
...IN OTHER NEWS, HOME DEPOT'S STOCK SURGED, POSSIBLY DUE TO THE TENS OF MILLIONS THEY EARNED SELLING DUCT TAPE AND OTHER ITEMS RECOMMENDED BY TOM RIDGE.
2004
HEY, REMEMBER WHEN TOM RIDGE SAID TO GET DUCT TAPE? THAT MADE NO SENSE, SUSAN.
NO SENSE AT ALL, LEMONT.
2005
...IN OTHER NEWS, TOM RIDGE HAS BEEN GIVEN A LUCRATIVE APPOINTMENT TO THE BOARD OF HOME DEPOT.
DARRIN BELL

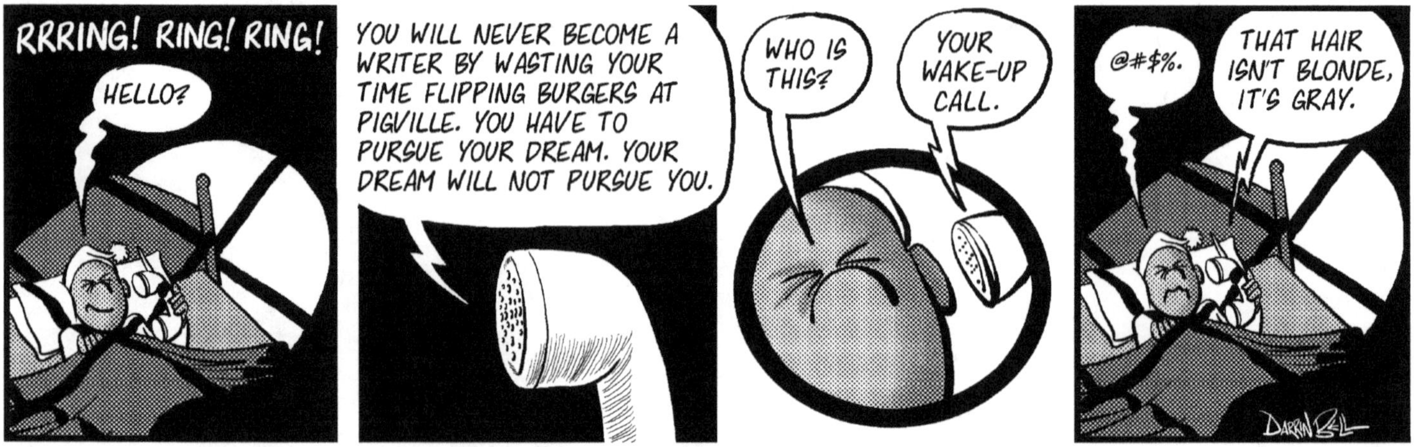
RRRING! RING! RING!
HELLO?
YOU WILL NEVER BECOME A WRITER BY WASTING YOUR TIME FLIPPING BURGERS AT PIGVILLE. YOU HAVE TO PURSUE YOUR DREAM. YOUR DREAM WILL NOT PURSUE YOU.
WHO IS THIS?
YOUR WAKE-UP CALL.
@#$%.
THAT HAIR ISN'T BLONDE, IT'S GRAY.
DARRIN BELL

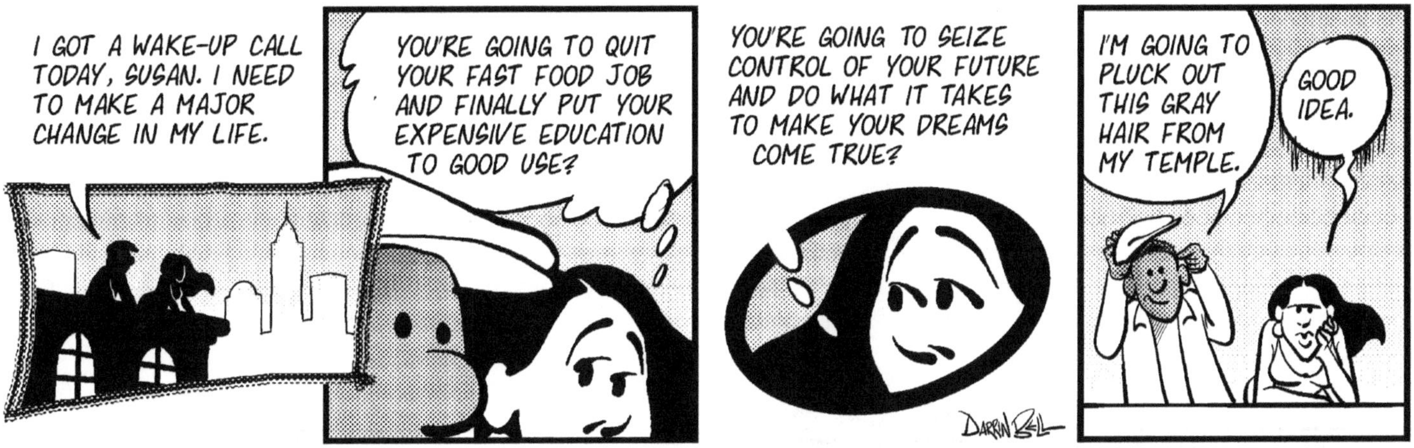
I GOT A WAKE-UP CALL TODAY, SUSAN. I NEED TO MAKE A MAJOR CHANGE IN MY LIFE.
YOU'RE GOING TO QUIT YOUR FAST FOOD JOB AND FINALLY PUT YOUR EXPENSIVE EDUCATION TO GOOD USE?
YOU'RE GOING TO SEIZE CONTROL OF YOUR FUTURE AND DO WHAT IT TAKES TO MAKE YOUR DREAMS COME TRUE?
I'M GOING TO PLUCK OUT THIS GRAY HAIR FROM MY TEMPLE.
GOOD IDEA.

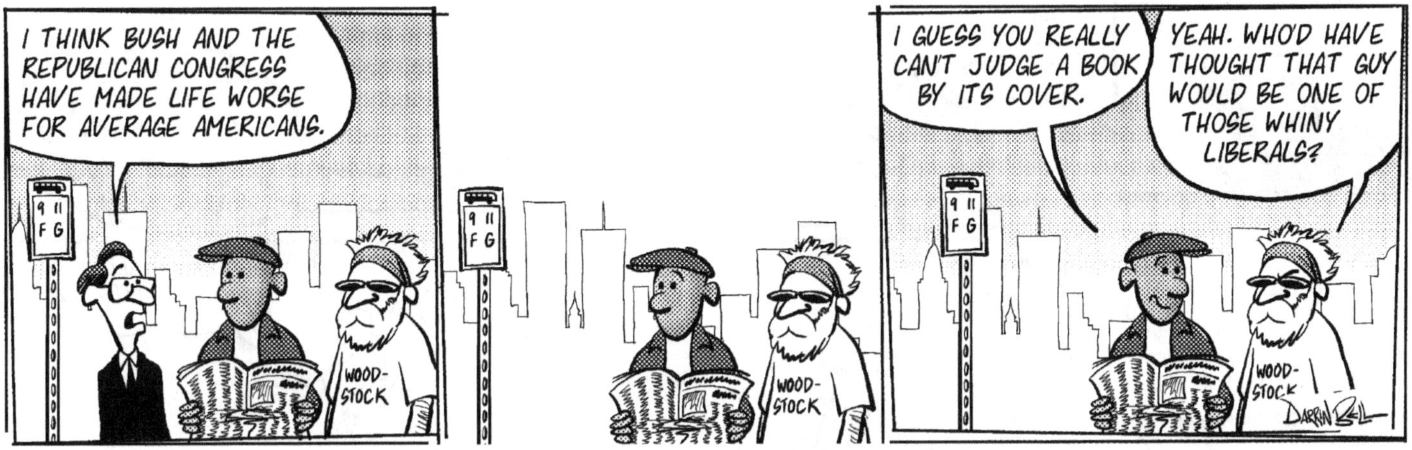
I THINK BUSH AND THE REPUBLICAN CONGRESS HAVE MADE LIFE WORSE FOR AVERAGE AMERICANS.
9 11
F G
WOOD-STOCK
I GUESS YOU REALLY CAN'T JUDGE A BOOK BY ITS COVER.
YEAH. WHO'D HAVE THOUGHT THAT GUY WOULD BE ONE OF THOSE WHINY LIBERALS?

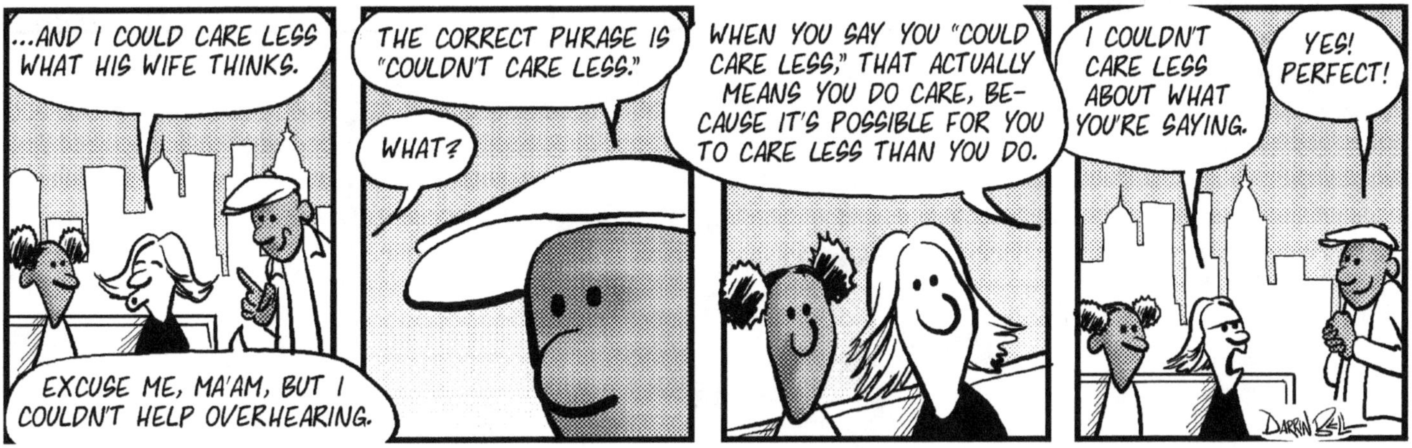
...AND I COULD CARE LESS WHAT HIS WIFE THINKS.
EXCUSE ME, MA'AM, BUT I COULDN'T HELP OVERHEARING.
THE CORRECT PHRASE IS "COULDN'T CARE LESS."
WHAT?
WHEN YOU SAY YOU "COULD CARE LESS," THAT ACTUALLY MEANS YOU DO CARE, BECAUSE IT'S POSSIBLE FOR YOU TO CARE LESS THAN YOU DO.
I COULDN'T CARE LESS ABOUT WHAT YOU'RE SAYING.
YES! PERFECT!

MAN, I WISH I'D NEVER LIED TO SUSAN. I SHOULDN'T HAVE SAID I LIKED HER BLONDE DYE-JOB.

I REALLY THOUGHT IT LOOKED AWFUL. I SHOULD HAVE TOLD HER SO. FRIENDS SHOULD ALWAYS TELL EACH OTHER THE TRUTH.

BUT LOOK AT HER -- SHE LOVES IT. AND EVERYONE ELSE SEEMS TO THINK IT LOOKS GOOD, TOO.

I GUESS I SHOULD JUST BE SUPPORTIVE AND NOT TELL HER WHAT I REALLY THINK ABOUT HER HAIR.

SHE'S HAPPY WITH HER HAIR, SO THE ONLY REASON TO TELL HER WHAT I REALLY THINK, AND RUIN HER HAPPINESS, WOULD BE TO ASSUAGE MY OWN GUILT ABOUT LYING -- TO MAKE MYSELF FEEL BETTER. AND THAT WOULD JUST BE SELFISH.

WELL I FEEL MUCH BETTER.

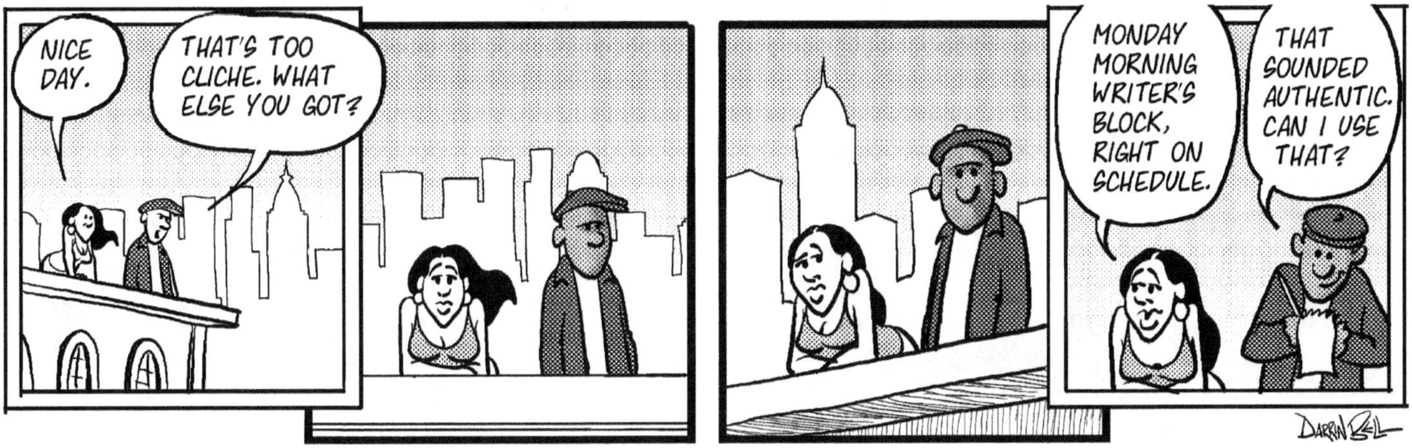
NICE DAY.
THAT'S TOO CLICHE. WHAT ELSE YOU GOT?
MONDAY MORNING WRITER'S BLOCK, RIGHT ON SCHEDULE.
THAT SOUNDED AUTHENTIC. CAN I USE THAT?
DARRIN BELL

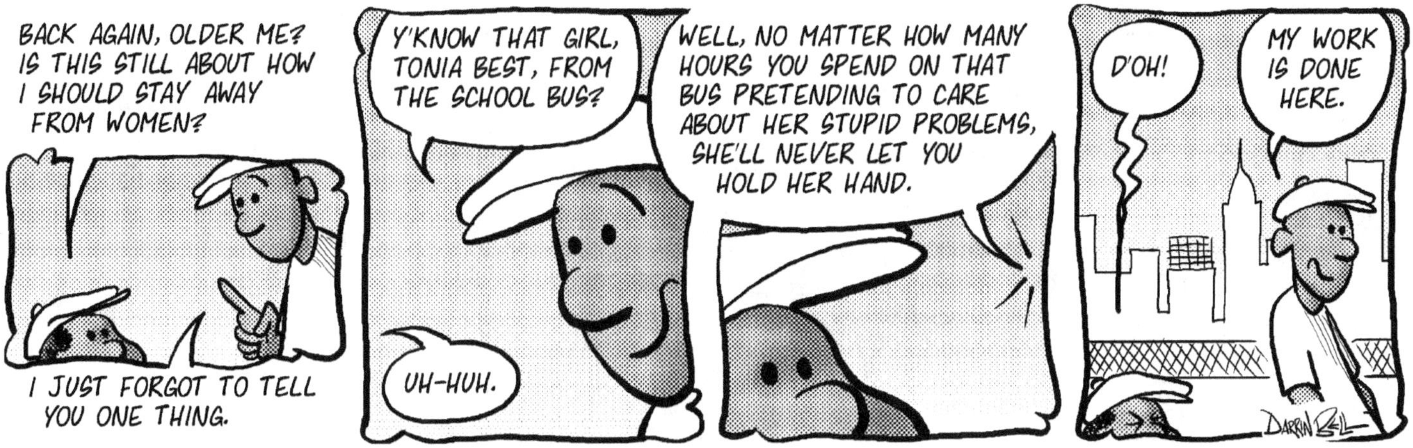
BACK AGAIN, OLDER ME? IS THIS STILL ABOUT HOW I SHOULD STAY AWAY FROM WOMEN?
I JUST FORGOT TO TELL YOU ONE THING.
Y'KNOW THAT GIRL, TONIA BEST, FROM THE SCHOOL BUS?
UH-HUH.
WELL, NO MATTER HOW MANY HOURS YOU SPEND ON THAT BUS PRETENDING TO CARE ABOUT HER STUPID PROBLEMS, SHE'LL NEVER LET YOU HOLD HER HAND.
D'OH!
MY WORK IS DONE HERE.
DARRIN BELL

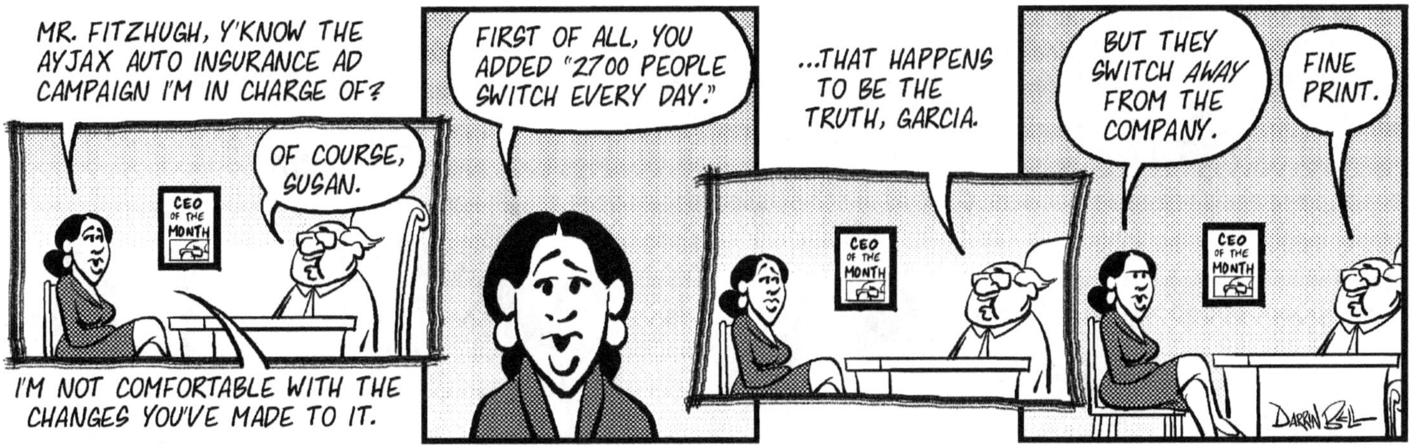
MR. FITZHUGH, Y'KNOW THE AYJAX AUTO INSURANCE AD CAMPAIGN I'M IN CHARGE OF?
OF COURSE, SUSAN.
CEO OF THE MONTH
I'M NOT COMFORTABLE WITH THE CHANGES YOU'VE MADE TO IT.
FIRST OF ALL, YOU ADDED "2700 PEOPLE SWITCH EVERY DAY."
...THAT HAPPENS TO BE THE TRUTH, GARCIA.
CEO OF THE MONTH
BUT THEY SWITCH AWAY FROM THE COMPANY.
FINE PRINT.
CEO OF THE MONTH
DARRIN BELL

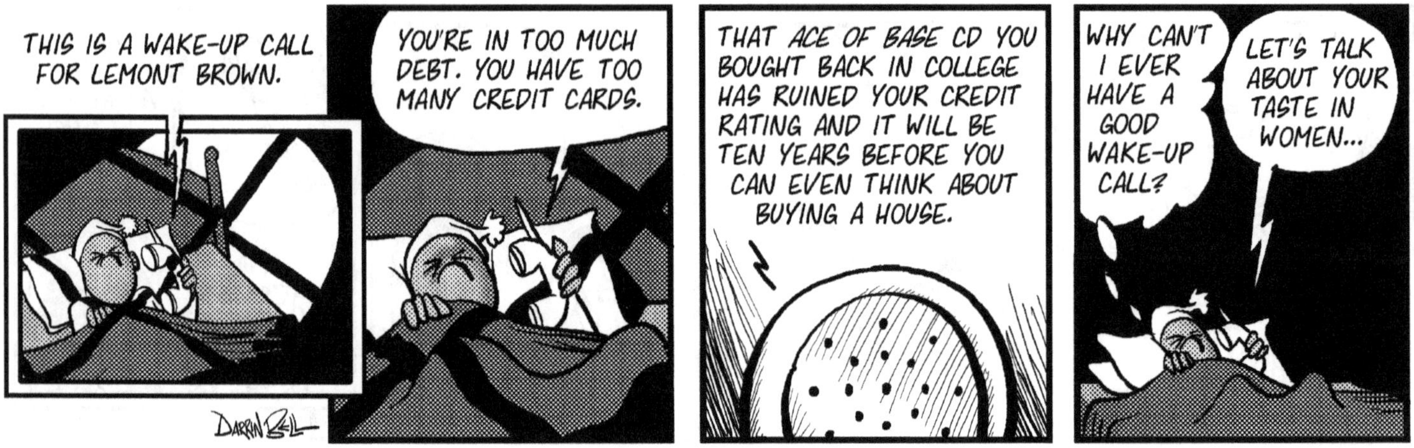
THIS IS A WAKE-UP CALL FOR LEMONT BROWN.
DARRIN BELL
YOU'RE IN TOO MUCH DEBT. YOU HAVE TOO MANY CREDIT CARDS.
THAT ACE OF BASE CD YOU BOUGHT BACK IN COLLEGE HAS RUINED YOUR CREDIT RATING AND IT WILL BE TEN YEARS BEFORE YOU CAN EVEN THINK ABOUT BUYING A HOUSE.
WHY CAN'T I EVER HAVE A GOOD WAKE-UP CALL?
LET'S TALK ABOUT YOUR TASTE IN WOMEN...

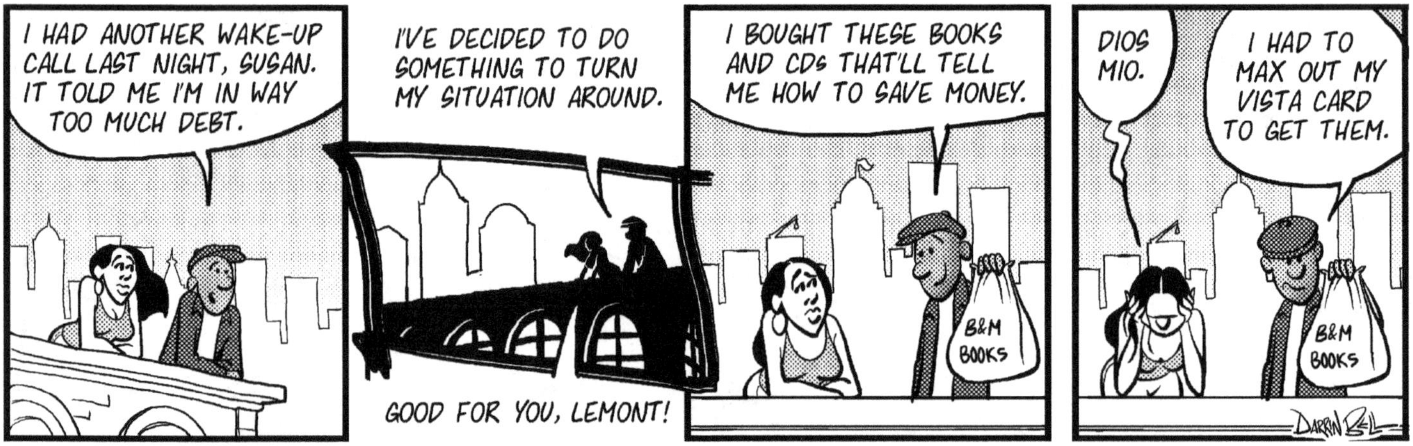
I HAD ANOTHER WAKE-UP CALL LAST NIGHT, SUSAN. IT TOLD ME I'M IN WAY TOO MUCH DEBT.
I'VE DECIDED TO DO SOMETHING TO TURN MY SITUATION AROUND.
GOOD FOR YOU, LEMONT!
I BOUGHT THESE BOOKS AND CDs THAT'LL TELL ME HOW TO SAVE MONEY.
B&M BOOKS
DIOS MIO.
I HAD TO MAX OUT MY VISTA CARD TO GET THEM.
B&M BOOKS
DARRIN BELL

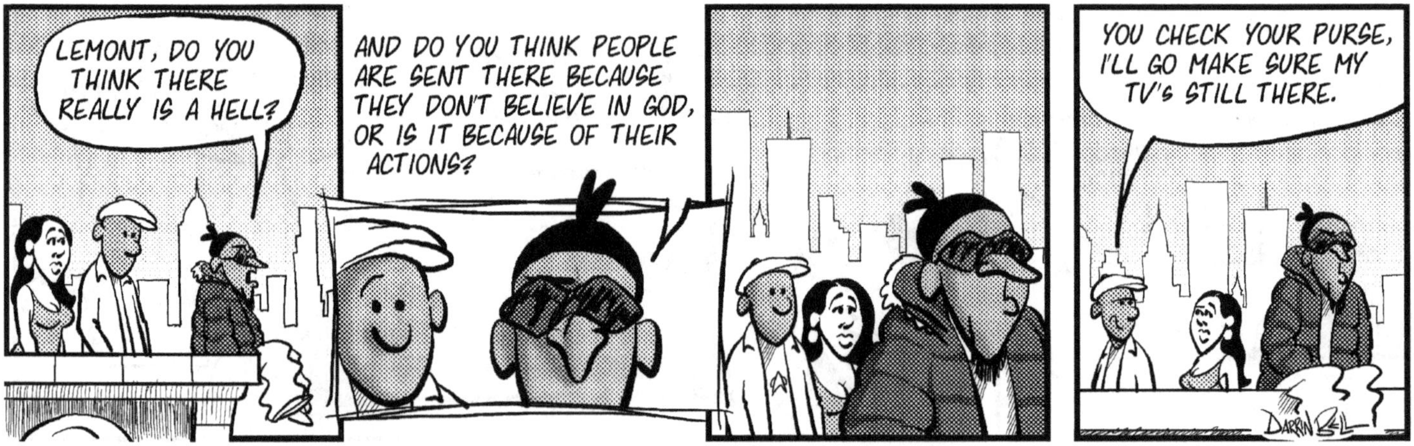
LEMONT, DO YOU THINK THERE REALLY IS A HELL?
AND DO YOU THINK PEOPLE ARE SENT THERE BECAUSE THEY DON'T BELIEVE IN GOD, OR IS IT BECAUSE OF THEIR ACTIONS?
YOU CHECK YOUR PURSE, I'LL GO MAKE SURE MY TV's STILL THERE.
DARRIN BELL

48 HOUR FITNESS
WHAT?
DARRIN BELL

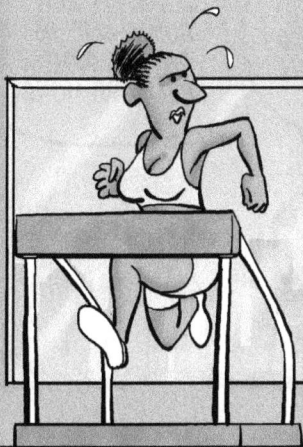

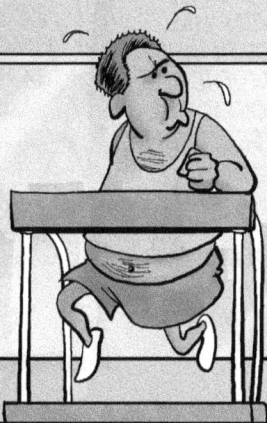

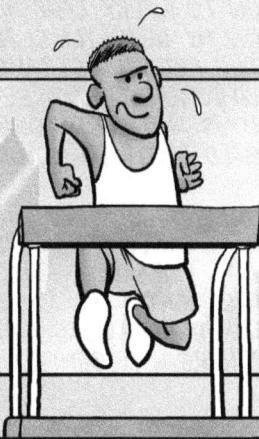

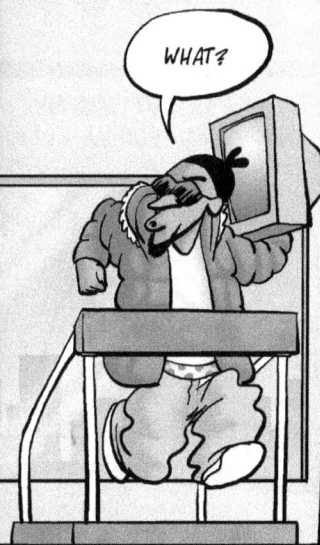

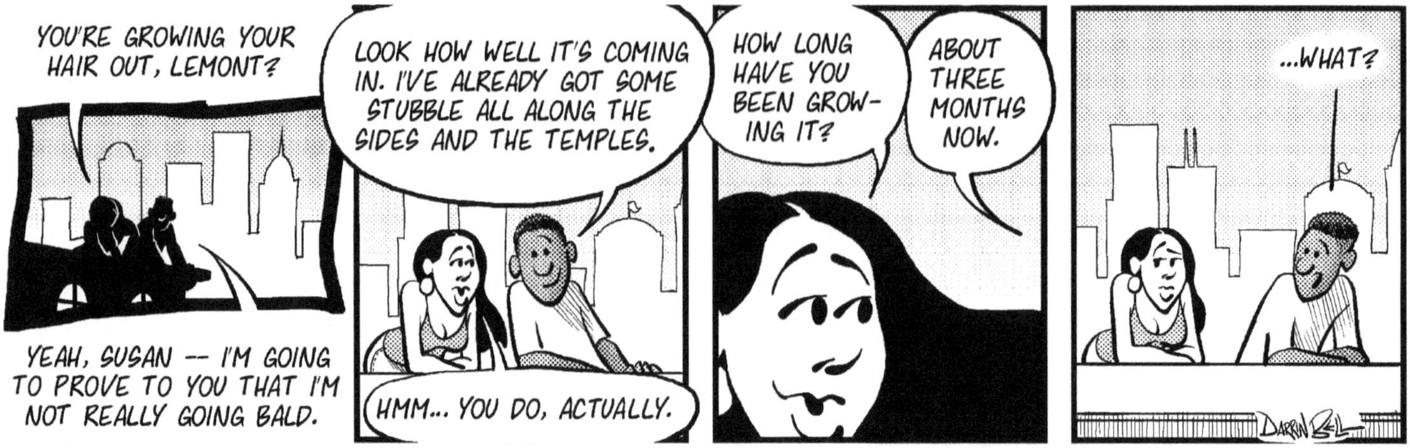
YOU'RE GROWING YOUR HAIR OUT, LEMONT?
YEAH, SUSAN -- I'M GOING TO PROVE TO YOU THAT I'M NOT REALLY GOING BALD.
LOOK HOW WELL IT'S COMING IN. I'VE ALREADY GOT SOME STUBBLE ALL ALONG THE SIDES AND THE TEMPLES.
HMM... YOU DO, ACTUALLY.
HOW LONG HAVE YOU BEEN GROW-ING IT?
ABOUT THREE MONTHS NOW.
...WHAT?
DARRIN BELL

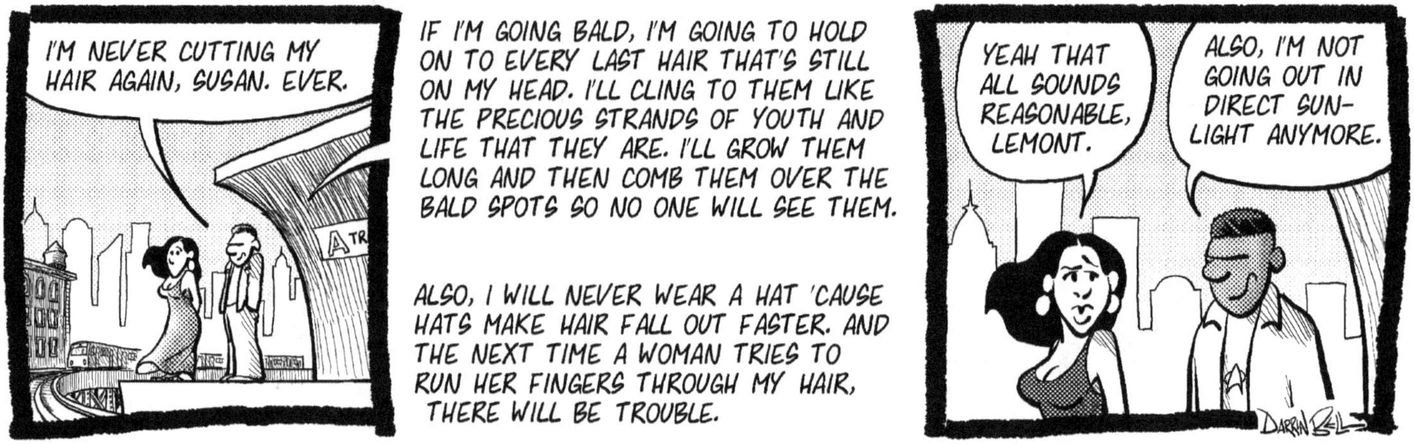
I'M NEVER CUTTING MY HAIR AGAIN, SUSAN. EVER.
IF I'M GOING BALD, I'M GOING TO HOLD ON TO EVERY LAST HAIR THAT'S STILL ON MY HEAD. I'LL CLING TO THEM LIKE THE PRECIOUS STRANDS OF YOUTH AND LIFE THAT THEY ARE. I'LL GROW THEM LONG AND THEN COMB THEM OVER THE BALD SPOTS SO NO ONE WILL SEE THEM.
ALSO, I WILL NEVER WEAR A HAT 'CAUSE HATS MAKE HAIR FALL OUT FASTER. AND THE NEXT TIME A WOMAN TRIES TO RUN HER FINGERS THROUGH MY HAIR, THERE WILL BE TROUBLE.
YEAH THAT ALL SOUNDS REASONABLE, LEMONT.
ALSO, I'M NOT GOING OUT IN DIRECT SUN-LIGHT ANYMORE.
DARRIN BELL

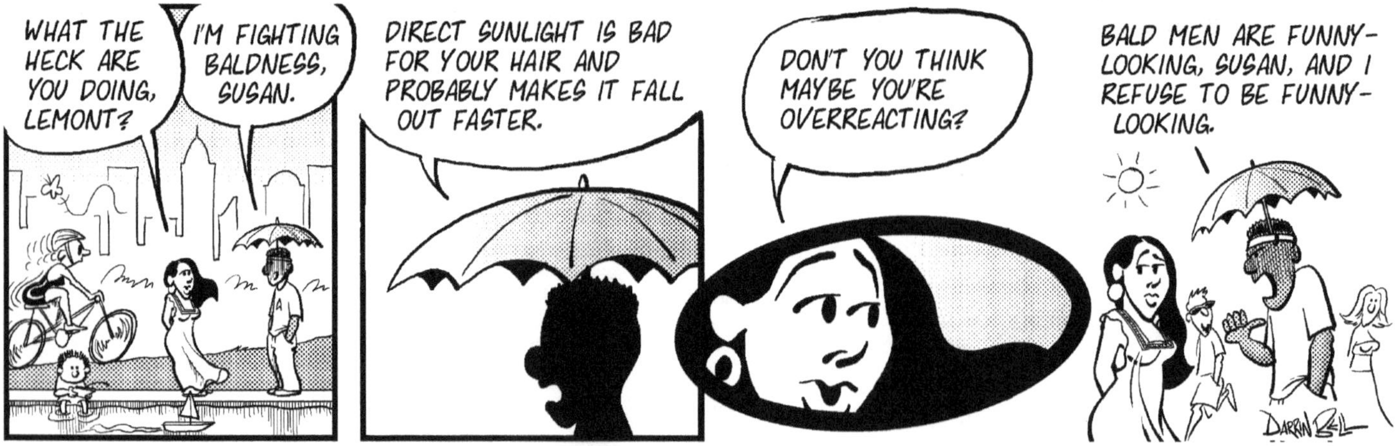
WHAT THE HECK ARE YOU DOING, LEMONT?
I'M FIGHTING BALDNESS, SUSAN.
DIRECT SUNLIGHT IS BAD FOR YOUR HAIR AND PROBABLY MAKES IT FALL OUT FASTER.
DON'T YOU THINK MAYBE YOU'RE OVERREACTING?
BALD MEN ARE FUNNY-LOOKING, SUSAN, AND I REFUSE TO BE FUNNY-LOOKING.
DARRIN BELL

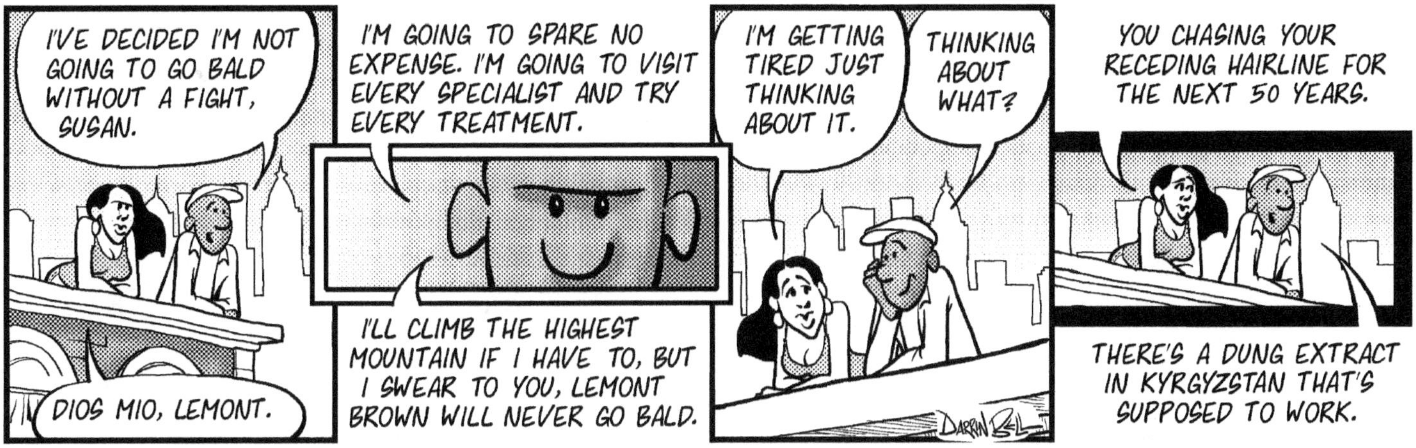
I'VE DECIDED I'M NOT GOING TO GO BALD WITHOUT A FIGHT, SUSAN.
DIOS MIO, LEMONT.
I'M GOING TO SPARE NO EXPENSE. I'M GOING TO VISIT EVERY SPECIALIST AND TRY EVERY TREATMENT.
I'LL CLIMB THE HIGHEST MOUNTAIN IF I HAVE TO, BUT I SWEAR TO YOU, LEMONT BROWN WILL NEVER GO BALD.
I'M GETTING TIRED JUST THINKING ABOUT IT.
THINKING ABOUT WHAT?
YOU CHASING YOUR RECEDING HAIRLINE FOR THE NEXT 50 YEARS.
THERE'S A DUNG EXTRACT IN KYRGYZSTAN THAT'S SUPPOSED TO WORK.
DARRIN BELL

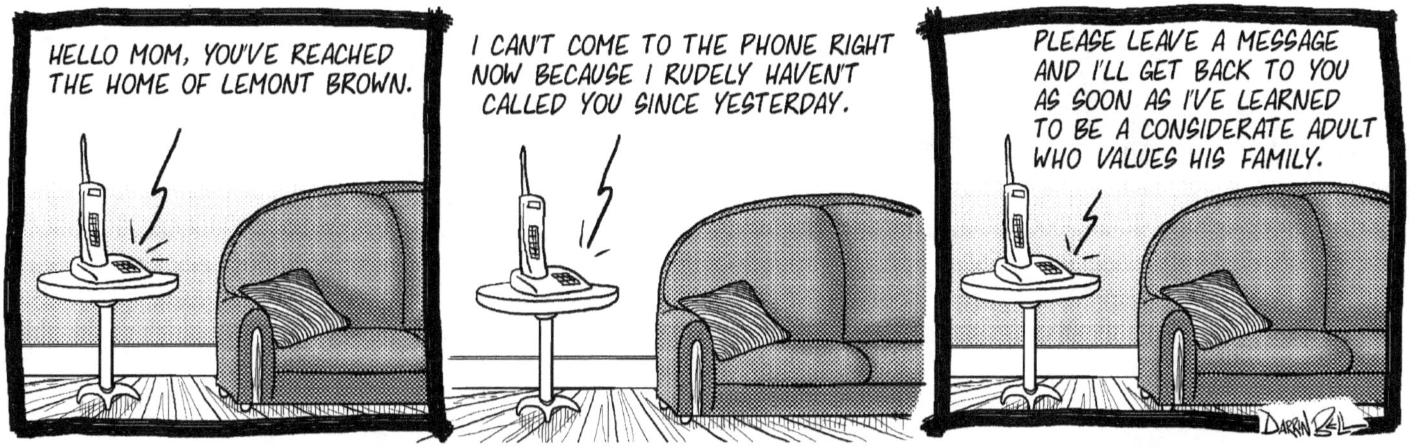
HELLO MOM, YOU'VE REACHED THE HOME OF LEMONT BROWN.
I CAN'T COME TO THE PHONE RIGHT NOW BECAUSE I RUDELY HAVEN'T CALLED YOU SINCE YESTERDAY.
PLEASE LEAVE A MESSAGE AND I'LL GET BACK TO YOU AS SOON AS I'VE LEARNED TO BE A CONSIDERATE ADULT WHO VALUES HIS FAMILY.
DARRIN BELL

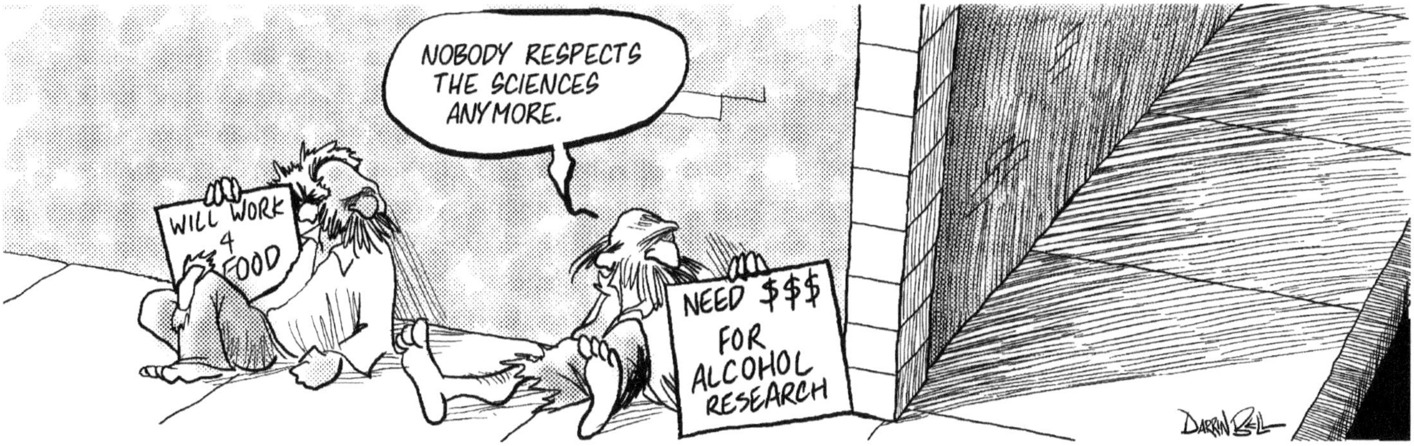
NOBODY RESPECTS THE SCIENCES ANYMORE.
WILL WORK 4 FOOD
NEED $$$ FOR ALCOHOL RESEARCH
DARRIN BELL

LEMONT, WHY DO YOU ALWAYS INSIST ON WALKING ON THE OUTSIDE OF THE SIDEWALK, CLOSER TO THE STREET?
IT'S AN OLD CUSTOM, SUSAN. IT'S CHIVALRY. IT SENDS A MESSAGE TO EVERY GUY OUT THERE THAT HE'D BETTER NOT MESS WITH YOU, 'CAUSE YOU'RE UNDER MY PROTECTION.
THE STREETS ARE VERY DIFFERENT PLACES FOR WOMEN THAN THEY ARE FOR MEN.
YOU'RE RIGHT. IF YOU'RE A WOMAN, EVERY STRANGE MAN YOU COME ACROSS ON THE STREET IS A POTENTIAL VICTIM.
DARRIN BELL
YOU MEAN "POTENTIAL ATTACKER."
THUMP!
WHAT WAS THAT YOU SAID?
I'M JUST HUMORING YOU BY LYING HERE MOTIONLESS.

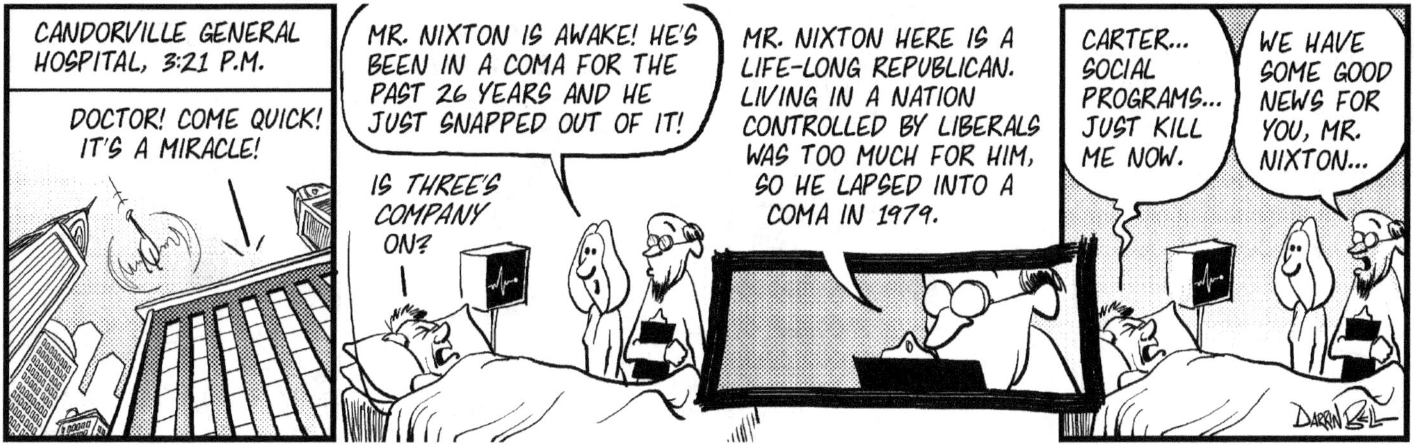
CANDORVILLE GENERAL HOSPITAL, 3:21 P.M.
DOCTOR! COME QUICK! IT'S A MIRACLE!
MR. NIXTON IS AWAKE! HE'S BEEN IN A COMA FOR THE PAST 26 YEARS AND HE JUST SNAPPED OUT OF IT!
IS THREE'S COMPANY ON?
MR. NIXTON HERE IS A LIFE-LONG REPUBLICAN. LIVING IN A NATION CONTROLLED BY LIBERALS WAS TOO MUCH FOR HIM, SO HE LAPSED INTO A COMA IN 1979.
CARTER... SOCIAL PROGRAMS... JUST KILL ME NOW.
WE HAVE SOME GOOD NEWS FOR YOU, MR. NIXTON...
DARRIN BELL

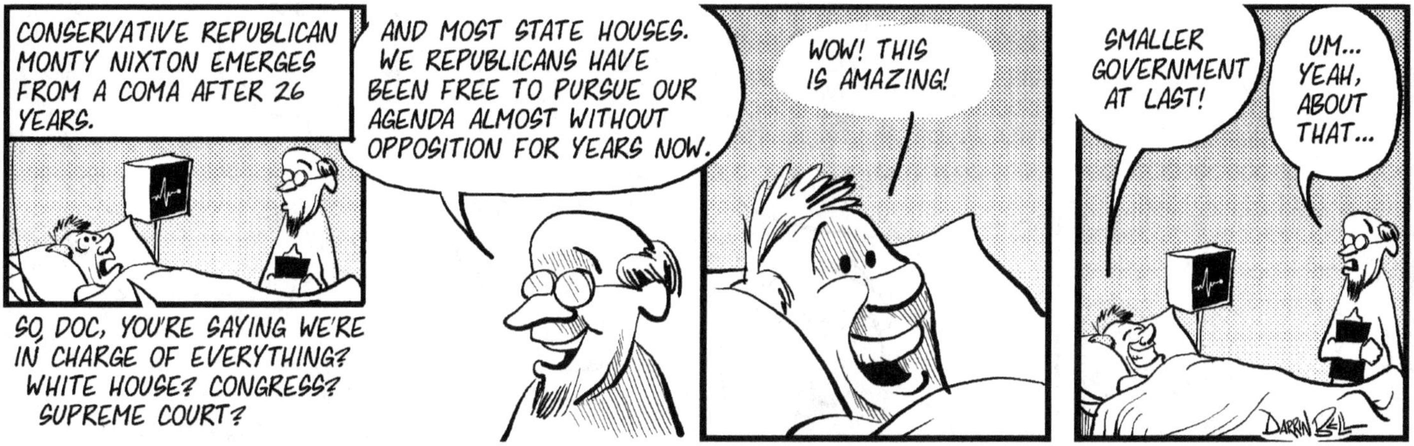
CONSERVATIVE REPUBLICAN MONTY NIXTON EMERGES FROM A COMA AFTER 26 YEARS.
SO, DOC, YOU'RE SAYING WE'RE IN CHARGE OF EVERYTHING? WHITE HOUSE? CONGRESS? SUPREME COURT?
AND MOST STATE HOUSES. WE REPUBLICANS HAVE BEEN FREE TO PURSUE OUR AGENDA ALMOST WITHOUT OPPOSITION FOR YEARS NOW.
WOW! THIS IS AMAZING!
SMALLER GOVERNMENT AT LAST!
UM... YEAH, ABOUT THAT...
DARRIN BELL

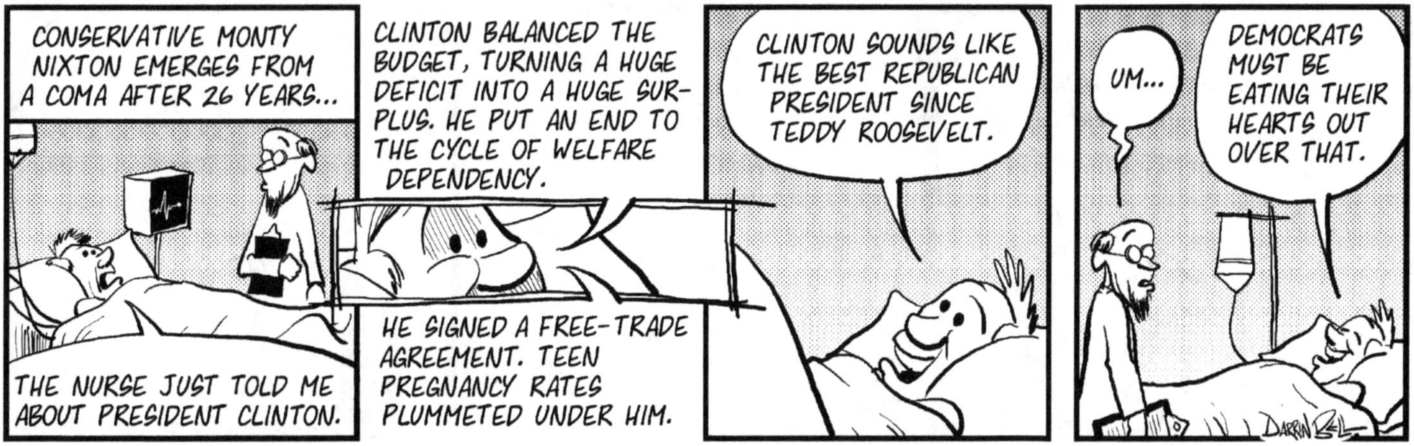
CONSERVATIVE MONTY NIXTON EMERGES FROM A COMA AFTER 26 YEARS...
THE NURSE JUST TOLD ME ABOUT PRESIDENT CLINTON.
CLINTON BALANCED THE BUDGET, TURNING A HUGE DEFICIT INTO A HUGE SURPLUS. HE PUT AN END TO THE CYCLE OF WELFARE DEPENDENCY.
HE SIGNED A FREE-TRADE AGREEMENT. TEEN PREGNANCY RATES PLUMMETED UNDER HIM.
CLINTON SOUNDS LIKE THE BEST REPUBLICAN PRESIDENT SINCE TEDDY ROOSEVELT.
UM...
DEMOCRATS MUST BE EATING THEIR HEARTS OUT OVER THAT.
DARRIN BELL

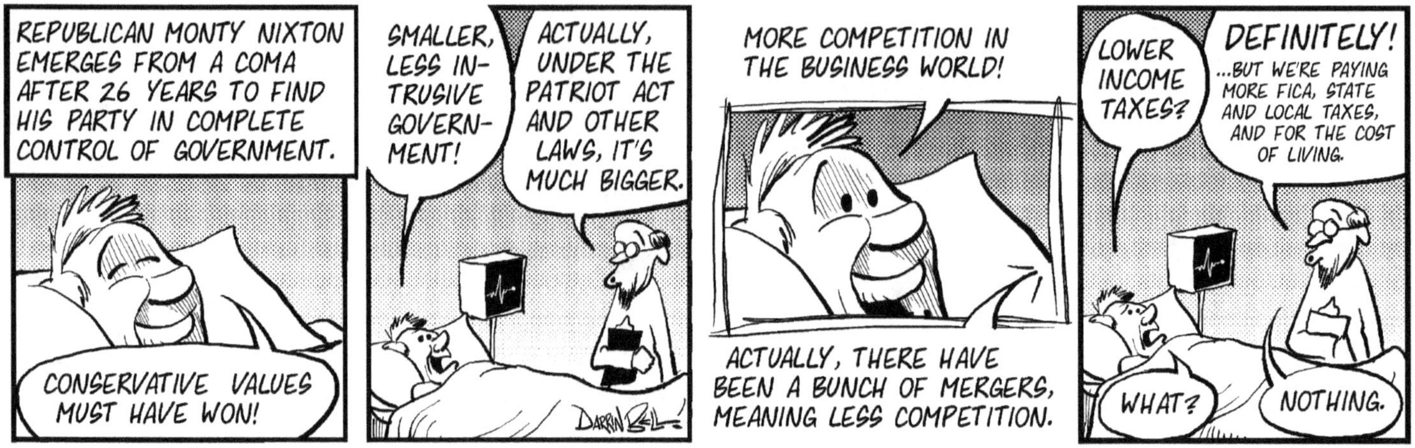
REPUBLICAN MONTY NIXTON EMERGES FROM A COMA AFTER 26 YEARS TO FIND HIS PARTY IN COMPLETE CONTROL OF GOVERNMENT.
CONSERVATIVE VALUES MUST HAVE WON!
SMALLER, LESS INTRUSIVE GOVERNMENT!
ACTUALLY, UNDER THE PATRIOT ACT AND OTHER LAWS, IT'S MUCH BIGGER.
MORE COMPETITION IN THE BUSINESS WORLD!
ACTUALLY, THERE HAVE BEEN A BUNCH OF MERGERS, MEANING LESS COMPETITION.
LOWER INCOME TAXES?
DEFINITELY!
...BUT WE'RE PAYING MORE FICA, STATE AND LOCAL TAXES, AND FOR THE COST OF LIVING.
WHAT?
NOTHING.

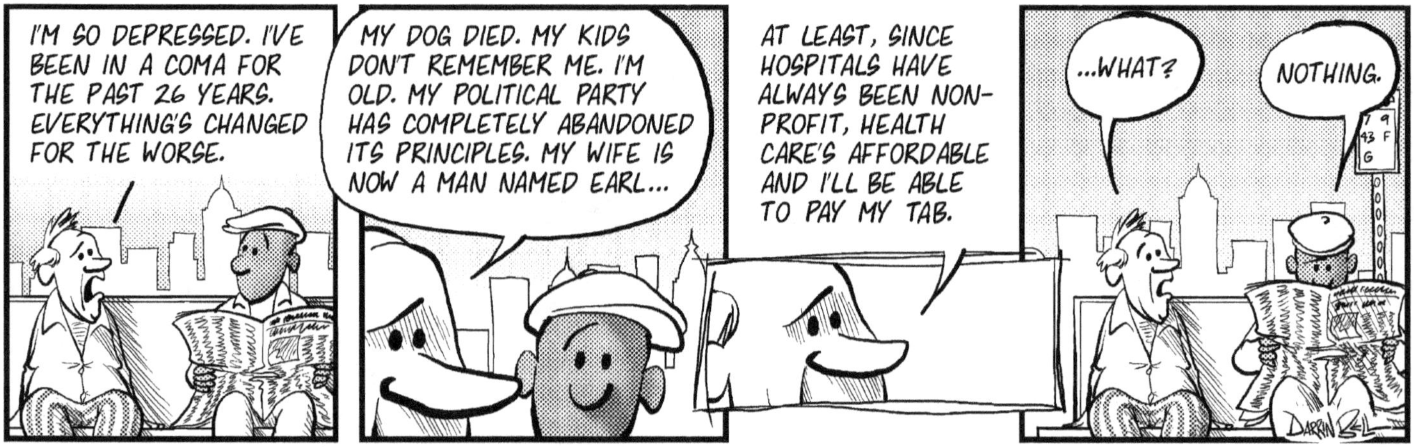
I'M SO DEPRESSED. I'VE BEEN IN A COMA FOR THE PAST 26 YEARS. EVERYTHING'S CHANGED FOR THE WORSE.
MY DOG DIED. MY KIDS DON'T REMEMBER ME. I'M OLD. MY POLITICAL PARTY HAS COMPLETELY ABANDONED ITS PRINCIPLES. MY WIFE IS NOW A MAN NAMED EARL...
AT LEAST, SINCE HOSPITALS HAVE ALWAYS BEEN NON-PROFIT, HEALTH CARE'S AFFORDABLE AND I'LL BE ABLE TO PAY MY TAB.
...WHAT?
NOTHING.

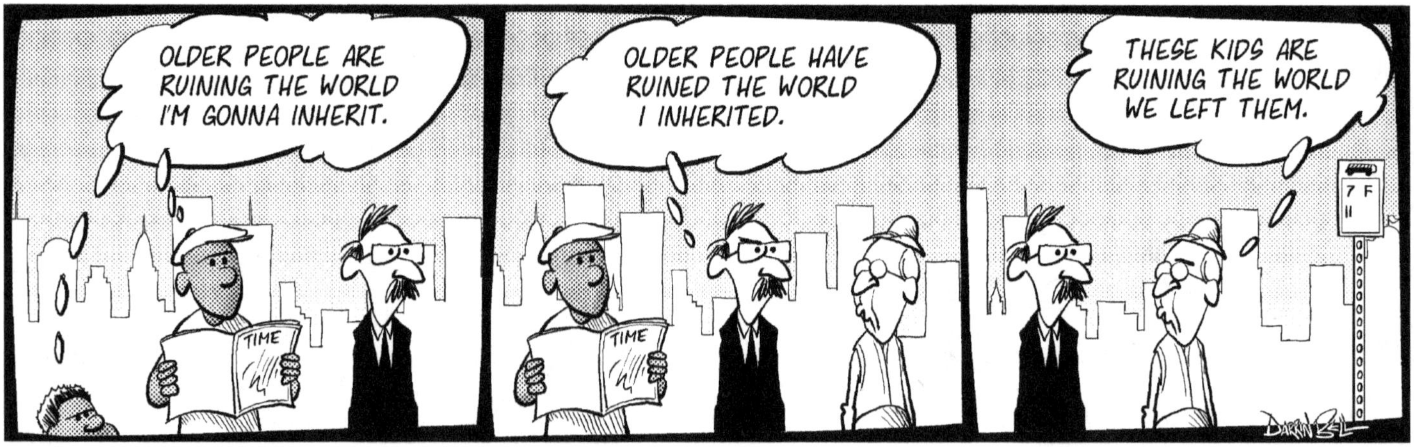
OLDER PEOPLE ARE RUINING THE WORLD I'M GONNA INHERIT.
OLDER PEOPLE HAVE RUINED THE WORLD I INHERITED.
THESE KIDS ARE RUINING THE WORLD WE LEFT THEM.

I'M BOB ROBERTS. TODAY ON THE SUNDAY MORNING POLITICAL SHOW, THE HOT TOPIC IS THE REPUBLICAN ATTEMPT TO BAN THE FILIBUSTER OF JUDICIAL APPOINTEES.
Sunday Morning Political Show
HERE TO REPRESENT THE REPUBLICAN CONTENTION THAT DEMOCRATIC FILIBUSTERING OF 10 OF BUSH'S 215 NOMINEES IS AN UNPRECEDENTED ABUSE OF POWER IS REPUBLICAN SENATOR BILL FRIST.
DARRIN BELL
REPRESENTING THE OPPOSING ARGUMENT, WE HAVE REPUBLICAN SENATOR BILL FRIST FROM THE YEAR 2000, WHO PARTICIPATED IN A FILIBUSTER OF RICHARD PAEZ, ONE OF BILL CLINTON'S JUDICIAL NOMINEES.
HE ALSO SUPPORTED THE BLOCKING OF 60 OTHER CLINTON JUDICIAL AND AMBASSADORIAL NOMINEES.
BOB, MY YOUNGER SELF HAS IT ALL WRONG. THE FOUNDING FATHERS NEVER REALLY INTENDED FOR THE MINORITY PARTY TO HAVE ANY MEANINGFUL INPUT IN THE SENATE.
THEY REALLY INTENDED FOR THE MAJORITY PARTY TO RULE WITH ABSOLUTE POWER.
WITH ALL DUE RESPECT, BOB, MY OLDER SELF IS A FASCIST.
AND MY YOUNGER SELF IS JUST A LIBERAL OBSTRUCTIONIST!

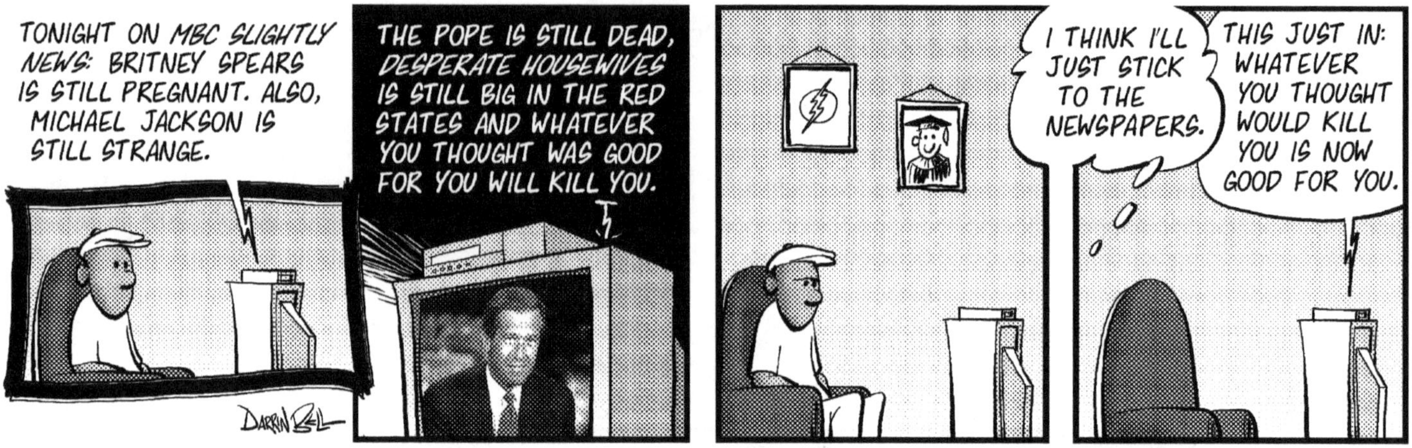
TONIGHT ON MBC SLIGHTLY NEWS: BRITNEY SPEARS IS STILL PREGNANT. ALSO, MICHAEL JACKSON IS STILL STRANGE.
THE POPE IS STILL DEAD, DESPERATE HOUSEWIVES IS STILL BIG IN THE RED STATES AND WHATEVER YOU THOUGHT WAS GOOD FOR YOU WILL KILL YOU.
I THINK I'LL JUST STICK TO THE NEWSPAPERS.
THIS JUST IN: WHATEVER YOU THOUGHT WOULD KILL YOU IS NOW GOOD FOR YOU.
DARRIN BELL

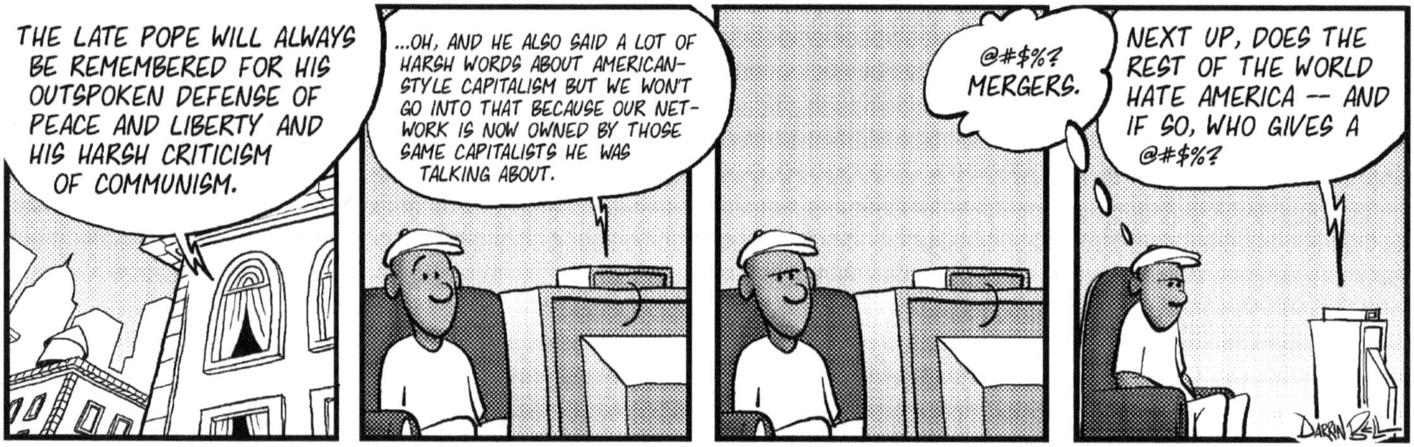
THE LATE POPE WILL ALWAYS BE REMEMBERED FOR HIS OUTSPOKEN DEFENSE OF PEACE AND LIBERTY AND HIS HARSH CRITICISM OF COMMUNISM.
...OH, AND HE ALSO SAID A LOT OF HARSH WORDS ABOUT AMERICAN-STYLE CAPITALISM BUT WE WON'T GO INTO THAT BECAUSE OUR NETWORK IS NOW OWNED BY THOSE SAME CAPITALISTS HE WAS TALKING ABOUT.
@#$%? MERGERS.
NEXT UP, DOES THE REST OF THE WORLD HATE AMERICA -- AND IF SO, WHO GIVES A @#$%?
DARRIN BELL

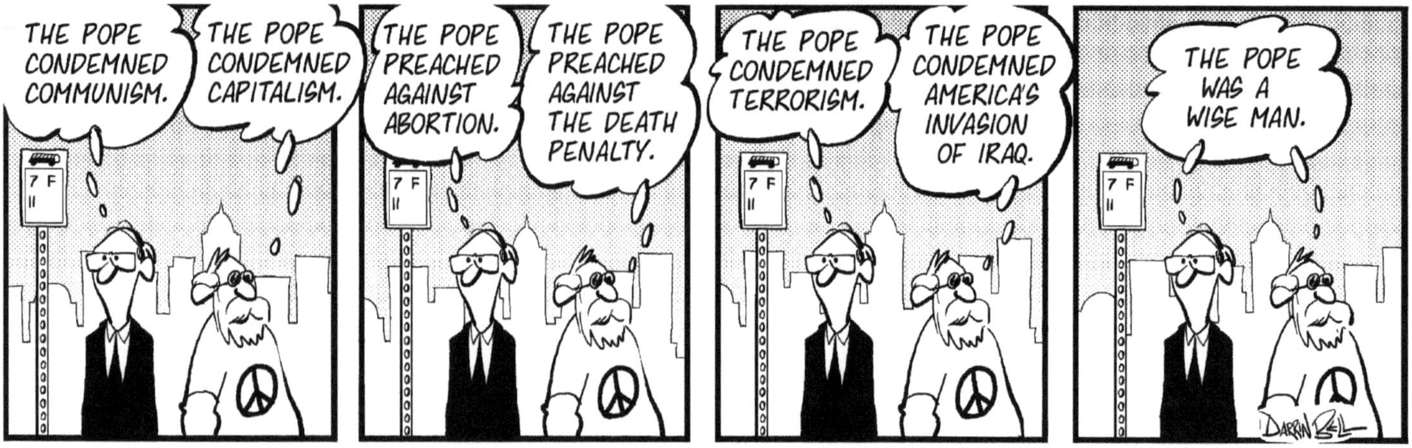
THE POPE CONDEMNED COMMUNISM.
THE POPE CONDEMNED CAPITALISM.
THE POPE PREACHED AGAINST ABORTION.
THE POPE PREACHED AGAINST THE DEATH PENALTY.
THE POPE CONDEMNED TERRORISM.
THE POPE CONDEMNED AMERICA'S INVASION OF IRAQ.
THE POPE WAS A WISE MAN.
DARRIN BELL

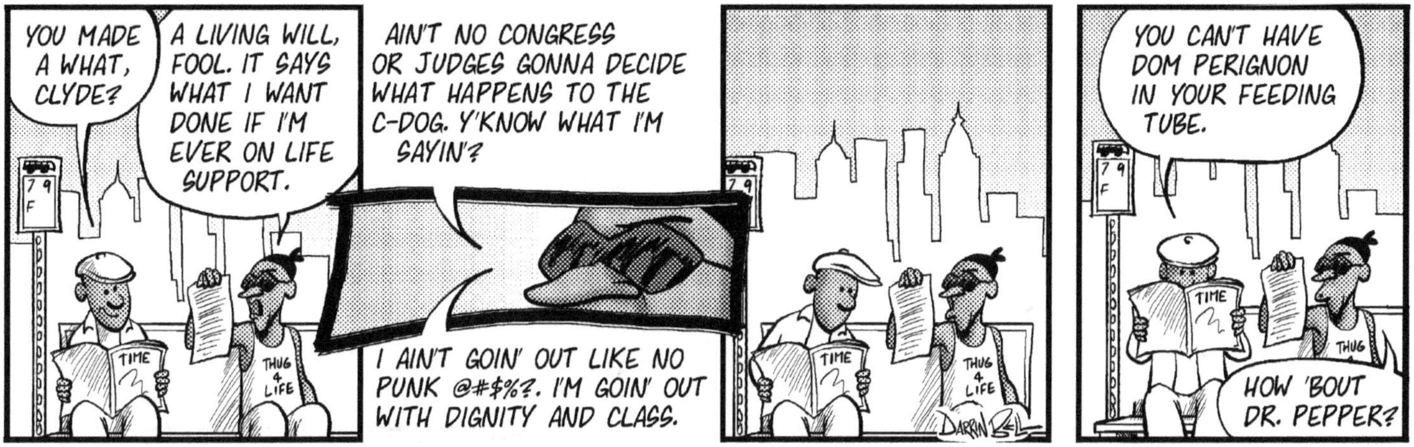
YOU MADE A WHAT, CLYDE?
A LIVING WILL, FOOL. IT SAYS WHAT I WANT DONE IF I'M EVER ON LIFE SUPPORT.
AIN'T NO CONGRESS OR JUDGES GONNA DECIDE WHAT HAPPENS TO THE C-DOG. Y'KNOW WHAT I'M SAYIN'?
I AIN'T GOIN' OUT LIKE NO PUNK @#$%?. I'M GOIN' OUT WITH DIGNITY AND CLASS.
YOU CAN'T HAVE DOM PERIGNON IN YOUR FEEDING TUBE.
HOW 'BOUT DR. PEPPER?
DARRIN BELL

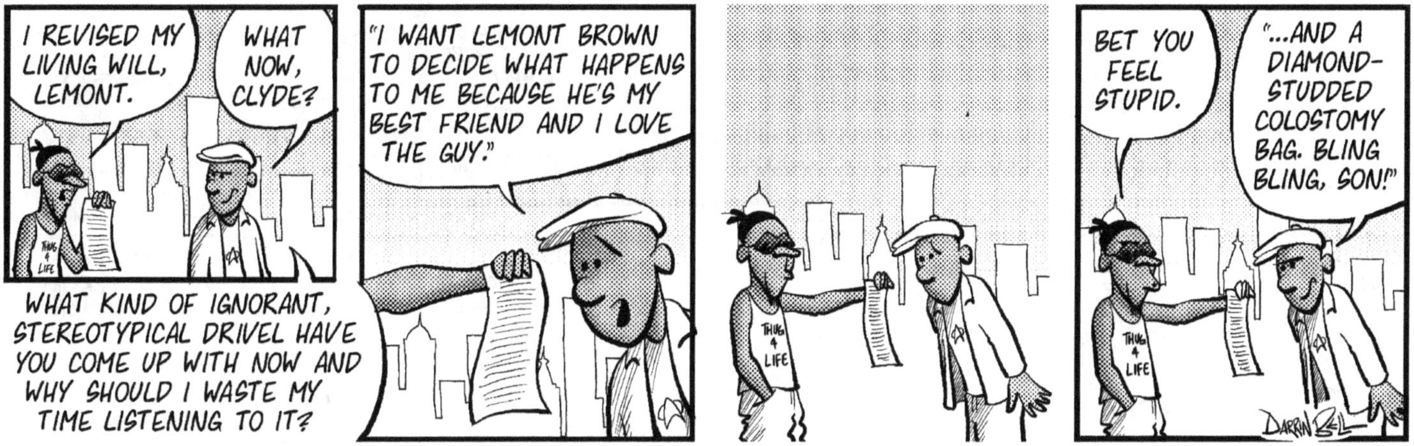
I REVISED MY LIVING WILL, LEMONT.
WHAT NOW, CLYDE?
WHAT KIND OF IGNORANT, STEREOTYPICAL DRIVEL HAVE YOU COME UP WITH NOW AND WHY SHOULD I WASTE MY TIME LISTENING TO IT?
"I WANT LEMONT BROWN TO DECIDE WHAT HAPPENS TO ME BECAUSE HE'S MY BEST FRIEND AND I LOVE THE GUY."
BET YOU FEEL STUPID.
"...AND A DIAMOND-STUDDED COLOSTOMY BAG. BLING BLING, SON!"
DARRIN BELL

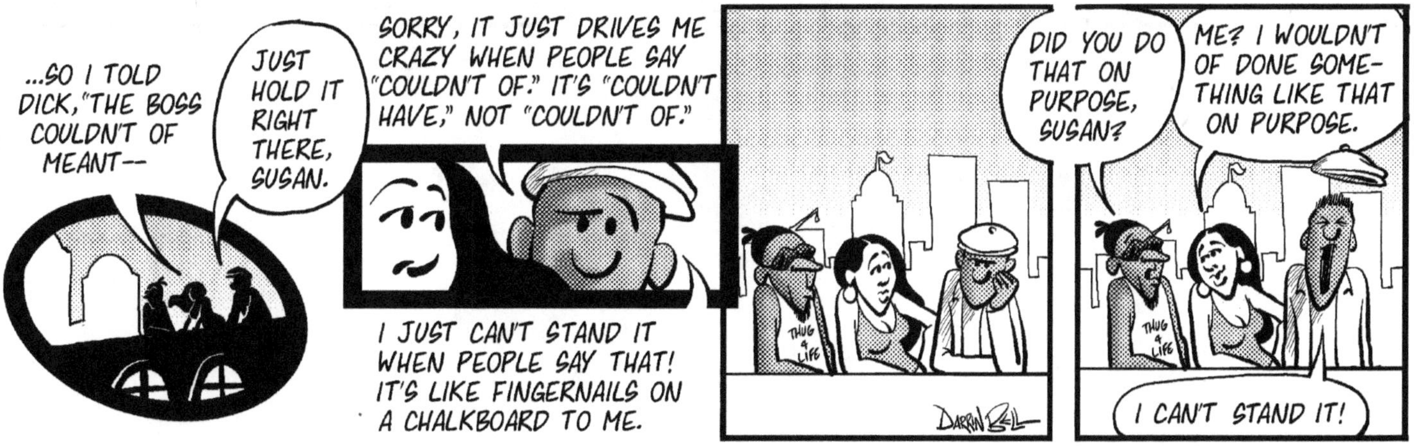
...SO I TOLD DICK, "THE BOSS COULDN'T OF MEANT--
JUST HOLD IT RIGHT THERE, SUSAN.
SORRY, IT JUST DRIVES ME CRAZY WHEN PEOPLE SAY "COULDN'T OF." IT'S "COULDN'T HAVE," NOT "COULDN'T OF."
I JUST CAN'T STAND IT WHEN PEOPLE SAY THAT! IT'S LIKE FINGERNAILS ON A CHALKBOARD TO ME.
DARRIN BELL
DID YOU DO THAT ON PURPOSE, SUSAN?
ME? I WOULDN'T OF DONE SOMETHING LIKE THAT ON PURPOSE.
I CAN'T STAND IT!

TODAY ON THE SUNDAY MORNING POLITICAL SHOW, WE CONTINUE OUR DISCUSSION ABOUT THE FILIBUSTER.

TODAY'S TOPIC: REPUBLICAN CLAIMS THAT DEMOCRATS ARE BLOCKING SEVEN JUDICIAL NOMINEES OUT OF BIGOTRY AGAINST CHRISTIANITY.

WE'RE JOINED BY REPUBLICAN SENATOR STROM THURMOND FROM 1957.

THANK YOU, BOB. THE DEMOCRATS ARE BIGOTS, PURE AND SIMPLE.

...AND I SHOULD KNOW, SEEING AS HOW I STILL HOLD THE RECORD FOR FILIBUSTERING MORE THAN 24 HOURS, TRYING TO STOP THE CIVIL RIGHTS ACT.

WE'RE ALSO JOINED BY REPUBLICAN SENATOR BILL FRIST.

THANKS, BOB. IN 1998 I SAID NOTHING WHEN MY PARTY BLOCKED A CLINTON AMBASSADORIAL APPOINTEE WHO WAS GAY, SO I FEEL I'M MORE THAN QUALIFIED TO TALK ABOUT BIGOTRY.

DARRIN BELL

OH THIS IS JUST TOO MUCH.

WE'RE ALSO JOINED BY FUNDAMENTALIST CHRISTIAN TONY PERKINS OF "FAMILY RESEARCH COUNCIL."

BOB, I KNOW BIGOTRY, SEEING AS HOW I BOUGHT KKK GRAND WIZARD DAVID DUKE'S MAILING LIST IN 1996 FOR $82,000...

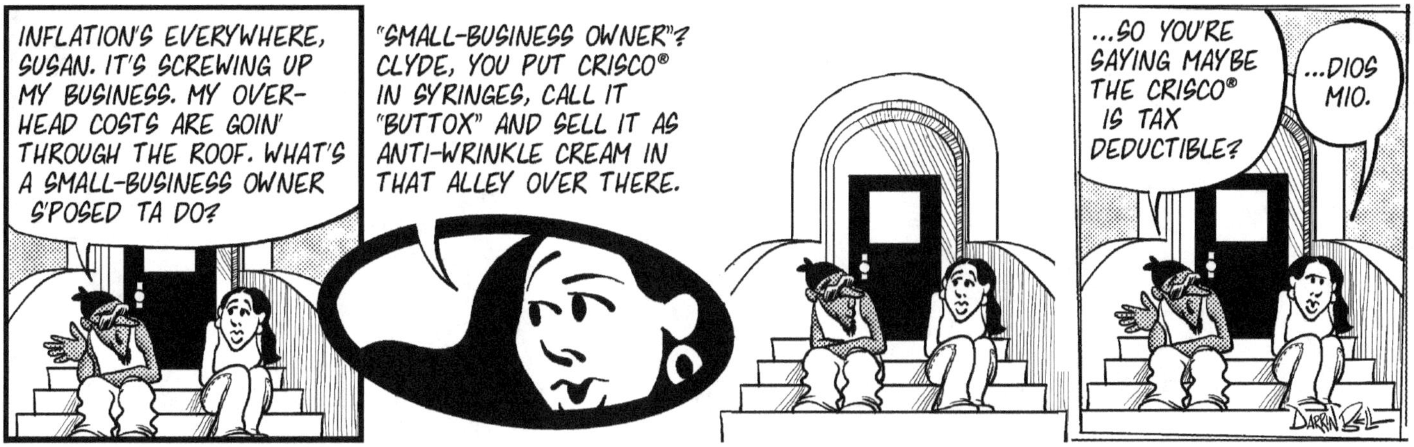
INFLATION'S EVERYWHERE, SUSAN. IT'S SCREWING UP MY BUSINESS. MY OVER-HEAD COSTS ARE GOIN' THROUGH THE ROOF. WHAT'S A SMALL-BUSINESS OWNER S'POSED TA DO?
"SMALL-BUSINESS OWNER"? CLYDE, YOU PUT CRISCO® IN SYRINGES, CALL IT "BUTTOX" AND SELL IT AS ANTI-WRINKLE CREAM IN THAT ALLEY OVER THERE.
...SO YOU'RE SAYING MAYBE THE CRISCO® IS TAX DEDUCTIBLE?
...DIOS MIO.
DARRIN BELL

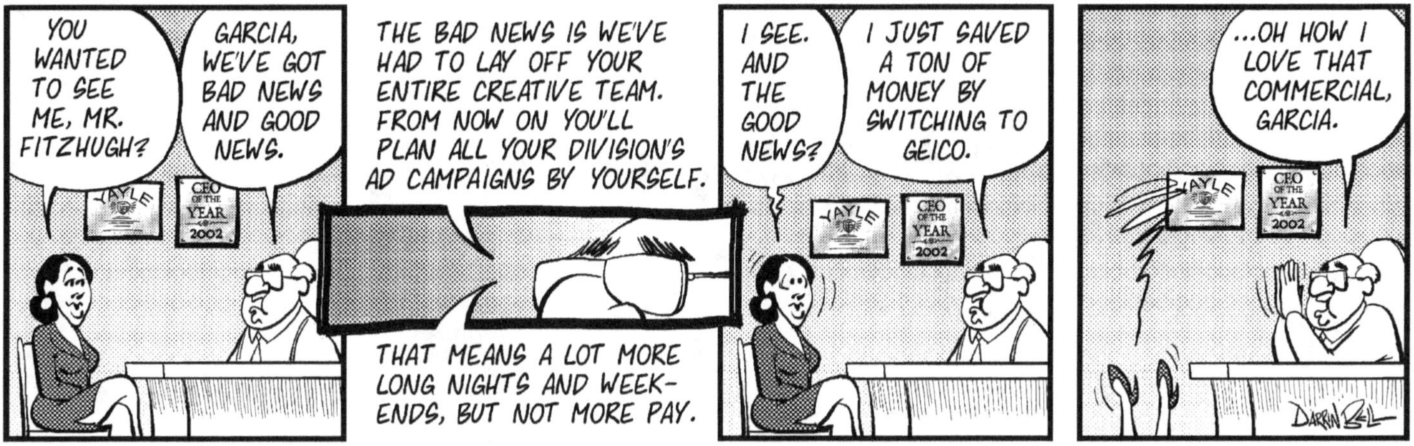
YOU WANTED TO SEE ME, MR. FITZHUGH?
GARCIA, WE'VE GOT BAD NEWS AND GOOD NEWS.
YAYLE
CEO OF THE YEAR 2002
THE BAD NEWS IS WE'VE HAD TO LAY OFF YOUR ENTIRE CREATIVE TEAM. FROM NOW ON YOU'LL PLAN ALL YOUR DIVISION'S AD CAMPAIGNS BY YOURSELF.
THAT MEANS A LOT MORE LONG NIGHTS AND WEEK-ENDS, BUT NOT MORE PAY.
I SEE. AND THE GOOD NEWS?
I JUST SAVED A TON OF MONEY BY SWITCHING TO GEICO.
...OH HOW I LOVE THAT COMMERCIAL, GARCIA.
DARRIN BELL

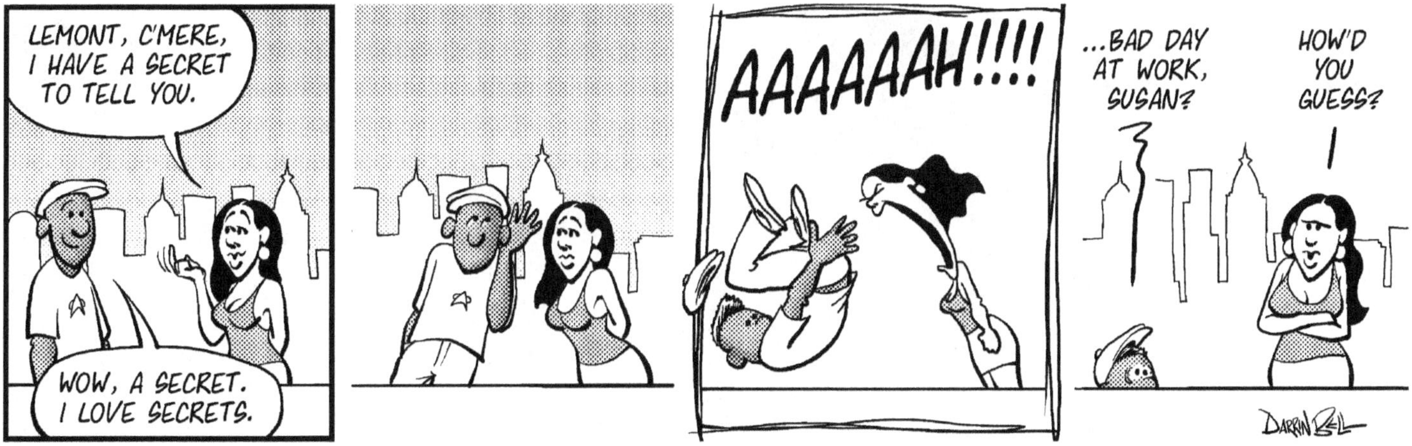
LEMONT, C'MERE, I HAVE A SECRET TO TELL YOU.
WOW, A SECRET. I LOVE SECRETS.
AAAAAAH!!!!
...BAD DAY AT WORK, SUSAN?
HOW'D YOU GUESS?
DARRIN BELL

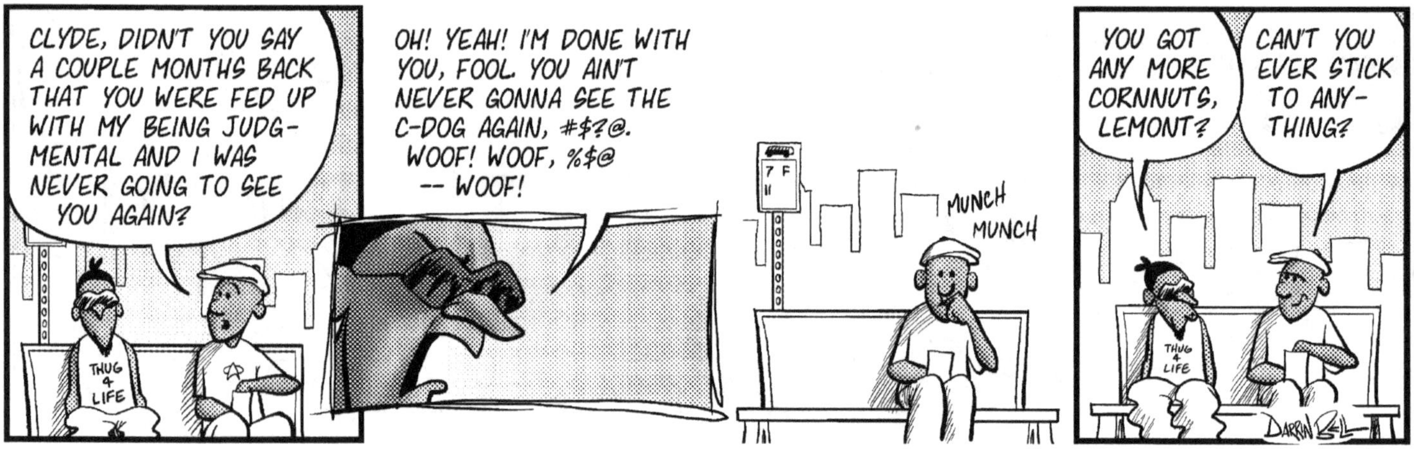

CLYDE, DIDN'T YOU SAY A COUPLE MONTHS BACK THAT YOU WERE FED UP WITH MY BEING JUDG-MENTAL AND I WAS NEVER GOING TO SEE YOU AGAIN?
THUG 4 LIFE
OH! YEAH! I'M DONE WITH YOU, FOOL. YOU AIN'T NEVER GONNA SEE THE C-DOG AGAIN, #$?@. WOOF! WOOF, %$@ -- WOOF!
MUNCH MUNCH
YOU GOT ANY MORE CORNNUTS, LEMONT?
CAN'T YOU EVER STICK TO ANY-THING?
THUG 4 LIFE
DARRIN BELL

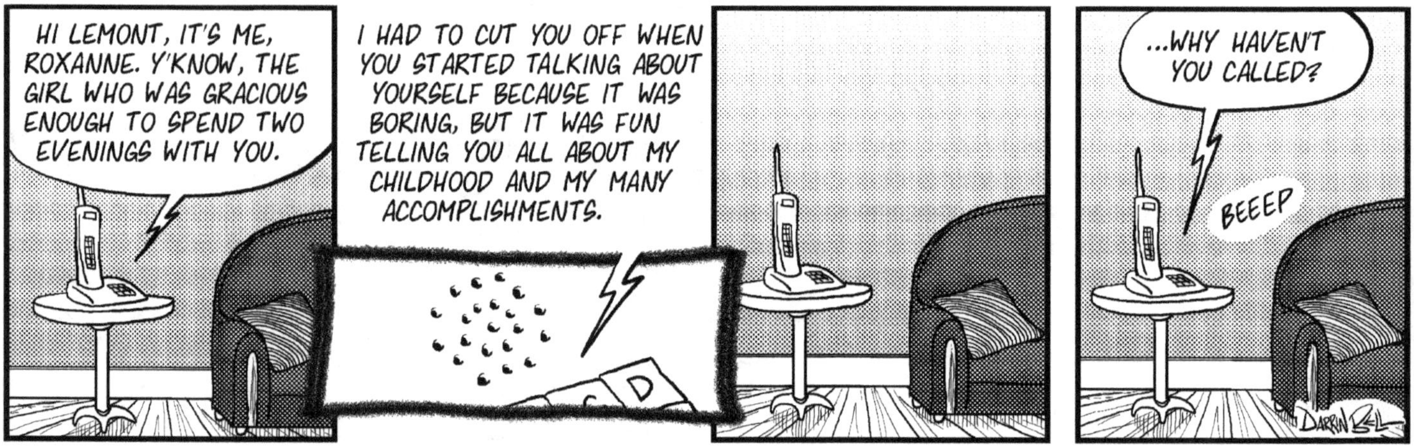

HI LEMONT, IT'S ME, ROXANNE. Y'KNOW, THE GIRL WHO WAS GRACIOUS ENOUGH TO SPEND TWO EVENINGS WITH YOU.
I HAD TO CUT YOU OFF WHEN YOU STARTED TALKING ABOUT YOURSELF BECAUSE IT WAS BORING, BUT IT WAS FUN TELLING YOU ALL ABOUT MY CHILDHOOD AND MY MANY ACCOMPLISHMENTS.
...WHY HAVEN'T YOU CALLED?
BEEEP
DARRIN BELL

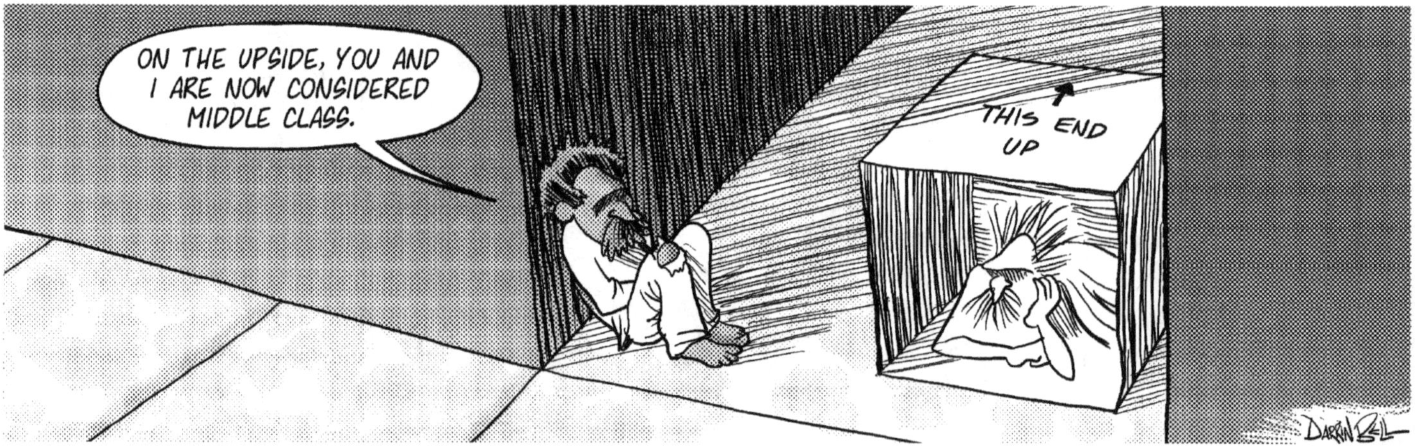

ON THE UPSIDE, YOU AND I ARE NOW CONSIDERED MIDDLE CLASS.
THIS END UP
DARRIN BELL